A HISTORY OF ISL.

Wael B. Hallaq is already established as one of the most eminent scholars in the field of Islamic law. In his latest book, the author traces the history of Islamic legal theory from its beginnings until the modern period. The analysis includes a comprehensive account of the early formation of the theory, focusing on its main themes and arguments and examining the synchronic and diachronic developments that gave rise to a rich variety of doctrines within that theory. The specific relationship between socio-religious reality and the production of legal theoretical discourse is also explored in some detail. The book concludes with a discussion of modern thinking about the theoretical foundations and methodology of Islamic law, presenting an outline of the methodological difficulties encountered by modern reformers and some of the solutions they have offered to reformulate legal theory.

In organization, approach to the subject and critical apparatus, the book is the first of its kind, and will be an essential tool for the understanding of the subject of Islamic legal theory in particular, and Islamic law in general. This, in combination with an accessibility of language and style, will guarantee a wide readership among students and scholars, and anyone interested in Islam and its evolution.

A HISTORY OF ISLAMIC LEGAL THEORIES

AN INTRODUCTION TO SUNNĪ *UṢŪL AL-FIQH*

WAEL B. HALLAQ
McGill University

CAMBRIDGE
UNIVERSITY PRESS

CAMBRIDGE UNIVERSITY PRESS
Cambridge, New York, Melbourne, Madrid, Cape Town, Singapore,
São Paulo, Delhi, Dubai, Tokyo, Mexico City

Cambridge University Press
The Edinburgh Building, Cambridge CB2 8RU, UK

Published in the United States of America by Cambridge University Press, New York

www.cambridge.org
Information on this title: www.cambridge.org/9780521599863

First published 1997
First paperback edition 1999
Reprinted 2003, 2004, 2005

A catalogue record for this publication is available from the British Library

Library of Congress Cataloguing in Publication Data
Hallaq, Wael B., 1955-
A history of Islamic legal theories: an introduction to Sunni
usūl al-fiqh I Wael B. Hallaq.
p. cm.
Includes bibliographical references and index.
ISBN 0521590272 (hardback)
1. Islamic law - Interpretation and construction. 2. Islamic law–
History. I. Title.
LAW <ISLAM 7 Hallaq 1997>
340.5'9-dc21 96-45194 CIP

ISBN 978-0-521-59027-3 Hardback
ISBN 978-0-521-59986-3 Paperback

CONTENTS

PREFACE

PERHAPS there is no better way to introduce this book than to explain its title. The choice of the plural form "theories" is of course deliberate, intending to convey the distinct message that the present field of enquiry is by no means reducible to a monolithic set of ideas divorced from various historical processes. A central aim of the book is then to show that *uṣūl al-fiqh*, the theoretical and philosophical foundation of Islamic law, constituted an umbrella under which synchronic and diachronic variations existed. The plan of the book manifests this concern for unraveling the most essential features of these variations. In the first chapter, I discuss the evolving principles of jurisprudence, from their rudimentary beginnings down to the end of the third/ninth century, when *uṣūl al-fiqh* came into existence as an integral legal methodology. Of the three centuries covered in this chapter, the second receives a treatment that is largely in agreement with the conventional understanding in the field, an understanding first propounded by Joseph Schacht. With regard to the first/seventh and, especially, the third/ninth centuries, I offer a generally different interpretation. In the case of the first century, I subscribe neither to the traditional view that Islamic law, as a more or less mature system, began during or immediately after the lifetime of the Prophet, nor to the relatively recent view which places the rudimentary beginnings of this law around the end of the first century of the Hijra (ca. 715 A.D.). My own explorations have led me to take a middle position between the two existing views. Concerning the third/ninth century, I argue against the prevailing notion that legal theory, as it came to be known later, was the product of the second/eighth century and that Ibn Idrīs al-Shāfiʿī was its architect.

The second and third chapters offer, as compendiously as possible, an account of the central themes of *uṣūl al-fiqh* as they had developed by the end of the fifth/eleventh century. The purpose behind this account is twofold: to give a synchronic view of the various doctrines as well as to set the stage for a discussion of diachronic variations, the concern of the fourth chapter. In the latter, I discuss the major components in the world of legal and social practices, together with intellectual trends, that gave rise to a rich variety of doctrines within *uṣūl al-fiqh*. The specific relationship between socio-religious reality and the production of legal theoretical discourse is illustrated in detail in the fifth chapter where I use the writings of the Andalusian jurist Abū Isḥāq al-Shāṭibī as a case-study. This analysis of Shāṭibī also aims to show that the conventional wisdom about the nature and purpose of his theory is erroneous.

My choice of Shāṭibī as the subject of the fifth chapter has a third justification. His theory, together with Ṭūfī's (which I discuss in the fourth chapter), constitute a significant source on which modern reformers have drawn. That these reformers as well as modern scholars misunderstood both the motives and, therefore, substance of Shāṭibī's theory informs our understanding not only of the intellectual construction of modern legal reform but also how history is distorted (unwittingly, of course) in the service of the present. The last chapter offers a general view of modern thinking about the theoretical foundations and methodology of Islamic law. The number of sources here is staggering and, by necessity, I was compelled to be highly selective in the choice of figures I discuss. Although far from exhaustive, this chapter attempts to present an outline of the methodological difficulties encountered by modern reformers and some of the solutions they offered to reformulate legal theory.

The subtitle is no less significant. This book is also deliberately written as an introduction, intended to appeal to a wide readership both within and without the field of Islamic studies. Although I advisedly avoided a comparison with other legal systems (for I believe such an exercise on an introductory level distorts a genuine perception of Islam and Islamic law), it is hoped that comparative lawyers will find in this book a useful tool. Students of religious studies and comparative religion should also be able to benefit from it. The book, however, is primarily addressed to those in the field of Islamic studies. Unfortunately, until now there has been no text that presents students interested in Islamic law as well as Islamicists at large with an intelligible, manageable account of Islamic legal theories. This introduction is designed to fill the existing gap.

It will be immediately noted that the subject of this book falls entirely within the Sunnī tradition. The Shīʿite and other legal theories are appreciably different both in their historical development and, consequently, structure. No doubt they stand on their own, and, like their Sunnī counterpart, they demand an independent treatment. Thus no apology is in order for excluding non-Sunnī legal theories.

In treating the theoretical works, I have, quite expectedly, taken full note of their declared purpose, namely, to set forth a methodology by means of which a highly qualified jurist can *discover* God's law. This approach clearly implies that the chief task of the jurist, who masters the apparatus of *uṣūl al-fiqh*, is represented in a confrontation with the primary sources of the law, a confrontation whose purpose is to discover rulings for unprecedented cases. However, legal theories played another (rarely and vaguely articulated) role, involving the justification and re-enactment of time-honored and long-established legal rules and of the processes of reasoning that produced and continued to sustain them. Put differently, this other role consisted of a reasoned defense of the *madhhab*, the legal school and its authoritative, standard doctrine. Theoretically, and as a matter of principle, *uṣūl al-fiqh* would function in the same fashion in the spheres both of rule-creation and rule-justification. It is precisely due to the absence of difference at this level of abstract theorization that I have not given much attention to legal theory's second role, although it constitutes, in its own right, a rich and promising field of enquiry.

The introductory nature of this work dictates that Arabic technical terms be kept to a minimum, which I have attempted to do throughout. However, I did not think it judicious to exclude these terms entirely, since, on the one hand, they present the new student with the key concepts used in *uṣūl al-fiqh* and, on the other, they make it easier for those who are interested in the original Arabic texts to trace the discussions there. Also kept to a minimum are the notes; wherever possible they have been placed at the ends of paragraphs to prevent interruption in reading. Instead of cluttering the text with references to sources that inform a particular discussion and that have been consulted in writing the book, I have opted to list the relevant sources at the end, signaling those that are important for further reading (see the references).

Although this book represents a somewhat revisionist outlook, there is no doubt that it is indebted to previous and current scholarship in the field. In some instances, I have drawn on earlier writings of mine, and this I duly acknowledge in the appropriate places. A number of scholars have given me the benefit of their valuable comments. David Powers read chapters 1, 4 and 5; Bernard Weiss chapters 2 and 3; and John Voll chapter 6. Farhat Ziadeh read the entire manuscript. To all of these generous colleagues, I record my deep gratitude. Finally, I should also record a long-standing debt to Steve Millier for the care he has taken in editing the manuscript and for his crucial assistance as a librarian.

1

THE FORMATIVE PERIOD

INTRODUCTION

IN its developed form, Islamic legal theory came to recognize a variety of sources and methods from and through which the law might be derived. Those sources *from* which the law may be derived are the Quran and the Sunna or example of the Prophet, both of which provide the subject matter of the law. Those sources *through* which the law may be derived represent either methods of legal reasoning and interpretation or the sanctioning instrument of consensus (*ijmāʿ*). Primacy of place within the hierarchy of all these sources is given to the Quran, followed by the Sunna which, though second in order of importance, provided the greatest bulk of material from which the law was derived. The third is consensus, a sanctioning instrument whereby the creative jurists, the *mujtahid*s, representing the community at large, are considered to have reached an agreement, known retrospectively, on a technical legal ruling, thereby rendering it as conclusive and as epistemologically certain as any verse of the Quran and the Sunna of the Prophet. The certitude bestowed upon a case of law renders that case, together with its ruling, a material source on the basis of which a similar legal case may be solved. The *mujtahid*s, authorized by divine revelation, are thus capable of transforming a ruling reached through human legal reasoning into a textual source by the very fact of their agreement on its validity. The processes of reasoning involved therein, subsumed under the rubric of *qiyās*, represent the fourth source of the law. Alternative methods of reasoning based on considerations of juristic preference (*istiḥsān*) or public welfare and interest (*istiṣlāḥ*) were of limited validity, and were not infrequently the subject of controversy.

Now, the declared, and indeed main, purpose of Islamic legal theory was to formulate rulings (*aḥkām*) concerning cases whose solutions had not been explicitly stated in the first two material sources.[1] And these constituted the greater part of the law. The formulation of solutions entailed developing a rich variety of interpretive methods by means of which the legal effects of the Quran and the Sunna could be determined. It also entailed the elaboration of a theory of abrogation, whereby one Quranic verse or Prophetic report is deemed to repeal another verse or report. Furthermore, there arose the need to establish the authenticity or inauthenticity of Prophetic reports, since it is in these that the Sunna of the Prophet is expressed and embedded. Probing authenticity meant scrutinizing the transmitters of each report and the modes of its transmission. This in turn led to a classification of reports in accordance with the epistemic value each enjoyed.

It is with this broad outline in mind that we shall attempt to sketch the stages through which the sources of law evolved during the first three Islamic centuries. We shall argue that by the end of the second/eighth century, legal theory had emerged in only a rudimentary form, and that it was not until the beginning of the fourth/tenth century that it reached the final stage of its formation as an integrated methodology.

Before we proceed, however, two historiographical remarks are in order. First, it is my assumption, justified by the absence of noteworthy evidence to the contrary, that the Quran originated during the lifetime of the Prophet and that it reflected events and ideas that occurred then. Therefore, whatever the Quran says about an event or an idea during the Prophet's lifetime, I take to be an authentic representation of that event or idea. Second, but more historiographically problematical, is the authenticity of the reports about the deeds and utterances of the Prophet. Goldziher, Schacht and Juynboll,[2] among others, argued that we have good reason to believe that Prophetic reports were fabricated at a later stage in Islamic history and that they were gradually projected back to the Prophet. Schacht placed the beginnings of the Sunna, and the verbal reports that came to express it, toward the end of the first century A.H. and the beginning of the second (ca. 720 A.D.), whereas Juynboll conceded that they may have surfaced a quarter of a century earlier.[3] However, mounting recent

[1] Another important function of legal theory, one that is assumed and rarely articulated in works of *uṣūl al-fiqh*, is the justification and "re-enactment" of the processes of legal reasoning behind existing rules. An example of this justification and re-enactment is found in Taqī al-Dīn ʿAlī al-Subkī, *Takmilat al-Majmūʿ*, 12 vols. (Cairo: Maṭbaʿat al-Taḍāmun, 1906), X, 13–98.

[2] I. Goldziher, *Muslim Studies*, ed. S. M. Stern, trans. C. R. Barber and S. M. Stern, 2 vols. (London: Allen & Unwin, 1967–71), II, 17–251; Joseph Schacht, *The Origins of Muhammadan Jurisprudence* (Oxford: Clarendon Press, 1950); G. H. A. Juynboll, *Muslim Tradition: Studies in Chronology, Provenance and Authorship of Early Ḥadīth* (Cambridge: Cambridge University Press, 1983).

[3] For a useful summary of the views about the origins of Prophetic Sunna, see David S. Powers,

research, concerned with the historical origins of individual Prophetic reports,[4] suggests that Goldziher, Schacht and Juynboll have been excessively skeptical and that a number of reports can be dated earlier than previously thought, even as early as the Prophet. These findings, coupled with other important studies[5] critical of Schacht's thesis, go to show that while a great bulk of Prophetic reports may have originated many decades after the Hijra, there exists a body of material that can be dated to the Prophet's time. Therefore, I shall not *a priori* preclude the entirety of Prophetic reports as an unauthentic body of material, nor shall I accept their majority, even though many may have been admitted as authentic (*ṣaḥīḥ*) by the Muslim "science" of *ḥadīth* criticism.

THE QURAN AS A LEGAL DOCUMENT

While it is true that the Quran is primarily a book of religious and moral prescriptions, there is no doubt that it encompasses pieces of legislation, strictly speaking. In propounding his message, the Prophet plainly wished to break away from pre-Islamic values and institutions, but only insofar as he needed to establish once and for all the fundaments of the new religion. Having been pragmatic, he could not have done away with all the social practices and institutions that prevailed in his time. Among the multitude of exhortations and prescriptions found in the Quran, there are many legal and quasi-legal stipulations. For example, legislation was introduced in select matters of ritual, alms-tax, property and treatment of orphans, inheritance, usury, consumption of alcohol, marriage, divorce, sexual intercourse, adultery, theft, homicide and the like.

Muslim jurists and modern scholars are in agreement that the Quran contains some 500 verses with legal content. In comparison to the overall bulk of Quranic material, the legal verses appear exiguous, giving the erroneous impression that the Quran's concern with legal matters is merely

Studies in Qur'an and Ḥadīth: The Formation of the Law of Inheritance (Berkeley: University of California Press, 1986), 2 ff. See also Harald Motzki, "The *Muṣannaf* of ʿAbd al-Razzāq al-Ṣanʿānī as a Source of Authentic *Aḥādīth* of the First Century A.H.," *Journal of Near Eastern Studies*, 50 (1991): 1 f.

4 See, for instance, Powers, *Studies in Qur'an and Ḥadīth*, 8 and generally; David S. Powers, "The Will of Saʿd b. Abī Waqqās: A Reassessment," *Studia Islamica*, 58 (1983): 33–53; Motzki, "The *Muṣannaf*," 1–21; Uri Rubin, "'Al-Walad li-l-Firāsh': On the Islamic Campaign against 'Zinā'," *Studia Islamica*, 78 (1993): 5–26.

5 Notable of these studies are those by M. M. Azami, *Studies in Early Hadith Literature* (Beirut: al-Maktab al-Islāmī, 1968); M. M. Azami, *On Schacht's Origins of Muhammadan Jurisprudence* (New York: John Wiley, 1985); Nabia Abbott, *Studies in Arabic Literary Papyri*, II (Chicago: University of Chicago Press, 1967), 5–83; Fuat Sezgin, *Geschichte des arabischen Schrifttums*, I (Leiden: E. J. Brill, 1967), 53–84 and generally.

incidental. At the same time, it has frequently been noted by Islamicists that the Quran often repeats itself both thematically and verbatim. If we accept this to be the case, as Goitein has argued, it means that the proportion of the legal subject matter (in which repetition is virtually absent) to non-legal subject matter is larger than is generally thought. And if we consider the fact that the average length of the legal verses is twice or even thrice that of the average non-legal verses, it would not be difficult to argue, following Goitein, that the Quran contains no less legal material than does the Torah, which is commonly known as "The Law."[6]

Even in Mecca, Muhammad already thought of the community that he hoped to create in terms of a political and social unit. This explains his success in organizing the Arab and Jewish tribes into a body politic immediately after arriving in Medina. The so-called Constitution he drafted there points to a mind highly skilled in formulaic legal documents, which is hardly surprising in light of the legal thrust of the Quran and the role Muhammad himself had played as an arbitration judge (*ḥakam*). In Medina, Muhammad continued to act in the latter capacity for some time, relying in his decisions, so it seems, upon the prevailing customary law and tribal practices. From the Quran we learn that at a certain point after his arrival in Medina, Muhammad came to think of his Message as one that carried with it the Law of God, just as the Torah and the Gospel did. Sūra 5, revealed at Medina, marshals a list of commands, admonitions and explicit prohibitions concerning a great variety of issues, from eating swine meat to theft. Throughout, references to the Jews and Christians and to their respective scriptures recur. In 5:43 God asks, with a sense of astonishment, why the Jews resort to Muhammad in his capacity as a judge "when they have the Torah which contains the Judgment of God." The Quran continues: "We have revealed the Torah in which there is guidance and light, [and by which] the Prophets who surrendered [to God] judged the Jews, and the rabbis and priests judged by such of Allah's Scriptures as they were bidden to observe." In the next two verses, the Quran turns to the Christians, saying in effect that God sent Jesus to confirm the prophethood of Moses, and the Gospel to reassert the "guidance and advice" revealed in the Torah. "So let the People of the Gospel judge by that which God had revealed therein, for he who judges not by that which God revealed is a sinner" (5:47).

This clearly demonstrates that the Quran considered the Jews and Christians not only as possessors of *their own* respective divine laws, but also

[6] See S. D. Goitein, "The Birth-Hour of Muslim Law," *Muslim World*, 50, 1 (1960), 24. The next three paragraphs draw in part on this article.

as bound by the application of these laws. If the Jews and Christians were so favored, then what about the Muslims? The Quran here does not hesitate to provide an explicit answer: "We have revealed unto you the Book [i.e., the Quran] with the truth, confirming whatever Scripture was before it . . . so judge between them by that which God had revealed, and do not follow their desires away from the truth . . . *for we have made for each of you* [i.e., Muslims, Christians and Jews] *a law and a normative way to follow.* If God had willed, He would have made all of you one community" (5:48=; italics mine). Of course, God did not wish to do so, and He thus created three communities with three sets of laws, so that each community could follow *its own* law. And as was the case with the Christians and Jews, Muhammad is repeatedly commanded throughout the Quran[7] to judge by what God has revealed unto him, for "who is better than God in judgment?" (5:49–50).

Goitein argues that Sūra 5, or at least verses 42–50 therein, was precipitated by an incident in which certain Jewish tribes resorted to the Prophet to adjudicate amongst them. It is unlikely that such an incident took place after 5 A.H., since the repeated reference to the rabbis implies a substantial Jewish presence in Medina, and this could have been the case only before the end of the fifth year of the Hijra. Be that as it may, the incident seems to have marked a turning point in the Prophet's career. Now he began to think of his religion as one that should afford the Muslim community a set of laws separate from those of other religions. This may also account for the fact that it is in Medina that the greatest bulk of Quranic legislation took place.

This is not to say, however, that the Quran provided Muslims with an all-encompassing or developed system of law. What the Quranic evidence mentioned above does indicate is a strong tendency on the part of the Prophet toward elaborating a basic legal structure.[8] This tendency finds eloquent testimony in the stand of the Quran on the matter of the consumption of date- and grape-wine. In the Meccan phase, wines clearly were permitted: "From date-palm and grapes you derive alcoholic drinks, and from them you make good livelihood. Lo! therein is indeed a portent for people who have sense" (16:67). In Medina, the position of the Quran changes, expressing an ambivalent sense of dislike toward alcoholic beverages. "They ask you [i.e., Muhammad] about wine and gambling. Say: 'In

[7] Quran 2:213; 3:23; 4:58, 105; 5:44–5, 47; 7:87; 10:109; 24:48, generally. Q. 5:44, for instance, states: "He who does not judge by what God has revealed is a disbeliever."

[8] That Muhammad had upheld a law particular to the new religion is also attested in the Armenian chronicle written in the 660s and attributed to Bishop Sebeos. See P. Crone and M. Cook, *Hagarism: The Making of the Muslim World* (Cambridge: Cambridge University Press, 1977), 7.

both there is sin, and utility for people'" (2:219). The sense of aversion subsequently increases: "O you who believe, do not come to pray when you are drunken, till you know what you utter" (4:43). Here, one observes a provisional prohibition which relates to consuming alcohol only when Muslims intend to pray. Finally, a categorical command is revealed in 5:90–91, whereby Muslims are ordered to avoid alcohol, games of chance and idols altogether.[9] It is interesting that the final, decisive stand on alcohol occurs in Sūra 5 which, as we have seen, marks a turning point in the legislative outlook of the Prophet.

This turning point, however, should not be seen as constituting an entirely clean break from the previous practices of the Prophet, for he had played all along the role of a judge, both as a traditional arbitrator and as a Prophet. The turning point marked the beginning of a new process whereby *all* events befalling the nascent Muslim community were henceforth to be adjudicated according to God's law, whose agent was none other than the Prophet. This is clearly attested not only in the Quran but also in the so-called Constitution of Medina, a document whose authenticity can hardly be contested.[10]

That all matters should have been subject to the divine decree must not be taken to mean that all problems encountered by Muhammad were given new solutions. Although a credible historical record of this early period is still awaited, we may assert that, with the exception of what may be called Quranic legal reform, the Prophet generally followed the existing pre-Islamic Arab practices. Two examples may serve to illustrate the point.[11] The first is the customary law of bartering unripe dates still on the palm tree against their equal value in picked dried dates. The second concerns the law of *qasāma* (compurgation), according to which, if the body of a murdered person is found on lands occupied by a tribe, or in a city quarter, domicile, etc., fifty of the inhabitants must each take an oath that they have neither caused the person's death nor have any knowledge as to those who did. Should there be less than fifty persons available, those who are present must swear more than once until fifty oaths have been obtained. By so

9 On the verses relating to intoxicants, see Muqātil b. Sulaymān, *Tafsīr al-Khams Mā'at Āya*, ed. I. Goldfeld (Shafā'amr: Dār al-Mashriq, 1980), 141–44; Abū 'Ubayd al-Qāsim b. Sallām, *Kitāb al-Nāsikh wal-Mansūkh*, ed. John Burton (Bury St Edmunds: St Edmundsburgh Press, 1987), 87–88.

10 For the Quran, see n. 6 above. On the Constitution of Medina, see R. B. Serjeant, "The 'Constitution of Medina'," *Islamic Quarterly*, 8 (1964): 3; reprinted in R. B. Serjeant, *Studies in Arabian History and Civilization* (London: Variorum, 1981).

11 Ritual laws, such as prayer and fasting, may be cited as additional survivals from pre-Islamic Arabia to the new religion. See S. D. Goitein, *Studies in Islamic History and Institutions* (Leiden: E. J. Brill, 1966), 73–89, 92–94.

doing, they free themselves from any liability, but are nonetheless not exempt from paying the blood-money to the agnates of the person slain. Both of these practices were recognized by later Muslim scholars as pre-Islamic customary practices that were sanctioned by the Prophet himself.[12]

JURISPRUDENCE IN THE FIRST CENTURY H. (CA. 620–720 A.D.)

During the few decades after the Prophet's death, when conquest was being undertaken and when the capital of the state was still in Medina, there were mainly two sets of principles and laws on the basis of which the leaders of the nascent Muslim community fashioned their conduct: pre-Islamic Arab customary law and the Quran. The former was still the only "system" of law known to the conquerors, and the latter contained and symbolized the Mission in whose name these conquerors were fighting. The importance of the Quran and its injunctions for the early Muslims can hardly be overstated. Early Monophysite sources inform us that when Abū Bakr, the first caliph (d. 13/634), deployed his armies to conquer Syria, he addressed his generals with the following words:

> When you enter the land, kill neither old man nor child . . . Establish a covenant with every city and people who receives you, give them your assurances and let them live according to their laws . . . Those who do not receive you, you are to fight, conducting yourselves carefully in accordance with the ordinances and upright laws transmitted to you from God, at the hands of our Prophet.[13]

In this passage the reference to the Quran is unambiguous, although one is not entirely sure whether or not the "upright laws" refer to legal ordinances other than those laid down in the Quran. Noteworthy, however, is the contrast drawn between the laws of the conquered nations and the law transmitted from God through the Prophet. Abū Bakr's orders to allow the mainly Christian inhabitants of Syria to regulate their affairs by their own laws echo the passages in the fifth Sūra, where each religion is enjoined to apply to itself its own set of laws. Here, Abū Bakr is implicitly and, later in the passage, explicitly adhering to the Quran's letter and spirit, and in a sense to the personal stand adopted by the Prophet on this issue which is inextricably connected with the very act of revelation. But more on this point later.

[12] See Muḥammad Ibn Ḥazm, *Muʿjam al-Fiqh*, 2 vols. (Damascus: Maṭbaʿat Jāmiʿat Dimashq, 1966), II, 838–39.

[13] Cited in S. P. Brock, "Syriac Views of Emergent Islam," in G. H. A. Juynboll, ed., *Studies on the First Century of Islamic Society* (Carbondale: Southern Illinois University Press, 1982), 12, 200.

The paucity of documentation on the early period makes it difficult for us to draw a complete picture of the sources from which legal practices were derived. However, it is fairly clear that the early caliphs, including the Umayyads, considered themselves the deputies of God on earth, and thus looked to the Quran as a source from which they could draw their legal decisions.[14] As evidenced in the orders he gave to his army, Abū Bakr seems to have generally adhered to the prescriptions of the Quran. Among other things, he enforced the prohibition on alcohol and fixed the penalty for its violation at forty lashes.[15] While his enforcement of this law indicates the centrality of the Quranic injunctions, it also demonstrates that beyond the Quranic prohibition there was little juristic experience or guidance to go by. For instance, the punishment for intoxication, thought to have been fixed arbitrarily, was soon altered by ʿUmar and ʿAlī to eighty lashes, apparently on the ground that inebriation was analogous to falsely accusing a person of committing adultery (*qadhf*), for which offense the Quran fixed the penalty at eighty lashes. ʿUmar, who was the first to impose the new penalty for inebriation, is also reported to have insisted forcefully on the Muslims' adherence to the Quran in matters of ritual, and these became an integral part of the law.

The increasing importance of the Quran as a religious and legal document manifested itself in the need to collect the scattered material of the Book and to establish therefrom a vulgate. ʿUthmān, who followed in the footsteps of his two predecessors in enforcing the rulings of the Quran, was the man who took charge of the task. The collection of the Quran must have had a primary legal significance, for it defined the subject matter of the text and thus gave the legally minded a *textus receptus* on which to draw. The monumental event of establishing a vulgate signified the rudimentary beginnings of what may be described as a "textual" attitude toward the Quran, an attitude which reached its zenith only centuries later.

During the ensuing decades, Muslim men of learning turned their attention to the explicit legal contents of the Quran. Again, the paucity of credible sources from this period frustrates our attempts at gaining a comprehensive view of historical developments. Nonetheless, from the scope of activities that took place in connection with developing a theory of abrogation, we can derive some clues as to the extent to which the Quran played a role in elaborating Islamic jurisprudence.

The rudimentary beginnings of the theory of abrogation seem to have

[14] See Patricia Crone and Martin Hinds, *God's Caliph: Religious Authority in the First Centuries of Islam* (Cambridge: Cambridge University Press, 1986), 56 and generally.

[15] ʿAbd al-Ghanī b. ʿAbd al-Wāḥid al-Jamāʿīlī, *al-ʿUmda fī al-Aḥkām fī Maʿālim al-Ḥalāl wal-Ḥarām*, ed. Muṣṭafā ʿAṭā (Beirut: Dār al-Kutub al-ʿIlmiyya, 1986), 463.

arisen in response to the need for reconciling what appeared to the early Muslims as seeming contradictions within the body of legal verses in the Quran. The most immediate concern for these Muslims was neither theology nor dogma – matters that acquired significance only later – but rather the actions through which they realized and manifested obedience to their God, in adherence to the Quranic command. In other words, Islam meant, as early as the middle of the first century, adherence to the will of God as articulated in His Book. Thus it was felt necessary to determine the Quranic stand with regard to a particular issue. When more than one Quranic decree was pertinent to a single matter, such a determination was no easy task. To solve such difficulties, questions about the chronological order in which different verses had been revealed became essential.

Although the Companions of the Prophet reportedly were involved in beginning such discussions, Muslim sources make relatively few references to their contributions to this field. It was the generation of the Successors that was closely associated with discussions on abrogation and with controversies about the status of particular verses. Ibrāhīm al-Nakhaʿī (d. 95/713), Muslim b. Yasār (d. 101/719), Mujāhid b. Jabr (d. 104/722) and al-Ḥasan al-Baṣrī (d. 110/728) were among the most prominent in such discussions.[16] Qatāda b. Diʿāma al-Saddūsī (d. 117/735) and the renowned Ibn Shihāb al-Zuhrī (d. 124/742) have also left us writings which attest to the beginnings of a theory of abrogation, a theory which by then had already been articulated in literary form.[17] Though their original works in all probability were subjected to redaction by later writers, the core of their treatises has proven difficult to dismiss as inauthentic.[18] Even if this core is reduced to a minimum, it manifests an awareness, on the part of these scholars, of the legal thrust of the Quranic text. For it is clear that the treatises were concerned exclusively with the ramifications of those verses that had direct bearing on legal issues.

It is likely that the theory of abrogation developed in a context in which some Quranic prescriptions contradicted the actual reality and practice of the community, thus giving rise to the need for interpreting away, or canceling out, the effect of those verses that were deemed inconsistent with other verses more in line with prevailing customs. However the case may be, the very nature of this theory suggests that whatever contradiction or problem needed to be resolved, this was to be done within the purview of

[16] See David S. Powers, "The Exegetical Genre *nāsikh al-Qur'ān wa-mansūkhuh*," in Andrew Rippin, ed., *Approaches to the History of the Interpretation of the Qur'ān* (Oxford: Clarendon Press, 1988), 119.

[17] Andrew Rippin, "Al-Zuhrī, *Naskh al-Qur'ān* and the Problem of Early *Tafsīr* Texts," *Bulletin of the School of Oriental and African Studies*, 47 (1984): 22 ff.

[18] Ibid.

Quranic authority. This is in agreement with the assertion that the Umayyad caliphs saw themselves not only as the deputies of God on earth, and thus instruments for carrying out God's justice as embodied in the Quran, but also as the propounders of the law in its (then) widest sense.[19] In addition to fiscal policy and the laws of war, they regularly concerned themselves with establishing and enforcing rules regarding marriage, divorce, succession, manumission, preemption, blood-money, ritual and other matters.[20] The promulgation of these rules was carried out in the name of the Lord, whose deputies these caliphs claimed to be.

At the same time, to say that all such promulgations originated, even indirectly, in the Quran would be to overstate the matter. The text comprises some 500 legal verses, and these cover a relatively limited number of legal issues and, furthermore, treat of them selectively. Thus the question that suggests itself here is what was the other material source, or sources, from which the law was derived? At the outset of this chapter mention was made of the Prophet's Sunna as the second source of the law according to later legal theory. To what extent, if at all, did first century jurisprudence draw on this source?

The term *sunna* means an exemplary mode of conduct and the perfect verb *sanna* has the connotation of "setting or fashioning a mode of conduct as an example for others to follow." During the first decades of Islam, it became customary to refer to the Prophet's biography and the events in which he was involved as his *sīra*. But while the latter term indicates a manner of proceeding or a course of action concerning a particular matter, the former, Sunna, describes the manner and course of action as something established, and thus worthy of being imitated.[21] For the contemporaries and immediate successors of Muhammad, an awareness of a particular Prophetic *sīra* did not entail an understanding that they were bound to follow the example of the Prophet's manner of conduct.

However, some evidence indicates that the Sunna of the Prophet became an established concept soon after his death. For the notion of *sunna* as model behavior had been in existence long before Muhammad began his mission. As early as the fifth century A.D., the Arabs of the north saw in Ishmael a sort of a saint who provided them with a model and a way of life.[22] In pre-Islamic Arabia, any person renowned for his rectitude, charisma and distinguished stature was, within his family and clan, considered to provide a *sunna*, a normative practice to be emulated. The poet al-

[19] Crone and Hinds, *God's Caliph*, 53. [20] Ibid.
[21] M. M. Bravmann, *The Spiritual Background of Early Islam* (Leiden: E. J. Brill, 1972), 138–39, 169.
[22] Irfan Shahid, *Byzantium and the Arabs in the Fifth Century* (Washington, D.C.: Dumbarton Oaks Research Library and Collection, 1989), 180.

Mutalammis, for instance, aspired to leave "a *sunna* which will be imitated."[23] The concept of *sunna* thus existed before Islam and was clearly associated with the conduct of individuals, and not only with the collective behavior of nations, as attested in the Quran.

Accordingly, it would be difficult to argue that Muhammad, the most influential person in the nascent Muslim community, was not regarded as a source of normative practice. In fact, the Quran itself explicitly and repeatedly enjoins Muslims to obey the Prophet and to emulate his actions. The implications of Q. 4:80 – "He who obeys the Messenger obeys God," – need hardly be explained. So too Q. 59:7: "Whatsoever the Messenger ordains, you should accept, and whatsoever he forbids, you should abstain from." Dozens of similar verses bid Muslims to obey the Prophet and not to dissent from his ranks.[24] Moreover, in Q. 33:21 it is explicitly stated that "in the Messenger of God you [i.e., Muslims] have a good example."

It may be argued that obedience to the Prophet was incumbent upon Muslims while the Prophet was alive, but that after his death they might have felt free to decide their own affairs as they saw fit, without his deeds and utterances being a model which they were bound to follow. But this argument is hard to accept in view of two considerations. First, Muhammad, like all the other leading figures who preceded him in pre-Islamic Arabia, represented a source of normative behavior for his contemporaries and successors; the association of certain individuals with an ideal *sunna* constituted an integral ingredient in the social value structure of Arabia, with or without Islam. Second, the Quran forcefully sanctioned this established structure and the place of the Prophet in it, and further enhanced his personal authority by bestowing on him the status of the Messenger of God. To obey him, by definition, was to obey God. In establishing his *modus operandi* as exemplary and worthy of being emulated by contemporary and later generations, the Prophet hardly could have received better support than that given by the society in which he lived and by the Deity he was sent to serve.

The most persuasive argument in support of the early origins of "the Sunna of the Prophet" is the term's attestation by the middle of the first century at the latest,[25] indeed, as early as 23 H., when ʿUthmān and ʿAlī, the two candidates for the caliphate, were asked whether they were prepared to "work according to the Sunna of the Prophet and the *sīra* of the two

[23] Bravmann, *Spiritual Background*, 139 ff. See also Zafar Ishaq Ansari, "Islamic Juristic Terminology before Šāfiʿī: A Semantic Analysis with Special Reference to Kūfa," *Arabica*, 19 (1972), 259 ff.

[24] See, e.g., Q. 3:32, 132; 4:59 (twice), 64, 69, 80; 5:92; 24: 54, 56; 33:21; 59:7.

[25] Ansari, "Islamic Juristic Terminology," 264; Crone and Hinds, *God's Caliph*, 59–61.

preceding caliphs," Abū Bakr and ʿUmar.[26] It is reported that, even earlier, ʿUmar referred to the decisions of the Prophet in a matter related to meting out punishment for adulterers, and in another in which the Prophet enjoined him to allot the distant relatives the shares of inheritance to which they were entitled.[27] Subsequently, the number of references to the "Sunna of the Prophet" increased, frequently with reference to concrete things said or done by the Prophet.[28] In a number of instances, however, the expression "Sunna of the Prophet" referred to no substantive or concrete matter, but rather to "right and just practice." This is also the connotation attached to many early references to the *sunna*s of Abū Bakr, ʿUmar, ʿUthmān and others. By such *sunna*s it was meant that these caliphs set a model of good behavior, not that they necessarily laid down specific rulings.[29]

From the foregoing, one concludes that a Sunna of some kind was associated with the Prophet. Whether this is the same Sunna attributed to him one or two centuries later is a question we will now attempt to answer. We must begin by looking at the content of Prophetic Sunna during the two or three decades following the Prophet's death. There is little doubt that the core of Sunnaic material that was inspired by the vitally important issues raised in the Quran represents a portrait of the actual Sunna enacted by the Prophet. It would be inconceivable that all these issues were confined to the Quran and excluded from the Sunna. Such matters as pertain to inheritance,[30] taxes[31] and property,[32] and which were dealt with in a range and variety more or less equal to the range and variety in which these matters were recorded in the Quran, are examples of authentic Sunna; their inauthenticity, in fact, cannot be established.[33]

As noted, Muhammad had an open mind toward those pre-Islamic Arab customs that he did not regard as endangering the establishment of his new religion.[34] The law of *qasāma* represented one such customary practice that he sanctioned and applied in a litigation that was brought against the Jews of Khaybar. The law was considered by later jurists as having been derived

26 Ansari, "Islamic Juristic Terminology," 263.

27 Juynboll, *Muslim Tradition*, 26–27. For other instances in which ʿUmar refers to the "Sunna of the Prophet," see Ansari, "Islamic Juristic Terminology," 263; Bravmann, *Spiritual Background*, 168–74.

28 Crone and Hinds, *God's Caliph*, 71 and generally, and sources cited in the previous two notes.

29 Crone and Hinds, *God's Caliph*, 55.

30 Powers, "The Will of Saʿd" 33–53; Powers, *Studies in Qur'ān and Ḥadīth*.

31 Juynboll, *Muslim Tradition*, 24–25.

32 Bravmann, *Spiritual Background*, 176, 229 ff.

33 See sources quoted in the previous three notes.

34 Numerous such customs and practices which were adopted by the new Muslim religion have been documented in Khalīl ʿAbd al-Karīm, *al-Judhūr al-Tārīkhiyya lil-Sharīʿa al-Islāmiyya* (Cairo: Sīnā lil-Nashr, 1990), 15–19, 23–26, 36–47, 71–82, 85–98.

from his Sunna; interestingly enough, they explicitly acknowledged that it originally had been a pre-Islamic practice.[35] The fifth-/eleventh-century jurist Ibn Ḥazm, admitting the Jāhilī origin of *qasāma*, declared that "it is not lawful to disregard [the law of] *qasāma*, since it is not permissible to adhere to some laws applied by the Prophet and cast aside others. For all [laws] come from God, and all are binding."[36] It is interesting to note here the transformation of a law from the "heretical" Jāhilī environment to the realm of the divine, a transformation accommodated through the agency of the Prophet.

Similarly, it was a pre-Islamic Arab practice to distribute any surplus of property (*faḍl al-māl*) for social and charitable purposes. The Prophet applied this principle, which the jurists later thought to be his practice. And inasmuch as it was considered a Prophetic Sunna, it became part of the Sharīʿa.[37]

In the second half of the first century, when the capital of the Islamic empire was transferred to Damascus, and vast territories came under Islamic rule, a third element became a constituent part of the Prophetic Sunna. This was the administrative and legal practices then prevailing in the newly occupied lands. The customary law of pre-Islamic Arabia continued to be applied with regard to many matters that were brought before the Umayyad rulers, but this law was obviously insufficient to deal with the varied and intricate problems that arose in the new provinces. These problems were solved by Muslim judges who often invoked laws that had prevailed prior to the Islamic conquest.[38] It was through the practice of these judges that the administrative and legal subject matter predominating in the provinces entered the body of the Prophetic Sunna. This process of assimilation was aided by the activities of religious scholars, and especially by story-tellers, who spread stories with ethico-legal content about the Prophet and his immediate followers. Although these stories were partly inspired by what the Prophet had actually done or approximately said, they also contain statements that expressed the local practices and norms prevailing in the conquered provinces; and these latter were endowed with the authority of the new religion by having been attributed either to the Prophet or to his Companions.

The enormous growth in the body of materials attributed to the Prophet

[35] Ibn Ḥazm, *Muʿjam al-Fiqh*, II, 838; see also ʿAbd al-Karīm, *al-Judhūr al-Tārīkhiyya*, 89–91.

[36] See, e.g., Ibn Ḥazm, *Muʿjam al-Fiqh*, II, 838.

[37] Bravmann, *Spiritual Background*, 176, 229 ff. Included in the Sharīʿa in the same fashion were prayer and fasting. See Goitein, *Studies*, 73–89, 92–94.

[38] See Gladys Frantz-Murphy, "A Comparison of the Arabic and Earlier Egyptian Contract Formularies, Part II: Terminology in the Arabic Warranty and the Idiom of Clearing/Cleaning," *Journal of Near Eastern Studies*, 44 (1985): 99–114.

and his Companions generated an interest, particularly among pious scholars, to investigate the soundness and authenticity of these materials and the credibility of those who narrated them. This interest gave rise to two fundamental concepts in first-century legal thought, namely, *ḥadīth* and *isnād* (the chain of transmission). The early and informal investigation of the credibility of informants gradually gave way to an increasing awareness of the importance of establishing criteria by which the sound – or what was thought to be sound – reports from the early paragons could be sifted from the massive body of spurious material. But it was not until the second and third centuries that this activity developed into a full-fledged science. The *ḥadīth*, on the other hand, represented reports or verbal transmissions which conveyed the contents of Sunna. Encapsulating the Sunna in *ḥadīth* was inevitable, since it was the only way in which the contents of the Sunna could be defined, transmitted and investigated.

At the end of the first century, the process of expressing the Sunna through the medium of verbal transmission was by no means complete. A Prophetic Sunna concerning a certain theological position, for instance, was known to Ḥasan al-Baṣrī although he was unable to produce a verbal transmission attesting to it.[39] It appears that the process of verbal transmission began some time after the demise of the generation of the Companions, who knew first hand what the Prophet was saying and doing. But verbal transmission, in the form that subsequently came to be known as *ḥadīth*, was only beginning to emerge and did not encompass the whole material of the Sunna, which was still being informally circulated by storytellers and others. This explains why Ḥasan al-Baṣrī could know of a "Sunna from the Prophet" but could not adduce a verbal transmission to express the contents of that Sunna.

By the end of the first century, a part of the Prophet's Sunna had become the subject of intense interest among certain groups. The Umayyad caliph ʿUmar II (99–101/717–19) is the first major figure associated with the collection of the Prophetic Sunna, or, at least, with that Sunna that touched on fiscal and administrative matters. Upon his accession to power, he is reported to have rebuked one of his administrators for not following the Sunna of the Prophet and for not abandoning "the innovations that took place after [the Prophet's] Sunna."[40] He is also reported to have asked Abū Bakr al-Anṣārī and others to "look for what there is of the *ḥadīth* of the Apostle and of his Sunna."[41] The task of coordinating the material he received from his subordinates was assigned to Zuhrī, and

[39] Ansari, "Islamic Juristic Terminology," 263–64.
[40] Cited in Juynboll, *Muslim Tradition*, 35.
[41] Cited in Abbott, *Studies*, 26.

copies seem to have been publicized in the provinces for the benefit of judges and administrators.[42] But ʿUmar's enterprise failed, for it appears that at that time disregarding the Prophet's Sunna was not yet looked upon as a serious matter.

The increasing importance of the Sunna toward the end of the first century represents only one expression of the rapidly growing tendency toward adopting revealed sources as the ultimate guide of Muslim conduct. It was in this period, we may recall, that the theory of abrogation was beginning to take shape. And it was in this period that the first generation of legists, such as the distinguished Ibrāhīm al-Nakhaʿī, were active, elaborating the core of a positive legal doctrine, particularly the branches of the law that dealt with rituals, inheritance, alms-tax, marriage, divorce and other matters. Significantly, it was during this period that the well-known "travel in search of knowledge" (*ṭalab al-ʿilm*) became a common practice. "Search for knowledge" meant at the time a search for the textual sources of Islam within the central lands of the empire, and *ḥadīth* was the foremost goal for students and scholars alike.

ʿIlm came to signify knowledge of the Quran and the Sunna. Its binary opposite was *raʾy*, that is, considered opinion. An opinion arrived at on the basis of *ʿilm* amounted to *ijtihād*, a term that was used ordinarily in conjunction with the word *raʾy*. *Ijtihād al-raʾy* thus meant the intellectual activity or the reasoning of the legal scholar whose sources of knowledge are materials endowed with religious (or quasi-religious) authority.[43]

At a time when the textual sources of religion were not yet established and when their controlling authority was far from exclusive, such practices as *raʾy* would not have been censured. In fact, by the eighth decade of the first century, the term was used to indicate sound and considered opinion. The poet ʿAbd Allāh b. Shaddād al-Laythī (d. 83/702) regarded the approval given by *ahl al-raʾy* (the people of good sense) to be a desideratum for acquiring a good reputation in society.[44] But this was soon to change. The increasing importance of religious texts gradually ousted *raʾy* from the realm of legitimacy. The beginning of this process seems to have been, again, associated with the last quarter of the first century, and, more particularly, with ʿUmar II. As caliph, he is said to have demanded of any judge he appointed that he be possessed of *ʿilm* and that he resort, when in doubt, to those who were adept in *ʿilm*, not *raʾy*.[45]

42 Ibid., 30–31. 43 Bravmann, *Spiritual Background*, 177–78, 193–94.

44 His poem is excerpted in Sayyid Aḥmad al-Hāshimī, *Jawāhir al-Adab fī Adabiyyāt wa-Inshāʾ Lughat al-ʿArab*, 2 vols. (Beirut: Mu'assasat al-Risāla, n.d.), I, 190. On the positive connotations of *ra'y* in the early period, see also Schacht, *Origins*, 128 (on the authority of Goldziher).

45 Juynboll, *Muslim Tradition*, 36.

JURISPRUDENCE IN THE SECOND CENTURY H. (CA. 720–815 A.D.)

Contrary to the notions currently prevalent among modern scholars, the overwhelming body of evidence indicates that Islamic jurisprudence did not begin around 100 H., but that the state of affairs as it existed at the turn of the second century constituted a further stage in a process of development that had begun much earlier. There is no evidence that distinguishes the period around 100 H. as a time in which new institutions or concepts came into being. Our centennial division must therefore be understood as a convenient way of presenting the material, and not as conforming to any chronology of significant events.

The last quarter of the first century saw an upsurge of intellectual legal activity in which Arab Muslims and non-Arab converts took part. Interest in legal issues no longer was limited to an elite who were privileged to have been affiliated with the Prophet or with his Companions. This increasing interest in these issues was reflected in the evolution of various centers of legal activity throughout the Islamic lands. In the beginning of the second century, the most prominent centers were the Hijaz, Iraq and Syria. Egypt became such a center soon thereafter.

During this period, legal activity drew on the Quran and on what was thought to be the practices of the Prophet and of the early Muslims who had surrounded him and who were vested with special religious authority by virtue of the presumption that they knew the Prophet's intentions at first hand. But to no lesser an extent was legal activity influenced by the administrative and judicial practices prevailing in the various provinces, and these differed from one region to another. As seen by the scholars of each region, their own practice constituted a *sunna*, a body of average doctrine that expressed both practical and ideal elements. Although the practical elements were in large part identical with administrative and judicial practices existing in each region, and thus were not necessarily the products of the Quran or the religious and ethical material related on the authority of the Prophet and his Companions, they were subjected, from the beginning, to a process in which they were gradually imbued with a religious and at times ideal element.

Injecting these practices with a religious element meant nothing more than claiming them to be doctrines enunciated or adopted by an earlier authority, usually a Successor or a Companion. But the attribution of doctrines to older authorities, which often was authentic, did not stop at the level of a Successor or a Companion. The differences among the geographical schools (as well as among scholars within each school) amounted in fact to a competition among conflicting doctrines. And in order to lend a doctrine an authority sufficient to guarantee its "success" over and against competing doctrine – say one attributed to a Companion – the chain of authority of the first doctrine was extended to the Prophet himself.

This process of projecting legal doctrines backward, mainly from the Successors to the Companions, and ultimately to the Prophet, was a lengthy one; it began some time toward the end of the first century and continued well into the third. The beginnings of this process are associated with the scholars of Iraq. The Kufans, in particular, appear to have been the first to attribute the doctrine of their school to Ibrāhīm al-Nakhaʿī, whose generation represented the earliest specialists in the law. The Iraqi scholars Ḥammād b. Sulaymān (d. 120/738) and Ibn Abī Laylā (d. 148/765) represent two successive stages in which there is a slow but steady growth in the body of Prophetic reports. By the time of the latter, who was a contemporary of Abū Ḥanīfa (d. 150/767), the reliance on Prophetic reports was still relatively insignificant. Abū Ḥanīfa, for instance, had a limited number of *ḥadīth*s at his disposal, and whatever he used was by and large considered suspicious by the later *ḥadīth* critics.

Another contemporary of Abū Ḥanīfa, the Syrian jurist Awzāʿī (d. 157/774), used relatively few Prophetic reports, though he often referred to the "Sunna of the Prophet." The technical relationship between the Sunna and the reports that express it is still tenuous in Awzāʿī, for he considers an informal report or a legal maxim without *isnād* sufficient to attest to the Prophetic Sunna. But like the great majority of his contemporaries and immediate predecessors, Awzāʿī viewed the practice (=*sunna*) of his community as having been continuous since the Prophet, and as having been maintained throughout by the caliphs and the scholars. Awzāʿī, in other words, projects the entire body of his doctrine, including elements of provincial customary practice, back to the Prophet, without, however, feeling bound to adduce formal reports.[46] That the legists in the first and second centuries thought their doctrines to carry an authority extending back to the Prophet is clear. Also clear is the fact that these doctrines encompassed, aside from the Quran, two types of legal material that hailed from two radically different sources. The first was Arabian, associated with the pre-Islamic laws and customs that were practiced or approved by the Prophet, and the second provincial, gradually but systematically assimilated into the normative practices of the Muslim community, practices that were perceived by Muslims to derive from the Sunna of the Prophet. However, by the time of Abū Ḥanīfa and Awzāʿī, it was still largely immaterial to

[46] Schacht, *Origins*, 70 ff.

express the body of doctrine embodying these practices in the form of reports from the Prophet.

It was the generation that flourished in the second half of the second century that began, albeit inconsistently, to anchor its doctrines in Prophetic reports. The increasing reference to reports coincided with another process in which reports were projected, more than ever before, to the Prophet himself. Again, the Iraqis stood in the forefront: their doctrines were not only the most advanced in technical legal thought, but also reflected the highest stage of development in the construction of a body of Prophetic *ḥadīth*, both in content and transmission. Although the doctrine of Abū Yūsuf (d. 182/798), a student of Abū Ḥanīfa, already represented an advance over that of his master, it was Aḥmad b. Ḥasan al-Shaybānī (d. 189/804) who insisted for the first time that no legal ruling can be valid unless it is based upon a binding text, by which he meant the Quran and Prophetic *ḥadīth*, although reports from the Companions still played some role in his doctrine. The elimination of the role of the Companions' reports from the construction of the law was completed by Muḥammad Ibn Idrīs al-Shāfiʿī (d. 204/820) who insisted, consistently and systematically, that the Quran and the Sunna of the Prophet are the sole material sources of the law.

Shāfiʿī's theory of *ḥadīth*, which represented a middle position between two extremes, was by no means universally accepted at the time. On the one hand stood a group of scholars who thought that all human conduct must be firmly regulated by authoritative texts, and that human reasoning has no place in religious matters. On the other hand stood the rationalists, many of whom belonged to the Muʿtazilite movement, who attempted to discredit such texts and held the Quran sufficient to explain everything. They dismissed reports conveyed through single (or a few) chains of transmission and demanded that for a report to be accepted it must be transmitted by many from many. Some Iraqi scholars, probably associated with the Muʿtazilites, set aside any report that was contradicted by another, and instead resorted to their own reasoning. They were also inclined to dismiss reports by maintaining that they were applicable to the Prophet alone, not to his followers. Like the rationalists, they rejected solitary reports, but argued that a report might be accepted if it is related through at least two lines of transmission, by analogy with the accepted number of witnesses in the law of evidence.[47]

With the emergence of a powerful movement which aimed at anchoring

[47] On these groups as well as on the development of the *ḥadīth* movement in the second century, see ibid., 27 ff., 40 ff., 47 ff., 51, generally.

all law in religious, authoritative texts, the nature of legal thinking changed. The concepts of *raʾy* and *ijtihād*, and the types of reasoning they encompassed, underwent a change in both structure and meaning. By the middle of the second century (and perhaps earlier), the term *raʾy* indicated two types of reasoning. The first was free human reasoning based on practical considerations and bound by no authoritative text. The second was free reasoning based on such a text and motivated by practical considerations. With the growth of the religious movement during the second century, the first type of reasoning was gradually abandoned in favor of the second, and even this was to undergo, in turn, two significant changes. On the one hand, the attribution of the authoritative texts constituting the bases of this kind of reasoning and ascribed to a class lower than that of the Prophet were gradually upgraded to the status of Prophetic Sunna. Shāfiʿī's doctrine represents the culmination of this process. On the other hand, the quality of reasoning was to change in favor of stricter and more systematic methods. Even the term *raʾy*, having been so deeply associated with arbitrary forms of reasoning, was completely abandoned and replaced by other terms which came to acquire positive connotations. *Ijtihād* and *qiyās* were two such terms, encompassing all forms of methodical reasoning on the basis of the Quran and the Sunna.

The transformation from the old ways of reasoning subsumed under *raʾy* to the new methods of *qiyās* and *ijtihād* was gradual. By the middle of the second century we find that the Iraqis, and even the Medinese, at times introduce under *raʾy* strict and systematic methods of reasoning. By the beginning of the third/ninth century, *raʾy*, as both a technical term and a method of free reasoning, seems to have lost, for the most part, its grounds in legal discourse. The alternatives, *qiyās* and *ijtihād*, became widespread after the time of Shāfiʿī, and their adoption was in no small measure due to the fact that they were not associated with the now derogatory connotation of arbitrary opinion. We recall that *ijtihād*, even when coupled with the term *raʾy*, indicated, as early as the first century, reasoning based on authoritative texts (*ʿilm*).

It is clear that labels for types of reasoning in this period were far from fixed, and that *raʾy*, for instance, could encompass as well strict forms of reasoning concerning a particular case. It appears that the rulings reached through these forms of reasoning were later identified with *qiyās*, and those associated with free human reasoning with *istiḥsān*, a term that came into use around the middle of the second century.[48] Systematic legal reasoning in turn was often, but certainly not always, described as *qiyās*, which seems

[48] Ibid., 112.

to have encompassed at least two distinct methods. The first was analogy, that is, when two cases are "brought together" due to a common meaning. The Iraqis and the Medinese, and later Shāfiʿī himself, resort to it, but do not call the common meaning *ʿilla* (*ratio legis*), a term that emerged only later. The Iraqis also subsume under *qiyās* the *a fortiori* argument in both of its forms, the *a maiore ad minus* and the *a minore ad maius*.[49]

Ever since the formation of the geographical schools of law took shape during the first half of the second century H., the idea of consensus had played a significant role in sanctioning their doctrines. The concept of consensus (*ijmāʿ*) had been in existence since pre-Islamic times, and referred to the conscious formal agreement of the tribe.[50] In the early schools, consensus expressed the average doctrine on which the scholars and the community, whether in a particular region or at large, were in agreement. For the Iraqis, consensus extended in theory to all countries, but in practice it had a local character. On matters related to general practice, all Muslims were deemed to participate in forming consensus, whereas on technical points of the law, the scholars had a monopoly. The Medinese, on the other hand, while at times sharing with the Iraqi concept its claim to universality, limited their consensus to the common practice at Medina. Be that as it may, once a doctrine became subject to consensus it was considered, by those who were party to it, final and immune from error.[51]

Although consensus, in one form or another, had always been part of the make-up of the geographical schools of law, there was no attempt at first to anchor it in any authoritative text. With the growth in the body of *ḥadīth*, however, and with the concurrently increasing tendency to ground all law in the Sunna of the Prophet, there were attempts toward the end of the second century to justify consensus on the basis of Prophetic reports. The earliest and most notable attempt was made by Shaybānī who declared on the authority of the Prophet that "Whatever the Muslims see as good is good (*ḥasan*) in the eyes of God, and whatever they see as bad is bad in the eyes of God." But Shāfiʿī seems to have rejected this report since it clearly smacks of *istiḥsān*, a principle he abhorred. Instead, as we shall see, he resorted to other Prophetic reports as well as to the Quran.

Shāfiʿī flourished in a period when a powerful group of traditionalists advanced the thesis that nothing that the Muslim community says or does should escape the sanction of the Quran and the reports of the Prophet. At the same time, this group militated against a tendency that had become entrenched in Islam since the first century, namely, the tendency to ignore

49 For the logical properties of these arguments, pp. 96–99 below.
50 Bravmann, *Spiritual Background*, 194–98.
51 Schacht, *Origins*, 82, 85, 88.

the Prophetic reports and insist on human reason as the final judge on matters not regulated by the Quran. Shāfiʿī elaborated his concept of how the law should be formulated against the backdrop of a reality thoroughly permeated by the conflict between the traditionists and the rationalists. His concept constituted in effect a rudimentary theory of law, a theory that was in one sense caused by, and in another the result of, that conflict.

THE BEGINNINGS OF LEGAL THEORIZATION

Shāfiʿī's legal theory, as indeed all his *corpus juris*, underwent a transformation from what is known as the "old doctrine" to the "new," in which he seems to have reached a fresh understanding of the law. Reportedly born in Palestine and raised in the Hijaz, Shāfiʿī lived in the major centers of learning, where he became exposed to all the influential trends of legal learning. We do not know at what point of his life he decided to abandon the "old doctrine," but it is highly likely that it was in Egypt after 198/813, some six years before his death. There he seems to have revised his treatise on some aspects of legal theory, a treatise he titled *al-Kitāb*, but which subsequently came to be known as *al-Risāla*. Both words mean "epistle," this being an accurate description of the work which was originally written for, and then in fact sent to, ʿAbd al-Raḥmān b. Mahdī, who died in 198/813–14.

The *Risāla* reportedly was the first work written on legal theory to be designated as *uṣūl al-fiqh*, a compound term which appeared much later. In this treatise, Shāfiʿī attempted to set forth a theory that describes, and in fact prescribes, the methods by means of which law is formulated. As suggested earlier, the work constituted a reaction to the trends and movements that prevailed in second-/eighth-century jurisprudence. In order to understand the thrust of the work, we shall examine it according to the same manner and arrangement in which it is presented by Shāfiʿī.

Shāfiʿī opens his work with a reference to two types of communities, one that worshipped idols and possessed no divine book, and another that did possess one which it altered and corrupted. The latter are the Jews and Christians, while the former are the pre-Islamic, polytheistic Arabs of the Peninsula. The peninsular Arabs, however, were sent a Prophet, Muhammad, who conveyed to them a Book, and they have thus become bound by the wishes of God as expressed in that Book. Now in possession of scripture, they have become duty-bound to cast their personal predilections and desires aside and to abide by the dictates of an all-encompassing revelation. Nothing that befalls Muslims, severally and collectively, is neglected in the Book. The Muslim community and its affairs, we are to understand, are sublime enough to command the attention of God Himself. What seems to be here an ennoblement of the human condition is nothing more than an assertion directed against contemporary rationalists who held that man can determine the quality of his acts by his own reason and without the intervention of a deity.

The recipients of a divine revelation, Muslims are duty-bound to attempt to gain and augment *ʿilm*, that is, knowledge of the scripture in its direct as well as oblique meanings. For God has revealed His precepts in a variety of forms. In one form, He unequivocally states in the Quran certain rulings, such as those related to prayer, alms-tax, pilgrimage, fasting, etc. In another form, the rulings are stipulated in the Quran in general terms, the details of which the Prophet has laid down in his Sunna. God has also decreed certain rulings through His Prophet, without there being any reference to them in the Quran. Finally, the revealed texts, the Quran and the Sunna, provide, in the absence of explicitly formulated rulings, indications and signs (*dalālāt*) which lead to the discovery of what God intended the law to be. In sum, God left nothing outside the compass of His decree; revelation is all-inclusive.[52]

It is noteworthy that the all-inclusiveness of revelation means, in Shāfiʿī's view, not only that positive law must ultimately rest on the divine texts, but also that the methods by which that law is discovered must rest on those same texts. The Quran as a source of law hardly needed any justification, though the same cannot be said of the Sunna of the Prophet, as we shall see. The preoccupation of Shāfiʿī's *Risāla* was primarily to justify the authoritative bases of, first, the Sunna, and, second, consensus and *qiyās*. Aside from the fact that the Quran's authority was seen as self-evident, it was too well established as a source of law to warrant any justification. But this was not the case with the three remaining sources. In advocating a paramount place for Prophetic Sunna in the law, Shāfiʿī was addressing, if not reacting to, those who resorted to any means by which they could diminish its juristic role. And in advocating *qiyās*, he was responding to the traditionists who spurned reason as a means of expounding the law. Consensus, or its binary opposite, disagreement (*ikhtilāf*), acquires importance in Shāfiʿī's legal theory mainly as a result of the differing methods used by the jurists in interpreting the texts and in reasoning on their basis. Otherwise, Shāfiʿī's chief concern was with the Sunna and its ramifications in the law.

Having enumerated the types of language in which God chose to reveal His legal judgments, Shāfiʿī goes on to establish the authoritative basis of

52 Muḥammad b. Idrīs al-Shāfiʿī, *al-Risāla*, ed. Muḥammad Sayyid Kīlānī (Cairo: Muṣṭafā Bābī al-Ḥalabī, 1969), 15 ff. Henceforth quoted as *Risāla*.

the method by which the linguistic signs and indications must be interpreted in order for them to yield what the jurist believes to be God's law. The justification of this method, which he calls *ijtihād* as well as *qiyās*, rests with the Quranic injunction to pray in the direction of the Kaʿba: "Turn your [Muhammad's] face towards the Sacred Place of Worship, and you [Muslims], wherever you may be, turn your faces [when you pray] towards it" (2: 144, 150). Shāfiʿī argues that in their prayer Muslims are commanded to face the Kaʿba even when it is beyond the range of their sight. They are under the obligation to attempt to discover the direction of the Holy Site by seeking, through the exercise of their mental faculties, indications and signs which might lead them to know that direction. For after all, he maintains, God has stated that He created stars, mountains, rivers, light, darkness, etc., so that the Muslims may be guided by them (Q. 6:97, 16:16). The strict implication of these verses is that Muslims are not at liberty to pray in the direction they deem desirable, but rather are bound to exert the utmost mental effort in seeking the location of the Kaʿba. By analogy, he deduces, Muslims are under an obligation to determine the legal values governing their conduct, values that are hidden in the language of the texts.[53]

Once Shāfiʿī has established the textual, authoritative basis of *ijtihād* (=*qiyās*), he delimits the scope of this method. Obviously, when the Book or the Sunna provides the legal solution to a particular problem, no inference is needed. But when there arises a new case for which the texts provide no express solution, the exercise of *ijtihād* becomes not only necessary but obligatory. In the absence of a formulated textual solution, the jurist must look for a parallel textual case for which a solution is provided. If the new case has the same *ratio legis* (*maʿnā*; lit. meaning) as that given to the parallel textual case, the ruling in the text must be transferred to the new case. But such a *ratio legis* is not always capable of identification, in which event the jurist must locate all cases in the texts that resemble the new case, and must transfer the ruling of the most similar case to the new case at hand. These two methods, one based on a *ratio legis*, the other on a similitude, are, together with the *a fortiori* argument, the exclusive constituents of *ijtihād* (=*qiyās*). Any inference that is governed by less than the strict implications and significations of the texts is invalid and hence impermissible. It is on these grounds that Shāfiʿī spurned *istiḥsān*, a method of reasoning that he regarded as based merely on free human reasoning guided by personal interests and whims. *Istiḥsān*, he thought, amounts to indulging in base pleasures.[54]

[53] *Risāla*, 16–18.

[54] Ibid., 219–44; Muḥammad b. Idrīs al-Shāfiʿī, *Kitāb al-Umm*, 7 vols. (Cairo: al-Maṭbaʿa al-Kubrā al-Amīriyya, 1325/1907), VII, 267–77.

Shāfiʿī at this point abandons the discussion of *ijtihād*, only to come back to it toward the end of the treatise. There he stipulates the conditions that the jurist must fulfill in order to qualify for practicing *ijtihād*, including knowledge of the Arabic language, of the legal contents of the Book, of its particular and general language, and of the theory of abrogation (*naskh*). The jurist must be able to employ the Sunna in interpreting those Quranic verses that are equivocal, and in the absence of a Sunna he must be aware of the existence of a consensus which might inform the case at hand. Finally, he must have attained majority, be of sound mind, and willing and ready to exert his utmost intellectual effort in solving the case.[55]

Shāfiʿī then turns to the Quran and insists that no foreign vocabulary may be found in it and that it was revealed in pure Arabic. He considers a masterly knowledge of the Arabic language to be one of the qualities necessary for a "proper understanding" of the texts. Knowledge of areas required for such understanding include, among others, the theory of abrogation, the texts containing commands and prohibitions (*amr/nahy*), consensus and disagreement (*khilāf*). Although Shāfiʿī does not explain why he chooses to discuss these areas of knowledge, we can infer that he deems them to be necessary for the practice of *ijtihād*, because they constitute a safeguard against arbitrary interpretation of the texts.

Another aspect of such knowledge relates to general and specific (*khāṣṣ/ʿāmm*) words used in the Quran. In a brief discussion, Shāfiʿī introduces some principles of hermeneutics and remarks that at times a general Quranic text is particularized by a Prophetic Sunna. This brings him to a rather lengthy exposition of the binding force of Prophetic Sunna, a theme that recurs throughout the treatise. The constant and consistent attention accorded the role and function of the Sunna, and the sheer bulk of the discussions devoted to it, constitute eloquent testimony to Shāfiʿī's motive for composing the *Risāla*. It would not be an exaggeration to state that the treatise represents a defense of the role of Prophetic reports in the law, as well as of the methods by which the law can be deduced from those reports. Any concern with topics that appear on the surface to be unconnected with the Prophetic Sunna and *ḥadīth* has ultimately to bear, directly or obliquely, upon the Sunna and its role in the law.

The Sunna, Shāfiʿī argues, may correspond to, overlap or depart from Quranic rulings. The fact that the Prophet followed the commands of God is evidence that his Sunna conforms, and represents a parallel, to the Quran. That it overlaps with the Quran means that it agrees with the Quran on general principles, while providing additional details explaining these

[55] *Risāla*, 211–19.

principles, thus going beyond the scope of the Book. The Sunna departs from the Quran in the sense that it provides legislation on matters on which the Quran is silent.[56]

Only with regard to this last category, Shāfiʿī remarks, were the scholars in disagreement. They disagreed on this category only insofar as its source of authority is concerned, not on its validity as such. One group of scholars has argued that since God made it incumbent upon Muslims to obey the Prophet – a point that is of central importance in Shāfiʿī's *Risāla* – He mandated to His Prophet the power to legislate where the Quran is silent. Another group rejected this category altogether, arguing that there is nothing in the Sunna that has not been laid down in the Quran. Shāfiʿī mentions other groups who proffered other explanations, and then goes on to explain those types of the Sunna that are supported by the Book and those that are not. In either case, it is clear to Shāfiʿī that nothing whatsoever in the Sunna contradicts the Quran; the Sunna merely explains, supplements or particularizes the Quran.

At this point Shāfiʿī devotes a lengthy discussion to the relationship of the Sunna to the Quran, including the abrogation of one by the other. To illustrate the harmonious relationship between the two sources, he discusses their contribution to the construction of the law of marriage. In His Book, God has forbidden men to have sexual relations with women except through marriage and concubinage. The Prophet's Sunna came to complement this decree by providing details for what constitutes a valid marriage. Accordingly, the Prophet stipulated that for a marriage to be valid, the woman who is a *thayyib* (non-virgin), a divorcée or a widow must express her consent, and furthermore that there must be two witnesses who will attest that the marriage contract was concluded. From the Prophetic stipulation that such a woman must express her consent it is inferred, Shāfiʿī maintains, that her counterpart, the man, must also express his consent. If the woman has not been previously married, she must be given in marriage by a guardian who is usually the nearest male agnate. Shāfiʿī includes this last condition without specifying the source from which it was derived. Dowry is recommended; it is neither obligatory nor a condition for a valid marriage. We know that it does not constitute such a condition because the Quran does not require it. On what grounds he deems it to be recommended, Shāfiʿī does not say.[57]

Further regulations pertaining to marriage are provided by the two textual sources. The Quran prohibited marriage between a man and his wife's sister. The Prophet went farther and considered marriage between a

[56] Ibid., 52. [57] Ibid., 54 ff., 58 ff., 61 ff., 68 ff.

man and his maternal and paternal aunts to be prohibited. The Quran allows a man to marry up to four wives, and the Prophet prohibited more than four. He also prohibited marriage to a woman during the waiting-period that follows her divorce or the death of her husband. The Sunna provides a multitude of other regulations which represent supplements to the Quran or details for general principles laid down therein.

Later on in the treatise, however, Shāfiʿī cautions that some Prophetic reports, though authentic and sound, must not be extended to govern new cases. Those reports that came to qualify or mitigate a Quranic judgment are intended to regulate only those specific cases for which they were enacted, and they ought not to be used in *qiyās*. The same principle applies to a universal Sunna that was qualified by the Prophet himself for the purpose of making an exception in a particular case. The Sunna, for instance, decrees that the blood-money paid for the murder of a male or a female person is a hundred or fifty camels, respectively. The Prophet, however, ruled that for the murder of a fetus the blood-money due is five camels, irrespective of the fetus's sex. The report about the fetus, which makes no distinction between sexes, is applicable exclusively to the murder of fetuses. Shāfiʿī, however, does not expound on the criteria for determining which reports are to be treated as limited to the particular cases they govern and which are not.[58]

Once the authority and the relationship of the textual sources have been established, Shāfiʿī moves on to a second level of analysis, one that is principally epistemological. Knowledge (*ʿilm*) according to Shāfiʿī is of two types: one type belongs to the generality, that is the community-at-large, the other belongs to the specialists, namely, the legal scholars. The first type, being textual, is widespread among all people, and is transmitted from the generality by the generality. The fact that it is transmitted in this manner, we are to understand, guarantees its authenticity and precludes the possibility of any disagreement on its substance as well as on its transmission. All this, coupled with the fact that its interpretation is subject to no disagreement, renders it certain. Examples of this type of knowledge are the five prayers and the obligation to fast in Ramadan.[59]

The second type of knowledge is not to be found in the Book, nor can most of it be attested in the Sunna. Whatever Sunna there is to sustain this knowledge, it is transmitted by channels fewer than those through which the first type is reported. To put it differently, it is transmitted from a few by a few, and these are the specialists. This knowledge, being subject to

[58] Ibid., 237–44.

[59] Ibid., 154 ff. On this and other related issues, see Norman Calder, "*Ikhtilāf* and *Ijmāʿ* in Shāfiʿī's *Risāla*," *Studia Islamica*, 58 (1984): 57 ff.

varying interpretations and derived by means of *qiyās*, can yield only probability.

In contradistinction to the first type of knowledge whose apprehension and performance is incumbent upon all Muslims, the second type entails duties for only a few. Shāfiʿī here argues, again on the basis of textual evidence, that certain religious responsibilities incumbent upon Muslims may be considered fulfilled if a sufficient number of individuals perform them. Such is the obligation to conduct holy war against the infidels; if part of the Muslim community performs that task, the obligation imposed upon the entire community is waived. Those who do not participate in waging the war are not guilty of sin, since the act of launching war is performed on their behalf, and yet those who do participate will acquire a double reward. From this it is deduced that some of the Muslims, here the legists, must be in charge of probing and interpreting the law on behalf of the entire community, since it is incumbent upon the community to attempt to discover God's law so that they may order their lives in accordance with it.[60]

The uncertainty surrounding the second type of knowledge requires that Shāfiʿī explain how it is to be employed in the construction of the law. It must be established that Prophetic reports related by a few from a few, technically known as solitary traditions (*khabar al-khāṣṣa* or *khabar al-wāḥid*), go back as far as the Prophet. He who transmits them must be trustworthy, pious, of sound mind, and knowledgeable of the meaning of the report he relates. He must convey the reports verbatim and must avoid narrating the meaning in his own language. For should he misunderstand the meaning of the report he is narrating, he would in effect be changing the contents of the report. Thus a literal transmission would safeguard against any change in that meaning.[61]

The aggregate of these conditions is not alone sufficient to establish the authority of the solitary report, although they do go as far as to make such authority highly probable. Therefore, in order to render it completely binding, Shāfiʿī invokes the practice of the Prophet, citing a number of cases in which the Prophet accepted and acted upon reports conveyed to him by a single person. Furthermore, he claims that a consensus in the past and in recent times has been reached on the authoritativeness of solitary reports.[62]

Like the solitary report, consensus too must rest on textual evidence. When consensus is reached on the basis of an unambiguous text, then the force of the text, Shāfiʿī seems to argue, justifies consensus, since the text, being certain, allows for no disagreement whatsoever. Such a consensus

[60] Ibid. [61] *Risāla*, 160. [62] Ibid., 175 ff.

would, in effect, be tantamount to knowledge of the first type – knowledge conveyed by the generality from the generality. But even if consensus is not known to be based on a text, the community, when it arrives at such a consensus, is deemed infallible since it cannot in its entirety be ignorant of the Sunna of the Prophet. We know, Shāfiʿī argues, that the community can agree neither on an error nor on a matter that is contrary to the Prophet's Sunna. The authority for this knowledge stems from two reports, from which Shāfiʿī deduces, by a rather strained argument, that the majority cannot fall into error.[63]

Thus, it is obvious that, for Shāfiʿī, all knowledge possessed by the generality and transmitted from the generality is certain, whereas knowledge that is the domain of the specialists is not. Accordingly, a consensus of the specialists that is transmitted by the specialists is not certain. Neither is any ruling arrived at by means of *qiyās* or *ijtihād*, for these are methods of reasoning and interpretation that are susceptible to error.

When the texts explicitly state the ruling of a case, then there should be no room for doubt whether or not it is God's intention. However, when the texts provide only indications and signs, the jurist then must attempt to find out the divine intention, although there is no guarantee that the ruling he reaches will be identical with that which is lodged in God's mind. But such a ruling must be accepted as true, insofar as it is derived from the texts. The justification for this is again found in the Quranic injunction that Muslims, wherever they are, must turn toward the Kaʿba when they pray. The obligation to pray in the direction of the Kaʿba, when it is out of their sight, is tantamount to the obligation to find out God's ruling without it being explicitly stated in any text. In locating the direction of the Kaʿba the believers have been provided with stars, mountains, rivers, day and night as instruments of guidance; and in disclosing God's law, they have been likewise provided with textual indications and signs.

Shāfiʿī's analogy serves to introduce a related matter. Just as two men may determine the location of the Kaʿba differently, so may two jurists arrive at different solutions to the same legal problem. Obviously, one of them must be in error, though more often than not this cannot be determined. Whatever the case, they are equally obligated to attempt to discover the law, and they are both rewarded for their efforts. To maintain that because error is possible no *ijtihād* should be undertaken is tanta-

[63] Abū Bakr Aḥmad Ibn al-Ḥusayn al-Bayhaqī (d. 458/1065) reports that Shāfiʿī also resorts to a Quranic verse in justification of consensus, namely, 4:115. See his *Aḥkām al-Qurʾān*, 2 vols. (Beirut: Dār al-Kutub al-ʿIlmiyya, 1975), I, 39. For a detailed treatment of this issue, see W. B. Hallaq, "On the Authoritativeness of Sunnī Consensus," *International Journal of Middle East Studies*, 18 (1986): 431 ff.

mount to arguing that no prayer should be performed until certainty about the location of the Kaʿba is attained – an argument that is plainly objectionable.

Toward the end of the treatise, Shāfiʿī reintroduces the subject of *qiyās* and *ijtihād*, which he had dealt with in the beginning of his work. We recall that he already discussed two forms of analogical argument under the rubric of *qiyās*, one based on a *ratio legis*, the other on a similarity. He now introduces a third argument under the nomenclature of *qiyās*, namely, the *a fortiori* inference, in both of its forms, the *a minore ad maius* and the *a maiore ad minus*. "If God forbids a small quantity of a substance, we will know that a larger quantity is equally forbidden . . . and if He permits a large quantity of something then a lesser quantity of the same thing is *a fortiori* permitted." Interestingly, Shāfiʿī's example in illustration of the use of this inference derives from ethical rather than strictly legal subject matter. Quoting Q. 99:7–8 ("He who does good an atom's weight will see it [in the Hereafter] and he who does ill an atom's weight will see it"), he remarks that the reward or punishment of those who do good or evil more than an atom's weight will be, respectively, greater.

In establishing the general principles of legal reasoning, Shāfiʿī insisted that no legal ruling can be propounded if it is not ultimately anchored in the Book of God and/or in the Sunna of His Prophet. In fact, it can be safely stated that Shāfiʿī's purpose in writing the *Risāla* was to define the role of the Prophetic Sunna in the law, and to establish the methods of reasoning and interpretation by means of which the law can be deduced from it. It is no wonder then that the bulk of the treatise is devoted to a discussion of the Sunna, its types, interpretation, and its function in elaborating the Sharīʿa. Nearly everything else seems tangential, discussed to a greater or lesser extent in order to shed light on, or expound, the Sunna. In insisting on Prophetic Sunna as the only binding textual authority next to the Quran, Shāfiʿī was arguing for a law that would be exclusively divine in its origin, and this required that he explain the manner in which non-textual sources – i.e., consensus and *qiyās* – may be utilized while maintaining the fundamental proposition that law derives from the Divine will.

With its predominant interest in, and elaboration of, the legal science of Prophetic reports, it may appear that the *Risāla* discusses legal theory only inadvertently. This is further evidenced by the manner in which non-Sunna topics are dealt with. Not only are they given less than a full, and far from systematic, treatment, but they are scattered throughout the treatise as if they were subservient to more central themes and imperatives. This in fact is obviously the case. In theorizing about the law, it was clearly the Prophetic Sunna that was Shāfiʿī's first and last concern.

THE EMERGENCE OF LEGAL THEORY

Modern scholarship has accorded Shāfiʿī the distinction of being the founder of the science of legal theory (*uṣūl al-fiqh*), and his *Risāla* is now thought to be not only the first work expounding the subject, but the model that later jurists and theoreticians strove to imitate. This conception of Shāfiʿī as the "Master Architect" of legal theory has as its corollary the notion that, once he elaborated his theory, *uṣūl al-fiqh* came into existence and that later authors simply followed in his footsteps. In other words, an unbroken continuity in the history of legal theory is assumed between Shāfiʿī's *Risāla* and the later writings on the subject.

Recent research has shown that such a continuity never existed and that the image of Shāfiʿī as the founder of *uṣūl al-fiqh* is a later creation.[64] There is ample evidence in the sources to show that even as late as the end of the third/ninth century, legal theory as we now know it, and as we assume it to have issued from Shāfiʿī's work, had not yet come into existence. It is striking that that century produced no complete treatise on *uṣūl al-fiqh*. In fact, Shāfiʿī's *Risāla* is rarely mentioned in the writings belonging to that century, and, furthermore, it elicited neither commentary nor refutation by the authors of that period, when the genre of commentary and refutation became a part of the written discourse. On the other hand, with the advent of the fourth/tenth century, Shāfiʿī's *Risāla* attracts a number of commentaries and at least two rebuttals. It is also no coincidence that with the appearance of commentaries on, and refutations of, the *Risāla*, there emerges for the first time a sizable number of complete works of *uṣūl al-fiqh*, works that treat of this discipline as an *organically structured* and comprehensive methodology.

The absence of interest in Shāfiʿī's legal theoretical discourse may be explained in part by the fact that the *Risāla* does not offer an exposition of a legal theory proper. The treatise, as we have seen, is largely preoccupied with *ḥadīth*, and offers only a few basic principles: (1) that law must be derived exclusively from revealed scripture; (2) that the Prophetic Sunna constitutes a binding source of law; (3) that contradiction exists neither between the Sunna and the Quran nor among verses or *ḥadīth*s within each of these two sources; (4) that the two sources complement each other hermeneutically; (5) that a legal ruling derived from unambiguous and widely transmitted texts is certain and subject to no disagreement, whereas a ruling that is inferred by means of *ijtihād* and *qiyās* may be subject to dis-

[64] For this and the following paragraphs, see W. B. Hallaq, "Was al-Shafiʿi the Master Architect of Islamic Jurisprudence?," *International Journal of Middle East Studies*, 25 (1993): 587–605.

agreement; and finally (6) that *ijtihād* and *qiyās*, as well as the sanctioning instrument of consensus, are prescribed by the revealed sources.

A brief comparison of the subject matter of the *Risāla* with that of later works of legal theory reveals that a host of questions, fundamental and indeed indispensable to *uṣūl al-fiqh*, are entirely absent from the *Risāla*. Questions of legal language, which occupy on average one-fifth to one-fourth of the space in later treatises, are virtually non-existent in the *Risāla*. Other questions pertaining to consensus, abrogation, legal reasoning, causation etc. also receive little attention, if any.

Admittedly, the absence from the *Risāla* of a number of fundamental elements of legal methodology does not entirely explain the marginal status of the work during the century that followed its author's death. After all, the work, notwithstanding its predominant occupation with *ḥadīth*, offers certain guiding principles of legal interpretation and reasoning. Another reason why the treatise failed to interest Shāfiʿī's immediate successors appears to be the unprecedented synthesis that Shāfiʿī attempted to create between the theses of the then two major camps dominating the sphere of law. Among the aforementioned propositions that Shāfiʿī brought together in the *Risāla*, the first four were addressed to the rationalists, whereas the sixth was aimed at the traditionalists. But Shāfiʿī's theory, embodying this synthesis, appealed neither to the traditionalists nor to the rationalists. For not only did his theory represent a clean break from the prevalent doctrines, but also he himself does not seem to have belonged to either camp. Evidence from the sources strongly suggests, contrary to the conventional wisdom which places Shāfiʿī squarely in the traditionalist camp, that for the traditionalists Shāfiʿī was involved with the rationalists and Muʿtazilites, and that for the rationalists, he was no minor advocate of some fundamental traditionalist doctrines.[65] Both charges could be substantiated, and rightly so, in the very synthesis that Shāfiʿī put forth.

The failure of the *Risāla* to arouse the interest of jurists during the century after its author's death may also be explained in terms of the direction taken by the religious and legal movement in the course of the second/eighth and third/ninth centuries. As we have seen, the beginning of the second/eighth century witnessed the initial stages of the development of Islamic law and jurisprudence. This phase may be characterized as one in which human reasoning, commonly known as *raʾy*, was predominant. By the middle of the century another competing movement stressing the role of Prophetic reports was on the rise. At the time Shāfiʿī wrote

[65] Ibid., 592 ff.

his *Risāla*, the rationalist movement was only beginning to decline, and this may have been due to the rapid increase in the volume of Prophetic reports that had infiltrated the domain of law. Shaybānī's positive law exhibits, perhaps better than any other, this stage of development, in which *ḥadīth*s constitute an important, but by no means exclusive, element in the law. In Shāfiʿī, as we have seen, revelation – the Quran and the Prophetic reports – represents the ultimate source of law, and *raʾy*, as an expression of rationalist and utilitarian tendencies, is to be wholly expunged. This is precisely where Shāfiʿī was a jurist on his own: while he unconditionally rejected *raʾy* and insisted on the overriding authority of the two primary sources, he salvaged certain elements of what had come under the rubric of *raʾy* and molded them into arguments that may be used in law only insofar as they derive their premises from revelation.

But Shāfiʿī's was not the ultimate synthesis which universally reconciled the doctrines of the rationalists and the traditionalists. After Shāfiʿī, the pendulum of the religious movement shifted farther toward anti-rationalism. The careers and legal doctrines of Aḥmad b. Ḥanbal (d. 241/855) and Dāwūd Ibn Khalaf al-Ẓāhirī (d. 270/883), dominating the legal scene for most of the third/ninth century, exemplify the drastic shift toward traditionalism. While both approved of Shāfiʿī, they went much farther in their emphasis on the centrality of scripture and on the repugnant nature of human reasoning in law. Their positions, however, were by no means identical. Ibn Ḥanbal, as we can glean from his positive law, did not favor the practice of *qiyās*, unless it was absolutely necessary. Dāwūd, on the other hand, rejected it categorically.

There emerges here a clear pattern: Shāfiʿī's predecessors resort to *raʾy* with little attention to the Sunna. Shāfiʿī regulates *raʾy* in the form of *qiyās* and assigns it a role subsidiary to that of the revealed sources, though it remains an essential part of his methodology. Ibn Ḥanbal avoids *qiyās*, but not completely. Dāwūd completely rejects it in favor of a literal reading of the two primary sources. In both time and doctrine, then, Shāfiʿī's position is located midway between the early *raʾy* libertinism and the later Ẓāhirite conservatism.

The rationalist movement, on the other hand, began to experience a process of decline after the middle of the third/ninth century. From this point on, the rationalists drew closer to the traditionalists, but only in one sense: namely, they could no longer afford to ignore the scripture as the exclusive foundation of the law, and they were compelled to submit to the divine decree as the first and last judge of human *sharʿī* affairs. This concession to revelation is clearly attested in the jurisprudential writings of the later Muʿtazilite masters, such as ʿAbd al-Jabbār (d. 415/1024) and Abū

Ḥusayn al-Baṣrī (d. 436/1044). On the other side, the traditionalists had to make some concessions. Soon, for instance, the Ḥanbalites, among others, were to disregard their eponym's dislike for *qiyās*, and allow their legal methodology to become virtually interchangeable with that of the other schools. It is significant that those who did not make these concessions, such as the ultra-traditionalist Ḥashwiyya[66] and the Ẓāhirites, were ultimately doomed to extinction.

What may be seen as a reconciliation between the traditionalists and the rationalists – a reconciliation that began to manifest itself only toward the very end of the third/ninth century – may also be seen as a general acceptance of the rudimentary principles of Shāfiʿī's thesis. But until the end of that century, this thesis remained in the minority, and none of Shāfiʿī's followers appears to have defended it. Muzanī (d. 264/878), who was Shāfiʿī's chief disciple and the most likely candidate to have carried on his master's mission, leaned more toward rationality than toward *ḥadīth*, and in any case is universally thought to have diverged from the legal methodology set by Shāfiʿī.

It was not until the illustrious Shāfiʿī jurist Ibn Surayj (d. 306/918) and the generation of his younger contemporaries that the traditionalist–rationalist compromise was finally articulated. Acknowledged as the most distinguished and faithful follower of Shāfiʿī, Ibn Surayj was universally held to be the jurist who single-handedly defended the Shāfiʿite school and raised it to prominence. He and his disciples combined a knowledge of traditionalism and rationalism, with the result of conceptualizing legal theory as a synthesis between rationality and the textual tradition. Thus, Ibn Surayj must be credited with paving the way for his students, who discoursed on this synthesis and elaborated it in greater detail. This explains why the first and foremost Shāfiʿite authors who did write works on *uṣūl al-fiqh* were his students, such as Ibn Ḥaykawayh (d. 318/930), Ibrāhīm al-Marwazī (d. 340/951), Abū Bakr al-Fārisī (fl. ca. 350/960), Ibn al-Qāṣṣ (d. 336/947), Abū Bakr al-Ṣayrafī (d. 330/942), and al-Qaffāl al-Shāshī (d. 336/948), to mention only a few.

With the rise of *uṣūl al-fiqh* in the beginning of the fourth/tenth century, and as a reaction to the increasingly widespread claims that the early Ḥanafite masters were the founders of the discipline, the image of Shāfiʿī as the exponent and founder of *uṣūl al-fiqh* begins to take form. About a century later the image becomes firmly rooted, as attested in the literature treating of Shāfiʿī's scholarly virtues (*manāqib*). In the earliest work of

[66] On the Ḥashwiyya, see A. S. Halkin, "The Ḥashwiyya," *Journal of the American Oriental Society*, 54 (1934): 1–28.

manāqib available to us, the author, Abū Ḥātim al-Rāzī (d. 327/938), allots a number of chapters to Shāfiʿī's excellent knowledge of the law. In one chapter, which consists of about fifty-one lines (the work as a whole consists of about 2,400 lines), the author discusses Shāfiʿī's proficiency in what he calls *uṣūl al-ʿilm*, by which he clearly means *uṣūl al-fiqh*. Even here, however, the *Risāla* is never mentioned, and nowhere in the entire treatise does Shāfiʿī appear as the founder of the discipline. In the entire treatise, the *Risāla* is mentioned only twice, and then in passing. In both instances, it is referred to in the context not of law but, significantly, of Prophetic reports.

Over a century later, Bayhaqī (d. 459/1066) wrote another work on Shāfiʿī's *manāqib*. For Bayhaqī, Shāfiʿī is now not only a genius of *uṣūl*, but the unrivaled founder of the discipline. The *Risāla*, for its part, is mentioned over eighteen times, and, moreover, receives a comprehensive treatment. In contrast to Rāzī's 51 lines, Bayhaqī allocates a staggering 160 pages, out of a total of 918, to Shāfiʿī as an *uṣūlī*. The depiction of Shāfiʿī as the founder of *uṣūl al-fiqh* is similarly drawn by later authors of the *manāqib* genre. In Fakhr al-Dīn al-Rāzī (d. 606/1209), Shāfiʿī becomes to *uṣūl al-fiqh* "what Aristotle was to logic."[67]

Sometime before Bayhaqī wrote, but certainly after Abū Ḥātim al-Rāzī, Shāfiʿī's image as the founder of *uṣūl al-fiqh* became firmly established. It is not a coincidence that the intervening period between these two authors coincides with the career of Abū Muḥammad al-Juwaynī (d. 438/1046), the last commentator on the *Risāla*. That Shāfiʿī's treatise failed to attract further commentary in the decades and centuries that followed helps to explain the role that Shāfiʿī, as the founder of the discipline, was required to play in his school. Once his image as the founder was established, commentaries on his treatise ceased forever. In a field in which commentaries were the norm, the discontinuity of interest in commenting on the *Risāla* also explains the irrelevance of the work's themes to the far more complex and different methodology of *uṣūl al-fiqh*.

It is a generally accepted view that the *Risāla* represents the first attempt at synthesizing the disciplined exercise of human reasoning and the complete assimilation of revelation as the basis of the law. Since Islamic law finally came to accept this synthesis, we have long been led to believe that *uṣūl al-fiqh* as we know it began with Shāfiʿī. But Shāfiʿī's theory, propounding this synthesis, appeared at a time in which not many were willing to embrace it. For Shāfiʿī's theory to have prevailed immediately after its publication would have required that both the rationalists and the tradi-

[67] Hallaq, "Was al-Shafiʿi the Master Architect," 599 f.

tionalists should have abandoned their doctrines once and for all. But this certainly did not happen. In fact, the traditionalists rejected his *qiyās*, and the rationalists were reluctant, to say the least, to accept his thesis that revelation is the first and last judge of human affairs. It was only toward the end of the third/ninth century that a genuine synthesis was created between rationalism and traditionalism. With the emergence of this synthesis, whose causes and characteristics are yet to be studied, the way to *uṣūl al-fiqh* was finally paved. And once this science bloomed, at the hands of Ṣayrafī, Qaffāl and their likes, the rudimentary synthesis created by Shāfiʿī a century earlier became relevant and was thus rejuvenated in the form of commentaries on the *Risāla*. By attributing all the ramifications of the synthesis to Shāfiʿī, his successors made him, *ex post facto*, the founder of *uṣūl al-fiqh*.

2

THE ARTICULATION OF LEGAL THEORY: I

INTRODUCTION

ONE of the central problems associated with the history of Islamic legal theory is the marked absence of works written not only in the third/ninth century but also in the fourth/tenth. As we have seen, the lack of literature from the third/ninth century is causally connected with the very development of legal theory, which was to emerge only as late as a century after Shāfiʿī's death. But the fact that we have virtually no works from the following century is not so much to be associated with the development of legal theory as with the sheer historical fact – or accident – that such works have simply failed to reach us. Those works that have succeeded in surviving the ravages of time[1] are either incomplete or so compressed that it is virtually impossible to draw from them an adequate picture which might represent the state of development of theory in the fourth/tenth century. An account of this development must thus await the publication of several key works written by the chief theorists of the time.

The earliest period from which we have an extensive record is the fifth/eleventh century, which can claim a special status in the field of legal theory for more than one reason. First, this century is associated with a stage in which the major problems of legal theory were addressed, thus paving the grounds for subsequent, finer analyses. Second, it witnessed the proliferation of a staggering number of works, almost unprecedented, as far as we know, in the history of the field. Third, it produced some of the most creative and brilliant legal theorists (*uṣūlists*) of Islam, theorists whose

[1] E.g., Aḥmad b. Muḥammad al-Shāshī, *Uṣūl al-Shāshī* (Beirut: Dār al-Kitāb al-ʿArabī, 1982); Aḥmad b. ʿAlī al Rāzī al-Jaṣṣāṣ, *Uṣūl al-Fiqh al-Musammā al-Fuṣūl fī al-Uṣūl*, ed. ʿUjayl Jāsim al-Nashamī, I (Kuwait: Wizārat al-Awqāf wal-Shu'ūn al-Islāmiyya, 1985); and ʿAbd al-Jabbār al-Asadabādī *al-Mughnī fī Abwāb al-Tawḥīd wal-ʿAdl*, ed. Amīn al-Khūlī, XVII (Cairo: al-Dār al-Miṣriyya lil-Ta'līf wal-Nashr, n.d.).

works were to become influential in the subsequent development of *uṣūl al-fiqh*. It is with the major issues and the fundamental problems raised by these theorists that we shall be concerned in this and the following chapter.

While there is broad agreement among these *uṣūlist*s as to what constitutes the fundamental subject matter of legal theory, their works display remarkable differences. Such differences manifest themselves mainly on two levels: the first is the exclusion or inclusion of certain subjects, and the second is the extent to which a subject, when included, is discussed, emphasized or deemphasized.

Unlike the rudimentary, and somewhat haphazard, structure of Shāfiʿī's legal theory, the fifth-/eleventh-century theories show an acute awareness of structure. The fact that the law derives from the divine scriptures, both directly and obliquely, dictated, in the eyes of the *uṣūlist*s, a particular structure within which topics were configurated and related to each other. The direct and oblique derivation of the law from the revealed texts required the elaboration of an epistemology in which the distinction between probability and certainty played a central role. The comprehensive textual basis of the law demanded the articulation of a linguistic typology, a science of legal language proper. The textual nature of the law also gave rise to the development of a methodology whose task it was to discern the epistemological value of the texts according to the strength or weakness of their transmission, as well as according to the qualitative clarity of their linguistic implications. And as we have already observed in Shāfiʿī's theory, the solution to the problem of conflicting texts was found in the theory of abrogation.

This concern for structure carried over into the next level of investigation. Once the relevant text had gone through these processes of linguistic classification, authentication and repeal, it entered the final stage of interpretation and reasoning, where the jurist reached the desideratum, the legal ruling. But before subjecting the relevant text to his reasoning, the jurist was assumed to know the law upon which a consensus (*ijmāʿ*) had been reached, since such law constituted a binding *corpus juris* on the basis of which solutions for new cases of law were derived. Thus, in order to determine what law was subject to consensus he was required to know what were the conditions that rendered a consensus valid and, consequently, binding. It is this structural order that dominated all theoretical exposition.

EPISTEMOLOGY

One of the most salient features of legal theory is the epistemological distinctions that permeated nearly all its elements. These distinctions were not unconnected with those made in theological enquiries (*ʿilm al-kalām*), since law was seen as derivative of the mother science, theology. It was the function of the latter to prove the existence of God, His attributes, prophecy, revelation and all fundaments of religion, whereas law presupposed these theological conclusions and indeed built on them. In these two disciplines, therefore, knowledge is viewed as an attribute that exists in the mind of God and in the minds of created beings. The knowledge of God, whose study is the domain of the theologian, is eternal, all-inclusive and defies any description. It is neither necessary (*ḍarūrī*) nor acquired (*muktasab*).[2]

Human knowledge, on the other hand, is created, and is susceptible to the categorization of necessary and acquired. Necessary knowledge is that which is imposed on the mind and can by no means be rejected or subjected to doubt. By definition, it is not acquired by means of inference. Rather, according to one classification, this knowledge is either *a priori* or derives from sense perception. *A priori* knowledge may, in turn, be divided into affirmative and negative. For example, knowledge of one's own existence, hunger or happiness is affirmative, whereas knowledge of the Law of Excluded Middle is negative. The existence of this knowledge in the mind is the result of neither thinking nor inference; it is simply posited there. This is perhaps why some jurists call this type "innate," while others label it as "intellectual" (*ʿaqlī*), namely, inherent in the mind *ab initio*. Sensory knowledge is also deemed necessary, since once a person sees, for example, a tree, she no more needs inference to know that what she has observed was a tree than she is able to dissociate her mind from that knowledge. Similarly, when my finger touches a flame, I need not reason that since my finger has touched the flame I should feel excruciating pain; I *immediately* feel it.

On the other hand, acquired knowledge is by definition attained through inference and reasoning. Unlike necessary knowledge, it does not grip the mind. The fact that it is not immediate, and is obtained only by inferential operations of the mind, renders it subject to falsification and error. This explains why this type of knowledge is thought to lead to probability (*ẓann*), whereas necessary knowledge leads to certainty (*yaqīn*, *qaṭʿ*).

[2] For this and the following discussion under this section, see Abū Isḥāq Ibrāhīm b. ʿAlī al-Shīrāzī, *Sharḥ al-Lumaʿ*, ed. ʿAbd al-Majīd Turkī, 2 vols. (Beirut: Dār al-Gharb al-Islāmī, 1988), I, 148–52; Abū al-Walīd b. Khalaf al-Bājī, *Iḥkām al-Fuṣūl fī Aḥkām al-Uṣūl*, ed. ʿAbd al-Majīd Turkī (Beirut: Dār al-Gharb al-Islāmī, 1986), 170–71; ʿAbd al-Qāhir al-Baghdādī, *Uṣūl al-Dīn* (repr.; Beirut: Dār al-Kutub al-ʿIlmiyya, 1981), 8 ff; Imām al-Ḥaramayn ʿAbd al-Malik Abū al-Maʿālī al-Juwaynī, *al-Kāfiya fī al-Jadal*, ed. F. Ḥusayn Maḥmūd (Cairo: Maṭbaʿat ʿĪsā Bābī al-Ḥalabī, 1399/1979), 3 ff.; Abū Ḥāmid Muḥammad b. Muḥammad al-Ghazālī, *al-Mankhūl min Taʿlīqāt al-Uṣūl*, ed. Muḥammad Ḥasan Haytū (Damascus: Dār al-Fikr, 1980), 42–62; Abū Ḥāmid Muḥammad b. Muḥammad al-Ghazālī, *al-Mustaṣfā min ʿIlm al-Uṣūl*, 2 vols. (Cairo: al-Maṭbaʿa al-Amīriyya, 1324/1906), I, 10 ff.

While certainty is not a matter of degree, probability may be. In the jargon of the Muslim jurists, to say that something is probable (*ẓannī*) is to mean that the possibility of its being true is in excess of 0.5, when certainty is 1.0. If the truth of a proposition, for example, is thought to be *ẓannī*, supporting or circumstantial evidence may increase the chances that it is true, thus elevating its probability to a higher degree. Depending on the quality and strength of evidence, the probability may be moderately increased, in which case it is termed *ghalabat al-ẓann*, or it may be increased to such a great extent that it may "border on certainty," in which event it is known as *al-ẓann al-mutākhim lil-yaqīn*. Other intermediate degrees of probability are also distinguished.

Though the issues of certainty and probability dominated legal discourse, the jurists distinguished at least two other categories of knowledge, namely, doubt (*shakk*) and ignorance (*jahl*). Doubt represents a state of knowledge where the probability in favor of the truth, say, of a proposition, is precisely equal to the probability of its being false. Ignorance, however, is believing something to be what it is not – it is plainly a state of error.

In legal theory, all knowledge is seen as being predicated upon the definition (*ḥadd*) of concepts and upon the relation of one concept to another. Delimiting definition, therefore, was essential for determining how concepts are to be defined, for it is through *ḥadd* that the reality of things can be known. The *ḥadd* is defined as the statement that includes those qualities that belong to a concept and excludes those that do not belong. Furthermore, the definition must be coextensive and coexclusive with the *definiendum*; namely, the definition must exist whenever the *definiendum* exists, and whenever the *definiendum* does not exist, the definition must not exist. The logical justification of this requirement is that if part of the definition of a thing is the quality of its being existent, then it is necessary, in order to validate the definition, that it be true that all things exist and that whatever exists must be a thing, just as, conversely, that which does not exist is not a thing, and that which is not a thing does not exist.

While this conception of definition was predominant among the jurists of the fifth/eleventh century, there seems to have been a minority, among them Imām al-Ḥaramayn al-Juwaynī (d. 478/1085), who tended to view definition in realist terms, thus coming close to the philosophical tradition. But it was Juwaynī's student, Ghazālī (d. 505/1111), who made a clean break, at least in theory, with the established legal tradition and incorporated, in the last work he wrote on legal theory, a lengthy introduction to Greek logic where he discusses the Greek philosophical principles concerned with definition.[3] This logic included, by definition, a theory of universals, Porphyry's five predicables, syllogistics, demonstration and a host of other subjects. Definition, according to the terms of this logic, can be attained by means of genus and differentia, categories entirely unacknowledged by the great majority of Ghazālī's contemporaries. It is to be noted, however, that Ghazālī, as well as all his successors who followed in his footsteps and incorporated the principles of logical theory into their works, still followed, to a significant extent, the traditional epistemology which already thoroughly permeated all aspects of legal theory. When concrete discussions were introduced, Ghazālī and those who followed his example analyzed matters in terms of certainty and probability, and of acquired and necessary knowledge. In the actual construction of substantive theoretical doctrines, therefore, the impact of Greek logic can hardly be discerned.

THE LEGAL NORMS

Islamic legal theory after Shāfiʿī came to recognize five values with which all legal acts must be labeled. In other words, when the jurist arrives at a legal solution for a new case of law, his decision must fall into one of five categories; the obligatory (*wājib*), the recommended (*mandūb*), the permissible (*mubāḥ*), the prohibited (*ḥarām*), or the repugnant (*makrūh*). The obligatory represents an act whose performance entails reward, and whose omission entails punishment. An example in point is prayer. The impact of epistemological distinctions is already evident in this category. The Ḥanafites distinguished two categories of the obligatory, the *wājib* and the *farḍ*, in accordance with the type of evidence on the basis of which the ruling has been reached. They argued that the *farḍ* is a legal norm arrived at by means of certain evidence, whereas the *wājib* is determined by means of probable evidence. That is to say, the former is based on clear textual indicants (*dalāʾil*; sing. *dalīl*) which admit of only one interpretation and which have been transmitted through so many channels that no doubt whatsoever can be cast on their authenticity. The latter, however, is based on indicants susceptible to more than one interpretation and their authenticity is only probable.[4]

Some jurists, such as Ghazālī, have given consideration to the element

[3] *Mustaṣfā*, I, 11 ff.

[4] For the discussion under this section, see Shīrāzī, *Sharḥ al-Lumaʿ*, I, 159–61; Aḥmad b. ʿAlī Ibn Barhān, *al-Wuṣūl ilā al-Uṣūl*, ed. ʿAbd al-Ḥamīd Abū Zunayd, 2 vols. (Riyadh: Maktabat al-Maʿārif, 1984), I, 75–81; Imām al-Ḥaramayn ʿAbd al-Malik Abū al-Maʿālī al-Juwaynī, *al-Burhān fī Uṣūl al-Fiqh*, ed. ʿAbd al-ʿAẓīm Dīb, 2 vols. (Cairo: Dār al-Anṣār, 1400/1980), I, 308–13; Ghazālī, *Mustaṣfā*, I, 65–79. See also Bernard Weiss, *The Search for God's Law: Islamic Jurisprudence in the Writings of Sayf al-Dīn al-Āmidī* (Salt Lake City: University of Utah Press, 1992), 93–109.

of time in the performance of an obligatory act. The issue at stake was whether such an act must be performed instantaneously or whether it tolerates a delay within a predetermined stretch of time. If a master commands his slave to tailor a garment "today," is the slave under the obligation to perform the task instantaneously or can he perform it later in the day? Ghazālī, representing a group of jurists, maintained that rationally (*ʿaqlan*) the slave would fulfill his obligation if he tailors the garment any time during the day. However, being rational, the argument is rather insufficient in legal and religious matters. The defense of this view is finally made to rest on a consensus established with regard to the penance due upon the violation of certain laws, a penance that requires the freeing of a slave or feeding sixty of the poor. Although such penance is obligatory, the violator of the law is entirely free to choose one or the other of these forms of expiation. In analogy with this choice, the obligatory act allows another type of choice, namely, the choice of the exact time at which the obligatory act is to be performed. But also in analogy with the limited choice between freeing a slave and feeding the poor, the act must be performed within a span of time during which the performance is still deemed lawful.

The second value, the recommended (*mandūb*), represents an act whose performance entails a reward but whose omission does not require punishment. As the purpose of this value is to encourage piety, omission does not constitute a violation of the law, since obedience to the Lawgiver is in any case fulfilled. Similarly, obedience is also attained in the third value or the permissible (*mubāḥ*; also known as the indifferent) act whose commission or omission is equally legitimate. In neither case is there a reward or punishment. However, this should not be understood to mean that the law has no position on this category of laws, as some of the Muʿtazilite theologians thought to be the case. Ghazālī maintains that although the revealed texts may offer neither direct nor oblique indications concerning the rulings of a number of legal cases, these texts have nonetheless laid down a universal principle to govern such cases. This is the principle that whenever the texts fail to command the commission or omission of an act, the Muslim has a free choice between the two.

The fourth category is the prohibited or impermissible act, which obviously entails punishment upon commission. On the other hand, the repugnant act is rewarded when omitted, but is not punished when committed.

Legal theory also laid down another taxonomy, pertaining not to the juridical value of acts as such, but rather to their validity. Subsumed under this taxonomy are the categories of the valid (*ṣaḥīḥ*) and the invalid (*fāsid*). A contract concluded in a lawful transaction, say one of hire, is not subject to classification in accordance with the five norms governing acts. While the act of hiring is itself classifiable, the contract is itself not, and can be deemed either valid or invalid. When a contract is valid, it is binding and produces full legal effects; when invalid it is not so. Being invalid, however, does not mean that it is entirely null and void, productive of no legal effect whatsoever – a category known as *bāṭil*. Rather, *fāsid* means that it is not effective, and that its consequences are not always binding by the operation of the law.

LEGAL LANGUAGE

In attempting to find the solution of a hitherto unsolved legal case, the jurist is confronted by the texts which constitute his ultimate frame of reference. His task begins with a search for a text that appears to be most relevant for the case at hand. Such relevance is determined by a multi-layered process in which the text is subjected to linguistic analysis. On the most general level, this analysis is of two types, one that relates to the identification of words, the other to the meaning or the semantic force of these words once they have been identified. While the latter belongs to legal reasoning associated with *qiyās* – a later stage in legal construction – the former appertains to linguistic interpretation *par excellence*.

The aim of linguistic interpretation is to determine whether, for instance, a word is ambiguous, univocal, general, particular, constituting a trope, a command, etc. Each word is analyzed in light of one or more of these categories, whose number and hermeneutical purview vary from one jurist to another. However, a number of these have been considered central to most theories, and it is with these that we shall be now concerned.

Tropology.[5]

It is the jurists' general presumption that words are normally used to indicate the meanings for which they were originally coined. This usage is a real one (*ḥaqīqa*), rather than metaphorical (*majāz*). When we hear the word "chicken" we presume, unless there is a good reason not to do so, that what is meant is the common domestic fowl. But the word may be used figuratively, i.e., as a trope, to refer to a person whom we think to be a coward. Until such a time as we can determine what is meant by "chicken," we will be unable to comprehend the signification of the language with which we are addressed.

[5] On tropology, see Shīrāzī, *Sharḥ al-Lumaʿ*, I, 169–75; Ghazālī, *Mustaṣfā*, I, 105; Ghazālī, *Mankhūl*, 74 f.; Ibn Barhān, *Wuṣūl*, I, 97–102.

The great majority of legal theorists maintain that most words in the Arabic language are used in their real sense. Some jurists, such as Abū Isḥāq al-Isfarā'īnī (d. 418/1027), are reported to have taken the position that tropes do not occur in the Arabic language, the implication being that the Quran is free of metaphors. A few others have admitted the existence of metaphors in the language, but rejected the claim that the Quran contains any such words. The majority, however, held the position that the Quran does contain metaphors, and in support of this they adduced, among others, Q. 19:4: "And the head has flared up with grey hair." It is clear that the head itself does not "flare up," and that the metaphor issues from the substitution of fire for hair.

In determining whether a word is being used in its real or tropical sense, the jurist may first resort to the authorities on language, such as Aṣmaʿī and Khalīl. The jurist can also exercise his own faculty of reasoning by investigating the word in the context of language. At times, a trope is easily identified, such as when a tall man is referred to as "a palm-tree." It is self-evident that the meaning of "palm-tree" in a context in which the term is clearly substituted for the name of the person cannot have the real palm-tree as referent. Furthermore, a trope can be tested by the method of coextensiveness, namely, that the real usage would apply to all trees of the family Palmae, but would not so apply to all tall things in the world. The exception, which happens to be tall men, is a tropical usage. Another test consists of whether or not we can subject a word to the same linguistic uses as those that connote real meanings. If we cannot, then it is a metaphor, for we would be taking it too far if we proceed to refer to the hands of a tall man as branches.

Be that as it may, the presumption of the jurist must be that all words in legal language ought to be treated as non-tropical unless there is textual evidence to the contrary. This presumption is related to the governing principle that every metaphor corresponds to a word with a real referent, but such words do not always have corresponding tropes.

The clear and the ambiguous.[6]

Words used in their real meanings are said to be either clear (*mubayyan*, *mufassar*) or ambiguous (*mujmal*). The latter category encompasses all expressions whose denotations are so general and imprecise that the hearer would be able to understand neither the intention of the speaker nor the

[6] See, e.g., Juwaynī, *Burhān*, I, 419 ff.; Shīrāzī, *Sharḥ al-Lumaʿ*, I, 446 ff.; Ghazālī, *Mustaṣfā*, I, 345 ff.; Bājī, *Iḥkām*, 189–90, 283 ff.

point he is making. The ambiguity stems from the fact that the referent of such words includes several attributes or different genera. In Q. 17:33 "And he who is killed wrongfully, we have given power (*sulṭān*) to his heir," the term "power" is utterly ambiguous, since it could refer to a variety of genera, such as retaliation, right to blood-money, or even the right to pardon the murderer. This ambiguity explains why the *mujmal* does not constitute a text whose legal effect is binding, for the ruling or the subject of that ruling would not be sufficiently clear as to enable Muslims to understand what exactly is being commanded. It is only when such words are brought out of the realm of ambiguity into that of clarity by means of other clear "speech" that the legal effects of the *mujmal* become binding.

Ambiguity is the result not only of the uses of vague language, as evidenced in the aforementioned verse, but also of homonymous nouns which designate more than one object. An example illustrating the difficulty is the English word "spring" which equally refers to the season of the year, to the natural source from which water issues, and to a coil of wire found in mattresses, machines, etc. Furthermore, ambiguity may accrue to an otherwise clear expression by virtue of the fact that it is associated with an ambiguous statement. For instance, Q. 5:1: "The beast cattle is made lawful unto you [for food]" is, as it stands, fairly clear. Immediately thereafter, however, the verse continues with the statement: "except for that which is unannounced for you," thus rendering the earlier statement ambiguous, since what is unannounced cannot be known until such time when that which is announced is documented in the texts.[7]

According to a widely accepted classification of legal language, words are either clear or ambiguous. Those that are ambiguous and can by no means be clarified remain without legal significance and hence are not productive of rulings. On the other hand, those words that are intrinsically unambiguous as well as those that are rendered clear after having been ambiguous belong to the category of the *mubayyan*, a category that encompasses virtually all types of functional legal language. The *mubayyan* is in turn divided into two major categories:

(1) the category of words that are clear insofar as the meaning of the language (*nuṭq*) in which they are conveyed is clear; and
(2) the category of words that are clear insofar as their linguistic implication (*mafhūm*) is clear.

Again, category 1 is divided into two subcategories in accordance with whether words are subject, or not subject, to more than one interpretation.

[7] Juwaynī, *Burhān*, I, 421.

Univocal language

Words of this type are known as *naṣṣ*, their meaning being so clear as to engender certitude in the mind. When we hear the word "four" we automatically know that it is neither three nor five, nor any other number. To know what "four" means we have no need for other language to explain the denotation of the word. It is simply self-sufficiently clear. Against those few who maintained that the *naṣṣ* rarely occurs in legal language, the majority of jurists argued that univocal language is quite abundant in the texts.[8]

Indeterminate language

Words whose signification is not readily obvious are of two types, the first of which are those whose meaning is so general (*ʿāmm*) that they need to be particularized if they are to yield any legal content. The second type includes words with two or more possible meanings, one of which, the *ẓāhir*, is deemed, by virtue of supporting evidence, superior to the others.[9]

The general and its particularization[10]

Words that equally include two or more individuals of the genus to which they refer are deemed general (*ʿāmm*). Thus all plurals accompanied by a definite article are general terms, e.g., *al-muslimūn* (the Muslims). Some jurists considered such words to belong to the category of the general even when not accompanied by a definite article. In addition to its function of defining words, this article serves, in the Arabic language, to render words applicable to all members of a class. Accordingly, when the article is attached to singular nouns, these nouns will refer to the generality of individuals within a certain class. *Al-insān* or *al-muslim* thus refers not to a particular individual, but, respectively, to human beings or to Muslims generally. Yet another group of words considered to be general is that of the interrogative particles, classified in Arabic as nouns.

A general word in the Quran or the Sunna may be particularized only by means of relevant words or statements provided by these texts. By relevant is meant words or statements that apply to the same genus denoted by the general word. Particularization (*takhṣīṣ*) thus means the exclusion from the

[8] Ghazālī, *Mankhūl*, 165–6; Abū al-Walīd b. Khalaf al-Bājī, *Kitāb al-Ḥudūd fī al-Uṣūl*, ed. Nazīh Ḥammād (Beirut: Mu'assasat al-Zuʿbī lil-Ṭibāʿa wal-Nashr, 1973), 42–43.

[9] Ghazālī, *Mankhūl*, 138 ff., 167–68; Abū Isḥāq Ibrāhīm b. ʿAlī Shīrāzī, *al-Lumaʿ fī Uṣūl al-Fiqh*, ed. Muḥammad al-Naʿsānī (Cairo: Maṭbaʿat al-Saʿāda, 1326/1908), 31–32.

[10] Shīrāzī, *Lumaʿ*, 16–22; Shīrāzī, *Sharḥ al-Lumaʿ*, I, 302 ff.; Ibn Barhān, *Wuṣūl*, I, 202 ff., 216 ff., 260 ff.; Juwaynī, *Burhān*, I, 318 ff.; Bājī, *Iḥkām*, 230 ff.; Ghazālī, *Mankhūl*, 153.

general of a part that was subsumed under that general. In Q. 2:238 "Perform prayers, as well as the midmost prayer," while the midmost prayer was specified it cannot be said to have been particularized. Particularization would have taken place if the verse were to read "Perform prayers except for the midmost one."

A classic example of particularization occurs in Q. 5:3 "Forbidden unto you [for food] is carrion" which was particularized by a Prophetic report allowing the consumption, among others, of dead fish. This example also makes it clear that the reports, including solitary ones, can, at least according to some jurists, particularize the Quran. So can the Quran, as one can expect, particularize the Sunna. The vast majority of jurists also held that within the Quran and the Sunna statements in one may particularize statements in the other, and vice versa.

There are at least two other types of particularization[11] that apply to two different texts. The first type of particularization takes place when a proviso or a condition (*sharṭ*) is attached to, or brought to bear upon, a general statement. Q. 3:97, for example, states: "And pilgrimage to the House is a duty unto God for mankind, for him who can find a way thither." It is plain here that the obligation to go on pilgrimage is waived in the case of those who have no means to perform it. The second type, on the other hand, is particularization by means of introducing into the general, not a condition, but a quality (*ṣifa*). This is known as the qualification (*taqyīd*) of an unrestricted (*muṭlaq*) word or statement. For instance, in cases where a man swears not to resume a normal marital relationship with his wife (*ẓihār*), but later does, the penalty fixed in the Quran is "freeing a slave" (58:3). But the penalty for accidental homicide is "freeing a believing slave" (4:92). The attribute "believing" has qualified, or particularized, the word "slave."

When a qualifying attribute is nowhere to be found in the texts, the unrestricted expression must be taken to refer to the general category subsumed under that expression. And when a qualified word appears without an object to qualify, the word must be taken to apply only to that which is subject to the qualification. However, some difficulties arise concerning the extent to which the principle of qualification should be applied when an unrestricted word meets with a qualifying attribute. In Q. 58:4, it is stipulated that the penalty for *ẓihār* is either "fasting for two successive months" or "feeding sixty needy persons." Unlike the general command to feed sixty persons, fasting here is qualified by the requirement that it be successive. Since these are two different types of penance, one relating to feeding, the

[11] Shīrāzī, *Sharḥ al-Lumaʿ*, I, 412–23; Bājī, *Iḥkām*, 279–83.

other to fasting, the qualification applicable to the latter must not be extended to the former. But when the two penances (or rulings) are of the same nature, the attribute must be taken to qualify the unrestricted word or sentence. For instance, Q. 2:282 ("when you sell one to another, have witnesses [attest to the sale]") is qualified by an earlier passage in the same verse stipulating "call to witness, from amongst you, two witnesses, and if two men are not available, then a man and two women."

In this case, both the qualified and the unrestricted rulings are one and the same, and they pertain to a single case, namely, concluding a contract of sale. But what would be the interpretative attitude in the event where the qualified and unrestricted rulings are identical, but the cases that give rise to them are different? Such is the case with *ẓihār* and accidental homicide. The penalty for the former is "freeing a slave," whereas for the latter, "freeing a believing slave" (Q. 58:3, 4:92). In such an event, the latter must be considered to qualify the former, a consideration said to be grounded in reasoning, not in the very language of the texts. That is to say, in the contract of sale God made it clear in the *language* (*lafẓ*) of the Quran that what he meant was witnesses of a certain sort, but in *ẓihār* and accidental homicide He did not provide *language* to this effect; we merely reason, on the basis of the text, that this was God's intention.

Equivocal language

We have previously intimated that equivocal words are classifiable into two broad categories, one encompassing general terms (*ʿāmm*), together with those we have called unrestricted (*mufaṣṣal*), and the second including words that are capable of more than one interpretation.[12] Through a process of interpretation, technically known as *ta'wīl*, one of the meanings, the *ẓāhir*, is deemed by the interpreter to be the most likely among the candidates, it being given extra weight by evidence that is absent in the case of the other possible meanings. An example of this sort of evidence would be language that took imperative (*amr*) or prohibitive (*nahy*) forms, to mention the two most significant linguistic types in legal hermeneutics.[13]

The jurists are unanimous in their view that revelation is intended to lay down a system of obligation, and that the imperative and the prohibitive forms (whose prototypes, respectively, are "Do" and "Do not do") constitute the backbone and the nerve of that system's deontology. Without coming to grips with the hermeneutical ramifications of these two forms, obedience to God can never be achieved. For it is chiefly through these that God chose to express the greatest part of His revelation.

[12] See p. 45 above. [13] Bājī, *Iḥkām*, 230 ff.

The imperative[14] There are few topics in Islamic legal theory that succeeded in arousing so much controversy as did the issue of the imperative form (*amr*). Even the very definition of the imperative became subject to disagreement. Some jurists, such as Ghazālī, defined it as "a statement by which a person is required to perform a commanded act." For Shīrāzī (d. 476/1083) and others, this definition fell short of including other essential elements. They maintained that the imperative represents "a statement by which a superior requests the performance of an act from an inferior." The opponents of this last definition objected to limiting the imperative to discourse that issues from a superior to an inferior, and argued that a command may be issued by an equal. Shīrāzī replied that when the imperative issues from an equal, it does not, properly speaking, constitute a command, but only a request (*ṭalab*), in which case the form itself would be used merely in the metaphorical sense.

Now, the first major point of disagreement concerning the imperative form centered around its legal effects. When someone commands another by saying "Do this," should this be construed as falling only within the legal value of the obligatory or also within that of the recommended and the indifferent? The Quran states "Hold the prayer" (2:43), a phrase that was unanimously understood to convey an obligation. At the same time, the Quran stipulates "Write [your slaves a contract of emancipation] if you are aware of aught of good in them," (24:33), language that was construed as a recommendation. Furthermore, in Q. 5:2, the statement "When you have left the sacred territory, then go hunting" was taken to indicate that hunting outside the Kaʿba is an indifferent act.

Adducing such texts as proof, a minority among the jurists held that the imperative form is a homonym, equally indicating obligation, recommendation and indifference. Others maintained that it signifies only recommendation. The majority of jurists, however, rejected these positions and held the imperative to be an instrument by means of which only obligatory acts are decreed. Whenever the imperative is construed as inducing a legal value other than obligation, such a construal would be based on evidence extraneous and additional to the imperative form in question. Conversely, whenever the imperative form stands apart from any contextual evidence (*qarīna*), it must be presumed to convey an obligation. The Shāfiʿite jurist

[14] Shīrāzī, *Sharḥ al-Lumaʿ*, I, 199–219; Ghazālī, *Mustaṣfā*, I, 411 f., 417–35; Ibn Barhān, *Wuṣūl*, I, 133–44; Bājī, *Iḥkām*, 190–201. For an exposition of a seventh-/thirteenth-century theory of the imperative, see Jeanette Wakin, "Interpretation of the Divine Command in the Jurisprudence of Muwaffaq al-Dīn Ibn Qudāmah," in Nicholas L. Heer, ed., *Islamic Law and Jurisprudence: Studies in Honor of Farhat J. Ziadeh* (Seattle and London: University of Washington Press, 1990), 33–52.

Bāqillānī (d. 403/1012) is said to have held that a judgment on the signification of the imperative form must be suspended (*tawaqquf*) until such time when it can be determined by means of additional contextual evidence. His position seems to be identical with that of the minority who viewed the imperative as a homonym, equally denoting the obligatory, the recommended and the permissible.

Once adopted by the majority, the position that the imperative form, in the absence of contextual evidence, indicates obligation was given added support by arguments developed by a number of leading jurists. The first set of arguments are, expectedly, drawn from both the Quran and the Sunna, and they are to the effect that when God commanded Muslims to perform certain acts He meant them as obligations that can only be violated on pain of punishment: "When it is said unto them: Bow down, they bow not down! Woe unto the repudiators on that day" (Q. 77:48–49).[15]

Those who argued for the position that the imperative form, when abstracted from contextual evidence, exclusively indicates recommendation adduced a report in which the Prophet is said to have declared: "If I command you [to perform an act] perform it to the best of your ability." This report was apparently construed as a categorical principle according to which the legal effect of the imperative form is to be mitigated to a degree falling short of the strict requirements of an obligation. The opponents of this position retorted that the said Prophetic report was solitary, leading to mere probability rather than to certainty. And it was universally held, as we shall see,[16] that any piece of evidence that is less than certain serves no purpose whatsoever in the establishment of principles in legal theory.

Furthermore, it was argued, words that are intended to impose an obligation can be easily distinguished from those that denote recommendation or prohibition. The mind simply knows that the words "Do this" mean obligation, and "Do this if you wish" indicate recommendation. The difference between these phrases, even in the complete absence of contextual evidence, is quite plain and indeed understood by the mind necessarily (*ḍarūratan*). However, should an imperative be construed as a recommendation – a case of rare occurrence, as Ghazālī assures us – it would only be construed as such on account of the overwhelming contextual evidence that transforms its original legal signification. Moreover, in the case of a recommendation, the performance or non-performance of an act is ultimately contingent upon the will of the person who is to perform it, whereas in the imperative, it is the will of the one who commands that is the decisive element.

[15] Other verses quoted are 24:63, 7:12, 9:38–39. [16] See p. 164 below.

Ghazālī argues that the significations of linguistic forms must be understood in accordance with what has been established by convention. This convention is known by means of multiply transmitted reports (*mutawātir*), since solitary reports and the faculty of intellect, the only other avenues, can be of no use here: the solitary report does not lead to certainty, and the intellect cannot decide on matters of language. Through multiply transmitted reports we know from past authorities what the convention with regard to the meaning of a word is, or we know that the Lawgiver has accepted and confirmed the meaning as determined by that convention. Such reports also inform us of the existence of any consensus in the community on how these words are to be understood, or, in the absence of a consensus, of how they have been understood by authorities whose rectitude and integrity would have prevented them from remaining silent when an error in language was committed. It is through one or more of these channels that the meaning, implication and use of the language is known.[17]

If the position that the imperative form indicates only obligation is to be adopted, then another problem arises concerning the number of times the commanded act must be performed. More precisely, the question was whether the commanded act, when it stands in isolation of contextual evidence, ought to be performed only once or continuously.[18] Again, the jurists were split on this issue, a minority opting for continuous performance and the majority for a single performance. All jurists, however, agree that when the imperative is accompanied by contextual evidence that limits the performance to a single instance or, alternatively, necessitates a continuous execution of the act, that evidence must be the ultimate determinant.

When abstracted from any contextual evidence, the imperative is deemed by the majority to necessitate a single performance. For, they argue, an imperative form such as "Pray" is equivalent to the perfect tense "I prayed" in that the latter constitutes sound and complete linguistic usage when the person who is commanded performs the act of praying once. So does the imperative form "Pray" entail the performance of a single prayer. This form, after all, is a derivative of the verb, and derivatives cannot transcend the limits set by that from which they are derived. If the expression "I prayed" is deemed an accurate and complete description after one prayer is performed, then the imperative "Pray" must also be considered a true and complete command generating only a single instance of performance.

[17] Ghazālī, *Mustaṣfā*, I, 422 ff.

[18] Shīrāzī, *Sharḥ al-Luma*ʿ, I, 219–28; Ghazālī, *Mustaṣfā*, II, 7–8; Ibn Barhān, *Wuṣūl*, I, 141–48; Bājī, *Iḥkām*, 201–07; Abū al-Ḥusayn al-Baṣrī, *al-Muʿtamad fī Uṣūl al-Fiqh*, ed. Muhammad Hamidullah et al., 2 vols. (Damascus: Institut Français, 1964–65), I, 108 ff.

In support of the position that the imperative requires continuous performance, some jurists argue that the Prophet's command "the wine-drinker should be flogged" is unanimously interpreted as requiring continuous flogging, until eighty lashes are administered. Against these jurists, the majority insists that this command is not devoid of contextual evidence. The command, they argue, can be properly interpreted, as it indeed was, only with the accompanying knowledge that the Prophet ordered this penalty as a deterrence against consuming alcohol, and such deterrence can be achieved only by continuous flogging, not by a single lash.

Thus a distinction must always be drawn between the imperative *qua* imperative and the contextual evidence that is extraneous to it but which drastically affects its denotation. The significance of this distinction becomes clear in the following example which was a subject of debate between a majority and a minority of jurists. The latter argued that if a servant is commanded to keep in his custody his master's goat while the master is absent, the servant would be deserving of rebuke should he release the goat after having held it for a certain time, but before his master returns. These jurists concluded that if the imperative entails a single instance of performance, the servant would not be liable for rebuke. The majority replied that the command in this example warrants repetition of performance – i.e., maintaining custody of the goat until the master's return – on the grounds of contextual evidence superadded to the command. For the command was not restricted to the very act of taking custody of the goat for a short period of time, but rather for the safe-keeping of the animal. And safe-keeping would not be possible if he had released the goat before his master's return.

Another argument adduced in support of the minority's position issues from the form of prohibition (*nahy*). They maintained that the imperative must be treated like prohibition in that the latter requires a continuous omission of the act prohibited, and that the imperative, being, in a sense, the antonym of prohibition, must entail continuous commission. The onus of drawing a clear distinction between the imperative and prohibitive forms rested with the majority who agreed that to prohibit an act is to negate it once and for all. However, in contrast to the command, prohibition of an act would be violated should the act be committed even once. If, for instance, I am commanded to pray, and, having prayed, I say "I have prayed," I would be deemed to have obeyed the command even if I thereafter cease to pray. Furthermore, if prohibition is qualified by the requirement that the act "should not be performed once," then it is the contrary of an imperative that is qualified by a requirement of a single performance;

the former would be considered fulfilled by continuous instances of omission whereas the latter would be so considered by a single instance of commission.

But what about the commands to pray and to fast, which are known to require continuous acts of performance? The position of the majority is that these commands, in and by themselves, do not require repeated performance. Praying five times a day, for instance, is not construed on the basis of a general command to pray, but rather on the grounds of a specific command to conduct prayer at five designated points of time during the day. And these times are explicitly stated in the law. Had the command been unqualified, the obligation would have been considered fulfilled by the performance of a single prayer.

However, the jurists distinguished at least three types of qualified commands. We have seen that in a command qualified by a specification of time the act must be performed in accordance with that stipulation. The second type is a command qualified by a condition (*sharṭ*), and this requires a single instance of performance. If I were to order my real estate agent to "Sell my house if it rains," the condition "if it rains" shall have no bearing whatsoever on the number of times the act is performed, for if the agent sells my house once he would be fulfilling his duty. The condition, however, affects only the circumstance (*ḥāl*) under which the act is performed – the house cannot be sold unless there is rain. This is to be distinguished from the third type where a command is qualified by a rationale (*ʿilla*), in which case the rationale is to be treated as contextual evidence requiring repeated performance of the act. An example in point is flogging the wine-drinker repeatedly.

The perception of the imperative as entailing repeated action seems to stem, at least in the mind of some jurists, from the assumption that since no specific time of performance is stipulated in the imperative, then no point of time has a priority over another insofar as performance of the act is concerned. And since all points of time are of equal importance, it was argued that the unqualified imperative requires performance at all times, and thus repeatedly. This argument is simply rebutted by the example of a person who is commanded, say, to eat an apple. As the time of performance is not specified, that person can eat the apple at any time, and once he does, he is deemed to have obeyed the command.

Now, the position that an imperative requires one instance of performance necessarily poses the problem of the time in which the act should be carried out after receipt of the command.[19] There seems to have

[19] Shīrāzī, *Sharḥ al-Lumaʿ*, I, 234–45; Ghazālī, *Mustaṣfā*, II, 2–7, 9–10; Bājī, *Iḥkām*, 212–15.

emerged three views concerning this matter: (1) the act ought to be performed instantaneously (*ʿalā al-fawr*); (2) instantaneous performance is not obligatory; and (3) judgment on the time of performance should be suspended until such additional textual evidence can be found as can support one or the other of the previous alternatives. It should be noted that the second view, espoused by the majority, is phrased thus advisedly, for no jurist has ever held the view that the performance of a commanded act must be deferred to an unspecified time in the future (*ʿalā al-tarākhī*).

Nonetheless, the jurists agree that the unqualified imperative, once it is communicated to the believers, must engender in their minds an instantaneous and permanent belief that it is binding, and they must have the instantaneous intention to carry out the commanded act. For to deny the binding authority of the divine command or to have no intention to implement that command, even for a fleeting moment, constitutes an act of disbelief. But it is one thing to *believe* that an act is binding, and to *intend* to perform it, and it is quite another to be under the obligation to perform it immediately after receipt of the command. The majority rejected the argument that since believing and intending are entailed by the very fact of the decreed command, immediate performance is also necessarily entailed. They maintained that whenever the divine command allows for latitude in the performance of an act, the Muslim may defer implementation but must instantaneously believe that the act is binding upon him and must have the intention of performing it immediately. This proves that in the unqualified imperative there exists no necessary relationship between believing and intending on the one hand, and immediate performance on the other. Besides, they add, believing and intending instantaneously are obligatory not by virtue of the very language of the imperative, but rather by the independent, though concomitant, fact that they constitute a prerequisite for obedience to God and His Prophet. The language of the imperative in and by itself contains nothing to the effect that the performance must be immediate.

The language of the unqualified imperative by definition denotes a command to perform an act without any specification of time and, for that matter, without delineating the manner in which it is to be carried out. Specification of the time and manner of performance is not inherent in the imperative form, but rather constitutes an additional element coupled with the imperative. Thus, whenever the commanded act is performed, it will be realized, and the person commanded will be deemed to have properly performed his duty and to have demonstrated obedience. Furthermore, it was argued, the commanded act must necessarily be implemented in a certain place and time. Now, just as there is nothing in the language of the unqualified imperative to indicate the place in which an act is to be carried out, there is likewise nothing in it to denote a specific time of performance.

The proponents of the view that the imperative requires immediate performance thought prohibition to be analogous to the imperative in that like the former the latter demands instantaneous observance. The majority replied that in prohibition the person must immediately refrain from the forbidden act, since if he does not do so, he cannot be said to have obeyed the will of God. In the imperative, on the other hand, any time he performs the act he can properly be described as having obeyed the will of God.

The argument from prohibition continued, however, to be utilized to defend the position of immediate performance. Since, as was commonly held, the commanded act implies that its opposite is forbidden, and since prohibition necessitates instantaneous omission, it was concluded that the imperative must also entail the immediate performance of the act. The opponents of this position, again the majority of jurists, advanced at least two arguments in its refutation. First, the analogy drawn between the imperative and prohibition is imperfect, as has been already established in the matter of performing the commanded act only once. Second, while it is true that the commanded act entails the omission of its opposite, it does so not by virtue of the direct meaning of the imperative's language, but rather by its implication. This simply means that the opposite act, which has become forbidden as a consequence of the issuance of the imperative, will become effective only when the imperative is implemented, for there is nothing inherent in the language of the imperative that has explicit and direct bearing upon the prohibited act. If this is the case, then consequently whatever the imperative commands will determine the status of the prohibited act. And since, as has been already argued, the unqualified imperative does not necessarily require immediate performance, the opposite act becomes prohibited only when the commanded act is performed.

As we have mentioned earlier, there emerged three views regarding the issue under discussion, the third of which was that judgment on the time in which the commanded act must be performed is to be suspended until additional evidence decides whether it is to be implemented instantaneously or not. The proponents of this view maintained that in this respect the imperative is similar to general words (*ʿāmm*) whose meaning cannot be determined until they are particularized by further evidence. Against these, the majority argued that the general word, it is true, does entail an ambiguity in that its language does not clearly refer to a specific individual, but rather to a genus or an indeterminate entity within that genus. Therefore, suspending judgment on the general is quite unavoidable. The unqualified imperative, however, does not involve such an ambiguity, as its language is entirely free from any reference to time. The linguistic contents of such an imperative pertain to nothing but the sheer performance of a particular act, and in this there is no room for ambiguity. In the imperative "Pray," the command is deemed fulfilled whether one prays while in illness, on a journey, fasting, etc. It is hardly reasonable, they contend, to suspend prayer just because the command failed to specify the condition in which the prayer must be held. Besides, the command, being unqualified, includes no reference whatsoever to any particular condition, and for that matter, to any particular point of time.

Thus far the discussion has revolved around imperatives that are unqualified, namely, imperatives that are abstracted from contextual evidence. However, the imperative form may at times appear in conjunction with additional stipulations, such as when the command affords the Muslim a choice in the performance of an act. When an oath is broken, for instance, it is commanded that atonement must consist of freeing a slave or feeding sixty of the poor. The atonement would be considered to have been successfully carried out once either of the two acts is performed. Should both acts be performed, one would be considered as obligatory penance and the other as voluntary, dedicated as a gesture of added piety.

In certain imperatives, the choice is not, as in the previous example, completely free, but rather predicated upon a variety of conditions. If a particular condition obtains, then the choice is eliminated. A case in point is *ẓihār*, whereby the husband sexually abandons his wife and later decides to resume his sexual relationship with her. A reprehensible act, the penance for it may consist of freeing a slave, of fasting or of feeding the poor, depending upon the financial capabilities and health of the person who breached the law. If he owns a slave, then the other options cease to exist; he must free the slave. On the other hand, if he owns no slaves and his health is in such a condition as to enable him to fast, then feeding the poor drops out as an option. But should he choose to do the three forms of penance, then he would be deemed to have complied with the law only insofar as he does that penance suitable to his particular circumstances. The other two would simply be voluntary acts, dictated by no command.[20]

It may be the case that in performing a commanded act, it becomes necessary to avoid another act or a thing whose omission is otherwise not commanded. The question that arises here is whether or not such an omission is always mandatory.[21] If the omission of an act or avoidance of a thing causes undue hardship, then such omission or avoidance is waived. For instance, prayer, commanded by the Lawgiver, presupposes the

[20] Shīrāzī, *Lumaʿ*, 11 ff.; Bājī, *Iḥkām*, 208 ff. [21] Shīrāzī, *Sharḥ al-Lumaʿ*, I, 263–64.

performance of ablution, and this cannot be carried out without ritually clean water. If it happens that the entire reservoir of water available to a person has been ritually contaminated (*najāsa*), and he has no access to other reservoirs, he would then be beset with immeasurable hardship, since his prayer would be deemed invalid without ablution in which ritually clean water is used. Accordingly, the command to use ritually clean water is waived in such a situation. It is clear, however, that should one be able to gain access, without undue hardship, to other uncontaminated reservoirs of water, then the waiver does not apply; ritually clean water must be used and that which is unclean avoided.

The prohibitive form.[22] Like the imperative, the prohibitive form (*nahy*) represents an utterance used by a superior to address someone in an inferior position. But whereas the imperative requires the commission of an act, the prohibitive calls for omission. Some jurists further argue that the omission dictated by prohibition is obligatory and is not classifiable under any other legal norm. In linguistic usage, the statement "Do not do such and such" (*lā tafʿal*) has a special form denoting a command to refrain from commission. For, it is argued, in customary usage, if a master prohibits his servant to perform a certain act, but the servant nonetheless performs it, the master would be considered to have taken appropriate action in rebuking or punishing the servant. Thus, in the convention of language, this special imperative form, provided it is divorced from contextual evidence, requires omission.

Unlike the imperative, prohibition requires immediate and constant omission of the act, for failure immediately to refrain from the performance of an act constitutes an act of performance, and this in turn represents a violation of the prohibition. In the hypothetical example of the prohibition "Do not kill unbelievers," obedience to the law does not take effect unless the Muslim avoids killing unbelievers, for if he kills even one, he would not be said to have obeyed the prohibitive command. Delaying obedience to the command furthermore implies that he did not avoid killing unbelievers. Thus, in order for obedience to be complete, the prohibited act must be omitted immediately and constantly, *ad infinitum*.

We have already seen that certain imperative commands afford the Muslim an unqualified choice in the performance of an act. In such a case, the obligation would be considered satisfactorily fulfilled once any of the acts is duly performed. Though the performance of an additional act is strictly deemed voluntary and does not constitute a fulfillment of the com-

[22] Ibn Barhān, *Wuṣūl*, I, 186–200; Shīrāzī, *Sharḥ al-Lumaʿ*, I, 291–301; Bājī, *Iḥkām*, 228–30.

manded obligation, it remains within the realm of legality. This is not the case, however, with the prohibition of one of two or more acts. If prohibition is predicated of any number of acts, only one act is prohibited and the rest are not. At no time can two of these acts be performed together. In illustration of this doctrine, the jurists advance the case of the prohibition to marry two or more women who are blood relatives. When a Muslim man marries a woman, he is not permitted to marry her sister or aunt while he is still married to her. In other words, he can marry any one in a group of women related by blood, but he is prohibited to enter into matrimony with any two of them at the same time.

Another issue in prohibition that runs parallel to the imperative is whether the binary opposite of a prohibited act must be performed. The jurists argue that if the prohibited act has no more than one opposite, then it would be an obligation to perform the opposite act. The prohibition of fasting during the Feast of Breaking the Ramadan Fast (*ʿĪd al-Fiṭr*) requires Muslims not to fast, and since eating is the only opposite to fasting, the prohibition of fasting must be taken to imply that eating is an obligation. If, on the other hand, the prohibited act has more than one opposite, then the performance of any one of these opposites would in effect constitute an omission of the prohibited act. Since the opposite of the prohibited act of adultery may be prayer, fasting, working, etc., the performance of any one of these acts represents, *ipso facto*, an omission of the act of adultery.

That the prohibited act should be omitted does not entail that the act must be regarded as falling under the legal value of impermissible. While a number of jurists held it to be impermissible, many legal scholars belonging to the Ashʿarite school of theology argued that the prohibited act may either be impermissible or repugnant. It is only with the aid of additional evidence, extraneous to the language of the prohibition, that the act can be distinguished as either impermissible or repugnant. In the absence of such evidence a judgment on the legal value of the act cannot but be suspended.

Nor should the prohibited act be construed as necessarily and absolutely invalid (*fāsid bi-iṭlāq*). True, such acts as theft and consumption of inebriants are prohibited on the grounds that they are malefactory. But other acts within the purview of the law may be prohibited though they do not fall into the latter category. Such is the case of fasting during the Feast of Breaking the Ramadan Fast. Although fasting on this day represents a violation of the command to feast, it is not absolutely invalid but merely repugnant. It is not absolutely invalid, since fasting is indeed prescribed to Muslims during the month of Ramadan. The argument that the prohibited act is absolutely invalid leads to the conclusion that God's law is contradictory, since fasting, for instance, would then be at once forbidden and prescribed.

Linguistic implication

It has already been noted that according to one *uṣūl* taxonomy, legal language bears either a meaning (*maʿnā*) or an implication (*mafhūm*). The imperative, for instance, embodies both a meaning and implication. The meaning (*maʿnā*) inheres in the very language of the command to perform an act; e.g., "sit down" denotes nothing but the order to be seated. The implication, on the other hand, is understood not directly from the semantic force of the language but rather from what can be indirectly inferred from it. Thus one of the implications of the command "sit down" is "do not stand up." There is nothing in the very language (*nuṭq*) of the command that can be construed as having a strict semantic relation to standing up – it is merely deduced from the language.

Since this category of linguistic implication has a direct bearing upon legal reasoning in general and *qiyās* in particular, it would be fitting to follow the lead of some jurists in postponing its discussion to the sections dealing with *qiyās*. Accordingly, the *a fortiori* and the *e contrario* arguments, constituting the main components of the category of linguistic implication, will be discussed in the next chapter where they will also serve to delimit the scope of the inferential procedure of *qiyās*.

PROPHETIC REPORTS: EPISTEMOLOGY, TRANSMISSION, AUTHENTICATION

The analysis of legal language presupposes that the texts embodying this language have been established as reliable insofar as their transmission is concerned. A text that has been transmitted by dubious channels is deemed to lack any legal effect even though its language may be explicit and unequivocal. Thus all texts must pass the test of both linguistic analysis and transmission before they are approached with a view to deriving legal rulings from them. The Quranic text, however, is not subject to the test of transmission, because, as we shall see later on, the mode of its transmission in the Muslim community excludes the possibility of any doubt or error. The reports of the Prophet, on the other hand, are subject to such a test.

Though it may seem self-evident that the Quran and the Prophetic Sunna constitute the material foundations of the law, Muslim intellectuals did not take such a fact for granted. That the Quran and the Prophethood of Muhammad are authoritative is a matter that is determined by the science of theology (*uṣūl al-dīn*), the offshoot of which is legal theory (*uṣūl al-fiqh*). Theology justifies and establishes the broad foundations of religion, including the existence of God, the truth of His Book and His Prophets, the last one of whom was Muhammad. Legal theory departs from the point where theology leaves off, assuming the truth of theology's postulates. Two such postulates are the truth and authoritativeness of the Quran and the Sunna as the foundations of the law.[23]

Postulating the Sunna as one of the foundations of the law does not necessarily preclude the possibility of questioning certain elements of it, for showing that an element is doubtful amounts to demonstrating that it does not partake in that Sunna. Nor do theology's postulates bear upon the delimitation of the scope of the Sunna or upon the analysis of its substance. These are tasks that squarely belong to the province of legal theory.

The first step in the discourse about the Sunna as a foundation of the law is to define its constitution. The Sunna, by definition, requires the involvement of the Prophet. The most direct form of involvement is his own utterances and actions. But also included in his Sunna are actions and utterances of others which he has seen or heard and of which he has tacitly approved. Such utterances and actions, once tacitly approved by the Prophet, acquire the same status as that accorded to his own statements and deeds. Even actions that he has not seen may, under certain circumstances, enter the body of the Sunna. If it can be established that a Companion, for instance, has behaved in a manner about which the Prophet could not have but known, and of which behavior the Prophet did not disapprove, the Companion's conduct is deemed to constitute part and parcel of the Prophetic Sunna. For example, the renowned Companion Muʿādh b. Jabal reportedly used to perform the evening prayer together with the Prophet and would thereafter regularly visit his own tribe, the Banū Salama, and would join them in performing the same prayer. His behavior, known to, and approved by, the Prophet, set a Sunna precedent concerning voluntary prayers, on the basis of which the jurists considered the first of a double performance of the same prayer (in this case the evening prayer) to be mandatory and the other voluntary.[24]

Whether the Sunna stems from the actions and utterances of the Prophet himself or not, it is subject to classification in accordance with the legal norms. Those actions that pertain to non-religious affairs, such as walking, sleeping, etc., are classified as permissible, where commission or omission entails neither reward nor punishment. Other actions and utterances may

[23] Juwaynī, *Burhān*, I, 84, 85; Ghazālī, *Mustaṣfā*, I, 6–7. [24] Shīrāzī, *Sharḥ al-Lumaʿ*, I, 561–62.

belong to one of three categories: (1) obeying God's command; (2) clarifying an ambiguous matter; or (3) setting a precedent. If the imperative form of the command is construed to be an obligation, or a recommendation, then the Sunna must be construed in accordance with that command. And if it is a clarification of an ambiguous text, the linguistic evidence surrounding that text must determine its legal value. However, if the Sunna represents an action or an utterance that is entirely new, some jurists argued that such a Sunna signifies an obligation unless contextual evidence shows it to be otherwise. Other jurists maintained that in and by itself it signifies neither obligation nor recommendation, and a judgment on it must be suspended (*tawaqquf*) until further evidence shows it to belong to one or the other value.[25]

Be that as it may, the Sunna, whatever legal value it embodies, is binding upon Muslims and is not applicable exclusively to the person of the Prophet unless explicit evidence proves it to be so confined. That the Sunna is binding upon Muslims has, as we have seen, been demonstrated by Shāfiʿī (as well as by later jurists) on the basis of the Quran which enjoins Muslims to obey the Prophet and not to swerve from his ranks.[26]

Inasmuch as it is binding, and in sheer bulk the most significant source of the law, the Sunna was constantly being exploited for raw legal material. Its transmission thus became a central concern for Muslim scholars, be they jurists, strictly so defined, or simply religious scholars interested in the promotion of religion. But the extent to which a particular Sunna was legally useful depended not only on its linguistic contents but also on the manner in which it was conceived to have been transmitted from the time of the Prophet. Being wholly or partly expressed in a *ḥadīth* (Prophetic report), a Sunna was deemed to carry with it an epistemic value that was measured according to the conditions under which it was transmitted. These conditions thus determined whether a report would be taken to yield certainty, probability, or a lesser degree of knowledge of no service to the law.

Attaining certainty in the transmission of a Prophetic report means that there is no doubt whatsoever concerning the fact that the report is authentic and genuine. This certainty occurs only in the recurrent (*tawātur*) mode of transmission where three conditions must be met. First, the report must reach us through channels of transmission sufficiently numerous as to preclude any possibility of error or collaboration on a forgery. Second, the very first class of transmitters must have a sensory knowledge of what the Prophet said or did. Third, these two conditions must be met at each stage

[25] Ibid., I, 545 ff.; Bājī, *Iḥkām*, 309–12. [26] *Risāla*, 43–54; Bājī, *Iḥkām*, 309 ff.

of transmission beginning with the first class and ending with the last hearer of the report.[27]

The recurrent mode of transmission yields necessary knowledge, wherein the mind is the recipient of the report's subject matter without exercising the faculty of reasoning or reflection. Put differently, upon hearing the recurrent report the mind has no choice but to admit the contents of the report *a priori* as true and genuine. Unlike acquired knowledge (*ʿilm muktasab*) which occurs to the mind only after it conducts inferential operations, necessary knowledge is lodged in the mind spontaneously. Upon hearing a report narrated by a single person, one is presumed to have gained probable knowledge of its contents and authenticity. In order to reach a level of necessary knowledge, we must hear the report relayed a sufficient number of times and each time by a different transmitter.[28]

The great majority of jurists maintain that a Prophetic report relayed through fewer than five channels of transmission cannot be considered recurrent since the acceptance of such a report necessarily involves reflection. Their argument for rejecting the report as recurrent stems from the procedural law of testimony. They argue that for a judge to admit the testimony of four witnesses in a court of law, he must exercise his faculty of reasoning in enquiring about their character in order to assert their trustworthiness. If it were the case that the testimony of four witnesses could result in necessary knowledge, then such an enquiry would be superfluous. And since the analogy between witnesses and transmitters was seen as valid, it was held that the knowledge conveyed by four transmitters is not necessary, but requires the intervention of the faculty of reasoning in ascertaining their reliability.[29]

Some jurists fixed the minimum number of transmitters at 5, while others set the number variably at 12, 20, 70 or 313. The choice of 70, for instance, was based on the alleged number of persons who followed Moses, while 313 represented the number of Muslim fighters who joined the Prophet in the battle of Badr. However, it is generally acknowledged that the number at which immediate knowledge obtains must be larger than five but cannot be exactly determined since it varies from one person to another. Each instance of transmission is surrounded by contextual evidence which may be known to one person but unknown to another. A

27 Shīrāzī, *Sharḥ al-Lumaʿ*, I, 572 ff.; Bernard Weiss, "Knowledge of the Past: The Theory of *Tawātur* According to Ghazālī," *Studia Islamica*, 61 (1985): 81–105; Wael B. Hallaq, "On Inductive Corroboration, Probability and Certainty in Sunnī Legal Thought," in Heer, ed., *Islamic Law and Jurisprudence*, 9–19.

28 Shīrāzī, *Sharḥ al-Lumaʿ*, II, 574–77; Hallaq, "Inductive Corroboration," 10 ff.

29 Juwaynī, *Burhān*, I, 570–73; Bājī, *Iḥkām*, 328–29.

person who is familiar with contextual evidence relevant to a particular report will attain necessary knowledge before another who is not. Theoretically, however, two persons who have equal knowledge of such evidence and who have heard the same number of transmitters are expected to attain necessary knowledge at the same time.[30]

Since knowledge of the recurrent report is necessary, involving neither reflection nor reasoning, it is argued that the hearer of the report does not know how and when he reaches such knowledge. Those who have never visited Mecca, for instance, know with certainty of its existence through hearing a multiplicity of reports to the effect that the city exists. But they have no way of knowing by which individual report they became certain of the existence of Mecca. Likewise, if a man were killed in the marketplace, and we are told by one person who has been to the market that such a murder took place, we would think that such an event has probably happened. But when we hear the same report from a number of persons, the probability in favor of the event having indeed occurred is increasingly strengthened in our mind until we become totally convinced that there has indeed been a murder in the marketplace. We do not know, however, at what individual report we have made the transition from the region of probability to that of certainty. The exact moment or stage at which knowledge becomes certain is, the legal theoreticians argue, as impossible to determine as the exact moment at which night ends and the light of day begins. The impossibility of determining the minimum number of recurrent reports necessary to engender certain knowledge takes us back to the intellect of the hearer as the ultimate point of reference. It is the moment at which a person realizes that he is completely certain of a reported matter which determines the number of reports, not the other way round; that is, the number may be decided only when conclusive knowledge has already been attained.[31]

The solitary reports (*āḥād*), on the other hand, do not lead to necessary knowledge, though under certain circumstances they may yield certainty that amounts to acquired knowledge. The ever-present need to investigate the reports' authenticity injects in our minds an element of reasoning and reflection which precludes the knowledge conveyed by these reports from being necessary and immediate. In the solitary report we are perfectly conscious of the process by which knowledge has entered our minds.[32]

Though some solitary reports may lead to acquired knowledge, the

[30] Juwaynī, *Burhān*, I, 569–70; Muḥammad b. Abī Yaʿlā al-Baghdādī Ibn al-Farrā', *al-ʿUdda fī Uṣūl al-Fiqh*, ed. Aḥmad Mubārakī, 3 vols. (Beirut: Mu'assasat al-Risāla, 1980), III, 856–57; Hallaq, "Inductive Corroboration," 12 ff. [31] Hallaq, "Inductive Corroboration," 12.

[32] Ghazālī, *Mankhūl*, 245 ff.; Shīrāzī, *Sharḥ al-Lumaʿ*, II, 578.

majority do not exceed the level of probability (*ẓann*). Thus, there are distinguished two types of solitary reports, one that results in certainty, the other in probability. Both types, however, lack the multiplicity of channels of transmission by which the recurrent report is passed through successive generations. Any report that fails to be transmitted through a recurrent number of channels is solitary, whatever the number of these channels. It then follows that the term "solitary" (like the Arabic "*āḥādī*") signifies a Prophetic report that is transmitted through one or more channels which never reach the number satisfied in *tawātur*.

The first type of the solitary reports is said to provide an authoritative basis for both certainty and practice, whereas the second type lacks the element of certainty. The presence of this element in the first type of solitary reports finds justification in the added evidence that these reports contain evidence that is absent from the second type. An example of such a report is one transmitted by a single person in the audience of a large group of people who happened to hear him and who raise no objection to him since they have themselves heard the statement or witnessed the event he has relayed. Their tacit approval of the report he transmitted constitutes corroborative evidence which removes all doubt concerning the truth of what he has relayed. But the certain knowledge conveyed in his transmission is not necessary since his credibility as a transmitter must be investigated, thereby introducing to the knowledge embedded in the report an element of reasoning and reflection.[33]

The multiplicity of the chains of transmission in the recurrent reports precludes the need to investigate the reliability of transmitters, a fact which explains why these reports yield certain and necessary knowledge. In the solitary reports of the first type the multiplicity of witnesses at the first tier of transmission represents the corroborative support that lends the report an epistemic value of certitude. The absence of this support subsequent to the first tier, however, makes it necessary to investigate the trustworthiness of each transmitter from the second down to the last one.

The second type of solitary reports that lead only to probability lacks the element of corroboration at the first tier of transmission. The absence of corroboration and of a sufficiently large number of transmitters at each tier of transmission fails to guarantee beyond doubt the genuineness of the report. At the same time, if the report proves to have been transmitted without interruption and if all the transmitters have passed the test of reliability, then the report is taken to yield probable knowledge that is admissible in matters of practice, but not in those that involve religious belief.

[33] Bājī, *Iḥkām*, 319.

Some jurists argued that solitary reports must not be resorted to in legal cases that have a wide range of applicability (*mā taʿummu bihi al-balwā*), since their authenticity cannot be conclusively ascertained. The majority, however, maintained that solitary reports may be employed in arriving at any legal ruling whether such a ruling involves a wide or a limited range of applicability. This view is held on the grounds that *qiyās* itself derives its authoritativeness from solitary reports. Since the rules inferred through the procedures of *qiyās* are admissible in all matters, be they limited or general, the rules based on solitary reports must likewise be admissible in all levels of application. Furthermore, it is argued that the Companions of the Prophet reached a consensus on the validity of solitary reports as a textual basis for rulings that bear upon matters of universal importance. This consensus renders solitary reports as valid as both the Quran and the recurrent Sunna in serving as a textual basis for solving such matters as pertain to practice.[34]

The lack of certainty in the transmission of the solitary reports compelled jurists to articulate the sources of authority that justify the use of these reports in matters of law. Reason, they argued, constitutes such a source, though it is in fact subsidiary to the religious argument that derives its force from the practice of the Prophet who depended on individual deputies in conducting the affairs of the provinces that came under his command. It was a single judge or governor from whom the Prophet learned of such affairs, and through whom he ruled distant regions. Such was the common practice of the Companions during and after the time of the Prophet.[35]

Now, by the fifth/eleventh century, Sunnī legal theory came to acknowledge another body of reports that were recurrent but were not identical with those which we have previously encountered. These latter are recurrent in their *lafẓ*, namely, each report represents a text which is transmitted identically, word by word, through all the channels in a recurrent fashion. That is why they are known as *lafẓī* recurrent reports. The other body of reports, however, is recurrent only insofar as the number of channels are concerned, but each channel, while containing a report that is textually different from the other reports, shares with those reports an identical meaning. Here, each report qualifies, technically speaking, only as solitary, but when there exists a *sufficient* number of such reports supporting one theme (*maʿnā*), then in their aggregate they are considered to yield certain and necessary knowledge, precisely like the *lafẓī* recurrent reports. And since their texts are worded differently but share the same theme, they are

[34] Shīrāzī, *Sharḥ al-Lumaʿ*, II, 606 ff.

[35] Ibn Barhān, *Wuṣūl*, II, 156–72; Bājī, *Iḥkām*, 334 ff.; Shīrāzī, *Sharḥ al-Lumaʿ*, II, 583–603.

known, in contradistinction to the *lafẓī* type, as thematic (*maʿnawī*) recurrent reports.[36]

The necessary knowledge resulting from the *maʿnawī* recurrent reports finds its logical justification in the inductive corroboration each report lends the others in supporting the truth of a single theme. The emphasis here is placed on the differences among the reports insofar as the chains of transmission and the verbal contents are concerned. The degree of probability attached to them individually is immediately eliminated once they are grouped together as one aggregate. Put differently, the possibility that these reports are individually false is immediately dismissed when, taken all together, they attest uniformly to a particular matter. In this, they become identical to the *lafẓī* recurrent reports in yielding necessary knowledge. Without being aware of the actual process of relaying the reports, the intellect augments knowledge until the point at which it becomes entirely certain of the information relayed. The process is purely corroborative. It is likened by jurists to drops of water or crumbs of bread; when they are continuously consumed they will eventually quench the thirst or satiate, but individually they are insufficient.[37]

Solitary reports may, at a certain stage of transmission, be interrupted, in the sense that one or more of the transmitters may be unknown. The early jurists are in agreement that if the transmitter with whom the report resumes after the interruption is known for his integrity and is reputed for transmitting only those reports that are sound, then his report is to be treated as a sound solitary report that results in a probable level of knowledge, fit for legal practice (*ʿamal*). However, a number of later jurists, including those theologians who discoursed on legal theory, dismissed such a report, arguing that it is deficient and should not, therefore, be admissible in the law.[38]

In some solitary reports the chain of transmission is not only complete but has multiplied during the third or fourth generation after the Prophet. Known as widespread (*mashhūr*, lit. well known), these reports were considered to yield certain, though acquired, knowledge. The assumption that the earliest generations could not, by virtue of having lived in so pristine a phase of Islam, have lied or conspired on a forgery, precludes the possibility that a given report should have been questionable in the early period of its life, when it was still solitary. And once it became highly circulated after the first generations, the great number of instances of transmission certainly secured its conclusiveness. But since a certain amount of conscious

[36] Shīrāzī, *Sharḥ al-Lumaʿ*, II, 569; Hallaq, "Inductive Corroboration," 19–21.
[37] Hallaq, "Inductive Corroboration," 20–21. [38] Bājī, *Iḥkām*, 349 ff.; Shīrāzī, *Lumaʿ*, 49.

thinking was involved in verifying the soundness of the report in its early phases, the knowledge obtained from it must remain acquired.[39]

We have seen on more than one occasion that the rectitude of the transmitter played a central part in determining the status and authenticity of Prophetic reports. Indeed, most of the qualities an impeccable transmitter had to have enjoyed revolved around rectitude. The attribute that was most valued, and in fact deemed indispensable, was that of being just (*ʿadl*), namely, being morally and religiously righteous, having committed no grave sin, and no more than a few minor ones. A just character seems to have implied another requirement, i.e., that of being truthful (*ṣādiq*) and incapable of lying. This requirement was intended to preclude either outright tampering with the wording of the transmitted text, or interpolating in it fabricated material. It also implied that the transmitter could not lie as to his sources, claiming that he had heard the report from an authority when he in fact did not. He had also to be fully aware and cognizant of the material he related, so as to transmit it with precision (*ḍabṭ*). Finally, he must not have been involved in any religious innovation (*bidʿa*), such as belonging to the Khārijī movement, for should he have been so involved, he would have been liable to produce heretical material for the sake of the movement to which he belonged. This last requirement strongly implied that the transmitter had to adhere to the Sunnī community, to the exclusion of the sectarian movements considered heretical.[40]

Only reports transmitted throughout all stages by persons who met these requirements may be admitted as sound. And no report may be deemed admissible until the integrity of the transmitter has been established. As is the case with witnesses, the integrity of a transmitter is confirmed by the attestation of a single witness who testifies that he, the transmitter, is trustworthy. Formally speaking, if the testimony is positive, it is sufficient for the witness to state briefly that the transmitter is just, but should it be negative, the witness is under the obligation to provide a detailed explanation for his testimony. A testimony in which the witness merely states that the transmitter is not trustworthy is insufficient to discredit the transmitter. On the other hand, should two witnesses contradict one another concerning the rectitude of a certain transmitter, the negative testimony is deemed to supersede the other, since it is assumed to be based on additional information about the character of the transmitter that is not available to the other witness.[41]

[39] Muḥammad b. Aḥmad Abū Sahl al-Sarakhsī, *al-Uṣūl*, ed. Abū al-Wafā al-Afghānī, 2 vols. (Cairo: Dār al-Maʿrifa, 1393/1973), I, 291–93.

[40] Ghazālī, *Mustaṣfā*, I, 155–62; Shīrāzī, *Sharḥ al-Lumaʿ*, II, 630–33; Sarakhsī, *Uṣūl*, I, 345–55.

[41] Shīrāzī, *Sharḥ al-Lumaʿ*, II, 614 ff.; Ibn Barhān, *Wuṣūl*, II, 186 ff.

The jurists agree that the verbatim relay of *ḥadīth* represents the best form of transmission. Some jurists also deem acceptable a thematic transmission of reports, provided that the language and meaning of the report are unambiguous, since an equivocal report may be thought by the transmitter to have a meaning that is different from its real meaning. The transmitter must also possess precise knowledge of the report's meaning, for if he does not, he might unwittingly convey to his audience a meaning that is at variance from that originally intended by the Prophet.[42]

Furthermore, it is preferable that the report be transmitted in full, although part of a report that is thematically unconnected with the other parts may be transmitted alone. Partial transmission, however, is inadmissible when the parts are interconnected or interdependent, as such transmission would amount to ignoring the overall context of the report, a context that may well affect the meaning of the transmitted part.[43]

Now, in seeking to solve a case of law the jurist might encounter two or more reports that are perceived to bear upon that case. If all the reports uniformly support a particular solution, then the jurist's ruling gains added support. A problem, however, may arise when such reports are seen to be relevant to the case, but are clearly contradictory. If they cannot be reconciled, the jurist must attempt to resort to the procedure of abrogation (*naskh*), whereby one of the reports is made to repeal the others. Failing this, he must seek to make one report preponderant over the others by establishing that a particular report possesses attributes superior to those found in the others. The criteria of preponderance (*tarjīḥ*) are relative to the mode of transmission (*isnād*) as well as to the subject matter (*matn*) of the report. There are several criteria to be met. First, a report whose transmitters are of age and are well known for their precision and good memory is deemed more reliable than another where one or more of its transmitters is a minor and/or lacks the attributes of good memory and precision. Second, a report that includes among its transmitters more jurists (*faqīh*s) than is found in another is clearly superior. Third, a report transmitted by more persons than is another gains added strength. Fourth, a report whose first transmitter was closer to the Prophet is considered superior to one whose first transmitter barely knew the Prophet. Fifth, a report relayed by one or more Medinese transmitters is preferable to one that is not transmitted by such persons. Last, but not least, a chain of transmission that is unconditionally approved by the authoritative *ḥadīth* scholars obviously

42 Bājī, *Iḥkām*, 384–85; Ibn Barhān, *Wuṣūl*, II, 187–91; Shīrāzī, *Sharḥ al-Luma'*, II, 645–47; Sarakhsī, *Uṣūl*, I, 355–57.

43 Shīrāzī, *Sharḥ al-Luma'*, II, 648–49. Incidentally, note the modernist critique of this feature in traditional theory, pp. 241 ff., below.

renders a report more reliable than one whose transmission is controversial.[44]

The subject matter also determines the comparative strength or weakness of a report. The first of the criteria for this is the thematic agreement of the contents of a report with other authoritative sources, such as a Quranic verse, another Sunna, or consensus. Such agreement amounts to a corroboration by these sources of the truth embedded in the report and thus grants it a status higher than a report that finds no such corroboration. Second, a report is deemed superior to another when the community acts upon a ruling derived from it, since this constitutes a consensus that attests to its veracity. Third, a report that conveys both an utterance and a deed of the Prophet is preferable to one that contains one or the other. Fourth, a report that affirms an act – such as standing up – takes precedence over one that negates the opposite act – e.g., sitting down, for the former is clearly more explicit than the latter insofar as the ruling is concerned. Fifth, a report whose legal effect is prohibition overrides one that results in permission with regard to the same matter; the reasoning here being that the former represents a safer recourse, since permitting what is otherwise a prohibited act is viewed by many jurists to be far more reprehensible than prohibiting a permissible act. This view, however, was controversial, and many other scholars consider the two reports to have an equal force.[45]

ABROGATION

When the jurist is faced with two conflicting texts relevant to a particular case the solution to which is pending, he must attempt to reconcile the texts by harmonizing them so that both may be brought to bear in resolving it. But should the texts prove to be so contradictory as not to be capable of harmonization, the jurist must resort to the theory of abrogation (*naskh*) with a view to determining which of the two texts repeals the other. Thus abrogation involves the replacement of one text, which would have otherwise had a legal effect, by another text embodying a legal value contradictory to the first.

The justification for the theory of abrogation derives from the common idea, sanctioned by consensus, that the religion of Islam abrogated many, and sometimes all, of the laws upheld by the earlier religions. It is a fundamental creed, furthermore, that Islam not only deems these religions legitimate but also considers itself to be the bearer of their legacy. That

44 Shīrāzī, *Sharḥ al-Luma*ʿ, II, 657–60; Bājī, *Iḥkām*, 735–44.
45 Bājī, *Iḥkām*, 745–52; Shīrāzī, *Sharḥ al-Luma*ʿ, II, 660–62.

Muhammad repealed his predecessors' laws goes to prove that abrogation is a valid hermeneutical instrument which was specifically approved in Q. 2:106: "Such of Our revelation as We abrogate or cause to be forgotten, we bring [in place] one better or the like thereof" and 16:101: "When We put a revelation in place of another, and God knows best what He reveals, they say: 'Lo, you are but inventing. Most of them know not.'" These verses were taken to show that abrogation is applicable to revelation *within* Islam.[46]

It is to be stressed that the greatest majority of jurists espoused the view that it is not the texts themselves that are actually abrogated, but rather the legal rulings comprised by these texts. The text *qua* text is not subject to repeal, for to argue that God revealed conflicting and even contradictory statements would entail that one of the statements is false, and this would in turn lead to the highly objectionable conclusion that God has revealed an untruth.[47]

Why there should be, in the first place, conflicting and even contradictory rulings is not a question in which the jurists were very interested. That such rulings existed, however, was undeniable, and that they should be made to abrogate one another was deemed a necessity. The criteria that determined which text is to abrogate another mainly revolved around the chronology of Quranic revelation and the diachronic sequence of the Prophet's career. Certain later texts simply abrogated earlier ones.

But is it possible that behind abrogation there are latent divine considerations of mitigating the severity of the repealed rulings? Only a minority of jurists appears to have maintained that since God is merciful and compassionate He aimed at reducing hardships for His creatures. Abrogating a lenient ruling by a less lenient or a harsher one would run counter to His attribute as a merciful God. Besides, God Himself has pronounced that "He desires for you ease, and He desires no hardship" (Q. 2:185). Accordingly, repealing a ruling by a harsher one would contravene his pronouncement. The opponents, however, rejected this argument. They maintained that to say that God cannot repeal a ruling by another which involves added hardship would be tantamount to saying that He cannot, or does not, impose hardships in His law, and this is plainly false. Furthermore, this argument would lead to the absurd conclusion that He cannot cause someone to be ill after having been healthy, or to be blind after having enjoyed perfect vision. As for the aforementioned Quranic verse (2:185), they reject it as an invalid argument since it exclusively bears upon hardships involved in a quite specific and limited context, namely, the

[46] Shīrāzī, *Sharḥ al-Lumaʿ*, I, 482–84, 489; Ibn Barhān, *Wuṣūl*, II, 13–21; Bājī, *Iḥkām*, 391 ff.
[47] Bājī, *Iḥkām*, 393.

fast of Ramadan. They likewise reject the Quranic verse 2:106 which states that God abrogates a verse only to introduce in its place another which is either similar to or better than it. What is "better," they argue, is not necessarily that which is more lenient and more agreeable, but rather that which is ultimately more rewarding in this life and in the hereafter. And since the reward is greater, it may well be that the abrogating text comprises a less lenient ruling than that which was abrogated.[48]

If God's motives for abrogation cannot be determined, then these motives cannot serve to establish which of the two conflicting legal rulings should repeal the other. The criteria of abrogation must thus rest elsewhere. The first, and most evincive, criterion may be found in an explicit statement in the abrogating text, such as the Prophet's pronouncement "I had permitted for you the use of the carrion's leather, but upon receipt of this writing [epistle] you are not to utilize it in any manner." Here, an earlier permission has been explicitly repealed by a prohibition.[49]

The second and most common criterion for abrogation is the chronological order of revelation, namely, that in point of time a later text repeals an earlier one. For instance, during the early phase of his mission, the Prophet declared the punishment for adultery to be a hundred lashes and banishment of the violater for a duration of one year. Later on, when a certain Māʿiz committed adultery, the Prophet did not resort to flogging or exile, but instead ordered that he be stoned. This latter practice, thought to be chronologically of later origin, was taken to represent a repeal of the earlier form of punishment. The difficulty that arises here is to determine the chronology of texts. The first obvious indication is one that appears in the text itself, as we have seen in the case of the carrion's leather. But such explicit statements are admittedly difficult to come by. Most other conflicting texts have to be dated by external evidence, and here the Companions' practices and pronouncements are invaluable since their attestation as to which of the Prophet's practices or statements came later in time is considered crucial for dating texts. Finally, in the event of failure to determine the chronological sequence of Prophetic reports by these methods, an examination of the first transmitter in each of the two conflicting reports becomes necessary. Such an examination may unravel which report occurred first in point of time, and this is rendered possible by establishing, for instance, that one of the two transmitters died before the other could have known the Prophet, which means that the report of the latter transmitter was subsequent to that of the former. This type of

[48] Shīrāzī, *Sharḥ al-Lumaʿ*, I, 493–95; Ibn Barhān, *Wuṣūl*, II, 25–27; Bājī, *Iḥkām*, 400–04.
[49] Shīrāzī, *Sharḥ al-Lumaʿ*, I, 515–17.

evidence was considered sufficient to conclude that the latter transmitter's report must have been posterior to that of the former.[50]

The third criterion is consensus. Should the community, represented by its scholars, agree to adopt a ruling in preference to another, then the latter is deemed abrogated since the community cannot agree on an error. The very fact of abandoning one ruling in favor of another is tantamount to abrogating the disfavored ruling. A number of jurists, however, rejected consensus as having the capability to abrogate, their argument being that any consensus must be based on the revealed texts, and if these texts contain no evidence of abrogation in the first place, then consensus as a sanctioning instrument cannot decide in such a matter. To put it differently, since consensus cannot go beyond the evidence of the texts, it is the texts and only the texts that determine whether or not one ruling can abrogate another. If a ruling subject to consensus happened to abrogate another conflicting ruling, abrogation would be due to evidence existing in the texts, not to consensus.[51]

If consensus is rejected as incapable of abrogating a ruling, it is because of a cardinal principle in the theory of abrogation which stipulates that derivative principles cannot be employed to abrogate all or any part of the source from which they are derived. This explains why consensus and juridical inference (*qiyās*), both based on the Quran and the Sunna, were deemed by the great majority of jurists, and in fact by mainstream Sunnism, to lack the power to repeal either Prophetic reports or Quranic verses.[52]

The other cardinal principle, quite often resorted to in jurisprudential arguments, is that an epistemologically inferior text cannot repeal a superior one. Thus a text whose truth or authenticity is only presumed (=probable: *ẓannī*) can by no means abrogate another text marked by certitude (*qaṭʿ*, *yaqīn*). On the other hand, texts that are considered of equal epistemological value or of the same species may repeal one another. This principle seems to represent an extension of Q. 2:106 which speaks of abrogating verses and replacing them by similar or better ones. Hence, it is a universal principle that like the Quran, concurrent reports may abrogate one another. And the same applies to solitary reports. Furthermore, according to the logic of this principle, an epistemologically superior text can abrogate an inferior one. Thus the Quran and the concurrent Sunna may abrogate solitary reports, but not vice versa.[53]

Within the Quran and the Sunna, moreover, a text expressing a pronouncement (*qawl*) may repeal another text of the same species, just as a

[50] Ibid., I, 517–19. [51] Ibn Barhān, *Wuṣūl*, II, 51–54.
[52] Ibid., II, 54–55; Shīrāzī, *Sharḥ al-Lumaʿ*, I, 512. [53] Shīrāzī, *Sharḥ al-Lumaʿ*, I, 505.

text embodying a deed (*fiʿl*) may repeal another text of the same kind. And in conformity with the principle that a superior text may repeal an inferior one, the abrogation of a "deed-text" by a "pronouncement-text" is deemed valid. For the latter is equal to the former in that it represents a statement relative to a particular ruling, but it differs from the former in one important respect, namely, that a "pronouncement-text" transcends itself and is semantically brought to bear upon other situations, whereas the "deed-text" is confined to the very situation that gave rise to it in the first place. A "deed-text" bespeaks an action that has taken place; it is simply a statement of an event. A "pronouncement-text," on the other hand, may include a command or a generalization that could have ramifications extending beyond the context in which it was uttered. Q. 6:135 and 155, taken to be "pronouncement-texts," enjoin Muslims to follow the Prophet. So does Q. 33:21: "Verily, in the Messenger of God you have a good example."[54]

Since one Quranic verse can repeal another, it was commonly held that a verse may abrogate a Prophetic report, particularly because the Quran is deemed to be of a more distinguished stature. In justification of this view, some jurists further argued that since the Quran is accepted as being capable of particularizing the Sunna, so it can abrogate it. Other jurists, while adopting the position that the Quran can repeal the Sunna, rejected the argument from particularization. Particularization, they held, represents an imperfect analogy with abrogation – the latter entails a total replacement of one legal text by another, whereas the former does not involve abrogation but merely delimits the scope of a text so as to render it less ambiguous.[55]

Be that as it may, the Quranic abrogation of the Sunna has also history to recommend it. A historical precedent in point is the Prophet's peace treaty with the Qurayshīs of Mecca whereby he agreed to return to Mecca all those who converted to Islam as well as those who wished to join his camp. But just before sending back a group of women who adopted Islam as a religion, Q. 60:10 was revealed, ordering Muslims not to continue with their plans, thereby abrogating the Prophet's practice as expressed in the treaty. Another instance of Quranic abrogation is 2:144 and 150 which command Muslims to pray in the direction of Mecca instead of Jerusalem, a direction the Prophet had decreed earlier.[56]

More controversial was the question of whether the Sunna can repeal the Quran. Those who espoused the view that the Quran may not be abrogated by the Sunna advanced Q. 2:106 which, as we have seen, states that

[54] Ibid., I, 498. [55] Ibid., I, 499–501. [56] Ibid., I, 499.

if God repeals a verse, He does so only to replace it by another which is either similar to, or better than it. The Sunna, they maintained, is neither better than nor equal to the Quran, and thus no report can repeal a Quranic verse. On the basis of the same verse they furthermore argued that abrogation rests with God alone, and this precludes the Prophet from having the capacity to abrogate.

On the other hand, the proponents of the doctrine that the Sunna can abrogate the Quran rejected the view that the Prophet did not possess this capacity, for while it is true that he could act alone, he spoke on behalf of God when he undertook to abrogate a verse. However, the central argument of these proponents revolved around epistemology: both the Quran and the concurrent reports yield certitude, and being of equal epistemological status, they can abrogate each other. Opponents of this argument rejected it on the grounds that consensus also leads to certainty but lacks the power to repeal. Moreover, they maintained, the epistemological equivalence of the two sources does not necessarily mean that there exists a mutuality of abrogation. Both solitary reports and *qiyās*, for instance, lead to probable knowledge, and yet the former may serve to abrogate whereas the latter may not. The reason for this is that these reports in particular, and the Sunna in general, constitute the principal source (*aṣl*) from which the authority for *qiyās* is derived. A derivative can by no means repeal its own source. And since, it was argued, the Quran is the source of the Sunna as well as superior to it, the Sunna can never repeal the Quran.[57]

A rather consequential disagreement also arose concerning the ability of solitary reports to repeal the Quran and the concurrent Sunna. A group of jurists, espousing the view that solitary reports can abrogate the Quran and concurrent Sunna, maintained that their position was defensible not only by a rational argument, but that such abrogation had taken place at the time of the Prophet. Rationally, the mere existence of the notion that a certain solitary report may constitute a substitute for a concurrent Sunna or a Quranic verse is sufficient proof that such a Sunna or verse lacks the certitude that is otherwise associated with it; and since certainty is lacking, the solitary report would not be epistemologically inferior to the Quran and the concurrent Sunna, and therefore it can abrogate them. It was further argued that solitary reports had been commonly accepted as being capable of particularizing the concurrent Sunna and the Quran, and if they had the power to particularize, they must have the power to repeal. But their most evincive argument in support of this position was perhaps that which drew on the dynamics of revelation at the time of the Prophet. A classical case

[57] Bājī, *Iḥkām*, 417–24.

in point is Q. 2:180 which decrees that "It is prescribed for you, when one of you approaches death, if he has wealth, that he bequeath unto parents and near relatives in kindness." This verse, some jurists argued, was abrogated by the solitary report "No bequest in favor of an heir." Since parents and near relatives are considered by the Quran as heirs, 2:180 was considered repealed, this constituting clear evidence that solitary reports can repeal the Quran and, *a fortiori*, the concurrent Sunna.

The opponents of this doctrine rejected any argument that arrogated to solitary reports an epistemological status equal to that of the Quran and the concurrent Sunna. The very possibility, they argued, of casting doubt on the certainty generated by these texts is *a priori* precluded. As they saw it, the solitary reports, being presumptive to the core, can by no means repeal the Quran and the concurrent reports. Furthermore, the attempt at equating particularization with abrogation is aborted by the fact that particularization involves the substitution of one piece of textual evidence for another by bringing together two texts to bear, *conjointly*, upon the solution of a given legal problem. Abrogation, in contrast, and by definition, entails the complete substitution of one text for another, the latter becoming devoid of any legal effect. The example of *qiyās* served to bolster this argument: this method of legal inference is commonly accepted as capable of particularizing the Quran and the Sunna, but it cannot, by universal agreement, repeal the textual sources. Finally, the occurrence of abrogation by a solitary report in the case of bequests was dismissed by the opponents of this doctrine as an instance of faulty hermeneutics. The solitary report "No bequest in favor of an heir" did not, they insisted, abrogate the aforementioned Quranic verse. Rather, the verse was abrogated by Q. 4:11 which stipulates that parents, depending on the number and the degree of relation of other heirs, receive fixed shares of the estate after all debts have been settled and the bequest allocated to its beneficiary. Specifying the parents' shares *subsequent* to the allocation of the bequest is ample proof that it is this verse that repealed 2:180 and not the solitary report. If anything, these jurists argued, this report came only to confirm the Quranic abrogation, and this is evidenced in the first part of the report, a part omitted by those who used it to support their case for the abrogation of Quranic verses by solitary reports. In its entirety, the report reads as follows: "God has given each one his due right; therefore, no bequest to an heir." The attribution of the injunction to God, it is argued, represents an eloquent attestation that the Prophet acknowledged and merely endorsed the abrogation of Q. 2:180 by 4:11.[58]

[58] Shīrāzī, *Sharḥ al-Lumaʿ*, I, 507–11; Bājī, *Iḥkām*, 426–27.

CONSENSUS

Considered a third source of law after the Quran and the Sunna, consensus (*ijmāʿ*) represented the ultimate sanctioning authority which guaranteed the infallibility of those positive legal rulings and methodological principles that are universally agreed upon by Sunnī scholars. The actual modalities of establishing the occurrence of a consensus on a particular issue are elusive indeed, and in any case, they seem to have lain outside the jurists' interest. Of direct concern to the theoreticians, however, was the authoritative basis of this sanctioning instrument and the conditions under which agreement becomes irrevocable.[59]

It was commonly maintained that the infallibility of the community as represented by its leading jurists (*mujtahid*s) cannot be guaranteed on the basis of reason. The argument that an entire community cannot agree on an error was flatly rejected on rational grounds, for both Christians and Jews, severally and aggregately, have managed to agree on many falsehoods, such as the doctrine of trinity and the crucifixion of Christ. Thus, the theory of consensus, which posits the infallibility of the community, was to be anchored in an authority other than reason, namely, revelation. Both the Quran and the Sunna, all jurists argued, provide evidence for the authoritativeness of consensus. Q. 4:115, among other verses, stipulates "And whoso opposes the Messenger after the guidance had been manifested unto him, and follows other than the believers' way, We appoint for him that unto which he himself had turned, and expose him unto Hell – hapless journey's end!" Admittedly, this verse, considered among all the verses to be most relevant for proving the authoritativeness of consensus, has no direct bearing upon the latter, for it does not speak of consensus *qua* consensus. This fact explains the lengths to which jurists have gone in order to bring this verse to bear upon consensus. Indeed, one can say with some confidence that there is no other verse or Prophetic report in the entire gamut of legal theoretical discussion that has attracted such lengthy commentary. Obviously, the aim of this commentary was to interpret the verse in such a way as to make it say that swerving from the path of the believers, who make up the community, warrants the same punishment of hellfire as dissenting from the Prophet's ranks.

The indirect relevance of this and other verses to consensus, though not openly admitted, is betrayed by the emphasis the jurists placed on the Sunnaic evidence, not only as a supplement to the Quran, but primarily as

[59] For consensus, see Shīrāzī, *Sharḥ al-Lumaʿ*, II, 665–710, 726 ff.; Bājī, *Iḥkām*, 435–99; Ghazālī, *Mustaṣfā*, I, 173–98; Ibn Barhān, *Wuṣūl*, II, 67 ff.

a self-contained proof for the authoritativeness of consensus. The concurrent verbal reports (*al-tawātur al-lafẓī*), however, contained nothing that might assist in solving the problem. All that was available were solitary reports to the effect that the community cannot altogether agree on an error. The reports "My community shall never agree on a falsehood" and "He who departs from the community ever so slightly would be considered to have abandoned Islam" are fairly representative of the themes conveyed by the rest of the reports. While these reports are of direct relevance to the authoritativeness of consensus, they give rise to the epistemological question of how they can, insofar as they are only probable, serve to prove a principle having the force of certitude. The answer lies in the nature of these solitary reports. Although solitary, these reports are not only numerous but, despite the variations in their wording, possess in common a single theme, namely, that through divine grace the community as a whole is safeguarded from error. The large number of the transmissions, coupled with their leitmotif, transforms these reports into the *maʿnawī* concurrent type, thus yielding certain knowledge of the subject matter they convey.

It is noteworthy that neither the Quranic nor the Sunnaic evidence relevant to the authoritativeness of consensus was seen as being guaranteed by consensus. Contrary to a widely held view, the authority and authenticity of revelation are not sanctioned by consensus and, therefore, no circularity is involved in the establishment of consensus as a source of law.

Nor is there any basis to the view that the centrality of consensus in Islamic jurisprudence means that the ultimate legislator is the community of Muslims, since it decides what portion of revelation is to be accepted and what is to be rejected. Legal theory is careful to state that no consensus whatsoever may be concluded without a basis in revelation, or, as the jurists put it, without a textual indicant (*dalīl*). Even if such an indicant cannot be deciphered in a consensus held, say, in the remote past, the underlying assumption must always be that such a consensus was concluded on the basis of revelation.[60]

This underlying assumption, coupled with the conclusive authoritativeness of consensus, gives rise to the doctrine that consensus is superior to the Quran as well as to the Sunna, in both of its types, the solitary and the concurrent. This superiority means that whenever a consensus is reached on a particular matter, the textual evidence resorted to in this consensus becomes, even though it may only be a solitary report, superior to any "competing" evidence, including evidence from the Quran and the con-

[60] On the authoritativeness of consensus, see Ghazālī, *Mustaṣfā*, I, 173–81; Ibn Barhān, *Wuṣūl*, II, 72–76; Shīrāzī, *Sharḥ al-Lumaʿ*, II, 665–82; Hallaq, "Authoritativeness."

current Sunna. The reasoning advanced in justification of this doctrine is that since the consensus of the community is infallible, the evidence of the texts set aside by consensus is deemed irrelevant, for if it were not so, the community would not have agreed on the basis of another piece of evidence. Thus, although it is consensus that bestows finalistic certitude on what is otherwise a probable text, it is this text itself that in turn justifies consensus.[61]

There appears to have been a group of scholars who denied the possibility that a consensus could be formed on the basis of probable evidence, in particular on the basis of *qiyās* which, being an inferential method, was universally deemed to yield probable knowledge. They argued that it is inconceivable for a large group of people to agree on an issue that lends itself to a variety of interpretations and which is capable of various ways of reasoning. The majority of theorists, however, rejected this position on the ground that although there may be a number of possible ways of reasoning, each yielding a different result, they all must depart from the same point, namely, the textual indicant. And despite the varied nature of the reasoning methods that are brought to bear upon that indicant, it is conceivable that all the reasoners, having departed from the same textual indicant, may reach the same ruling which might in turn become subject to consensus. A proof of this, it was argued, may be found in the actual existence of consensus on cases whose rulings were reached by legal inference. Furthermore, if taken to its logical conclusion, the argument of those who rejected consensus on the basis of inference would lead to the denial of the solitary reports altogether since the method by which such a report is authenticated is probable. Yet, it has often been the case that consensus was reached on rulings derived from solitary reports, this being sufficient proof that consensus may be reached on the basis of probable knowledge, including legal inference.[62]

Be that as it may, whatever the nature of the case upon which consensus is concluded, there remains the need to establish the actual occurrence of each consensus. Practically speaking, knowledge of the existence of consensus on a particular case is determined by looking to the past and by observing that the *mujtahid*s were unanimous with regard to the solution of that case. Theoretically, however, the occurrence of consensus is thought to be capable of determination by more formal criteria. Those whose opinions are counted in consensus may unanimously pronounce a solution or they may unanimously act upon it, or they may do both. In certain situations,

[61] Shīrāzī, *Sharḥ al-Luma'*, II, 682, 683 ff.

[62] Bājī, *Iḥkām*, 500–03; Shīrāzī, *Sharḥ al-Luma'*, II, 683–87.

some of the *mujtahid*s may actively agree on a particular case, while the rest of them, having knowledge of such an agreement, choose not to express their opinion on that matter. The former type of consensus, where all the *mujtahid*s are actively involved, is thought to be valid, since the possibility of dissenting voices is entirely eliminated. But in the latter type, the silence of some *mujtahids* by no means eliminates such a possibility. If anything, some jurists argued, silence may be due to intimidation or pressure – political or otherwise – and since this is conceivable, one can hardly argue that such a dubious agreement qualifies as consensus. The opponents of this view, on the other hand, argued that silence should not be attributed to such factors as intimidation or pressure. The habitual or customary course of events (*ʿāda*) has been that the *mujtahid*s never failed to express their opinions whenever they found themselves in disagreement with their peers; it follows that their silence must be taken to signify consent rather than dissent.[63]

Equally controversial was the issue of whether consensus is considered binding before all the *mujtahid*s belonging to a single generation die. There were those who maintained that if the qualified scholars in a generation agree on a matter of law, their agreement would not be binding until the last of them dies. This view is organically connected with another, namely, that no consensus may be reached if one of the *mujtahid*s of that generation changes his mind about the matter subject to consensus. Accordingly, death alone ensures that a change of mind does not take place, and that consensus becomes irrevocable. On the other hand, those who did not consider the demise of all *mujtahid*s to constitute a condition for the bindingness of consensus held a contrary view concerning the possibility of one or more *mujtahid*s rescinding their earlier opinions. To them, a *mujtahid* who rescinds his earlier opinion, an opinion already sanctioned by consensus, would be considered to have departed from the pale of the community, and this is tantamount to heresy. And since, on this view, consensus becomes irrevocable upon the actual agreement of the *mujtahid*s, the demise of these *mujtahid*s ceases to be a condition for bindingness.

Some Shāfiʿite jurists maintained that if all *mujtahid*s actively participate in forming a consensus then such a consensus is deemed binding before the death of these *mujtahid*s. However, if only some of them openly voice their agreement on an issue, while the rest of them express no opinion, then consensus cannot be considered to be binding until such time as the entire generation of these *mujtahid*s becomes extinct. Obviously, the rationale behind this position is that those who did not express an opinion may

[63] Shīrāzī, *Sharḥ al-Lumaʿ*, II, 690–97.

do so at a later time in their life, and their opinion may be at variance with that on which the others have agreed.

The majority of jurists, however, deemed consensus binding, whatever the modalities of agreement. And they rejected outright the proposition that bindingness is predicated upon the death of all the *mujtahid*s who participate in forming that consensus. They argued that there is nothing in the Quranic and Sunnaic evidence relevant to the authoritativeness of consensus that indicates, much less explicitly stipulates, that the demise of the *mujtahid*s is a condition for bindingness. Consensus, on this evidence, becomes authoritative, and thus binding, upon agreement and agreement alone. Furthermore, there is nothing in reason or revelation to suggest that the opinion of a legist becomes, or should become, authoritative only after his death. At any rate, they argued, insisting on this condition would amount to a complete nullification of the instrument of consensus since, strictly speaking, it is impossible to determine at what point of time a generation ends and another begins. There always are younger contemporaries who join those partaking in consensus, and before the death of the former yet other *mujtahid*s join their older contemporaries and so on. The impossibility of determining who is the last *mujtahid* deciding in a consensus simply leads to a paradox which can be avoided only by relinquishing the view that the death of the *mujtahid*s in an age is a prerequisite for rendering consensus binding.

The advocates and the opponents of the condition of death each maintained their own views on whether a younger contemporary's opinion is counted in a consensus formed by *mujtahid*s belonging to an older but still living generation. Expectedly, the proponents of the condition of death deemed such an opinion irrelevant in the deliberations of older contemporaries. But the great majority of jurists disagreed, and maintained that the elements of time and age are of no consequence whatsoever in matters of *ijtihād*. The sole criterion is the scholar's excellent legal knowledge, and once this is attained his opinion would be as valid as those of other living *mujtahid*s, even though they may be significantly older.[64]

Thus, the greatest majority of legal theoreticians held *ijtihād* to be the sole qualification necessary for partaking in the formation of consensus. Other personal attributes, such as being just or unjust, of renown or undistinguished, are deemed irrelevant, for what indeed counts in consensus is the capability to derive the law independently from the primary sources in accordance with recognized methods of interpretation and reasoning. From this it follows that laymen have no say in any consensus reached on

[64] Ghazālī, *Mustaṣfā*, I, 192–96; Shīrāzī, *Sharḥ al-Lumaʿ*, II, 697–701; Bājī, *Iḥkām*, 473.

a technical case of law, since they are not sufficiently qualified to tackle complicated legal questions. However, on non-technical matters where the law is fairly simple – such as the laws governing prayer, pilgrimage etc. – the community at large also partakes in the formation of consensus.[65]

It was the insistence of the Mālikites that the consensus of the scholars of Medina, the home town of Mālik b. Anas, constituted a binding authority which gave rise to the discussion of whether or not any region of Islamdom can independently form a consensus. Against the Mālikites, the adherents of the other schools argued that the Quran and the Sunna attest to the infallibility of the entire community, and that there is nothing in these texts to suggest that any segment of the community can alone be infallible. Furthermore, the non-Mālikites maintained that recognizing the consensus of a particular geographical area would lead to a paradox, since the opinion of a *mujtahid* who partakes, say, in a Medinese consensus would be authoritative in Medina but not so once he leaves the city. From this follows another objectionable conclusion; namely, that a particular geographical locale possesses as such an inherent capacity to bestow validity and authority upon the products of *ijtihād*. This not only makes no sense rationally, but it cannot be justified by the revealed sources; consensus is either that of the entire community (as represented by all its *mujtahid*s who live in a particular generation), or it is not a consensus at all.[66]

Thus far the discussion has revolved around consensus when it is reached on a particular case of law. It has been shown that the sanctioning power of consensus is thought to be capable of rendering all law subject to it certain, and being so certain it precludes the possibility of any future generation departing from it, either by setting it aside or by concluding a consensus on a matter contrary to it. But what about a generation of *mujtahid*s which, in addressing a legal question, reaches two solutions? Can the following generation of *mujtahid*s adopt one of the two solutions and thereby reach a consensus on it? Or, failing that, can they reach a third solution for the same question? Arguably, by arriving at two solutions for the same question, the earlier *mujtahid*s cannot be deemed to have reached a consensus on them, since agreement cannot be said to have taken place. The fact that they disagreed clearly means that the issue at hand is one open to interpretation and this leaves room for further *ijtihād* by later generations. In brief, the inability of the earlier generation of *mujtahid*s to reach an agreement on a single solution for that case indicates that it had not stipulated which of the two solutions is the true one, and thereby left the door

65 Shīrāzī, *Sharḥ al-Luma*ʿ, II, 720; Ghazālī, *Mustaṣfā*, I, 181–83.
66 Bājī, *Iḥkām*, 480–85; Ghazālī, *Mustaṣfā*, I, 187.

open for later *mujtahids* either to reach consensus on one of the two solutions or, failing that, to form an alternative, i.e., a third, solution.

It appears however that many legal theoreticians would deny a later generation the right to form a consensus on one of the two solutions reached by an earlier generation of *mujtahids* or even to put forth an alternative or third opinion. They maintain that by limiting the possible solutions to two, the earlier generation is thought to have irrevocably agreed that the truth lies within the confines of those solutions it had reached. In the view of these theoreticians, to argue that in holding two opinions there exists no evidence that a third opinion is permitted amounts to claiming that in reaching a consensus on one opinion there also exists no evidence that reaching a second opinion on the same case is invalid.[67]

[67] Ghazālī, *Mustaṣfā*, I, 198–201.

3

THE ARTICULATION OF LEGAL THEORY: II

INTRODUCTORY REMARKS

ARMED with the knowledge of hermeneutical principles, legal epistemology and the governing rules of consensus, the *mujtahid* is ready to undertake the task of inferring rules. Inferring rules presupposes expert knowledge in hermeneutics because the language of the texts requires what may be called verification; namely, establishing, to the best of one's ability, the meaning of a particular text as well as its relationship to other texts that bear upon a particular case in the law. For this relationship, as we have seen, may be one of particularization, corroboration or abrogation. Before embarking on inferential reasoning, the *mujtahid* must thus verify the meaning of the text he employs, and must ascertain that it was not abrogated by another text. Knowledge of the principles of consensus as well as of cases subject to the sanctioning authority of this instrument is required to ensure that the *mujtahid*'s reasoning does not lead him to results contrary to the established consensus in his school. This knowledge is also required in order to ensure that no case that has already been sanctioned by consensus is reopened for an alternative rule.

The certainty engendered by consensus places the rules subject to this instrument on a par with the Quranic and Sunnaic texts which are semantically unequivocal and which have been transmitted through a multiplicity of channels (*tawātur*). All other cases, however, are open either to a fresh interpretation or reinterpretation. Those open for fresh interpretation are novel cases (*nawāzil*; sing. *nāzila*) that befall the Muslim community, and they are considered to be infinite in number. Those open for reinterpretation are older cases of law for which the jurists proffered one or more solutions, but on which no consensus has been reached. The latter group of cases falls within the scope of juristic disagreement (*khilāfiyyāt*, *ikhtilāf*) and may therefore be subject to new ways of legal reasoning.

Now, the theorists recognize various types of legal reasoning, some of which are subsumed under the general term *qiyās*. Other types, which are somewhat controversial, come under the headings of *istidlāl*, *istiḥsān* and *istiṣlāḥ*. We begin with *qiyās*, unanimously considered in Sunnī jurisprudence as the fourth source (*aṣl*) of the law. The characterization of this method as a source must not, however, be taken in a literal sense. It is a source only insofar as it leads, as a method of reasoning, to the discovery of God's law on the basis of the revealed texts and of consensus.

QIYĀS

Analogy

The most important form of argument subsumed under *qiyās* is undoubtedly analogy, which constitutes the archetype of all legal arguments. In fact, the analogical argument employed in the law became, in the thought of some theologians and jurists, the archetype of all logical arguments, including syllogistics; the categorical syllogism was deemed to be both epistemologically equivalent and reducible to legal analogy.[1]

Among all topics of legal theory, analogy drew the most extensive exposition. In a typical treatise on the subject, it alone occupies an average of one-third of the total space, if not more. The main issues discussed relate to the constituents of the analogical argument, the conditions they must individually fulfill, and the principles that govern the relationships among them. These constituents are four: (1) the new case (*farʿ*) that requires a legal solution; (2) the original case (*aṣl*) embedded in the primary sources – the Quran, the Sunna and consensus; (3) the *ratio legis* (*ʿilla*), the attribute common to both the new case and the original case; and (4) the legal norm or the rule (*ḥukm*) which is attached to the original case and which, due to the similarity between the two cases, is transferred from that case to the new one. The archetypal example of legal analogy is the case of wine. The Quran stipulates that grape-wine is prohibited. If we have, say, a case involving date-wine for which we need to establish a legal norm (prohibition, permission, recommendation, etc.), we find that grape-wine is prohibited by the revealed texts, and that it shares the attribute of intoxication with date-wine, an attribute for which prohibition was legislated. Having established that the *relevant* attribute is common to both cases, we transfer

[1] See Wael B. Hallaq, trans. *Ibn Taymiyya against the Greek Logicians* (Oxford: Clarendon Press, 1993), xxxv ff.; Wael B. Hallaq, "The Logic of Legal Reasoning in Religious and Non-Religious Cultures: The Case of Islamic Law and the Common Law," *Cleveland State Law Review*, 34 (1985–86): 94–95.

the legal norm of prohibition from the case of grape-wine to that of date-wine.

In analogy, it is presumed that a new case is one the texts do not cover directly, and that there is a need for human agency to transpose the explicit decree in the texts to that case. Furthermore, for a new case to qualify as a *farʿ* (literally, a branch), it must bear a resemblance to a particular *aṣl* (literally source or stem; the metaphor of a tree here is unmistakable), for without a stem, so to speak, there can be no branch, and, tautologically speaking, the existence of a branch entails the existence of a stem.[2]

The original case, in which the legal norm is embedded, may be identified by means of either the texts or consensus. The texts, however, provide two types of case, with regard to the first of which the texts do not state the rationale behind the commands or prohibitions stipulated in them. Some cases in point are the number of the days of fasting, of prostrations in prayer, and the fixed times for performing certain rituals. No analogy may be drawn on the basis of such cases because the *ratio legis* cannot be uncovered and hence no extension to new cases is possible. In the second type of case, the *ratio legis* may be discerned, and it is here where the jurisconsult is able to extend the rule in the original case to the new. Furthermore, cases subject to consensus constitute the basis for analogical reasoning, since consensus renders such cases certain. Against a minority of jurists who rejected reasoning on the basis of consensus it was argued that since reasoning on the basis of the probable solitary reports (*khabar āḥād*) is admissible, consensus as a basis of reasoning must *a fortiori* be accepted. After all, consensus itself cannot take place unless the case subject to it has been solved in accordance with an original case in the texts, a case with which it has a common *ratio legis.*[3]

Some Ḥanafites and Shāfiʿites, among others, argued that even if consensus is not arrived at with respect to a new case, it may still serve as the basis for finding the rule for a yet unsolved case. In other words, these jurists argued that it is possible to base an analogy on a previous case which is in turn based on the revealed texts. Against this serial analogy, it was maintained that the *mujtahid* might lose sight of the *ratio legis* in the original case when drawing an analogy between the new case at hand and the second case arrived at on the basis of the original case. Usury, for instance, may be said to be prohibited in sale or barter of sugar on the basis of the original case in which usury is prohibited in the sale or barter of wheat. The

2 Ghazālī, *Mustaṣfā*, I, 7–9.

3 Shīrāzī, *Sharḥ al-Lumaʿ*, II, 825–26, 829–30; Bājī, *Iḥkām*, 640–41.

ratio legis for prohibition is said to be the fact of the commodity's being an edible foodstuff. Now, were there to arise a subsequent case pertaining to lead, the *mujtahid* may argue that usury in this instance is prohibited because lead shares with sugar the attribute of being measurable by weight. The *ratio legis* in the analogy between sugar and wheat is clearly not identical with that found between sugar and lead, and the *ratio* behind the prohibition in the original case is lost in the analogy between lead and sugar. This suffices, the opponents insist, to render such serial analogies invalid. On the other hand, the proponents of this type of analogy argue that if the jurisconsult establishes a different *ratio legis* in the inference that proceeds from sugar to lead, then both *ratio*s must be considered valid since the same rule of prohibition may have behind it two *ratio*s, and in this case they represent edibility and measurability by weight. From this it becomes clear that a single rule may be occasioned by more than one *ratio legis*. The death penalty, for example, is sanctioned for a variety of causes, such as murder, adultery (committed by a married person) and renouncing the religion of Islam. Conversely, a single *ratio* may occasion a variety of rules, such as in the case of menstruation which results in the prohibition of sexual intercourse, of fasting and of prayer.[4]

At the same time, the *ratio legis* may consist of one or more properties. The *ratio* of prayer, for instance, possesses two properties, namely, ritual purity and full legal capacity (i.e., being Muslim, free, of age and mentally sane). Likewise, the *ratio* of the penalty (*ḥadd*) for theft consists of five properties: (1) the taking away of something by stealth; (2) the stolen object must be of a minimum value (normally set at 10 dirhams or their equivalent); (3) the object must in no way be the property of the thief; (4) it must be taken out of custody; and (5) the thief must have full legal capacity. All of these properties must obtain for an act to qualify as theft punishable by cutting off the hand. Each property is necessary, although no single one by itself suffices to produce the *ratio legis*.[5]

In the aforementioned case of theft, the rationale behind the rule is comprehensible: stealing a particular object under certain circumstances qualifies as theft, and as a punishment and deterrent, the penalty of cutting off the hand is instituted. Likewise, the intoxicating property of wine renders it prohibited because intoxication incapacitates the mind and hinders, among other things, the performance of religious duties. In this example we comprehend the reason for the prohibition. Some properties, however, do not disclose the reason. We do not know, for instance, why edibility should be the *ratio legis* for the prohibition of usury; all we know is

[4] Shīrāzī, *Sharḥ al-Lumaʿ*, II, 830–32. [5] Ibid., II, 837.

that all objects possessing the property of edibility cannot be the subject of a transaction involving usury.

Now, the *ratio legis* may either be clearly stipulated in the original texts or it may be inferred by the jurisconsult. The inferred *ratio legis* finds its justification, *inter alia*, in the Prophetic report concerning one of the Prophet's lieutenants, Muʿādh b. Jabal. When he deployed Muʿādh to Yemen to govern and to act as a judge among the Yemenis, the Prophet is said to have asked him about the basis for his decisions when he could find no relevant revealed text, whereupon Muʿādh is reported to have replied: "I exercise my own legal reasoning" (*ijtihād*). The Prophet is said to have found the answer highly satisfactory. The clear implication of this report is that reasoning by inference, involving the derivation of the *ratio legis*, has been ratified by the Prophetic Sunna.[6]

The *ratio*, whether explicitly stated or inferred, may either bear upon a genus (*jins*) of cases or it may be restricted in its application to individual cases. If we say that the *ratio* of penal retaliation (*qiṣāṣ*) is both intentional homicide[7] and the religious equality of the murderer and the victim (for, according to some jurists, a Muslim may not be executed if he killed a non-Muslim, since they are not equal in status), then retaliation must obtain whenever the *ratio legis* obtains, and it must be waived whenever that *ratio* does not obtain. In other words, the *ratio* and the entire *genus* of cases involving intentional homicide and religious equality are concomitant.

However, the *ratio* may not be concomitant with the entire genus, but only limited to some members of that genus. If we say, for instance, that intentional homicide and religious equality must be punishable by death (*qatl*), the *ratio* would not be applicable to the whole genus of *qatl*, because the death penalty may result from other acts, such as committing adultery (in the case of married persons) and renouncing the religion of Islam. The validity of this type of *ratio* is justified by the common juristic understanding that the death penalty is induced by other reasons. As we shall see, without such an understanding, the *ratio* may be dismissed as invalid.

One of the most fundamental questions raised in legal theory is how a property, or a set of properties, is confirmed to be the *ratio legis* behind a

[6] Ibid., II, 845–46.

[7] Islamic law distinguishes at least two types of homicide, intentional (*ʿamd*) and unintentional (*khaṭaʾ*). The former, unlike the latter, usually entails the use of a deadly implement, such as a knife. The penalty for intentional homicide is retaliation or payment of blood-money, whereas for unintentional homicide it consists of blood-money and performance of the *kaffāra*, a form of religious expiation normally involving the manumission of a slave or feeding the poor. Abū ʿAbd Allāh Muḥammad al-Anṣārī al-Raṣṣāʿ, *Sharḥ Ḥudūd Ibn ʿArafa al-Mawsūm al-Hidāya al-Kāfiya al-Shāfiya*, ed. Muḥammad Abū al-Ajfān and al-Ṭāhir al-Maʿmūrī, 2 vols. (Beirut: Dār al-Gharb al-Islāmī, 1993), II, 613 ff.

certain rule in an original case. We have said that a *ratio* may either be stated or inferred. A *ratio* may be stated in the texts either explicitly or implicitly. An example of an explicitly stated *ratio* may be found in the Prophetic report relating to the barter of dates. When the Prophet was questioned about the legality of bartering ripe dates for unripe ones, he asked: "Do unripe dates lose weight upon drying up?" When he was answered in the affirmative, he remarked that such a barter is illicit. In this report, the language of causation is deemed explicit, for it is readily understood that the prohibition was instituted due to the fact that unripe dates become lighter in weight upon further maturity, and a barter involving these types of dates involves usury.[8]

But the *ratio* may be causally connected with its rule (*ḥukm*) in a less explicit manner. For example, from the Quranic verse "Say not 'Fie' to them [i.e., parents] neither chide them, but speak to them graciously" (17:23) one knows that uttering "Fie" is prohibited because it signifies a disrespectful attitude toward parents. If the mere utterance of "Fie" is prohibited, then striking one's parents is *a fortiori* prohibited. This last prohibition, engendered by the *ratio* of disrespect toward parents, is not explicitly stated in the texts, but is rather embedded in the language of revelation. (The *a fortiori* argument, however, was surrounded with controversy, as we shall see on pp. 96–99 below). Another example in point, illustrating a type of textual case that indicates the *ratio* by intimation (*tanbīh*), is the Prophetic report: "He who cultivates a barren land acquires ownership of it." The intimated *ratio* for ownership here is the cultivation of barren land. It is the semantic structure in this type of text that discloses the intimated *ratio*, for this structure is reducible to the conditional sentence "If . . ., then . . ." "If you rise up for prayer," the Quran states (5:6), "then you must wash . . ." The consequent phrase "then . . ." indicates that the *ratio* behind washing is prayer, and in the case of land, the *ratio* of owning a barren land is cultivating it.[9]

In the Prophetic Sunna, the sequence of events may also help in unraveling the *ratio* of a rule. If the Prophet behaves in a certain manner, and it is reasonably clear that he would not have behaved in this manner had it not been for the occurrence of a particular event or circumstance, it will be concluded that the *ratio legis* behind his action is that event or that circumstance. Similarly, any act precipitating a ruling by the Prophet is considered the *ratio* behind that ruling. When the Prophet knew that a man had sexual intercourse with his wife during the fasting hours of the month of

[8] Baṣrī, *Muʿtamad*, II, 775–77; Juwaynī, *Burhān*, II, 774 ff.; Shīrāzī, *Sharḥ al-Lumaʿ*, II, 844–45.
[9] Juwaynī, *Burhān*, II, 775; Baṣrī, *Muʿtamad*, II, 779–80.

Ramadan, he commanded him to free a slave. From this the *mujtahid* concludes that sexual intercourse during the fasting hours of Ramadan is the *ratio* for doing penance, one form of which is freeing a slave.[10]

Thus far we have spoken of the *ratio legis* that is stated in the texts with varying degrees of emphasis. The second type of *ratio*, we have said, is that which is inferred. Between these two types, however, stands a third, namely, a *ratio* determined by consensus. Such a *ratio* is originally inferred, which means it enjoys probability. But from being subject to consensus it becomes as certain as a *ratio* stated in the texts. By means of consensus, for example, it is determined that the full brother has priority over a half brother in matters of inheritance. The *ratio* in this case gains a strength equal to that of a *ratio* stipulated by the texts, and thus it functions as an original case according to which a new case may be solved. One such new case is guardianship over the marriage of one's sister; the bride's full brother, in the absence of the father, has priority over her half brother in assuming the role of a guardian (it being a condition for a valid marriage – in all the schools except the Ḥanafite in the case of a previously married woman – that the bride must be given in marriage by the closest agnate).[11]

The *ratio* may be inferred and verified through a variety of methods, all of which were subject to juristic disagreement. Here we shall be content to discuss the most important three, the first of which is suitability (*munāsaba*), considered by many theorists as the single most important method. Ghazālī, who presents perhaps the most extensive discussion of this method, argues, against those who claimed suitability to be a subjective method, that the *ratio legis* is established by means of a clear-cut rational argument, an argument "even the opponent cannot reject."[12] In the Quran, wine is forbidden because it possesses the property of inebriation, and inebriation incapacitates the mind, leading the intoxicated person to neglect his religious duties. If we were to assume, for the sake of argument, that the Quran did not stipulate the reason for the prohibition, we would still come to the understanding that the Quran prohibited the consumption of this substance because it leads to harmful consequences. This, Ghazālī insists, amounts to reasoning on the basis of suitability, since we, independently of revelation, know that there is a certain harm in allowing the consumption of wine and a particular benefit that accrues from its prohibition.

Since suitability is rationally conceived and emanates neither from the direct nor the oblique meaning of the revealed texts, its applicability to the

[10] Shīrāzī, *Sharḥ al-Luma'*, II, 855–56. [11] Ibid., II, 856–57; Baṣrī, *Mu'tamad*, II, 784–86.

[12] See his *Shifā' al-Ghalīl fī Bayān al-Shabah wal-Mukhīl wa-Masālik al-Ta'līl*, ed. Ḥamd al-Kabīsī (Baghdad: Maṭba 'at al-Irshād, 1390/1971). 143. For his discussion of this method, see pp. 142–266.

law cannot be universal. In other words, since the law cannot always be analyzed and comprehended in rational ways, reason and its products are not always in agreement with the legal premises and their conclusions. Suitability, therefore, may at times be relevant (*mulāʾim*) to the law, and irrelevant (*gharīb*) at others. No *ratio legis* may be deemed suitable without being relevant. Any irrelevant *ratio* becomes, *ipso facto*, unsuitable, and this precludes it from any further juristic consideration. The obligation to pray, for instance, is waived under circumstances of hardship. The *ratio* of hardship is deemed relevant to the spirit and positive commands of the law, since a great number of obligatory actions cease to be obligatory under extreme circumstances, such as illness and travel. But in the case of barring guardianship over divorced women who are of minor age, suitability is irrelevant, and therefore inadmissible. A divorcée who has reached the age of majority may remarry without a guardian, since she is thought to have acquired a sufficient degree of experience during her last marriage. This reasoning, though equally applicable to a divorcée who is a minor, is considered inappropriate in the context of the Sharīʿa since it runs counter to the aims of the law in protecting the interests and welfare of minors.

The ultimate goal of suitability is thus the protection of public interest (*maṣlaḥa*) in accordance with the fundamental principles of the law. But in determining the *ratio legis* by the method of suitability, the jurisconsult does not deal directly with the texts, since the *ratio legis* is not, strictly speaking, textual. Rather, he infers it through his rational faculty, but it must be in agreement with what may be called the spirit of the law. The law is known to prohibit that which is harmful and to protect and promote that which is beneficial to Muslims in this world and in the hereafter. Whatever is deemed detrimental to these benefits must be avoided, and whatever promotes harm must be prohibited. The constant and consistent promotion of benefit and exclusion of harm are the aims (*maqṣūd*) of the law, and it is to these goals that the rational argument of suitability must conform. The protection of life, private property, mind and offspring represents one of the aims of the law. Accordingly, the penalty of the murderer is death, a penalty instituted for the aim of deterring homicide. Similarly, wine is prohibited in order to safeguard the mind against malevolent and violent tendencies.

But the aims of the law are many and multi-faceted, and some are more fundamental than others. Ghazālī offers a hierarchical classification consisting of three levels, the first of which includes those aims that are considered indispensable (*ḍarūrāt*). Belonging to this level are the aforementioned central aims of protecting life, property, etc. This is complemented by a class of subsidiary aims that seek to sustain and enhance those central aims. For example, the consumption of a small quantity of wine is prohibited because it invites the consumption of a larger quantity. This prohibition is intended to give added support to the original and principal prohibition on drinking the genus of inebriating substances. Any *ratio legis* determined by suitability and falling within this area of the law must be treated according to the principles governing this level.

The second level, consisting of the necessary aims (*ḥājiyyāt*), is distinguished from the first in that the neglect of the indispensable aims causes severe harm to life, property, mind, etc., whereas aims classified as belonging to the second level are *needed* for maintaining an orderly society properly governed by the law. An example of these aims is the necessity to appoint a guardian for giving a female of minor age in marriage. Here, no life is threatened and no mind is corrupted; nevertheless, protecting certain interests, including those of the minor, are necessary for ensuring the orderly and just functioning of society.

Finally, the third, and least important, level is that which includes the aims of what Ghazālī calls "improvement" (*taḥsīn*, *tawsiʿa*) which merely enhances the implementation of the aims of law. The slave, for example, is denied the capacity to act as a witness because his menial social status and servitude impede his independent testimony. By this denial, the indispensable and necessary aims are not directly served, and in the absence of this denial, they are not harmed. But because of his impaired testimony, this denial serves to enhance the aims of the Sharīʿa.

To sum up, while suitability in and by itself is a rational method, it must conform to what may be called the spirit of the law, a spirit that dictates to what extent and in what circumstances suitability is to be accepted or not. The need for this conformity explains the distinction between relevant and irrelevant suitability, for what is considered irrelevant is nothing but a rational conclusion incompatible with the spirit, and therefore letter, of the law.

The second method by which a property is confirmed to be the *ratio legis* of a case is that of co-presence and co-absence (*ṭard wa-ʿaks*) of the *ratio* and the rule, known to later theorists as the method of concomitance (*dawarān*). According to this method, the rule must be concomitant with the *ratio*; that is to say, it must be present when the *ratio* is present, and must be absent when there is no reason for the *ratio* to be present. Only then will the jurisconsult confirm that the relationship between the rule and the *ratio* is one of efficacy (*taʾthīr*), namely, that the rule is necessarily entailed by the *ratio*. That inebriation is the *ratio* in prohibiting grape-wine is known by virtue of the concomitant relationship between intoxication and the legal value of prohibition. Before fermentation, prohibition is not predicated of grape-juice because the property of intoxication is not found in the juice.

Upon fermentation of the juice it becomes prohibited, and when wine turns into vinegar, the legal value of prohibition is waived, just as had been the case with juice.

Some theorists draw a clear distinction between the methods of concomitance and the efficacy of the *ratio*. In the aforementioned example of grape-juice provided by Ghazālī, the distinction is virtually obliterated; efficacy in Ghazālī is interwoven with concomitance. But for Shīrāzī, these are two distinct methods. The example of qualitative transmutation occurring in grape-juice is employed by Shīrāzī to illustrate the method of efficacy, where the property of intoxication *effects*, and is productive of, prohibition. According to Shīrāzī, however, the method of co-presence and co-absence, or concomitance, amounts to an analogy on the basis of the texts, whereby a property is judged to exist in a matter not stipulated by the texts due to its existence in a similar matter specified by these texts. Thus we judge that mares and mules are exempt from taxes on the ground that such taxes are waived for stallions, for if mares were taxable then stallions would be too.[13] Like all analogical inferences, this analogy does not engender certitude but only probability, albeit of the strong type (*ghalabat al-ẓann*). In rational inferences, too, the argument yields the same type of knowledge. In illustration, one theorist gives the following example:[14] if we see two men constantly in each other's company on Tuesday mornings, and we know that a lecture on legal theory normally takes place on these mornings, and we observe that on other days of the week they are never together, we conclude that the reason that brings them together on Tuesday mornings is their attendance of the lecture on legal theory. Conversely, when no lecture on the subject is given, they do not come together. Here, no absolute certainty can be attained, but the absence of other variables, such as the holding of another lecture on theology at the same time, leads us to believe that our conclusion stands, with the highest degree of probability, to be true.

For this method to yield a high degree of probability, both co-presence and co-absence of the *ratio* and the rule must be established. The theorists unanimously agree that co-presence alone is insufficient to confirm the concomitance of the rule with its *ratio*. For example, rice, possessing the properties of being both an edible and measurable substance, cannot be transacted usuriously; and a number of other commodities that cannot be transacted usuriously possess these two properties. But measurability by weight, according to the Shāfiʿites, does not qualify as a *ratio legis*, since there are other commodities, measurable by weight, that can be transacted usuriously. For measurability to stand as a *ratio*, it must be present where

13 Shīrāzī, *Sharḥ al-Lumaʿ*, II, 860–62.

14 Abū Ṭayyib al-Ṭabarī, as cited by Shīrāzī, ibid.

prohibition of usury is present, and absent where prohibition is absent; that is, all measurable commodities must not be transacted usuriously, and all transactions in which usury is prohibited must involve measurable substances. Thus to confirm the latter part of the equation, namely, that "all transactions in which usury is prohibited must involve measurable substances," amounts to resorting to the method of co-absence.[15]

Finally, the *ratio* may be verified through the method of classification and successive elimination (*al-sabr wal-taqsīm*), a method which consists of sorting out all *ratio*s deemed to be candidates, and by a process of successive elimination, arriving at one remaining *ratio*. Bread, for instance, cannot be subject to usurious transactions. According to the Shāfiʿites, there are three possible *ratio*s for the prohibition: measurability by weight, measurability by volume, or edibility. But bread, it is argued, cannot be sold by weight; nor can it be sold by volume. Thus, what remains is the *ratio* of edibility.[16]

When two or more *ratio*s seem to stand as equally valid candidates, and when such methods as classification and successive elimination fail to lead the jurisconsult to the single most probable *ratio*, then a series of considerations must be taken into account in order to make one *ratio* preponderate over the other(s). The first, and seemingly obvious, consideration is that a *ratio* derived from a text that leads to certainty supersedes one derived from a text whose language or mode of transmission engenders only probability. Similarly, a *ratio* stipulated in the texts is superior to one that is inferred from these texts.[17]

Second, the conflict may be between two texts that are both subject to consensus. Although such texts enjoy equally the epistemic status of certainty, their status may be analyzed on another level, thereby allowing the jurist to distinguish them in terms of precedence. For instance, when a consensus is reached upon two cases of law, cases which in turn function as the textual basis for solving further cases, epistemic precedence is given to that case (text) in which the *mujtahid*, or community of jurists, can decipher the textual basis of, and arguments leading to, the solution that became subject to consensus. For it may happen that later generations of *mujtahid*s are unable to uncover the texts and the line of reasoning employed by an earlier *mujtahid* in a particular case. However, if the textual evidence as well as the arguments can be deciphered in both of the competing cases, then the two cases are compared with a view to distinguishing them on other grounds.

15 Bājī, *Iḥkām*, 649–51; Shīrāzī, *Sharḥ al-Lumaʿ*, II, 864 ff.; Ibn Barhān, *Wuṣūl*, II, 275 ff.
16 Ghazālī, *Mustaṣfā*, II, 295–96; Ghazālī, *Mankhūl*, 350–52.
17 On the issue of preponderance, see Shīrāzī, *Sharḥ al-Lumaʿ*, II, 950–65.

Third, a text that has not been particularized is given precedence over another which has, the reason being that the manner in which particularization (*takhṣīṣ*) is applied may be considered by others to be invalid, or at least questionable, and thus the particularized text will be deemed weaker than the other.

Fourth, a text that has been stipulated by the Quran or the Sunna as constituting a basis for inference has precedence over one that lacks such a stipulation. An example in point is the Prophetic report relating to a woman who asked the Prophet whether or not she could perform pilgrimage on behalf of her father who died before he could perform this religious duty. The Prophet is reported to have asked her: "Would it do you any good if you paid back a monetary debt which your father had incurred?" Upon hearing the woman's reply in the affirmative, he said: "Then the debt owed to God is more important to pay back." Here, an analogy was drawn between pilgrimage and debt, the former being the basis for the latter. It is thus the report treating of pilgrimage that is considered the leading text in matters where children act on behalf of their parents in fulfilling a religious duty or a mundane transaction.

Fifth, a *ratio* in the original text which belongs to the same genus as that found in the novel case overrides another *ratio* belonging to a different genus. Whiskey, for instance, belongs to the same genus of grape-wine, a substance the consumption of which is prohibited by the original texts. If we assume, for the sake of illustrating the point, that the original texts also explicitly forbade the use of opium, then the text treating of grape-wine would be taken to override that which deals with opium, since whiskey, like wine, belongs to the genus of alcoholic beverages, whereas opium does not.

Sixth, a *ratio* corroborated by a number of texts supersedes another derived from a single text. However, some jurists, apparently a minority, rejected this view, arguing that the *ratio* in a text is not strengthened by multiple attestations.

Seventh, an affirmative *ratio* has precedence over a negative one. To say that fruits may not be subject to usurious transactions due to the *ratio* of edibility is preferable to saying that the prohibition is due to their being commodities that *cannot* be measured either by volume or by weight.

Eighth, a *ratio* on the basis of which a number of cases have been solved is superior to one that has served as a basis for solving a smaller number of cases. Again, the reason here being that by having been extended to a number of other cases, the *ratio*'s validity acquires added corroboration.

Ninth, a *ratio* that is co-present and co-absent with its rule (*ḥukm*) is, as we have seen, far stronger than one in which co-absence has not been shown. (In fact, the legal theoreticians agree that co-absence must be proven before a *ratio* can be considered valid).

Tenth, according to some jurists, a *ratio* that results in prohibition has precedence over one that dictates permission. These jurists argue that by adopting the rule of prohibition, no risk of violating the law is involved. To illustrate their point, they adduce the example of prohibition imposed on a man wishing to marry any one in a group of women suspected of including in it his sister (the assumption being that his sister, whose identity is no longer known, may be in the said group). Permission, on the other hand, may result in the man marrying his own sister.

Eleventh, and finally, a *ratio* that introduces a legal rule that did not exist before Islam (*al-ʿilla al-nāqila*) is superior to one that maintained the same rule throughout (*al-ʿilla al-mubqiya*), namely, before and after the advent of Islam. The significance of this view seems to be more theological than juridical.

Now, when arriving at a *ratio legis* for a legal rule, the jurisconsult must be able to defend the validity of that *ratio* against the objections of the opponent. In the medieval Islamic tradition, legal learning and juridical disputation as academic pursuits were, needless to say, intimately connected with legal practice. A doctrine upheld and applied by a jurisconsult to a particular case of law in the world of mundane reality was normally taken up again in the realm of academics, where it was discussed and disputed by the learned legists. This intermeshing of judicial practice and legal scholarship is amply documented by the sources, and is clearly evidenced in the structure of works treating of legal theory. Many works belonging to this genre included chapters devoted to the art of juridical disputation, properly called *al-jadal al-fiqhī*. In addition to the prescriptive-cum-descriptive theories concerning such issues as legal language, legal logic, abrogation, consensus, etc., works of legal theory included chapters that dealt with the manner in which a jurist must defend his doctrines against the opponent. And the subject of *ratio legis* received foremost attention in these chapters.

Thus, to safeguard the *ratio legis* against the critique of the opponent, the jurisconsult must take into account a number of considerations, the most important of which are the following: First, the jurisconsult must establish the property, the common denominator, in the original and novel cases in such a way as to preclude any objection to it on the part of an opponent. If the latter succeeds in casting doubt upon the attribute common to the two cases, then the jurisconsult's reasoning is refuted. In fact, the very process of reasoning by *qiyās* may be wholly subject to refutation. The reasoner must ensure before embarking on his task that the rule (*ḥukm*) he aims to reach by reasoning has not been stated in the texts. He would be an easy prey if the opponent could produce a revealed text in which the rule for the case in question is explicitly stated.[18]

Second, the *ratio legis* must be extracted from an established text, namely, a text that has not been, *inter alia*, abrogated by another. Similarly, the rule in the original text must also be unambiguous, and subject to no disagreement. The validity of the *ratio* itself would be highly questionable if the rule it produces cannot be known with certainty: one *ratio*, for instance, would not be deemed valid if it gives rise, at one and the same time, to both legal norms of prohibition and permission, or for that matter, to recommendation and reprehensibility. Only one, unambiguous, legal norm can issue from the *ratio*. Furthermore, the text from which a *ratio* is extracted must be extendable to other novel cases, and must not be of limited applicability. A text would be subject to the opponent's refutation if that opponent can prove that the text is limited in its applicability only to the Prophet himself, for, as we have noted, some texts concern the Prophet alone, and do not constitute legal subject matter for juridical inferences of general applicability.

Third, the *ratio* must be proven as efficacious (*mu'aththir*) in producing the legal rule; namely, it must be present wherever the rule is present. If the opponent is able to prove that the rule is present where the *ratio* is absent, then the *ratio* will be shown to be invalid. The aforementioned example of grape-wine and vinegar is a case in point.

Fourth, the lack of correspondence between the *ratio* and its legal rule, known as *naqḍ*, suffices to invalidate that *ratio* according to some theorists. Lack of correspondence is defined as the absence of the rule that would be otherwise generated by a certain *ratio*. Instead, the latter is made to produce a different rule because the reasoner decides to accept as efficacious only a part of it. This is known as the limitation of the *ratio legis* (*takhṣīṣ al-ʿilla*), an issue hotly debated in the context of *istiḥsān* (see pp. 110–11 below).

Fifth, the *qiyās* is undermined if the opponent can show that the employed *ratio*, without a change in any of its properties, generates a rule different from that reached by the reasoner. The ultimate test for the validity of either rule rests in efficacy (*taʾthīr*); whoever can demonstrate that the *ratio* is efficacious in producing the rule is considered to have followed the correct reasoning.

[18] On these considerations, see Ghazālī, *Mustaṣfā*, II, 347–50; Bājī, *Iḥkām*, 651 ff.

The a fortiori argument[19]

In addition to the archetypal analogical inference, the term *qiyās* encompassed non-analogical arguments. The primary textual premises in the Quran, the Sunna and consensus were conceived of as consisting of two basic categories, the first being those clear premises subject to only one interpretation, and the other being the ambiguous premises capable of varying interpretations. Clear premises (*nuṣūṣ*, pl. of *naṣṣ*) were said to engender necessary and immediate knowledge, namely, knowledge imposed upon the mind without reflection. This knowledge also obtains with regard to matters that are not explicitly stated in these premises, but only tacitly subsumed under these premises. Q. 5:3, for example, states: "Forbidden to you are carrion, blood, pork (*laḥm al-khinzīr*)." It was unanimously agreed that the expression *laḥm al-khinzīr* covers all types of pork, including wild boars, although the original reference was to domestic pigs. Although reasoning in this case can be cast in the syllogistic form, the legal theorists maintained that the conclusion "The meat of wild boars is forbidden" needs no inference since it is clearly understood from the very language of the Quranic verse. Thus, what formal logicians consider as purely deductive arguments were for these theorists nothing but linguistic propositions that lay outside inferential reasoning.

Between these linguistic propositions and the cases in which analogy was needed because revelation was entirely silent, there existed a grey area which attracted a great deal of theoretical discussion, at the center of which stood the *a fortiori* argument. Some jurists regarded this argument, in both of its forms, the *a minore ad maius* and the *a maiore ad minus*, as the most compelling form of *qiyās*. When God or His messenger forbids a small quantity of a certain matter, we conclude that a larger quantity of the same matter is also forbidden. Similarly, if the consumption, say, of a large quantity of a foodstuff is declared permissible, then a smaller quantity would also be permissible. An example of the first type of inference, the *a minore ad maius*, may be found in Q. 99:7–8: "Whoso has done an atom's weight of good shall see it, and whoso has done an atom's weight of evil shall see it." From this verse, it is understood that the reward for doing more than an atom's weight of good and the punishment for doing more than an atom's weight of evil are greater than that promised for an atom's weight. An example of the second type of argument, the *a maiore ad minus*, is the Quranic permission to kill non-Muslims who engage in war against

[19] Discussions in this and the following section draw on my article "Non-Analogical Arguments in Sunnî Juridical Qiyās," *Arabica*, 36 (1989): 287 ff.

Muslims. From this permission it is inferred that acts short of killing, such as the confiscation of the unbelievers' property, are also lawful.

Other theorists, however, argued that in these cases no inference is involved and that the matter is purely linguistic. The Ḥanafite jurist Sarakhsī (d. 490 or 495/1096 or 1101), for example, treats this issue as one that takes its premises from language, yielding a non-inferential, purely linguistic knowledge. In contradistinction to a higher linguistic category which contains statements that are expressly revealed in order to specify the rule of a particular case, this category of propositions is intended to legislate in matters that have not been explicitly specified but which are clearly understood from the language of these propositions. Legal questions in this category are denoted in the texts but not specifically stated. From Q. 17:23 "Say not 'Fie' to them [i.e., parents] neither chide them, but speak to them graciously," one knows that uttering "fie" is prohibited because it signifies a disrespectful attitude toward one's parents. The language of this injunction makes it abundantly clear that all words signifying actions of the same kind as well as actions exceeding in strength the uttering of "fie," such as striking one's parents, are prohibited. The intention behind the prohibition of uttering "fie" is to declare it prohibited for children to cause the least amount of harm to their parents. This, Sarakhsī maintains, is not a matter subject to reasoning by *qiyās*, but is rather a linguistic one, because the full extent of the meaning of "fie" is in fact encompassed by the meaning of harm. It thus follows that harmful things, which may range from expressing the sound of mere dissatisfaction to murdering one's parents, are forbidden by the uninferred specification of the Quran. Sarakhsī argues that in this category of language what may be considered the *ratio legis* is so obvious that the rule can be grasped by the mind without resorting to the method of *qiyās*.

This argument against including in *qiyās* the *a fortiori* argument had its counter-argument, with the Shāfiʿites as its chief exponents. Pinning the crux of the issue, Shīrāzī pointed out that *a fortiori* conclusions involve an inferential line of reasoning because the language of the texts does not explicitly state the rule with regard to matters implied. Striking one's parents, which is implied in the verse, cannot be understood from the word "fie." Only by implication can this term be taken to mean "any harm," and such an implication can be understood only through *qiyās*. Māwardī (d. 450/1058), another Shāfiʿite theorist, maintained that this *qiyās* is of the perspicuous type (*jalī*), which, among other types, is the closest to the unambiguous, self-explanatory texts. The ease with which *a fortiori* conclusions are reached derives from the fact that in such arguments the new case, though unspecified by the texts, comes under the meaning of these texts.

The absence of specification, Māwardī insists, draws a line between the legally clear texts, which require no reasoning whatsoever, and the perspicuous *qiyās*. In the clear texts, the case as well as its rule are explicitly stated, but in *qiyās* the rule is derived on the basis of another case. The word "fie" does not itself denote the meaning of "striking" or "insulting" and, conversely, "striking" and "insulting" are not used to describe the meaning expressed by the term "fie." A king or a prince, for instance, could order his guards to execute his own father without uttering the word "fie." Thus, the rule of prohibiting the striking of one's parents was *deduced* from the intention behind the prohibition of uttering the expression "fie," and not intuitively conceived from the very word itself.

In Ghazālī's view, the determinant in this question is the relationship between striking and the expression "fie." If "fie" conveys in linguistic usage the meaning of striking, then no *qiyās* is involved; on the other hand, if the prohibition of striking is understood from the *ratio legis* of the prohibition of uttering "fie," then such an inference is nothing but *qiyās*. The fact that such a *qiyās* is quite intuitive and that its conclusion can be reached with little analysis makes of it no less a *qiyās* than other inferences subsumed under that term. Ghazālī rejects the claim that the issue is linguistic. As shown in the example about the king, "saying not 'Fie'," in and by itself, does not imply a prohibition imposed on striking or on any other violent act. We instead deduce this prohibition through the *ratio* behind the necessity to respect parents, and the knowledge that uttering "fie" runs counter to such respect. This, Ghazālī insists, is the very course of reasoning known as *qiyās*.[20]

It is difficult to determine whether or not those theorists who argued that the *a fortiori* argument is linguistic were a minority. It seems, however, that their opponents (who espoused the view that the argument is rational) were, at the lowest estimate, somewhat more considerable than the former. The later jurist Shawkānī (d. 1255/1839), who was familiar with an impressive range of early and later works on the subject, approvingly reports, on the authority of earlier writers, that the majority of jurists held the view in favor of subsuming the *a fortiori* argument under *qiyās*.[21]

That the *a fortiori* argument was taken by a majority of theoreticians to be a form of *qiyās* does not necessarily mean that its logical property is analogical or inductive, since the argument can be reduced to a kind of asyllogistic inference due to its special logical feature of relational transitivity. The relationship between the subject and the predicate of the premises is transitive, and this precludes the inference from being subsumptive, and

[20] Ibid., 289–96, and sources cited therein.

[21] Muḥammad b. ʿAlī al-Shawkānī, *Irshād al-Fuḥūl ilā Taḥqīq al-Ḥaqq min ʿIlm al-Uṣūl* (Surabaya: Sharikat Maktabat Aḥmad b. Saʿd b. Nabhān, n.d.), 178.

thus from being syllogistic. In the proposition "Women are more intelligent than men," the relation "more intelligent" is transitive from women to men. This relationship is also said to be asymmetric, since there is no parity between the two as in "Women are as intelligent as men," but rather a comparison in terms of "more," "greater," "smaller," etc. It is this asymmetry that leads to the knowledge that striking parents is *more objectionable than* saying "fie" to them. Taking harm as the *ratio legis*, one concludes that if "fie" is prohibited, then striking is at least equally prohibited. Arguably, the absence of a necessary premise from the argument, namely, the harm in uttering "fie," renders it an enthymeme. The jurists, however, supplied the implied premise, which takes in a syllogism the position of a middle term. Thus, for Ghazālī the course of reasoning could be reduced to a deductive inference in which the major premise is "All harmful acts (directed against one's parents) are prohibited"; the minor premise "Striking is a harmful act"; and the conclusion "Striking (one's parents) is prohibited." But this reasoning is steps removed from the Quranic stipulation against saying "fie." The deductive inference on the basis of the verse would have been impossible had it not been presumed that "Striking is more harmful than saying 'fie' to one's parents," and that "harmful acts are prohibited." In this inference, the premises have not been originally stipulated but are themselves the conclusions of yet another inference, a fact that precludes the *a fortiori* from being a regular deductive argument.

Nor can the *a fortiori* argument be considered inductive. The fundamental difference between the two arguments lies in the relationship between the original and the new case. In analogy the inference proceeds from a particular to another particular, such as in the case of grape-wine and whiskey. The original and the new cases here stand on the same footing in that they are two equal particulars. In the *a fortiori* argument, on the other hand, there is no such parity between the cases. The original case always maintains a "greater" or "lesser" dimension than the new case. Added to this is the consideration that in analogy the rule (*ḥukm*) is inferred on the basis of a similarity that exists between the cases, whereas in the *a fortiori* the rule is *implied* without the prerequisite of drawing upon a similarity. It would therefore be consistent with the principles of logic to say that the *a fortiori* argument is asyllogistic, and has virtually nothing to do with the category of analogical inferences.

The reductio ad absurdum argument

Less controversial than the *argumentum a fortiori* was the *reductio ad absurdum* inference, defined as a course of reasoning in which the converse of a given rule of a case is applied to another case on the grounds that the *ratio legis* of the two cases are contradictory. The fundamental thesis of this argument is the establishment of a rule by demonstrating the falsehood or invalidity of its converse. It presupposes a premise whose conclusion is to be established as true; a converse of this premise is adduced with the view of establishing that the conclusion to which it leads is false or invalid. Once it is established that the conclusion of the second or converse premise is false or invalid, and that it stands in diametrical opposition to the conclusion of the first premise, the *mujtahid* reaches the conclusion that the first premise is true. The Mālikite theorist Bājī (d. 474/1081) gives the following example. We maintain that the *ratio legis* behind the prohibition on taking the organs of living animals is that the soul still resides in them; and it has been established that the rule of prohibition is induced by the *ratio legis*. From this we conclude that the soul does not reside in animal hair, for if it did, the taking of animal hair would have been, like the taking of organs, prohibited. Thus the absence of the *ratio* of prohibition in the taking of hair (which amounts to a *ratio* whose property is the converse of that found in organs) renders taking it from living animals lawful.[22]

According to Ghazālī, who attempted to analyze legal theory in terms of logic, the first step in the *reductio ad absurdum* argument is to reduce the first proposition into its component elements, and by invalidating these elements one by one, the entire proposition is proven false or invalid. One concludes that *īlā*ʾ is not a form of divorce by reasoning that if it were a form of divorce it would require a direct statement (*ṣarīḥ*) or an indirect declaration of intent (*kināya*) to the effect that the husband is divorcing his wife. *Īlā*ʾ, which merely involves a sworn testimony (*ḥilf*) to abstain from sexual intercourse for at least four months (after which divorce goes into effect) entails neither a direct statement nor an indirect declaration of intent. Therefore, we conclude that *īlā*ʾ is not a form of divorce. This line of reasoning, Ghazālī maintains, is reducible to two premises and a conclusion.[23] In syllogistic form, if divorce is *D*, *īlā*' is *I*, direct statement is *S*, and indirect declaration of intent is *K*, the argument can be put schematically as follows:

If *D* is *I*, then *I* is *S* and *K*
I is not *S* and *K*
———————————————
Therefore, *I* is not *D*

In Ghazālī's view then, the *reductio* argument as presented in this case seems to manifest the characteristics of the conditional hypothetical syllogism in

[22] *Iḥkām*, 673. [23] *Shifā*', 452.

the *modus tollens*. However, the classical features of the *reductio* argument exhibit the form of indirect reduction of the syllogism that "is a way of showing that if a certain syllogistic form is assumed to be valid, by assuming that its conclusion is false, a contradictory result follows, proved by a syllogism in the first figure. Hence, the original syllogism must be valid on pain of leading to a contradiction."[24] Be that as it may, the *reductio ad absurdum* argument, like the *a fortiori*, lacks all analogical features, despite the fact that it was considered a form of *qiyās* by the great majority of jurists.

A typology of qiyās

The above tripartite classification of *qiyās* into an analogical, an *a fortiori* and a *reductio ad absurdum* argument is clearly a logical one. It stems from our own analysis of the logical structure of legal argument, although we must recognize that the Muslim theorists did not, generally speaking, conceive of *qiyās* as being analyzable in these terms. The chief reason for advancing a logical analysis here lies in the misconception, rather widespread among modern students of Islamic jurisprudence, that *qiyās* amounts to no more than analogy. The theorists, on the other hand, were not particularly interested in an analysis of the logical structure of *qiyās*, for this structure had little, if any, bearing upon the issues that concerned them. Their concern lay elsewhere, namely, in the substantive relationship that exists between a linguistic proposition in the original texts and the new case or problem confronting the believer. In other words, their concern revolved exclusively around the degree to which the *ratio legis* makes itself manifest in the original texts, and its applicability, or lack thereof, to the new case at hand. Thus analysis of *qiyās* as an analogical, asyllogistic or syllogistic structure was for them largely an irrelevant issue. As jurists and "lawyers," the question that interested them was the degree to which a rule based on a particular *ratio* was thought to be probable.

This interest in the epistemological status of rules was instrumental in determining a particular typology of *qiyās*, a typology at the center of which stands the epistemological and ontological status of the *ratio legis*. According to this typology, *qiyās* is of two types, the first of which may be called causative inference (*qiyās ʿilla*), and the second indicative inference (*qiyās dalāla*).[25] According to the definition of some theorists, causative inference must be understood as being identical with the inference in which both the *ratio legis* and the rationale (*ḥikma*) behind the rule can be

24 R. M. Eaton, *General Logic* (New York: Longmans & Green, 1956), 128, cited in Hallaq, "Non-Analogical Arguments," 302.

25 Shīrāzī, *Sharḥ al-Lumaʿ*, II, 799–814; Bājī, *Iḥkām*, 626–31.

determined, whereas in an indicative inference the *ratio* can be identified, but without that rationale. Wine is pronounced prohibited because it is an intoxicant substance – intoxication being the *ratio legis*. We also know that intoxicants are prohibited because their consumption leads to objectionable behavior, such as neglecting prayer, belligerent attitudes and lack of control over one's own affairs. In this example of a causative inference, the rationale is known. But in indicative inferences, it is not. We know, for instance, that the *ratio legis* behind the prohibition of usury is, according to the Shāfiʿites, the fact of edibility. Wherever the feature of edibility exists, no usury is allowed. But God did not care to make the rationale behind this prohibition clear.

Other theorists did not take the distinction between these inferences to be a substantive one. For them the issue was largely formal. The distinction between them lies in the difference of stating the *ratio legis*. In the causative inference, both the *ratio* and the rationale are stated in such a manner as to create a causal relationship between them and the rule of the case. On the other hand, in the indicative inference the *ratio* is stated as concomitant with the rule, thus effacing any causal relationship. The *ratio* in this inference merely "indicates" or "alludes" to the rule. Thus, the difference between the two inferential types may be reduced to the mode in which the language of the original texts is stated. God could have said "pray, because the sun has set" and He could have said "when the sun sets, pray." The former injunction gives rise to the construction of a causative inference, whereas the latter does not. The relationship between sunset and prayer is not causal, but a matter of concomitance. The obligation to pray is merely "indicated" by the fact of the sun's setting.[26]

Within each of these two inferences there is distinguished two sub-categories according to the degree to which the *ratio legis* makes itself evident. The causative inference is thus divided into a perspicuous (*jalī*) and a concealed (*khafī*) *qiyās*. The former, in turn, encompasses at least four types: (1) that in which the *ratio legis* is explicitly stipulated in a language of causality, such as "because" or "for the reason that" or "in order not to"; (2) that in which the *ratio* is linguistically, not rationally, inferred, such as in the aforementioned example with regard to saying "fie" to one's parents; (3) that in which the *ratio* is discovered readily, without exercising much intellectual effort. An example in point is the Prophetic injunction "No one shall urinate in stagnant water" – we readily know that the reason for this prohibition is the introduction of impurities into water, and from this we infer that all ritually impure substances are prohibited; and (4) that in which

26 Shīrāzī, *Sharḥ al-Lumaʿ*, II, 799–80; Bājī, *Iḥkām*, 626–27, 630.

the *ratio* is established by consensus, such as in the case of Quranic penalties (*ḥudūd*) which were determined to have been instated *because* they represent a deterrent against committing crimes and other villainous acts.

Concealed *qiyās*, on the other hand, involves a process whereby the *mujtahid* infers – and not merely finds – the *ratio legis* from the original texts. Again, the theorists distinguish, in a descending order, various sub-categories of this inference according to the degrees in which the inferred *ratio legis* makes itself evident to the reasoner. The first of these is a *qiyās* in which the *ratio* is inferred from a property that appears conjoined with the rule. A case in point is the prohibition of usury in the Shāfiʿite school. The Prophet is reported to have forbidden the barter of unequal amounts of edible substances of the same kind. From this report, the Shāfiʿites inferred that the *ratio legis* in this case is edibility, for the prohibition seems to be conjoined, in the language of the report, with the property of edibility: thus, it was concluded that no edible foodstuff may be subject to usurious transactions.[27]

A *ratio legis* that seems connected to the rule in a less obvious way yields a concealed *qiyās* of a lower grade of probability. Upon hearing that a slave woman, whose husband was also a slave, was freed, the Prophet is said to have given her the choice between accepting freedom and rejecting it. It was inferred that the *raison d'être* of this choice was the fact that the woman was married to a slave who was not freed. The reasoner here assumes that a woman's right to accept or reject freedom is causally connected to the fact of her husband being a slave. Because the assumption of this connection has no textual indication or explicit specification to sustain it, it remains within the realm of mere probability, as opposed to high probability or certainty.

The last category of concealed *qiyās* is entirely based on inferential reasoning, but reasoning that follows the same dichotomous principles found in the method of concomitance (*dawarān*) in both of its components, copresence and co-absence (*ṭard wa-ʿaks*). But the theorists here describe this inference in terms of negation (*salb*) and affirmation (*wujūb*). To illustrate their point, the theorists give the following example: before they grow into full-fledged spikes, grain plants are not subject to the prohibition on usury; when spikes and grain seeds have fully grown, they become subject to this prohibition; but when they further grow to become wild grass, prohibition is waived. Therefore, we conclude that the prohibition of usury is concomitant with the *ratio*, which is that grain is a humanly edible foodstuff. The exclusive dependency of this category of *qiyās* on inferential reasoning

[27] Shīrāzī, *Sharḥ al-Lumaʿ*, II, 804–06.

renders its degree of probability even lower than that of the preceding category.

Now we turn to the indicative inference that the theorists conceive of as being based not on an explicitly specified or inferred *ratio legis*, but rather on a common factor (*jāmiʿ*) between the original and the new cases, a factor that indicates or points to a *ratio*. In this type of *qiyās*, it is assumed that a *ratio* does exist, but the locus of its existence is the mind of God, not the revealed texts. It is argued, for instance, that marrying off a virgin despite her disapproval is lawful, since marrying her off without securing her consent is permitted. This permission *indicates* the *ratio* in this case, namely, that her consent does not constitute a prerequisite for marriage. If her consent is not a prerequisite, then she may be married off whether she objects or not.[28]

The *ratio legis* may also be indicated by means of resemblance (*shabah*) between two cases, without, however, establishing this resemblance by means of efficacy (*taʾthīr*), as in the case of wine and whiskey. This type of *qiyās* was highly controversial, and a good number of theorists rejected it altogether. The classic example illustrating this inference, as well as the controversy over it, is the case of a slave's ownership. Some theorists argued that slaves, like freemen, must be permitted to own property. This, they argued, is justified on the grounds that slaves and freemen resemble each other in that they are human, responsible before the law, subject to legal penalties, capable of matrimony, of divorce, etc. Other theorists, on the other hand, rejected the analogy between slaves and humans insofar as the right of proprietorship is concerned. They maintained that slaves may not be granted that right because they resemble animals, not humans, in that they may be bought, sold, gifted, hired, used as a collateral, etc.[29]

The authoritativeness of qiyās[30]

Like consensus, but unlike the Quran and the Sunna, *qiyās* was not perceived as a revealed source of law and, as a derivative of the primary sources, it called for justification on the basis of these sources. The fundamental issues raised in this regard addressed the sources of the authority behind *qiyās*, as well as the epistemological status of this inferential method. The question whether or not this method could be justified by reason and rational argument, independently of revelation, was sure to lose any sig-

[28] Ibid., II, 806 ff.; Bājī, *Iḥkām*, 629.

[29] Shīrāzī, *Sharḥ al-Lumaʿ*, II, 812–14; Juwaynī, *Burhān*, II, 885 ff.

[30] On the authoritativeness of *qiyās*, see Baṣrī, *Muʿtamad*, II, 724–53; Shīrāzī, *Sharḥ al-Lumaʿ*, II, 757–87; Bājī, *Iḥkām*, 531–602; Ibn Barhān, *Wuṣūl*, II, 244–49; Ghazālī, *Mustaṣfā*, II, 234 ff.

nificance. *Qiyās* was a Sharʿī method, and no amount of human reasoning could single-handedly establish the authoritativeness and validity of any part of the divinely ordained law. Consequently, *qiyās* was to be justified by the revealed sources and their immediate product, that is, consensus, whose authoritativeness, as we have seen, was subject to similar arguments.

While a small minority of jurists espoused the view that the authoritativeness of *qiyās* cannot be justified with certitude, the great majority of Sunnī jurists held the view that the evidence in the two primary sources, together with consensus, proves that this method is authoritative with certainty. Even many of those who stood on the periphery of, or outside Sunnism, and who rejected *qiyās* on principle, admitted that perspicuous *qiyās* (*al-qiyās al-jalī*) and linguistic inferences (e.g., uttering "fie" before parents) represent two forms of authoritative and valid *qiyās*.

The strength of perspicuous *qiyās* lies in the fact that it is based on an explicit *ratio legis*. If the texts stipulate, for instance, that "Sugar is prohibited because it is sweet," we must affirm the rule of prohibition in all *loci* where sweetness is found. The necessity of universalizing the rule is understood from the language of the texts: "Sugar is prohibited because it is sweet" is the perfect equivalent of "Honey is prohibited because it is sweet." Anything sweet is prohibited. If only sugar was meant to be prohibited, then an absurdity ensues, since the stipulated *ratio legis* becomes utterly meaningless. It would then be expected, the theorists argue, that sugar should be prohibited without a *ratio* being specified. Therefore, the very existence of a stipulated *ratio legis* attests to the necessity of extending the rule to all other cases where the same *ratio* is found. This necessity argues for the authoritativeness of at least the perspicuous *qiyās*.

Of those non-Sunnī theoreticians who rejected *qiyās*, some argued that the Islamic religion is complete and that the Quran has provided answers to all issues that have confronted or might confront the Muslim community. They derived support for their thesis from Q. 6:38: "We have neglected nothing in the Book," and 5:3: "This day I have perfected your religion for you." Accordingly, they argued, *qiyās* is superfluous.

The opponents – the advocates of *qiyās* – agree that religion has been perfected in the Quran, but they do not see how the use of this method is rendered superfluous. For to have recourse to *qiyās* amounts in essence to having recourse to the Quran. Similarly, when *qiyās* appeals to the Prophetic Sunna or to consensus, it ultimately appeals to the Quran, since reference to the Sunna is enjoined by the Quran, and the authoritativeness of consensus is attested by both the Quran and the Sunna. Furthermore, it is argued, *qiyās* is an integral part of what has been called "perfection of religion," because the Quran, together with the Sunna and consensus it sanctions, confirms the need for it. Resorting to *qiyās* is thus no less legitimate than employing solitary reports or any other method or narrative that engenders probable knowledge.

But none of this categorically proves the authoritativeness of *qiyās*. The ultimate proof must rest with either the Quran, the Sunna or consensus; or an aggregate thereof. The Quranic passage that was considered to have the greatest bearing upon the authoritativeness of *qiyās* is 59:2: "So learn a lesson (*iʿtabirū*), O ye who have eyes." It was argued that the imperative verb *iʿtabirū* derives from the verbal noun *ʿubūr* which signifies the meaning of "crossing over" (as from one bank of a river to another), or making a passage from one place to another. The imperative form in the verse was thus construed to refer to "crossing over" from the original case to the new, and to the transference of the rule from the former to the latter.

No doubt the interpretation of the Quranic evidence seems somewhat strained, and many religious scholars and jurists have argued as much. The very controversy over the meaning of the passage suffices to relegate this evidence to the realm of probability, and proving the authoritativeness of *qiyās* with probability obviously leaves much to be desired; certainty must be attained.

Unable to find conclusive evidence in the Quran, the theorists turned to the Sunna, where a number of Prophetic reports were found to bear directly and obliquely upon the issue in question. But one report, said to be widespread (*mashhūr*), stood head and shoulders above the rest. This report has already been cited above in the context of the justification for accepting an inferred *ratio legis*. In the fuller form of this report, the Prophet is reported to have asked Muʿādh b. Jabal, when he dispatched him to Yemen to govern: "According to what will you judge?" Muʿādh replied: "According to God's Book." The Prophet then asked: "What if you do not find [in the book what you need]?" Muʿādh answered: "Then according to the Sunna of God's Prophet." The Prophet asked: "What if you do not find [in the Sunna what you seek]?" Muʿādh thereupon replied: "Then I exercise my own legal reasoning." The Prophet is said to have found the answer highly satisfactory. This report, the theorists maintain, shows that the Prophet approved of drawing inferences, which are understood to take their premises from the Book and the Sunna.

Furthermore, the Prophet himself is said to have employed such inferences. An example in point is the aforementioned report regarding a woman who asked the Prophet whether or not she could perform pilgrimage on behalf of her father who died before he could perform this religious duty.[31]

[31] See p. 93, above.

From this report, the Prophet is perceived to have drawn an analogy between pilgrimage and debt, where the former formed the basis of the latter.

Like the Quranic passage, these Prophetic reports are not considered conclusive, although their epistemological weakness does not stem from their meaning, which is fairly clear, but rather from the mode of their transmission. Neither of them is deemed concurrent, which means that they convey the information they contain with probability, albeit high probability. Again, certainty proves to be elusive.

Certainty nonetheless was seen to reside in consensus. In fact, the theorists seem to speak of more than one consensus. The Prophet's Companions are viewed as the first class of Muslim jurists who resorted to the use of *qiyās*, and universally agreed upon it as a legitimate method. And their consensus carries a particularly significant weight, since they are presumed, having been so close to the Prophet himself, to have known what he thought about, and how he dealt with, the matters befalling the Muslim community. Thus, if the Companions regularly resorted to *qiyās* and none of them objected to this practice, then their consensus is binding on two counts: their consensus *qua* consensus, and their intimate and unparalleled knowledge of the Prophet's behavior and methods in dealing with legal matters.

Later generations of jurists are also said, by those who held the authoritativeness of *qiyās* to be certain, to have reached consensus not only on the legitimacy of *qiyās* but also on the fact that jurisconsults and legists throughout the centuries and in all Muslim regions have made use of it, without a dissenting voice among them. Thus, it was argued that the cumulative effect of generational consensus proves, once and for all, that the authoritativeness of *qiyās* is known with certainty.

JURISTIC PREFERENCE (*ISTIḤSĀN*)[32]

In chapter 1, we took note of the fact that by the middle of the second/eighth century legal reasoning was neither consistently nor constantly sustained by textual evidence. Shāfiʿī, whose discourse centered around anchoring all law in revelation, perhaps had good reason to launch a scathing criticism against the early Ḥanafites who had not yet realized the necessity of basing all legal arguments on the revealed texts. It was

[32] On *istiḥsān*, see Sarakhsī, *Uṣūl*, II, 199–215; Shīrāzī, *Sharḥ al-Lumaʿ*, II, 696–74; Bājī, *Iḥkām*, 687–89; John Makdisi, "Legal Logic and Equity in Islamic Law," *American Journal of Comparative Law*, 33 (1985): 63–92; John Makdisi, "Hard Cases and Human Judgment in Islamic and Common Law," *Indiana International and Comparative Law Review*, 2 (1991): 197–202.

primarily Abū Ḥanīfa's doctrine that gave rise not only to the critique of Shāfiʿī but also to that of later jurists and theorists. This critique focused chiefly on those positive legal doctrines arising from his use of juristic preference. Indeed, Abū Ḥanīfa, together with his school, could never be forgiven for what was deemed by all the other schools to be an arbitrary form of legal reasoning.

After the third/ninth century, however, the Ḥanafite theorists took steps to dissociate themselves from the reputation of being arbitrary reasoners. Following the normative practice that had by then evolved as the unchallenged paradigm of juridical practice and legal scholarship, they insisted that no process of reasoning by means of juristic preference might rest on any grounds other than the revealed texts. In fact, with the emergence of a fully fledged legal theory after the third/ninth century, no Sunnī school could have afforded to hold a view in favor of a non-textually supported *istiḥsān*. Therefore, in the context of the articulation of legal theory we need not speak of a proto-Ḥanafite type of arbitrary inference; it simply did not exist. The systematic and technical modifications introduced into this form of argument rendered it acceptable to all legal schools, though as we shall see, controversy over some of its crucial features was never settled.

If juristic preference came to be systematically supported by the revealed texts, then what made it different from *qiyās*? All theorists agree that *istiḥsān* is nothing but a "preferred" form of legal argument based on *qiyās*, an argument in which a special piece of textual evidence gives rise to a conclusion different from that which would have been reached by *qiyās*. If a person, for example, forgets what he is doing and eats while he is supposed to be fasting, *qiyās* dictates that his fasting would become void, for the crucial consideration in *qiyās* is that food has entered his body, whether intentionally or not. But *qiyās* in this case was abandoned on the basis of a Prophetic report which declares fasting valid if eating was the result of a mistake. This last argument is thought to be "preferred" because it takes into account a text that would not have otherwise been employed in *qiyās* and that results in a different rule. To cite another example, *qiyās* requires that the object of a contract be present at the time of sale, since the absence of such an object entails risk (*gharar*). By juristic preference, based on a Prophetic report, it is determined that the *ʿarāyā* contract – in which unripe dates on the palm-tree are bartered against their value calculated in terms of edible dried dates – is lawful. The preference given to *istiḥsān* over *qiyās* led a number of theorists to maintain that the preference amounts to *tarjīḥ*, namely, giving one solution more weight than another.

The abandonment of *qiyās* in favor of juristic preference is determined not only by the revealed texts but also by consensus and necessity (*ḍarūra*).

Qiyās dictates that the contract of hire be *ab initio* void, since payment in this contract is extended over time, and extending payment over time violates one of the constitutive conditions in a valid contract. But the common practice of people over the ages has been to employ this type of contract in their daily transactions, and this is viewed as tantamount to consensus. This consensus is therefore deemed sufficient to annul the logical rule otherwise reached by *qiyās*; the reasoning here is that since consensus constitutes an instrument that sanctions law on a level of certainty, its force is equivalent to the revealed texts themselves, by which it was sanctioned in the first place.

Necessity, on the other hand, requires that in certain cases *qiyās* conclusions be set aside, such as in the matter of ritually impure wells. When an impurity comes into contact with the water in a well, it is determined by *qiyās* that the water therein also becomes ritually impure. Such a determination, however, is bound to cause serious hardship since, it is maintained, water is needed on a regular basis and is an essential item of daily life. The validity of averting undue hardship is justified by the Quran and the Sunna, and necessity and need, when not fulfilled, cause nothing but hardship. Thus, the use of water taken from ritually impure wells is deemed lawful by juristic preference, and the concept of necessity (and hence hardship), which justifies the departure from *qiyās*, is itself legitimized by the revealed texts.

Ultimately, then, conclusions reached by juristic preference reflect what may be termed the reasoned distinction[33] of textual evidence; and the distinction is viewed in terms of the strength or weakness of the *ratio legis*, strength and weakness being strictly matters of epistemology and ontology. In other words, the main issue comes down to a distinction between two *ratio*s, one establishing a commonality between the original case and the new one, and the other – while taking note of the rule generated by the first *ratio* – forming an exception to this rule based upon a more suitable and relevant text. This second type has been called, interestingly, a "preferred *qiyās*" (*al-qiyās al-mustaḥsan*).[34] An example in point is the analogy between predatory birds and predatory animals. Consumption of the former's flesh is deemed prohibited because the latter are stipulated by the texts to be ritually impure, and therefore prohibited. The *ratio legis* here is the impurity of the flesh of both kinds of animals. Consequently, food left by predatory birds is also considered impure and its consumption is thus prohibited, just as is the case with carcasses left by predatory animals. According to juristic preference, however, the food that predatory birds leave behind is lawful.

33 See Makdisi, "Legal Logic," 85.

34 Sarakhsī, *Uṣūl*, II, 204.

The reasoning involved here is this: when predatory animals eat, their own impurity is transmitted to the food through the saliva secreted in their mouths. But predatory birds eat by means of their beaks, which are formed of bone. Because predatory birds do not use their tongues when they eat, and because their beaks remain dry while doing so, no saliva is transmitted to the food they touch. Now, knowledge of the ritual purity of bones is derived from revelation which stipulates that the use of the bones of dead animals is lawful. Furthermore, this conclusion is bolstered by another Prophetic report which states that cats are ritually clean, and that whatever they touch is not rendered impure on account of their contact with it. The rationale for considering cats ritually pure is thought to be the hardship that may ensue from deeming them to be impure, since cats (one gathers) appear to have been a common pet. This is nothing but a juristic preference on the basis of necessity (*ḍarūra*), a principle that is brought to bear, as a subsidiary argument, upon the case of predatory birds. To consider the objects with which these birds come into contact as unlawful for consumption or use would also cause a great deal of hardship, since it is virtually impossible to prevent them from touching utensils that cannot be washed, for instance, in the desert.

Reasoning in this case is clearly grounded in both textual evidence, on the one hand, and the principle of necessity, on the other. On both sides of the argument, the conclusion runs counter to that reached by analogy, an insistence on which would have resulted in neglecting relevant, if not crucial, pieces of textual evidence and juristic principles. The introduction of the element of "dry bones" into the argument, together with its textual support, led to a change in the *ratio legis* which would have been otherwise taken into account without qualification in *qiyās*. But the change is significant and fundamental. Some theorists argued that the abandonment of the *qiyās*-based rule is in effect the result of abandoning the *qiyās*-based *ratio legis* altogether. The *ratio* in juristic preference is thus integral, being wholly unaffected by any limitation or curtailment.

This particular emphasis on the integral character of the *ratio legis* in juristic preference is nothing short of a loaded response to those theorists who held that preference requires the limitation of the *ratio legis* (*takhṣīṣ al-ʿilla*). Limitation occurs when the reasoner argues that the *ratio* of a case is *X* and the rule generated by *X* is *Y*, but due to an impediment (*māniʿ*) existing in the case, *X* is restricted in its scope; the resultant being a rule that is not *Y* but *Z*. To take the case of predatory animals, those who advocate limitation maintain that the *qiyās*-based *ratio* was limited due to the existence of an added consideration, namely, the ritual purity of bones.

The controversy over this issue, which caused much ink to flow from the pens of theorists, is thought by some jurists to be a merely verbal dispute.[35] But it is clear that the opposition to limitation has more to do with theological affiliation than with strictly legal considerations. The advocates of limitation are accused of having adopted the doctrines of the rationalist Muʿtazilites whose theology was shunned by a good number of Sunnī theorists.[36] Without going here into the theological dimensions of the dispute,[37] which has no direct relevance to law, we shall conclude this section by stating the main arguments against the limitation of the *ratio legis*, especially as expressed by the Ḥanafite theorist Ibn Sahl al-Sarakhsī.[38]

The validity of the *ratio legis*, Sarakhsī argues, stems from its extendibility (*taʿdiya*) to new cases. Conversely, a *ratio* incapable of being extended is invalid because it would exist without its effect. Now, allowing for an impediment to be part of the *ratio* does not, logically speaking, preclude the existence of other impediments in the other parts of the same *ratio*. And since impediments necessitate a rule different from that which would have been generated by the otherwise integral *ratio* (in the original *qiyās*), allowing for them would amount to having a presumably sound and valid *ratio*, but without this latter generating its own rule in new cases (a deficiency we have discussed above and which is known as *naqḍ*). Put differently, a *ratio* with impediments is tantamount to a *ratio* that cannot produce rules in new cases. In rational arguments, this is equivalent to having a cause without its effect, which would be absurd, since a cause must by definition have an effect, and if it does not, it would cease to be a cause.

Furthermore, the limitation of the *ratio legis* is shown to be invalid when, in the absence of impediments, the *ratio* produces a particular rule in a new case but cannot produce, with impediments, the same rule in another. The impediment, moreover, must be supported by the revealed texts with at least the same strength as that with which the *ratio* is supported; otherwise, it would not be fit to limit a *ratio* of a higher epistemic value. And if both the *ratio* and the impediment are of equal strength, then the latter can stand on its own in that it may function as an independent *ratio legis* which can be extended to new cases in which it generates its own rule. This clearly demonstrates, Sarakhsī maintains, that a *ratio* cannot be amalgamated with an impediment, for each must stand on its own. And if the latter is made to limit the scope of the former, thereby changing its rule altogether, then this would amount to abrogating a *ratio* by another – an idea no theorist would tolerate.

[35] See Aron Zysow, *The Economy of Certainty: An Introduction to the Typology of Islamic Legal Theory* (Ph.D. dissertation: Harvard University, 1984), 403–4, and sources cited therein, especially n. 513, p. 454. [36] See Sarakhsī, *Uṣūl*, II, 208.

[37] On these dimensions, see p. 135 below. [38] Sarakhsī, *Uṣūl*, II, 208 ff.

TEXTUALLY UNREGULATED BENEFITS (*MAṢĀLIḤ MURSALA*)

In our discussion of the *ratio legis* on pp. 88 ff., we have taken note of the role that public interest (*maṣlaḥa*; pl. *maṣāliḥ*) plays in determining suitability (*munāsaba*), a fundamental method of establishing and verifying the *ratio.* It is because of this relationship between the *ratio* and suitability that *maṣlaḥa* (and *istiṣlāḥ*, the act of reasoning on the basis of *maṣlaḥa*) is deemed an extension of *qiyās*, and thus most works of legal theory do not devote to it an independent section or chapter but treat it under suitability. Some later authors, however, included discussion of this matter in a chapter normatively designated as *istidlāl*, a chapter that usually covers all sorts of inferences that do not belong to the category of *qiyās.*[39]

One issue that arises in *istiṣlāḥ* relates to cases whose rules are derived on the basis of a rationally suitable benefit that is not sustained by textual evidence. This is called *al-maṣāliḥ al-mursala.* The great majority of theorists reject any conclusion that finds no support in the texts, be it motivated by public interest or otherwise. It is reported that Mālik (d. 179/795), the eponym of the Mālikite school, adopted conclusions that appear to serve such interests without these having the support of the texts. His later followers, however, deny that this ever took place. Be that as it may, no theorist after the third/ninth century advocated *maṣlaḥa mursala* in the sense attributed to Mālik. But many approved this method of reasoning if it could be shown that the feature of public interest adopted in a case was suitable (*munāsib*) and relevant (*muʿtabar*) either to a universal principle of the law or to a specific and particular piece of textual evidence. Thus, suitability and relevance are conditions necessary for a valid conclusion of *maṣlaḥa mursala.*[40]

Other theorists, such as Ghazālī, put the matter differently. We have seen that Ghazālī's hierarchy of legal aims (*maqāṣid al-sharīʿa*) included, at its top, the principles of protecting life, private property, mind, religion and offspring. If the feature of public interest in a case can be defined as serving any of these principles, and if it can also be shown to be certain (*qaṭʿī*) and universal (*kullī*), then reasoning in accordance with it is deemed valid. The condition of universality is intended to ensure that the interests of the Muslim community at large, and not only a limited segment of it, are served. The classical example offered in illustration of this condition is the

39 Hallaq, "Logic, Formal Arguments and Formalization of Arguments in Sunnī Jurisprudence," *Arabica*, 37 (1990): 317–18. For a useful discussion of the place of *maṣlaḥa* in the early and later works of legal theory, see Shawkānī, *Irshād*, 241–43. See also Ibn Barhān, *Wuṣūl*, II, 286–94.

40 For a detailed discussion about the relationship between *munāsib* and *mu'aththir* according to later authors, see Weiss, *Search for God's Law*, 615–20.

one in which an army of unbelievers captures a number of Muslims and uses them as a shield. If the shield is not attacked, the army of the enemy will succeed in its design to destroy the Muslim community. In order to repulse the enemy it is necessary to attack the shield, an act that is sure to result in killing many, if not all, the Muslims forming the shield. Although the individuals of this group are not guilty of any offense deserving of the death penalty, it is argued, according to *istiṣlāḥ*, that the killing of fellow Muslims is suitable (*munāsib*) in light of the accruing benefits. Here, the case of protecting the Muslim community at large, which will certainly face extermination if not defended *in this manner*, meets the three stipulated conditions: namely, universality, certainty and the protection of the necessary aims of the law.[41]

THE PRINCIPLE OF THE PRESUMPTION OF CONTINUITY (*ISTIṢḤĀB*)[42]

Inasmuch as it is only a principle, *istiṣḥāb* does not, strictly speaking, qualify as a method of legal reasoning, although many later theorists included it under the umbrella chapter of *istidlāl*, where it is at times discussed together with the methods of juristic preference and the textually unregulated benefits. According to this principle, a legal state of affairs is presumed to continue to be valid until there is reason to change this presumption. The principle of *istiṣḥāb*, however, was discussed from two angles of application, one concerning rational presumption of continuity (*istiṣḥāb ḥāl al-ʿaql*), the other, the presumption of continuity in a rule subject to consensus (*istiṣḥāb ḥāl al-ijmāʿ*).

It is generally agreed among the theorists that the rational presumption of continuity is a valid principle. An example of the application of this principle is the presumption that a sixth prayer each day is not mandatory, because the texts decree that only five are necessary. The jurisconsult may argue that as long as there is no evidence in the text to the effect that a sixth prayer is required, the presumption remains that only five are mandatory. If an opponent maintains that a sixth prayer is mandatory, then the onus of proof lies with him; he is required to produce textual evidence to sustain his allegation. Similarly, an inheritance cannot be claimed from a missing person, since the presumption must be that he is alive as long as there is no proof that he is dead (a presumption also known as *al-barāʾa al-aṣliyya*). If

41 Ghazālī, *Mustaṣfā*, I, 284–315.

42 See Ibn Barhān, *Wuṣūl*, II, 317–19; Ghazālī, *Mankhūl*, 372–73; Ghazālī, *Mustaṣfā*, I, 217 ff.; Shīrāzī, *Sharḥ al-Lumaʿ*, II, 986–87; Abū Isḥāq Ibrāhīm b. Alī al-Shīrāzī, *al-Tabṣira fī Uṣūl al-Fiqh*, ed. Muḥammad Ḥasan Haytū (Damascus: Dār al-Fikr, 1980), 526–29.

proof of his death is adduced, or if a claim of inheritance is made after a time too long for a human being to continue living, then his estate may be inherited by his relatives.

The presumption of continuity, however, must be sustained by reliable knowledge of the absence of evidence that might otherwise change this presumption. Knowledge of the absence of evidence is to be distinguished from the absence of knowledge of any evidence. Unlike the former knowledge, the latter is not admitted as a valid argument in favor of such a presumption: the absence of evidence to the contrary must be known with at least a degree of probability (*ẓann*). If it is argued that fasting during the month of Shawwāl is not required, it is not sufficient, to turn this presumption around, to maintain that knowledge to the contrary is absent. Rather, knowledge of evidence contrary to this presumption must be *shown* to be absent. Thus, it must be argued that if fasting were required during Shawwāl, such a requirement would have been stated in the texts, or, failing this, a large segment of the Muslim community would have known about it through some other means. The lack of textual evidence, coupled with the complete absence of any knowledge of this requirement in the community, go to show that the presumption of continuity is sustained by virtue of the knowledge that evidence to the contrary is absent.

The wide acceptance of the rational presumption of continuity is to be contrasted with the presumption of continuity on a matter subject to consensus, a position that has few adherents. The latter argue that the prayer of a person who has performed dry ablution (*tayammum*, i.e., washing with earth or sand in the absence of water) continues to be valid after that person has found out, while he is still praying, that water was available nearby. They maintain that consensus has been reached on the validity of the *tayammum*-prayer, and the validity backed by consensus is presumed to continue until the end of the prayer. This argument is rejected by the majority, who counter with the claim that consensus has been reached upon the validity of this type of prayer only when water is not found. Since allowing the *tayammum*-prayer is a license (*rukhṣa*),[43] granted as an acknowledgement of the existence of hardship entailed by the performance of a duty, the very knowledge of the availability of water renders the prayer void. Furthermore, the fact that some jurists consider this prayer void when water becomes available demonstrates that disagreement surrounds the issue. Where there is disagreement, there is, *ipso facto*, no consensus. Therefore, consensus on the validity of the *tayammum*-prayer ceases to exist

[43] See Aḥmad Ibn al-Naqīb al-Miṣrī, *ʿUmdat al-Sālik wa-ʿUddat al-Nāsik*, ed. and trans. N. H. Keller, *The Reliance of the Traveller* (Evanston: Sunna Books, 1991) 84–85. Further on *rukhṣa*, see pp. 177 ff. below.

when knowledge of the existence of water becomes present, and presuming the continuity of such a consensus in turn becomes untenable.

MONOTHEISTIC LAWS BEFORE THE ADVENT OF ISLAMIC REVELATION[44]

Some discussion in the works of legal theory is allocated to the highly theoretical issue of what legal norms should be attached to objects and acts before the advent of Islam. This issue is treated under the designation "the rule pertaining to things in their original state" (*ḥukm al-ashyāʾ fī al-aṣl*), namely, in the state existing before they have become subject to Islamic law in particular and to other monotheistic laws in general. The crux of the controversy generated by this question is whether things are prohibited, permissible or neither of the two. Those who argued in favor of prohibition maintained that since no revelation exists, it is safer to assume they are prohibited. For if we make this assumption, we never run the risk of committing unlawful acts. On the side of permissibility, on the other hand, stood those who argued that if we know a thing to be beneficial and harmless to all people, then, in the absence of revelation, we can only assume it to be lawful. All agree that justice is good, and if we label an act as just, there would be no conceivable reason why it should not be considered lawful. A third group, however, rejected the foregoing arguments, saying, in effect, that judgment on all things before the coming down of revelation should be suspended (*ʿalā al-waqf*). Human reason, they insist, is incapable of knowing whether a certain thing is good or bad, and therefore it cannot play a role in deciding legal values. God alone has the power to do so, and judgment must be postponed until He speaks!

While this issue seems to be of purely theoretical significance, the question of whether or not the Prophet adopted non-Muslim, monotheistic laws after he received revelation is not so theoretical. For the answer to this question, and it was by no means uniform, determined in turn whether or not a theorist would accept Christian and Jewish scriptures as a source of the law in cases where Islamic revelation is silent. This explains why the section in which this question is treated in works of legal theory comes under the general title "Sources of law subject to disagreement."[45]

In chapter 1, we have seen that some time after the migration to Medina, the Prophet began to think of his new religion as capable of providing its believers with laws similar to those existing in Christianity and Judaism.

44 Bājī, *Iḥkām*, 681–86; Shīrāzī, *Sharḥ al-Lumaʿ*, II, 977–86.

45 See, e.g., Muwaffaq al-Dīn Ibn Qudāma, *Rawḍat al-Nāẓir wa-Junnat al-Munāẓir*, ed. Sayf al-Dīn al-Kātib (Beirut: Dār al-Kitāb al-ʿArabī, 1401/1981), 142.

Before that turning point, however, this was not the case, and constant reference to the two religions as natural predecessors of Islam was in fact common. As reflected in the Quran, this fact of transformation provided the material for legal theorists to argue in favor of, and against, the proposition that the Prophet adopted laws belonging to the Christian and Jewish denominations.[46] The Quran contained variable evidence to satisfy both sides of the argument.

Those who held that the Prophet never adhered to non-Muslim laws advanced a number of arguments, the first and foremost of which is Q. 5:48, which states: "We have made for each of you [i.e., Muslims, Christians and Jews] a law and a way to follow. If God willed, He would have made all of you one community." This verse, it was argued, indicates that for every prophet a legal system was divinely decreed, and that no prophet is to follow a legal order ordained for another. Furthermore, a number of reports attest to the fact that the Prophet prohibited his companions from issuing rules in accordance with Christian and Judaic laws. He is said to have rebuked ʿUmar when he found him holding fragments from the Torah. Indeed, if the Prophet considered himself bound by these laws, he would have been in the practice of searching for legal rules in Christian and Judaic laws, and would have made it incumbent upon his Companions to do the same. But he did not. Finally, it is argued that the community's consensus has been that the Sharīʿa is the only law for Muslims, and that the Christian and Jewish laws are not binding upon them.

The proponents of the opposite position also argued on the basis of Quranic and Sunnaic evidence. Of the five verses cited in support of their argument, verse 5:48 is the most direct: "Lo, We did reveal the Torah, wherein is guidance and light, by which the Prophets who became Muslims [lit. surrendered] judged the Jews, and the rabbis and the priests [judged] such of God's Scripture as they were bidden to observe." And in the Sunna, the Prophet is known to have decided in some penal cases according to Jewish law, and to have referred to the Torah not only in the matter of stoning adulterers, but also in his dispute with the Jews themselves. If the Prophet did not consider the Torah, the embodiment of Jewish law, as authoritative and binding, he would not have referred to it so frequently. Now, against the aforestated interpretation of verse 5:48, it was argued that assigning to each prophet a legal system does not necessarily preclude a prophet from drawing in part on the laws of another prophet. As to the other textual arguments advanced by those who advocated non-reliance on Christian and Jewish laws, it was maintained that Muhammad's opposition

46 Ghazālī, *Mustaṣfā*, I, 245–60.

to the earlier scriptures, as evidenced in his rebuke of ʿUmar, was directed toward the corruptions that crept into them, not toward them as Christian and Jewish scriptures *per se.*

LEGAL REASONING AND ITS PRACTITIONERS: *IJTIHĀD AND MUJTAHID*S

In his *Mustaṣfā*, Ghazālī depicts the science of legal theory in terms of a tree cultivated by man. The fruits of the tree represent the legal rules that constitute the purpose behind planting the tree; the stem and the branches are the textual materials that enable the tree to bear the fruits and to sustain them. But in order for the tree to be cultivated, and to bring it to bear fruits, human agency must play a role. Thus, the additional element making up the metaphor is the set of cultivation methods, the principles of legal reasoning and hermeneutics, employed so that the tree may bear the fruits. Finally comes the human agent himself, without whom the tree can have no existential purpose.[47] Throughout this and the last chapter, we have discussed the first three constituents of legal theory. We shall now turn to the "cultivator," the human agent whose creative legal reasoning is directed toward producing the fruit, the legal norm. The jurist (*faqīh*) or jurisconsult (*muftī*) who is capable of practicing such legal reasoning is known as the *mujtahid*, he who exercises his utmost effort in extracting a rule from the subject matter of revelation while following the principles and procedures established in legal theory. The process of this reasoning is known as *ijtihād*, the effort itself.

We have already intimated that the province of legal reasoning and interpretation, properly called *ijtihād*, does not extend over the entire range of the law. Excluded from this province is a group of texts which unambiguously state the legal rules of a number of cases. The certainty (*qaṭʿ*) generated by these texts *ab initio* precludes any need for reinterpretation. Some cases in point are the prohibitions imposed, by textual decree, on adultery, homosexuality, and consumption of grape-wine. Also excluded are those cases subject to consensus, the sanctioning instrument that generates certainty. In all other spheres of the law, *ijtihād* is not only admissible but is also considered a religious duty incumbent upon those in the community who are learned enough to be capable of performing it; this duty is known as *farḍ kifāya*.[48]

But what are the conditions a person must fulfill in order for him to qualify as a *mujtahid*? The great majority of these conditions have to do with

[47] Ibid., I, 8–9. [48] Shīrāzī, *Sharḥ al-Lumaʿ*, II, 1035.

the accumulation of expert knowledge in a number of areas. First, he must possess an adequate understanding of the nearly 500 legal verses in the Quran; he need not commit them to memory, but must know how to retrieve them efficiently and quickly when he needs to do so. Second, he must be familiar with the *ḥadīth* collections relevant to law, and must be proficient in the techniques of *ḥadīth* criticism so he can examine the authenticity and epistemological value of the reports he needs in his reasoning. If for any reason he is not proficient in these techniques, he may rely upon those collections in which Prophetic reports have been scrutinized, and which have been accepted as credible by the major jurists who preceded him. Third, he must be knowledgeable of the Arabic language so that he can understand the complexities involved, among other things, in metaphorical usages, in the general and the particular, and in equivocal and unequivocal speech. Fourth, he must possess a thorough knowledge of the theories of abrogation, so that he does not reason on the basis of an abrogated verse or report. Fifth, he must be highly proficient in the entire range of the procedures of inferential reasoning. Sixth, he must know those cases that have become subject to consensus, for he must not attempt to reopen a case on which a consensus has been reached. However, it is not required of him to know all cases of substantive law.[49]

Nor is he required to be of a just and trustworthy character (*ʿadl*). He may be unjust, and still be a skilled jurist who can exercise *ijtihād*. This does not mean, however, that the product of his *ijtihād* is binding upon other Muslims, be they legists or laymen. We shall see, on the other hand, that one of the conditions of the *mujtahid*-jurisconsult is a just character, since the office of the jurisconsult, unlike that of the *mujtahid qua mujtahid*, is a public one.[50]

Finally, some theorists maintained that one of the conditions of *ijtihād* is an adequate knowledge of theological doctrines, such as the proofs for the existence of God, His attributes, prophecy, etc. Many theorists, however, rejected this requirement, arguing that detailed theological knowledge is not directly related to that sphere of learning necessary for discovering the law. All the *mujtahid* needs to possess in this respect is a firm belief in God and the Muslim faith.[51]

Once a person fulfills these conditions, he, being a *mujtahid*, can no longer follow the *ijtihād* of others, but must, whenever he is presented with a case, find for it a solution if he is capable of doing so. The reason for this is that no *mujtahid* is infallible, and that his opinion extracted through *ijtihād* is as valid as that of another. This is why it is also held that a *mujtahid* must

[49] Baṣrī, *Muʿtamad*, II, 929–32; Shīrāzī, *Sharḥ al-Lumaʿ*, II, 1033–35.
[50] Ghazālī, *Mustaṣfā*, II, 350. [51] Ibid., II, 352.

never follow the opinion of a lesser *mujtahid.* Only if he is incapable of solving a particular case may he resort to the opinion of another *mujtahid.*[52]

The majority of jurists held the doctrine of *tajzi'at al-ijtihād*, namely, permitting a jurist to practice *ijtihād* in a particular branch of the law when he is unequipped to practice it in others. A jurist who is proficient in matters of inheritance and whose knowledge of arithmetic is proficient may perform *ijtihād* in the area of inheritance, although he may be at the same time utterly incapable of *ijtihād* in other matters such as sales, family law and contracts. The opponents of this doctrine argued that dividing the scope of *ijtihād* is detrimental, since a case of *ijtihād* may be organically connected to another which may lie in an area of the law of which the limited *mujtahid* has little knowledge. The majority opposing this position does not address the issue of the organic connections within the law, a fact that is surprising given the interconnectedness of various areas of substantive law. Rather, the majority's counter-argument consists in appealing to the practice of the Prophet's Companions and the early doctors of the law who are reported to have frequently refused to issue legal opinions for new cases because they did not know all the answers. This practice, it is maintained, constitutes a consensus regarding the validity of *tajzi'at al-ijtihād*, and those who reject the doctrine are thus charged with violating this consensus.[53]

At the outset of this section we commented on the province of *ijtihād* as being confined to the realm of probability; wherever certainty exists *ijtihād* must be set aside. In other words, the *mujtahid*'s territory is entirely devoid of certitude, and what he must deal with is strictly confined to probability and even conjecture. Thus, the possibility of his going astray on a case of law is not inconsiderable. Now, this salient feature of legal theory gave rise to an important question: What if a *mujtahid* is wrong either in the conclusions at which he arrived, or in the very methodology he followed in order to reach these conclusions? Is he to be punished in the hereafter for his mistake? Or is he to be rewarded at least for his commitment to fulfill the religious duty entrusted to him? And since the province of *ijtihād* is probabilistic, can two *mujtahid*s who reach two contradictory solutions for the same case both be considered right?

It appears that the majority of theorists held the view that only one may be deemed right and that he is to be rewarded doubly in the hereafter. Doubly, because he fulfilled the obligation of practicing *ijtihād,* on the one hand, and succeeded in arriving at the correct rule, on the other. He who errs is to be rewarded only once, and this in recognition of his effort in fulfilling the obligation with which he was entrusted. God, it is argued,

52 Bājī, *Iḥkām*, 723 ff. 53 Ghazālī, *Mustaṣfā*, II, 353–54.

nowhere made it a requirement that a *mujtahid* reach the correct rule of a case; all He obligated him to do is to exercise his utmost effort in seeking this rule.[54]

Among the Sunnī theorists, there seems to be no disagreement on the view that a *mujtahid*, in being right or wrong, does not commit a sin of any kind. Again, the justification of this view does not rest in the need for tolerance in an area heavily charged with all sorts of uncertainty, wherein error, if not tolerated, will make *ijtihād*, and with it an entire legal system, impossible. Rather, the justification of this view lies in Prophetic reports and consensus. The Prophet is reported to have said: "If the judge exercised his *ijtihād* and reached the correct result, he is rewarded twice; if he is wrong then only once." From the domain of consensus, the theorists refer to the practice of the Companions who did not consider each other to have committed a sin when they were in error. It is argued that this common practice constitutes a consensus to the effect that error is admitted in *ijtihād*. Furthermore, the community at large is said to have reached a consensus on the necessity of scholarly disputations and on the need to hold special sessions for conducting these disputations among the jurisprudents. If all *mujtahid*s were correct in their reasoning, then there would be no point in holding such sessions, for, after all, the purpose of such sessions is to demonstrate that one of the disputing jurists is right and the other wrong.[55]

The plurality of legal doctrine also provides an argument in favor of the view that only one *mujtahid*'s opinion on a case of law is correct, and that those of the others are not. It cannot be said, it is argued, that the divergent rules reached by two or more *mujtahid*s on a single case are all wrong, since this clearly means that the community as a whole has been wrong in following erroneous law, when in fact the community is incapable of falling into error. If, on the other hand, it is argued that all such rules are correct for the case in question, then this would amount to violating the principle of non-contradiction. Therefore, only one rule is correct and the others are wrong. On the basis of this principle, it is argued that the principle of Equivalence of Proofs (*takāfu' al-adilla*)[56] is inadmissible in legal science since only one of a case's contradictory rules can be correct. The rejection of the latter principle means that the preponderance (*tarjīḥ*) of one *ijtihād* procedure over another is indispensable.[57]

The foregoing arguments indicate the existence of two groups of theo-

[54] Bājī, *Iḥkām*, 708 ff.; Shīrāzī, *Sharḥ al-Luma'*, II, 1044–45, 1049–71; Ghazālī, *Mankhūl*, 453–57.
[55] Bājī, *Iḥkām*, 708–11.
[56] Shīrāzī, *Sharḥ al-Luma'*, II, 1071–72; further on this philosophical principle, see Moshe Perlmann, "Ibn Hazm on the Equivalence of Proofs," *The Jewish Quarterly Review*, n.s. 40 (1949/50): 279–90.
[57] Shīrāzī, *Sharḥ al-Luma'*, II, 1044–45.

rists who argued for and against the doctrine that all *ijtihād* conclusions concerning a single case are correct.[58] The opponents of this doctrine maintained that when the *mujtahid* is faced with two contradictory rules pertaining to a single case, and when he cannot determine which of the two is the correct one, he must either suspend judgment because he is unable to weigh one over the other, or have recourse to the decision of another *mujtahid* who was able to distinguish one rule as superior to its rival. The proponents of this doctrine, on the other hand, were divided among themselves: some maintained that he should suspend judgment, while the others adopted the view that he should choose either of the two rules as he sees fit. The reasoning behind this seemingly arbitrary choice is the equal strength of textual evidence and lines of reasoning leading to both rules. That this equivalence is possible and valid is proven by the fact that it exists in certain spheres of the law. In the area of penance, for instance, the law obliges those who break their fast in Ramadan to do penance, and here a choice is given between feeding the poor or freeing a slave; it is entirely up to the violator to choose between the two penalties. Similarly, the principle of equivalence is resorted to in the law of preemption, which may be defined as the right of a person to substitute himself for the purchaser in a sale of property by virtue of an interest he has as a co-owner, a sharer in right of way, or an adjoining neighbor. When two co-owners or equally adjoining neighbors lay a claim, as preemptors, to a property for sale, the judge has no choice but to give both of them equal shares in that property. This equal division is necessary due to the perfect equivalence in the strength of both claims. But unlike the judge, the *mujtahid* cannot issue two rules on one and the same case. Nor can his choice in favor of one rule be deemed arbitrary. Moreover, against suspending judgment and in favor of choosing, it is argued that it is often the situation that a case requires an immediate solution, and in the absence of another *mujtahid* who is able to weigh the contradictory evidence, a choice must be made instantaneously. Otherwise, the judicial process itself will come to a halt.[59]

FOLLOWING AUTHORITATIVE OPINIONS: *TAQLĪD*

Legal theorists draw a sharp distinction between *mujtahid*s and non-*mujtahid*s, the latter being commonly known as the "followers" or "imitators" (*muqallidūn*; pl. of *muqallid*) of the former. In other words, anyone who is

[58] On this question, see Imām al-Ḥaramayn ʿAbd al-Malik Abū al-Maʿālī al-Juwaynī, *Kitāb al-Ijtihād*, ed. ʿAbd al-Ḥamīd Abū Zunayd (Damascus: Dār al-Qalam, 1408/1987), 34–64; Ibn Barhān, *Wuṣūl*, 341–51.

[59] Shīrāzī, *Sharḥ al-Lumaʿ*, II, 1075 ff.; Ghazālī, *Mustaṣfā*, II, 378–82.

not a *mujtahid* is a *muqallid.* The class of *muqallid*s is in turn divided into those who are jurists and those who are laymen. The chief characteristic common to both is their inability, when faced with a question of law, to reason on the basis of textual evidence. Their access to the law can be had only through referring to the reasoning of the *mujtahid*, whose opinion they are obliged to follow. This obligation is deemed necessary because it cannot be expected of all members of the community to rise to the level of *mujtahid*s, for this would require that they devote all their energies and time to attaining a sophisticated knowledge of the law which would in turn mean that no one would be able to acquire any other skill. As a consequence, society, whose functioning depends on all sorts of professions, would become impossible. And since *ijtihād* is a *farḍ kifāya*, a duty to be fulfilled by only a limited number of qualified persons, all laymen and non-*mujtahid* jurists are under the obligation to follow the guidance of the *mujtahid*s. This obligation is further justified by the Companions' practice as well as by Q. 16:43 which states: "Ask the people of Remembrance if you do not know." Here, the "people of Remembrance" is taken to refer to the *mujtahid*s. Some of the Companions are reported to have been less than proficient in legal matters, and they were in the practice of asking the other Companions for opinions on matters that had befallen them. The complete absence of the latter's disapproval of this practice indicates that they were in unanimous agreement, in what is considered a consensus, that *taqlīd* is perfectly legitimate.[60]

Although the layman's knowledge of the law is perceived to be insignificant, a group of theorists maintained that he is under the obligation to seek the advice or follow the opinion of the more learned *mujtahid*, if there are two or more of them. This was contested by other theorists who insisted that imposing this obligation upon the layman is unduly demanding, for it would require of him that he know what constitutes legal knowledge and who stands in possession of this knowledge. The aforestated verse 16:43, they further argue, does not make distinctions between the classes of learned men who should be consulted, and its generalizing nature indicates that asking any of the people of Remembrance is endorsed.[61]

That the layman must follow a *mujtahid* is a requirement subject to no dispute. The layman is charged with the responsibility of enquiring about the credentials of the legist whom he consults. He must ask at least one, and preferably two, persons whom he considers of trustworthy character. If only one *mujtahid* is to be found in the layman's town, then he may consult him without conducting such an enquiry. If more than one is avail-

[60] Shīrāzī, *Luma*ʿ, 84–85; Ghazālī, *Mankhūl*, 472–73, 488–94.
[61] Ghazālī, *Mustaṣfā*, II, 390–92; Juwaynī, *Burhān*, II, 1342–43.

able, the majority of theorists maintained that he may consult any one of them, with the proviso that he establish the *mujtahid*'s credentials.[62]

The *mujtahid* himself, however, is not entitled to follow the doctrine of another *mujtahid*, whether or not the solution to the case he is presented with is required urgently. Some theorists espoused the view that if the *mujtahid* cannot provide an immediate answer to the case under consideration, and this case requires an immediate solution, then he may resort to an opinion already formulated by another *mujtahid.* Still others, who seem to have been a minority, maintained that he may follow such an opinion whether or not a solution is immediately required. In support of their view, the first group of theorists argued that for the opinion to be valid, it must be the product of the jurist's own *ijtihād.* This condition is perfectly analogous to the requirement of ritual ablution in prayer; without the performance of ablution, prayer can never be valid. Since *ijtihād* is established as a religious obligation (*farḍ*), it must be practiced in every case by those who are qualified. If it is not practiced, then their opinion would have no validity. But what if the case under consideration is of some urgency, and the *mujtahid* cannot provide a solution in time? The answer given by some theorists is this: the layman should act as he sees fit, and when the *mujtahid* arrives at a solution at a time when the problem still persists, then the layman must adhere to that solution. This argument draws on the law appertaining to prayer. If the Muslim believer finds neither water nor sand to perform ablution, he must still pray, without ritual cleansing. If he, at a later time, comes by water or sand, then he must pray again after having washed himself with either substance.[63]

THE JURISCONSULT (*MUFTĪ*)

By now it should become clear that our theorists equate the *mujtahid* with the *muftī*, the jurisconsult proper. Throughout their writings, the two terms are used synonymously.[64] Whatever scholarly credentials the *mujtahid* must possess, the jurisconsult must enjoy too, but with one difference: the latter, according to the majority, must not only be of just and trustworthy character, but he must be known to take religion and religious matters quite seriously. If a person meets all these requirements, then it is his obligation to issue a legal opinion (*fatwā*; pl. *fatāwā*) to anyone who comes before him for this purpose. Interestingly, he is equally under the obligation to teach law to anyone who wishes to acquire legal knowledge, for disseminating legal

62 Juwaynī, *Burhān*, II, 1342.
63 Ghazālī, *Mustaṣfā*, II, 384–86; Juwaynī, *Burhān*, II, 1339–40.
64 Wael B. Hallaq, "*Iftā'* and *Ijtihād* in Sunnī Legal Theory: A Developmental Account," in Khalid Masud, Brinck Messick and David Powers, eds., *Islamic Legal Interpretation: Muftīs and their Fatwās* (Cambridge: Harvard University Press, 1996), 33–43.

(=religious) knowledge was perceived to be as meritorious as issuing legal opinions. In both activities there was involved a promotion of religion, the ultimate form of worship. The obligation to teach law seems to be an idealized requirement reflecting the reality of legal education and legal practice where professors of law in the medieval colleges normally held the office of *muftī* as well.[65]

We have taken note of the obligation imposed on those who are qualified to perform *ijtihād*. The jurisconsult is thus under the obligation, when he is the only one available in a certain locality, to issue legal opinions and teach whenever he is asked to do so. Only when other *mujtahid*s are available is he absolved of this duty. For only when such a request is met is the obligation dispensed with, and the community at large would then be considered to have fulfilled its duty.[66]

A group of theorists maintained that the jurisconsult must be prepared to exercise *ijtihād* a second time with regard to a case of law for which he had already provided an answer. Others rejected this view, arguing that his first *ijtihād* would be valid for the same case if it were to occur again.[67]

It often happened that a layman obtained more than one opinion for the particular problem that had befallen him. When the opinions were identical, it was a proof, in a court of law, that the case had no other solution. But what if the solutions were at variance? Three positions were taken in this regard. The first was that the layman may choose any one of them and discard the others, for *mujtahid*s, as we have seen, are equal in their attempt to unravel the law of God. They all operate within a sphere of probability. The second position did not allow the layman this freedom, but dictated that he must adhere to the opinion of the jurisconsult who is most just, trustworthy and learned in the law. This position seems to reflect what was indeed the actual practice, where the opinions of distinguished jurists seem to have unfailingly had the upper hand. The third required the layman to adopt the least lenient of the opinions, the reasoning being that it is safer to do so. If the legality of a certain beverage was in question, and two opinions were issued on this matter, one prohibiting and the other permitting its consumption, then it is safer, according to this position, to adhere to the rule of prohibition. If he follows the rule of permission, and it happened that God meant it to be prohibited, then he would be in sin. This, however, does not seem to have been the opinion of the majority. It appears that the first position was the most prevalent of all.[68]

[65] Shīrāzī, *Sharḥ al-Lumaʿ*, II, 1033–35; Ghazālī, *Mustaṣfā*, II, 350–53.
[66] Shīrāzī, *Sharḥ al-Lumaʿ*, II, 1035.
[67] Juwaynī, *Burhān*, II, 1343–44; Shīrāzī, *Sharḥ al-Lumaʿ*, II, 1035–37.
[68] Shīrāzī, *Sharḥ al-Lumaʿ*, II, 1038–39; Juwaynī, *Burhān*, II, 1344–45.

4

THE LEGAL TEXT, THE WORLD AND HISTORY

INTRODUCTION: THE THEORETICAL CONSTANTS

AS a theoretical construct, the Sunnī theory of law has, since its beginnings, operated on two levels of discourse between which a clear distinction must be drawn if we are to gain an adequate understanding of what this theory and its history are about. The first level of discourse represents a substructure that is thoroughly bound by the unalterable proposition of the divine command. Here, no amount of interpretation or intellectual manipulation could change the basic givens underlying, or the presuppositions governing, this discourse. The components of the discourse surrounding this first level may thus be characterized as theoretical constants, incapable of transmutation despite the changing pressures of time and social exigencies. Conceptually, any change in the fundamental assumptions operating on this level was thought to be tantamount to a complete abandonment of (Sunnī) Islam as a religion.

Sunnism as a religious and, thus, a legal identity was defined by the founding principles of legal theory. That is to say, the acceptance or rejection of these principles, which squarely belong to the first level of theoretical discourse, determined, respectively, one's affiliation to, or dissent from, the Sunnī fold. It was not without good reason that this fold was labeled *ahl al-sunna wal-jamāʿa*, referring to the main body of Muslims (*jamāʿa*), the Sunnīs, who united around a set of principles and tenets upon which they *agreed* (*ijtamaʿū ʿalā*) in the form of a consensus (*ijmāʿ*), to uphold as the distinguishing mark of their identity. This designation therefore bespeaks the sanctioning effect of consensus on the basic ingredients of Sunnism; and this is why rejecting these ingredients – the principles making up the first level of theoretical discourse – amounted to rejecting the *jamāʿa*, the Sunnī fold.

Aside from certain rudimentary theological tenets – the acceptance of which was not a prerequisite for practicing law, but consent to which was nonetheless implied in the fact of adhering to the law – Sunnī *uṣūl al-fiqh* is based upon a number of fundamental assumptions that I have characterized as the constants of legal theory. It goes without saying that the Quran and the Sunna of the Prophet constitute the two principal components of these assumptions; and these are assumptions in the sense that they form the universal basis of the law. But no less important are the two other "sources" of the law, consensus and *qiyās*.

These four components are considered constants only insofar as they are broadly defined as the foundations of the legal system. Under this broad definition come the essentials of a hermeneutic without which no understanding of the two textual sources may be possible. In addition to the doctrine of abrogation, these essentials include the theories of language discussed in the second chapter, such as indeterminacy, equivocality, the general and the particular, real usages and tropes, and the divine command. Similarly, the consensus of the community, represented by its *mujtahid*s, and the umbrella method of legal reasoning, *qiyās*, constitute, in their essential form, part and parcel of these constants. No person could reject any of these constants and still claim affiliation with Sunnism. Consensus and *qiyās* have become the defining features of Sunnism no less than the Quran and the Sunna. A learned person can debate what we may call the subsidiary elements of these constants; he may argue, without calling into question his affiliation with Sunnism, that there are no ambiguous terms in the Quran, that *mutawātir* reports do not yield knowledge with certainty, or that the authoritativeness (*ḥujjiyya*) of *qiyās* as a method or of consensus as a sanctioning instrument is far from certain, but he cannot keep intact this affiliation and still question the overall validity of any of these "sources."

Thus the line distinguishing constants and non-constants (or the second level which we shall call variables) is one that separates a "source" as a broadly accepted postulate or set of postulates from ways of understanding, interpreting and reinterpreting this source. This line is the norm that distinguishes, for instance, between the acceptance in principle of *qiyās* as a legitimate method and the outright rejection of the analogy of similitude (*qiyās shabah*). In adopting this and similar positions, no contradiction ensues. Indeed, this manner of dealing with the sources set the standard, and without it no Islamic legal theory could have come into existence. Just as the variables presuppose the constants, the constants are insufficient in themselves to supply the total sum of legal theory without the variables. To use a biological metaphor, the constants represent the skeleton, while the variables provide the flesh that gives form and life to the whole of the body. The question then is: What are these variables?

THE VARIABLES OF LEGAL THEORY

To continue with our metaphor, understanding a living organism requires not only an understanding of its physiological constitution but also the environment in which it lives and coexists with other organisms. This also requires a study of its growth and the surrounding elements influencing its later development. In legal theory, this translates into an investigation of the variables that constitute the collectivity we call *uṣūl al-fiqh*, both diachronically and synchronically. To understand this theory, it is necessary to understand not only the constants (a perception that has long dominated the field) but also the role of the variables that give each theory its distinctive color, and each theorist his unique individuality. They are of many types and manifest themselves in multifaceted ways.

Contents and arrangement of subject matter

One symptom of these variables is the fact of the controversy over the subject matter of legal theory. It is rare to find two works of legal theory covering identical subjects. A mere glance at the subject matter of theories in one century or over a span of several centuries reveals astonishing differences. And many a theorist shows a deep awareness of what subjects are appropriate or inappropriate for inclusion in legal theory. Ghazālī, for one, criticized those theorists who, he thought, committed excesses in treating of issues relating to theology, positive law and Arabic grammar. Shāṭibī (d. 790/1388) followed suit, criticizing the inclusion of subjects that have no bearing upon the acknowledged function and purpose of legal theory, namely, the discovery of substantive legal rules. A survey of randomly selected topics reveals that they were included in certain works but altogether left out of others. One such topic is *al-ʿazīma wal-rukhṣa*, *ʿazīma* indicating the binding force of a ruling without consideration of mitigating hardship, and *rukhṣa* representing the mitigation of a rule by substituting for it a more lenient one, due to some hardship.[1] Greek logic, juridical dialectic and linguistic prepositions (*ḥurūf*) are three other topics that were included in some works and excluded from others.

While these topics were excluded from certain theories for one reason or another, they found their way into a large number of other theories, influential or otherwise, so as to allow them to secure a place in the history of *uṣūl al-fiqh*. Whether or not the *kalām* theory of knowledge or the juridico-linguistic prepositions were discussed in a particular work, they

[1] Further on *ʿazīma* and *rukhṣa*, see pp. 177 ff. below.

nonetheless were present in the larger field of theoretical discourse. A jurist may have chosen to exclude from his *written* theoretical discourse the subject of prepositions, but he could not pretend that legal hermeneutics could possibly function without recourse to some theory of prepositions. Even if the theory could function without the exposition of a particular subject – as may be claimed in the case of logic – knowledge of this subject would usually be so enshrined in the larger intellectual milieu that it could often be taken for granted.

Other issues, however, could not have been taken for granted, issues that seem to have been introduced into a particular theory in an *ad hoc* manner, and which do not seem to resurface in other theories. Two examples in point are found in the works of Ghazālī and Ṭūfī (d. 716/1316). In his *Mustaṣfā*, Ghazālī discusses, in a section of the chapter on *taqlīd*, the Taʿlīmī[2] notions of this concept, which he vehemently criticizes and refutes.[3] We hardly need to stress the effect of Ghazālī's religious and political environment on his choosing to introduce this issue into his theory. It seems safe to assume that the changing political landscape after Ghazālī, especially the decline of the Fāṭimid threat, rendered this discussion and criticism irrelevant to other theorists, which explains its ephemeral existence in legal theory at large.

A less ephemeral issue appears in Ṭūfī's *Sharḥ Mukhtaṣar al-Rawḍa*,[4] a commentary on Ṭūfī's own abridgment of Ibn Qudāma's (d. 620/1223) work *Rawḍat al-Nāẓir*. The issue is the preponderance of one legal school over another, an issue that seems to have been first raised by the Muʿtazilite theologian and legist ʿAbd al-Jabbār (d. 415/1024). We have seen in chapters 2 and 3 that the doctrine of determining preponderance (*tarjīḥ*) in works of legal theory concerns itself with two main areas: Prophetic reports and the *ratio legis*. Available sources indicate that the *tarjīḥ* of one legal school (*madhhab*) over another is not an issue subject to discussion, either in the chapters devoted to *tarjīḥ* or elsewhere. But Ṭūfī in his commentary devotes a number of pages to this matter, concurring, in general terms, with ʿAbd al-Jabbār on the view that the principle of *tarjīḥ* legitimately may be brought to bear upon the legal schools,[5] thus justifying the inclusion of this discussion in his work. Espousing the legitimacy of this type of *tarjīḥ* means, as Ṭūfī explicitly states, that in principle any jurist or layman may weigh one school against another, thereby determining which, in his view, is the stronger of the two in terms of evidential textual support and legal reasoning.

[2] On the Taʿlīmīs, see ʿAbd al-Karīm al-Shahrastānī, *al-Milal wal-Niḥal*, ed. William Cureton (Leipzig: Otto Harrassowitz, 1923), 147 ff. [3] *Mustaṣfā*, II, 387–89.

[4] Ed. ʿAbd Allāh al-Turkī, 3 vols. (Beirut: Mu'assasat al-Risāla, 1407/1987).

[5] *Sharḥ Mukhtaṣar al-Rawḍa*, III, 682–87.

Another manifestation of the differences in works of legal theory is the arrangement of subject matter. Here, too, it is seldom the case that two theorists follow a single pattern. Some jurists began their works with an exposition of the legal norms, followed by the four sources of the law, the controversial sources, legal language, *qiyās*, *ijtihād*, *taqlīd* and *tarjīḥ*. Others, who objected to this arrangement, preferred to begin with an exposition of the legal language, and then to proceed to other issues, their reasoning being that virtually all questions of legal theory depend on the language of revelation, and an understanding of this language paves the way for the topics that follow. Yet others chose to begin with logic or a *kalām* theory of knowledge, thereafter taking up the legal norms, the four sources, legal language, and so on. Thus, the treatment of a particular issue, such as the legal status of things before revelation (*ḥukm al-ashyā᾿ qabla wurūd al-sharʿ*), may be found among the first chapters in certain works, whereas in others it is postponed until toward the end. Be that as it may, the arrangement of subject matter is by no means a matter of coincidence or personal preference; rather, it must be seen to reflect the theorist's particular perception of the interconnectedness of the parts and their relationship to each other, and this, in turn, reflects the uniqueness and distinctive quality of each theorist's views of what theory is and how it can fulfill its purpose. In fact, the theorists are known to have developed a variety of methods (*ṭuruq*; sing. *ṭarīqa*) of arrangement. Ṭūfī, for instance, allots a lengthy discussion to at least six distinct methods which belonged to Abū Isḥāq al-Shīrāzī, Ghazālī, Fakhr al-Dīn al-Rāzī (d. 606/1209), Qarāfī (d. 684/1285), Ibn al-Ṣayqal and Āmidī (d. 630/1232). After discussing these, he offers a method of his own. In his *Mustaṣfā*, Ghazālī declares that he advances in this work a unique method of arrangement;[6] and our sources confirm the truth of his declaration.

A matter related to the contents of theoretical works and their arrangement is the level of emphasis placed on the treatment of these contents. The degree of importance allotted to juristic preference and public interest in the various works is an obvious case in point. At times, certain central topics of legal theory were discussed in such great detail as to justify publishing them as separate, independent works. Two such examples are Ibn Taymiyya's (d. 728/1327) treatise *Mas'alat al-Istiḥsān* which deals with juristic preference,[7] and Ghazālī's treatise *Shifā' al-Ghalīl*, a substantial volume treating exclusively of the *ratio legis*.[8]

[6] See Ibid., I, 101–08; Ghazālī, *Mustaṣfā*, I, 4.

[7] See *Mas'alat al-Istiḥsān*, ed. George Makdisi, "Ibn Taymīya's Autograph Manuscript on *Istiḥsān*: Materials for the Study of Islamic Legal Thought," in George Makdisi, ed., *Arabic and Islamic Studies in Honor of Hamilton A. R. Gibb* (Cambridge, Mass.: Harvard University Press, 1965): 454–79.

[8] See the References.

Theoretical justification

The variables of legal discourse are also reflected in theoretical developments that ensued as a result, among other things, of the concomitant changing perception of substantive law. We have seen that the formative period of legal theory came to a close toward the end of the third/ninth century, with the appearance of theorists such as al-Qaffāl al-Shāshī and Abū Bakr al-Ṣayrafī. This development took place well over a century subsequent to the maturation of substantive law as reflected in the works of Shaybānī and Shāfiʿī. We have also noted the extent to which early substantive law lacked a systematic and coherent methodology, a methodology that, after the formative period, became unfettered in taking the revealed texts as its point of departure and as its exclusive and ultimate frame of reference.

The legacy of the second/eighth century was a substantive legal corpus based on a methodology that did not always meet the rigorous standards of later theorists. Inferences labeled as *qiyās* often left much to be desired in the eyes of these theorists, for they were nothing more than forms of arbitrary reasoning that were easily characterized as *raʾy* and *naẓar*. In fact, the converse was also true. In certain cases, reasoning, appearing under the labels of *ra'y* or *naẓar*, was nothing short of systematic, full-fledged *qiyās*.[9] But these were no more than labels. What was at issue was the positive legal rulings arrived at in the first and second centuries of Islam which became the acknowledged body of law whose guardians and advocates were, among others, these very theorists. Of course, a reformulation of the substantive legal rulings belonging to the early period in accordance with the systematic demands of later legal theory was out of the question. For this, if it were to be carried out on any significant scale, would amount to a grave violation of consensus. It would have constituted a deliberate and conscious departure from that law on which the early fathers and eponyms had agreed. More serious was the glaring implication of such a step, namely, an acknowledgement that the law that constituted the foundation of earlier Muslim society was wrong. It need hardly be stated that such an acknowledgement would have amounted to an outright condemnation of the ways adopted by the Muslim predecessors.

If early substantive law was not to be modified in content on any considerable scale, then it had to be theoretically justified in one way or another. When Abū Ḥanīfa resorted to juristic preference, he showed that

[9] For a detailed study of the forms of legal reasoning in the second/eighth century, see Schacht, *Origins*, 269–328.

he did not always feel himself to be bound by either the spirit or the letter of the revealed texts. One example must suffice. All later jurists agree that to prove an act of adultery, four witnesses must testify to the fact that the act took place, and their testimonies must be uniform. Any discrepancy among these testimonies will nullify all the testimonies. Abū Ḥanīfa is reported to have upheld (and we have no reason to doubt the attribution) the validity of such testimonies even when each one of the four witnesses testifies that the act of sexual intercourse took place in a different corner of the house.[10] Now, this opinion seems to have been abandoned in the later Ḥanafite school. The transformation is illustrative of the problem's ramifications. All cases that did not, in their underlying reasoning, accord with the later methodology of *qiyās* were to be accommodated under a different methodology with different criteria relative to both the ontology and the epistemology of the *ratio legis*. And the issue of the limitation of the *ratio*, with all the attending controversy, represents one of the results of this accommodation.

It was this accommodation that rendered the method of juristic preference acceptable to the later theorists of the Mālikite, Shāfiʿite and Ḥanbalite schools. The justification for abandoning one *qiyās* in favor of another – the crux of juristic preference – was made so palatable that even the Ḥanbalites came to adopt it, as attested in the writings of Ibn Taymiyya.[11] It seems that the Shāfiʿites stood alone in questioning this method, for while they finally came to accept its legitimacy as a method of legal inference, they do not seem to have contributed, like the Ḥanbalites, to its further theoretical elaboration. There is good reason to believe this attitude to be the outcome of Shāfiʿī's attack on the early practice of *istiḥsān*.[12] Here, Shāfiʿī, we might say, left behind a legacy that was to haunt his followers for many centuries.

Ḥanafism shares with Mālikism a similar history. Inferences driven by *naẓar* and *raʾy* were not exclusively the province of the Ḥanafites. Mālik, for instance, had the lion's share of such practices. But whereas those cases of *naẓar* and *raʾy* were labeled by the Ḥanafites as "juristic preference," the Mālikites generally subsumed them under the designation of public interest (*istiṣlāḥ*; *maṣlaḥa*). There may be two reasons for this difference, the first having to do with the nature of the assumptions underlying the reasoning in such cases. The philosophy behind abandoning a certain *qiyās* in favor of an inference grounded in assumptions of public interest appears to be different from the assumptions of juristic preference. The former claims to

10 Shīrāzī, *Sharḥ al-Lumaʿ*, II, 970. 11 See his *Masʾalat al-Istiḥsān*, 454–79.

12 Shāfiʿī's critique of *istiḥsān* is mainly expressed in his "*Kitāb Ibṭāl al-Istiḥsān*" in *al-Umm*, VII, 267–77. See also Schacht, *Origins*, 121–22.

protect a wider class of interests than does the latter. Second, Shāfiʿī's scathing criticism of Ḥanafite juristic preference, which seems to have been perceived by his successors as quite potent, appears to have dissuaded the Mālikites from this mode of reasoning. The alternative was to associate all cases that did not fall under *qiyās* with the notion and method of public interest.

It is significant that the terms *maṣlaḥa* and *istiṣlāḥ*, in their technical or even quasi-technical connotation, did not exist in the first two, and probably three, centuries A.H., when substantive law became fully developed. A modern scholar has maintained that he was not able to find traces of *istiṣlāḥ* before the fifth/eleventh century,[13] but this view must now be revised. Currently available sources indicate that some time toward the end of the third/ninth century and the beginning of the fourth/tenth, the concept surfaced in legal discourse.[14] By the middle of the fifth/eleventh century, notions of public interest not only became an identifiable element of legal reasoning but also entered into the domain of *qiyās* to become, as we have seen, an essential ingredient in the doctrine of suitability (*munāsaba*).

Ghazālī seems to have been among the foremost theorists to elaborate a detailed doctrine of *munāsaba*, and, thus, of public interest. In his *Shifā'*, he brought the latter topic to the forefront of discussion.[15] But his efforts pale into insignificance when compared with those demonstrated by Shāṭibī, who managed to weave an entire theory, both imposing and impressive in structure, around the doctrine of *maṣlaḥa*.[16] The point to be made here is that the doctrine of *maṣlaḥa* evolved from obscure beginnings, to become in the fifth/eleventh century[17] an essential component of *qiyās*, and in less than three centuries after Ghazālī, it acquired such a prominent status that a whole theoretic was erected around it. In chapter 6, we shall see that *maṣlaḥa* was utilized by a number of modern thinkers as the backbone of their reformist theories.

Developments in the domains of public interest and juristic preference went hand in hand with another major development without which the growth of legal theory as a whole would have been stunted. This was the central development of the *ratio legis*, which would have, in its fifth-century form, bewildered Shāfiʿī, Ibn Ḥanbal and their contemporaries. In addition to the indigenous juristic needs for a further advancement of this theory,

[13] See R. Paret, "Istiḥsān and Istiṣlāḥ," *Shorter Encyclopaedia of Islam* (Leiden: E. J. Brill, 1974), 184–86.

[14] See W. B. Hallaq, "Considerations on the Function and Character of Sunnī Legal Theory," *Journal of the American Oriental Society*, 104 (1984): 686.

[15] *Shifā'*, 142–266.

[16] See chapter 5, below.

[17] And perhaps earlier. But demonstrating that *maṣlaḥa* had become an essential component of *qiyās* should await the publication of works on legal theory from the fourth/tenth century.

there became available to the theorists, who themselves were involved in several other fields of intellectual endeavor, a body of logical discourse that was imported from Greece. The translation of Greek logical works throughout the second half of the third/ninth century and thereafter provided these theorists with certain material that bore directly upon their legal theorization, especially in the area of legal causation.[18] By the end of the fifth/eleventh century the process by which this material was assimilated seems to have come to an end. Subsequently, developments in the theory of the *ratio legis* continued, but the impulse and material for these developments came from within, from the massive body of theoretical discourse in the fields of law and theology.

To be sure, the assimilation of Greek logical elements was selective, for by the time legal theory became affected by the flood of translations it had already formed its basic character. What was to be adopted had to fit the needs of theory as it had developed by the fifth/eleventh century; but most of all, it had to be harmonious, or capable of being harmonized, with the prevailing assumptions. This is why, in the area of causation, identifying the precise elements that were assimilated is a difficult task and one that defies any sure assessment. The appropriation of Greek logical elements in other aspects of theory is more readily identifiable, as we shall see.

Whether or not the Islamic legal notion of induction was influenced by Greek logic, it is certain that this notion played a major role in later developments of legal theory. By the fifth/eleventh century, induction (*istiqrāʾ*) in the realm of law began to gain ground, as appears from the emergence of the principle of the thematic induction of Prophetic reports (*tawātur maʿnawī*).[19] We recall the crucial function that this principle played in solving the problem of the authoritativeness of consensus, a problem that found no solution for over three centuries. Until the beginning of the fifth/eleventh century, the textual evidence that was adduced in justification of authoritativeness consisted of Quranic verses and Prophetic reports that, taken individually, did not engender certitude. But the problem of authoritativeness could not be solved without conclusive evidence, for the theorists insisted that consensus is a "source" of the law that engenders certitude. If it enjoys certitude, it must be anchored in textual evidence that is certain, and this was as yet unavailable. It was the theorists of the fifth/eleventh century who articulated the principle of thematic induction of Prophetic reports as a response – we have good reason to believe – to the challenge raised by the issue of authoritativeness. By arguing that the aggregate weight of the multitude of solitary reports

[18] On this see Hallaq, "Logic, Formal Arguments," 315–58.

[19] See pp. 64–65 above.

testifying to the notion that the community can never agree on an error was epistemologically tantamount to the recurrent reports (*mutawātirāt*), the theorists finally managed to settle the question.

In its fifth-/eleventh-century form, the principle of thematic induction of solitary Prophetic reports was only a prelude to what was to come later, paving the way for more significant developments in the structure of legal theory. Induction was to play an increasingly important role in many theories, and in some, it played a central role. By the seventh/thirteenth century, induction became, according to Qarāfī, one of the "indicants" of the law, that is to say, the means by which law may be discovered.[20] The importance of induction is signified by its place in the order of the indicants classified by Qarāfī; it comes next to the Quran, the Sunna, consensus, *qiyās*, the reports of the Companions, public interest, the principle of the presumption of continuity, and customary law – this last being admitted in law on the principle of presumption. But this was not all. Induction became, for the theorists, a way of thinking. Discourse produced after the sixth/twelfth century was markedly different from that of the preceding period. One significant feature of the discourse of the later period is the repeated reference to the principle of induction in legal argumentation and reasoning. An argument based on an inductive survey of relevant particulars was deemed as authoritative as any other. But perhaps the most outstanding attestation of the central role of induction appears in Ṣhātibī's theory, which represents a unique and powerful marriage between the expanded notions of public interest and this logical principle (see chapter 5 below).

The assimilation of logical and theological principles

By now, it is clear that legal theory as an aggregate of ideas and principles did not exist in a vacuum but rather drew in some measure on relevant contributions made in other fields of intellectual endeavor. The influences exerted by these fields on formulating certain aspects of theory constituted some of the variables about which we have been speaking. From the field of theology (*kalām*) were appropriated certain fundamental elements that became an integral part of many, if not most, legal theories. Indeed, the prevailing epistemology in mainstream legal theory owes much to theology, although it is at times difficult to determine which of the two, legal theory or theology, influenced the other in this particular area.

However, theological doctrines were as much subject to refutation as to

[20] *Sharḥ Tanqīḥ al-Fuṣūl fī Ikhtiṣār al-Maḥṣūl fī al-Uṣūl*, ed. T. ʿAbd al-Raʾūf Saʿd (Cairo: Maktabat al-Kulliyyāt al-Azhariyya, 1973), 445, 448.

adoption. The fact that the legal theorists thought it worthwhile to devote some of their energy to the rebuttal of certain theological doctrines indicates the relevance of these doctrines to the issues raised in legal theory. And it seems that most of this energy was expended in defense of the Ashʿarite conception against Muʿtazilite theology. This is demonstrated by the central rationalist tenet which was intensely discussed in the opening sections of treatises on legal theory. This is the Muʿtazilite tenet that human acts are either good or bad, and that the mind, independent of revelation, is capable of determining which act is good and which bad.[21] It is only such ethical values as those related to acts performed in religious rituals, such as prayer and pilgrimage, that cannot be so determined, and must be judged by the dictates of revelation. The relevance of this tenet to the concerns of legal theory is readily obvious, for it runs in diametrical opposition to the most fundamental principle of Sunnī jurisprudence, namely, that God decides on all matters and that the human mind is utterly incompetent to function as a judge of any human act. It is not difficult to see why such a problem occupied, insofar as the order of subject matter is concerned, a primary place. They needed, at the very outset, to dispose of any *Weltanschauung* that contravened their own basic premise of a law squarely grounded in divine deontology.

On certain issues, legal theory was indirectly influenced by the rationalist doctrine. A strictly legal issue may be subject to a significant dispute, not on the grounds of any legal consideration but rather because accepting one view or another logically implies an admission of the validity of a spurned theological doctrine. A case in point is the issue of the limitation of the *ratio legis* (*takhṣīṣ al-ʿilla*). When Sarakhsī, for instance, rejected the validity of the principle of limitation, he was doing so in light of the theological implications to which this principle leads.[22] Limitation was interpreted as a situation where one would have a *ratio* without its expected ruling, which, in rational argument, is tantamount to having a cause without its effect. It is a fundamental assumption of Muʿtazilī doctrine that humans have an ability to act prior to their action. The acceptance of the principle of limitation therefore implied an outright acceptance of this rationalist doctrine, one that generated a great deal of opposition among the Sunnī theorists. It is highly likely that Sarakhsī's rejection of the limitation of the *ratio legis* was principally motivated by his opposition to this rationalist doctrine.

On the other hand, Ashʿarite doctrines of *kalām* gained currency among the theorists, many of whom did belong to this theological school. One

[21] Ghazālī, *Mustaṣfā*, I, 55 ff.; Juwaynī, *Burhān*, I, 87–94. See also Weiss, *The Search for God's Law*, 83–88. [22] Sarakhsī, *Uṣūl*, II, 208–15.

Ashʿarite doctrine in particular had a bearing on legal causation, and it was thoroughly incorporated into the greatest majority of legal theories. Unlike the Muʿtazilites, the Ashʿarites maintained that man is incapable of knowing the rationale (*ḥikma*) behind God's commands and that God is not obliged to command what is good for His subjects. The legal cause embodied in the *ratio legis* is nothing but a "sign" which signifies the legal rule but does not actually "effect" it. It is in this sense that a *ratio legis* may be seen as an occasioning factor, as one scholar has recently characterized it.[23] This Ashʿarite conception of occasionalism dominated a large segment of legal theory until the nineteenth century, although one can find exceptions, as exemplified by the illustrious Granadan theorist Abū Isḥāq al-Shāṭibī.[24]

In the initial stages of its development, legal theory seems to have incurred another debt to *kalām*, namely, dialectic (*jadal* or *munāẓara*,) which occupied a prominent place in the overall structure of this theory. Defining the precise extent of this debt is not an easy task, for *kalām* itself was influenced in this respect by the new Greek ideas that infiltrated Muslim religious sciences. Whether the dialectical method entered legal theory via *kalām* or was directly borrowed from Greek translations is a question that must await further research. But that the Muslim art of dialectic was significantly influenced by the Greek sources seems beyond dispute. And here, as elsewhere, borrowing was highly selective, as suggested by the distinction drawn between the dialectic of the philosophers – who, in the view of the orthodox, are not far removed from heresy – and the "good dialectic" (*al-jadal al-ḥasan*) which was harmonious with the spirit of law and legal theory.

By the middle of the fourth/tenth century, entire treatises on juridical dialectic appear to have come into existence, and the name of al-Qaffāl al-Shāshī is associated with the first composition on "good dialectic."[25] Writings on the subject steadily grew, culminating in such imposing and recondite contributions as Juwaynī's *al-Kāfiya fī al-Jadal*. Beginning with the fifth/eleventh century, dialectic as a method of argumentation was incorporated into works of legal theory, a practice that became increasingly popular in the following centuries.

In one sense, dialectic constituted the final stage in the process of legal reasoning, in which two conflicting opinions on a case of law are set against

[23] See Weiss, *The Search for God's Law*, esp. 593.

[24] See his *al-Muwāfaqāt fī Uṣūl al-Aḥkām*, ed. M. Muḥyī al-Dīn ʿAbd al-Ḥamīd, 4 vols. (Cairo: Maṭbaʿat Muḥammad ʿAlī Ṣubayḥ, 1970), II, 3–4.

[25] W. B. Hallaq, "A Tenth–Eleventh Century Treatise on Juridical Dialectic," *Muslim World*, 77 (1987): 198, n. 6; Abū Isḥāq Ibrāhīm b. ʿAlī al-Shīrāzī, *Ṭabaqāt al-Fuqahā'*, ed. Iḥsān ʿAbbās (Beirut: Dār al-Rā'id al-ʿArabī, 1970), 112.

each other in the course of a disciplined session of argumentation with the purpose of establishing the truthfulness of one of them. The aim of this exercise, among other things, was to reduce disagreement (*ikhtilāf*) among legists by demonstrating that one opinion was more acceptable or more valid than another. Minimizing differences of opinion on a particular legal question was of the utmost importance, the implication being that truth is one, and for each case there exists only one true solution.

This function of narrowing down disagreements by establishing where truth resides rendered the art of disputation – also known as *adab al-baḥth wal-munāẓara* – essential to legal theory, although one can find numerous treatises that do not devote any space to a discussion of this art. The systematic effect of dialectic on the modes of exposition of legal theories is readily obvious, reflecting the background against which this theory grew to maturity. The most common method of exposition – though exceptions are many– is that of the question-answer: "If someone says such and such, we reply with such and such." But this method is versatile, and an analysis of the logical structure of questions, and especially answers, shows that theorists adopted for their use the entire gamut of arguments we nowadays subsume under logic and rhetoric.

An equally salient feature of legal theory, which we characterize as one of the variables of legal discourse, is Greek formal logic. That this logic did not make an entry into legal theory until the end of the fifth/eleventh century is a matter that must await further enquiry. The fact is that logic had to wait over two centuries after its introduction to the intellectual landscape of Islam before it was accommodated in legal theory, accommodation for which Ghazālī must receive full credit, although the Ẓāhirite Ibn Ḥazm (d. 456/1062) had taken the first step some half a century before him. The credit must go to Ghazālī because his new enterprise fell squarely within the contours of Sunnī jurisprudence, whereas Ibn Ḥazm's remained outside it.

Ghazālī begins his work *al-Mustaṣfā* with an introduction containing a fairly detailed exposition of logic. Although he makes the reading of this introduction voluntary, he explicitly asserts that he who possesses no knowledge of logic has, in effect, no genuine knowledge of any science. When he proceeds to the legal part of his work, however, no sign of any formal logical analysis can be detected, and his treatment of the subject stands squarely within the traditional discourse of legal theory. What he seems to have intended in his treatise was not to revolutionize legal analysis but rather to insist on the necessity of logic as the only effective tool by which all inferences can be molded according to a rational design. In his *Shifā' al-Ghalīl*, a work which he wrote earlier in his career, he analyzes legal arguments in terms of syllogistics,[26] and in his logical work, *Miʿyār al-ʿIlm*, he illustrates the three figures of categorical syllogism together with their moods through examples drawn not only from theology and philosophy but also from law. Here he also discusses conjunctive and disjunctive syllogisms, *reductio ad absurdum* and induction.[27] It is quite obvious that in doing so Ghazālī wished to bring closer to the mind of jurists and legal theorists an understanding of the structure of these inferences, although he did not attempt to analyze legal cases through the medium of these arguments. Nor is there any effort at identifying, in terms of formal and non-formal logic, the distinctive structure of legal logic. The only exception to this, however, is the case of analogy; following in the footsteps of Aristotle and the Arabic logicians,[28] Ghazālī argues that in order for analogy to be valid, it must be converted to the first figure of the syllogism. In a chapter in his *Shifāʾ al-Ghalīl*, he goes farther in the direction of formalizing legal logic by attempting to analyze a wide variety of legal arguments in terms of syllogistics.[29]

Ghazālī's contribution to the formalization and logical analysis of legal arguments was paralleled by another to epistemology, and it is in these two interconnected areas of philosophical enquiry that his legacy was to persist. Let us begin with epistemology, which became the conceptual framework in which many, but by no means all, legal theories were grounded. Following the Arabic logicians since the beginning of the fourth/tenth century, many legal theorists held that the acquisition of knowledge is one of the tasks of logic. Logic, then, was seen as the tool by means of which sound human knowledge can be derived and augmented, thereby serving not only as a set of tautologies, but also as an epistemic system, a theory of knowledge proper. Accordingly, it was held that to avoid an infinite regress, the mind must be seen as proceeding from some *a priori* or even preexistent axiomatic knowledge to new concepts (*taṣawwurāt*) by means of definitions (*ḥudūd*; sing. *ḥadd*). If we know what "rationality" and "animality" are, we can form a concept in our minds of "man," who is defined as "a rational animal." It is through definitions, then, that concepts are formed.

Once concepts are acquired, the mind can proceed to a more advanced level of knowledge by predicating one concept or another. Having formed the concepts "man" and "intelligent," for example, we can formulate the

26 *Shifāʾ*, 435–55, translated in Hallaq, "Logic, Formal Arguments," 338–58.

27 *Miʿyār al-ʿIlm fī Fann al-Manṭiq*, ed. Sulaymān Dunyā (Cairo: Dār al-Maʿārif, 1961), 134–65.

28 Here I follow Nicholas Rescher in adopting the term "Arabic" rather than "Arab" to refer to those logicians who wrote in the Arabic language irrespective of their ethnic origin. N. Rescher, "The Impact of Arabic Philosophy on the West," in N. Rescher, *Studies in Arabic Philosophy* (Hertford: University of Pittsburgh Press, 1966): 147–48.

29 See n. 26 above.

judgment (*taṣdīq*), true or false, that "man is intelligent." A more advanced level of knowledge may be achieved by ordering judgments in such a manner as to obtain an inference – be it syllogistic, inductive, analogical or otherwise.[30] Here, theorists part company with philosophers, arguing that what philosophers call a syllogism (*qiyās*) is nothing more than an inference whose premises are certain, whereas juridical *qiyās* encompasses premises that are probable. The difference lies in the epistemic quality of the premises, for the form and structure of analogy do not differ from those of the syllogism in that both types of premises require the subsumption of a particular under a general.[31]

The culmination of the argument in favor of equating the philosophical syllogism with juridical *qiyās* perhaps finds its best expression in the writings of the Ḥanbalite jurist and theologian Taqī al-Dīn Ibn Taymiyya, who insisted that the syllogism, by virtue of form alone, cannot lead to a conclusion that engenders certainty.[32] It is the subject matter of the argument, he argued, not its form, that determines the truth of the conclusion. If the certainty of the premises in an analogy can be proven, then juridical *qiyās* is no weaker than the syllogism. Both arguments yield certitude when their subject matter is veridical, and they result in mere probability when their subject matter is uncertain. A syllogistic mode of reasoning will not result in a certain conclusion by virtue of form alone.

We recall that in analogy, when the new case proves to be equivalent to the original case, the rule in the latter case is transferred to the former. In the prototypical example of wine, grape-wine was prohibited due to its intoxicating quality, a quality that justifies the transference of prohibition to a new case, say, date-wine. The syllogism, for its part, consists of the same elements. The middle term in a syllogism is the *ratio legis* in analogy, and the major premise, which contains the major and middle terms, is equivalent in analogy to the concomitance (*talāzum*) or necessary relation between the *ratio legis*, on the one hand, and the original and new cases, on the other. Whatever is required to prove the truth and certainty of the universal premise in a syllogism will be required to prove that the *ratio legis* is for certain always concomitant with the rule. In other words, the means by which we establish the truth of the proposition "All intoxicants are

30 See, for example, Ibn Qudama, *Rawḍat al-Nāẓir*, 14–5; Qarāfī, *Sharḥ Tanqīḥ al-Fuṣūl*, 4 ff. For a detailed account of this theory, see Harry A. Wolfson, "The Terms *Taṣawwur* and *Taṣdīq* in Arabic Philosophy and their Greek, Latin and Hebrew Equivalents," *Muslim World*, 33 (1943): 114–28; Hallaq, trans., *Ibn Taymiyya*, xiv ff.

31 Hallaq, trans., *Ibn Taymiyya*, xxxv ff.; Hallaq, "Logic of Legal Reasoning," 94–95.

32 For Ibn Taymiyya's critique, see his *al-Radd ʿalā al-Manṭiqiyyīn*, ed. ʿAbd al-Ṣamad al-Kutubī (Bombay: al-Maṭbaʿa al-Qayyima, 1368/1949), 200–01, 211–12, 213, 214; and Hallaq, trans., *Ibn Taymiyya*, xxxv ff., and paras. 190–91, 216–18, 222–23.

prohibited" are identical with those by which we prove that whenever there is a given intoxicant, prohibition obtains. Conversely, the *ratio legis* of a rule may be refuted by the same means by which the universality of the premise in a syllogism may be questioned. If there is good reason to doubt the analogy "Men are corporeal, analogous to dogs, mules, elephants, etc.," then there is as good a reason to doubt the major premise, "All animals are corporeal." Thus, if the predication of the rule in the original case is questionable, then the transfer of that rule to the new case cannot be possible. Similarly, any doubt concerning the relational predicability between animality and corporeality is reason to question the universality of the major premise in the syllogism.

Establishing the universal character of the major premise is thus equivalent to verifying that whenever there is a *ratio legis* there is a rule. Furthermore, the methods of establishing the *ratio legis*, chiefly those operating according to the principle of *iṭṭirād*,[33] guarantee that for a *ratio* to be accepted as valid in one case it must be valid in others. Therefore, the difference between juridical analogy and the philosophical syllogism is that in the latter the universal subject and predicate are completely abstracted from the particulars, whereas in the former the predicate is affirmed of the subject insofar as one case is concerned, though such an affirmation is possible only through an examination of a certain number of other relevant cases.

We must hasten to add, however, that a large number of legal theorists did not share Ibn Taymiyya's views concerning the superiority of analogy over syllogism. For while Ibn Taymiyya opposed Greek logic altogether, they did not. What they found acceptable was the view, advocated by Ibn Taymiyya and others, that analogy can be reduced to the syllogistic form. Even as staunch a Ḥanbalite traditionalist as Ibn Qudāma thought of the syllogism as the methodological foundation of any science, be it rational or legal. Following in the footsteps of Ghazālī, Ibn Qudāma opens his treatise on legal theory with an introduction to logic, in which he not only discusses the theories of *taṣawwur*, *taṣdīq* and *ḥadd*, but also delineates the types of the syllogism, the conditions for their validity and the manner in which they may be made to serve the law.[34] He expounds the three figures of the categorical syllogism together with the hypothetical and the disjunctive syllogisms, and in illustration of their workings he gives legal examples. Arguments in all fields of knowledge, he says, must conform to the syllogistic rules, and for analogy to be valid it, too, must be reducible to the first

[33] On *iṭṭirād*, see pp. 90–92, 95, above.

[34] See his *Rawḍat al-Nāẓir*, 14–29. For a more detailed treatment of the theorists' writings on logic, see Hallaq, "Logic, Formal Arguments."

syllogistic figure. Ibn Qudāma's views on formal logic and their relation to the structure of legal arguments plainly attest to the persistence of the Ghazālian thesis.

A different approach integrating logic into law appears in Ibn Qudāma's younger Shāfiʿite contemporary Sayf al-Dīn al-Āmidī, who, like Ghazālī, was heavily involved in the study of Greek logic and philosophy. That Āmidī does not open his work with an introduction to logic must not obscure the fact that he was committed to the formal conception of legal science, no more nor less than Ghazālī and Ibn Qudāma were. He does, however, begin his work with some notes to the effect that knowledge of any science comes about through *taṣawwur* and *taṣdīq*, and that on the basis of these the legal indicant, the *dalīl*, can be brought to bear upon legal inference. Here, he classifies the indicant into three types, the rational, the revelational and that which is a combination of both. The rational indicant yields rational knowledge mostly used in theology and other rational fields, whereas the revelational indicant is derived from the religious textual sources. The third type is a rational argument which takes its premises from revelation.[35]

Toward the end of his work, Āmidī devotes a chapter to discussion of the indicant that is independent of *qiyās*, a chapter he entitles *istidlāl*,[36] namely, arguments based on the *dalīl*. In this chapter, he, like Ibn Qudāma, expounds the types of syllogistic arguments, with examples derived from substantive law. But unlike Ibn Qudāma and Ghazālī before him, Āmidī, having drawn a line between syllogistics and *qiyās*, does not maintain that the latter's validity is contingent upon its being reducible to the first syllogistic figure. This conception of the logical structure of *qiyās* and its relationship (or absence of such a relationship) with syllogistics does not seem to be substantively consequential for the actual processes of legal reasoning, but rather represents a purely theoretical concern.

The Mālikite theorist Ibn al-Ḥājib (d. 646/1248) shows the same commitment to the integration of logic into legal theory as did his predecessors Ghazālī, Ibn Qudāma and Āmidī.[37] In the tradition of those theorists who anchored legal theory in law, language and theology (*kalām*), Ibn al-Ḥājib devotes some space at the beginning of his work to each of these. Taftāzānī (d. 791/1388), one of the more important commentators on Ibn al-Ḥājib's treatise, remarks that instead of dealing in the section on *kalām* with substantive theological issues related to God and prophethood, Ibn al-Ḥājib

[35] Abū al-Ḥasan ʿAlī Sayf al-Dīn al-Āmidī, *al-Iḥkām fī Uṣūl al-Aḥkām*, 3 vols. (Cairo: Maṭbaʿat ʿAlī Ṣubayḥ, 1968),I, 8 f. [36] Ibid., III, 175 ff. See also Weiss, *Search for God's Law*, 655 ff.

[37] See his *Muntahā al-Wuṣūl wal-Amal fī ʿIlmayy al-Uṣūl wal-Jadal*, ed. Muḥammad al-Naʿsānī (Cairo: Maṭbaʿat al-Saʿāda, 1326/1908), 2–11.

dwells on logic.[38] Discussing logic under the guise of *kalām* must be attributed, in the view of Jurjānī (d. 816/1413), to the fact that law, being a religious discipline, cannot be openly grounded in a science as suspicious and alien as logic, and since *kalām*, the crown of religious sciences, has come to be inclusive of logic, it is used as a cover under which logic is subsumed. If this, Jurjānī says, shows anything it is that there is a genuine need for logic in legal theory.[39] In his super-commentary on Jurjānī, Harawī goes so far as to say that nothing of *kalām* is relevant to the needs of the law except logic.[40]

Logic-oriented theorists constituted only one group among their peers. Although it is difficult to quantify them, it can be safely assumed that those who did not integrate logic into their theories were many. If we are to accept one of the traditional classifications of theorists into those who wrote on the subject from a *kalām* viewpoint and those who wrote on it from a juridical perspective, it is arguable that the logic-oriented theorists largely, if not entirely, belonged to the former group. But whatever their number, and whatever the extent to which they were willing to anchor legal theory in a formal logical structure, one thing seems obvious, that is, the inconsequential effect of formal logic, in both its definitional and syllogistic contributions, on the actual modalities and substantive procedures of legal reasoning. To put it in more concrete terms, it is hard to discern the presence of formal logic in the legal reasoning exercised by judges and jurisconsults with regard to ordinary, day-to-day problems arising in Muslim societies. The task of the theorist cannot, admittedly, be reduced to merely satisfying needs arising from daily life. The theorist was a lawyer, a jurist and, no less, an intellectual. The theoretical exigencies posed by the needs of mundane reality were not the exclusive province of the theorist's discourse. His concern extended to the far reaches of the theoretical domain; theory and theoretical constructs were to be taken, and perhaps rightly so, to their extreme. Those theorists who cherished Greek logic aimed to utilize it in their theory to the farthest extent possible. Their approval of this logic implies that they adhered to a conception of knowledge based on the theory of essences, which was, in turn, inextricably connected with a realist theory of universals as well as with Porphyry's five predicables.[41] All this gave them an appealing logical, epistemological and, ultimately, conceptual framework which seemed superior to the traditional *kalām* theory of knowledge. The pedigree of the Greek formula appeared

[38] See his *Ḥāshiya ʿalā Sharḥ al-ʿAḍud al-Ījī*, 2 vols. (Cairo: Maktabat al-Kulliyyāt al-Azhariyya, 1973), II, 283. [39] Ibid., I, 38–39.

[40] See his *Ḥāshiya ʿalā Ḥāshiyat al-Muḥaqqiq al-Sayyid al-Sharīf al-Jurjānī*, 2 vols. (Cairo: Maktabat al-Kulliyyāt al-Azhariyya, 1973), I, 39. [41] On these, see Hallaq, trans., *Ibn Taymiyya*, xiv–xx.

more firmly anchored in a time-honored epistemology than in the traditionally, but more recently, accepted doctrine. Logic was the *organon* of philosophy and of all forms of knowledge, including legal theory. It is in this external intellectual framework that legal theory is to be placed, and it is this framework that constitutes the contribution of logic to legal theory.

Cumulative growth and later developments

In addition to the variables created in legal theory by the assimilation of logical, theological and other elements, a number of internal, substantive developments contributed additional variables. We characterize these as "internal" because they emanate from those components of legal theory that constituted, in contradistinction to "alien" Greek logic and extraneous theology, its elemental subject matter. Consider, for instance, the controversy surrounding the existence of *mujtahid*s, an issue not raised, in any form or manner, before the sixth/twelfth century. Toward the end of that century, or perhaps the beginning of the seventh/thirteenth, the controversy became part of the theorists' formal discourse. Āmidī is the first author known to us to have devoted a special section to the discussion of this issue. The polemical character of his account betrays the origins of this controversy, which seems to have been associated with a scholarly disputation between the distinguished Ḥanbalite jurist Ibn ʿAqīl (d. 513/1119) and an anonymous scholar belonging to the Ḥanafite school. In this disputation, Ibn ʿAqīl refuted the argument of his Ḥanafite opponent, who had maintained that the "gate of judgeship" was closed because *mujtahid*s no longer existed. Ibn ʿAqīl's insistence that *mujtahid*s must, and do, exist at all times became the standard Ḥanbalite position, against which the Shāfiʿite Āmidī put forth his objections. Joining the majority of Shāfiʿites were both the Ḥanafites and Mālikites who maintained that it is conceivable that at a particular time or age a *mujtahid* may be nowhere to be found. A minority of Shāfiʿites seem to have sided with the Ḥanbalites.[42]

What is relevant to us here is the manner in which this issue emerged from a scholarly disputation into a formal discussion in virtually all later theories. In his disputation with the Ḥanafite adversary, Ibn ʿAqīl employs a common-sense argument: no textual evidence is cited either by him or by the Ḥanafite jurist. It is to be noted that the focus of the disputation was the "gate of judgeship," not the "gate of *ijtihād*" as such. In Āmidī's account, as well as in all later discussions of the matter, the citation of

[42] On this issue, see Wael B. Hallaq, "Was the Gate of Ijtihād Closed?" *International Journal of Middle East Studies*, 16, 1 (1984): 22–26; Wael B. Hallaq, "On the Origins of the Controversy about the Existence of Mujtahids and the Gate of Ijtihād," *Studia Islamica*, 63 (1986): 129–30.

textual evidence becomes normative. According to Āmidī, the Ḥanbalites and some Shāfiʿites adduced two sets of arguments in favor of their position, one textual (*sharʿī*), the other rational (*ʿaqlī*). The former consisted of three Prophetic reports, the contents of which validate the view that at all times learned men (=*mujtahid*s) will lead the community of Muhammad, and that sound religious knowledge will constantly accompany Muslims throughout all time until the Day of Judgment. The rational argument, on the other hand, derives from the premise that the practice of *ijtihād* is a religious duty (*farḍ kifāya*) incumbent upon the qualified jurists and jurisconsults, and the abandonment of this duty would mean that the community as a whole has fallen short of fulfilling God's command. But the rationale behind this command is perceived to be the preservation of the Sharīʿa, for without *ijtihād* the law may cease to function, this having the grave implication that the Muslim community will no longer abide by the Divine law.

Against the three Prophetic reports adduced by the Ḥanbalites and their Shāfiʿite supporters in this issue, Āmidī advanced five reports to the effect that the Sharīʿa will steadily deteriorate and jurists will ultimately become extinct. The rational argument is countered with the claim that *ijtihād* is not an incumbent religious duty when it is possible to maintain the operation of the Sharīʿa on the basis of laws which had been elaborated throughout the centuries.[43]

Now, this controversy, to which the theorists after Āmidī devoted a special section in their works, was expanded to include further arguments, some of which pertained to the question of whether or not the legal system was, at any point in its history, actually devoid of *mujtahid*s.[44] The point to be made here is that legal theory continued to grow by introducing into its discourse new issues that had become pertinent to its needs. Theory had to respond to the mundane reality of the judicial system and the world of practice.

There is perhaps no better illustration of the response of theory to the changing reality of the world than the discussion of the relationship between the offices of the *mujtahid* and that of the jurisconsult, the *muftī*. Until the middle of the fifth/eleventh century, all theorists whose works are available to us maintained that for a jurisconsult to be qualified to issue legal opinions (*fatwā*s), he must have attained the rank of *mujtahid*. As we have seen in chapter 3, for a jurist to become a *mujtahid* he must fulfill a number of requirements, including an expert knowledge of the sciences of the Quran and the Sunna, as well as of the Arabic language, the doctrines

43 Āmidī, *Iḥkām*, III, 253–54.

44 For a discussion of these theorists, see Hallaq, "Was the Gate of Ijtihād Closed?," 23 ff.

of consensus and abrogation, and the art of legal reasoning. If a jurist is able to fulfill these requirements in only one area of the law, say inheritance, some theorists allow him to issue legal opinions only within the area in which he can practice *ijtihād*. Otherwise, any one who falls short of attaining the rank of a full or partial *mujtahid* may not issue legal opinions.[45]

About a century later, this doctrine underwent a fundamental change, again first reflected in Āmidī's work, although the initial traces of the shift away from the conventional doctrine are already evident in a non-theoretical work by Abū al-Walīd Ibn Rushd (d. 520/1126).[46] Āmidī now devotes to the issue a special section entitled "Whether a Non-*mujtahid* is Permitted to Issue Legal Opinions According to the School of a *Mujtahid*." We must emphasize that in the earlier theories of which we have spoken the issue is discussed in passing, normally in the chapter devoted to *ijtihād*. The initial indication of the change in Āmidī appears in the subtitle he gives to the section, "as it is the custom nowadays." But Āmidī also makes himself more explicit, saying that a *mujtahid* who is knowledgeable of the methodology of the independent *mujtahid* whom he follows and who is capable of deriving rules in accordance with this methodology is entitled to issue legal opinions. Admittedly, however, Āmidī's theory does not go so far as to approve of the practice he himself acknowledged to exist, a practice in which non-*mujtahid*s indeed functioned as jurisconsults.

But Āmidī's younger contemporary, Ibn al-Ḥājib, did concede the reality of juridical practice. He maintained that a jurist who is "knowledgeable of the doctrine of a legal school and who is able to reason properly, but who is not himself a *mujtahid* . . . is entitled to issue *fatwā*s."[47] By the middle of the seventh/thirteenth century, this doctrine had become commonplace. Ibn Daqīq al-ʿĪd (702/1302) is reported to have gone as far as to maintain that the predication of issuing legal opinion upon the attainment of *ijtihād* leads to immense difficulties, and that if the jurisconsult is known to be trustworthy and sufficiently knowledgeable of the teachings of his school then he should be considered a qualified jurisconsult. Ibn Daqīq even asserted that in his time there was a consensus on the legitimacy of this practice.[48]

Beginning in the seventh/thirteenth century, the view that a *muqallid* may function as a jurisconsult seems to have gained universal acceptance,

[45] For a detailed discussion of this issue, see Hallaq, "*Iftā'* and *Ijtihād* in Sunnī Legal Theory."

[46] See his *Fatāwā Ibn Rushd*, ed. Mukhtār b. Ṭāhir al-Talīlī, 3 vols. (Beirut: Dār al-Gharb al-Islāmī, 1978), III, 1494–1504. [47] See his *Muntahā al-Wuṣūl*, 165.

[48] Cited in Ibn Amīr al-Ḥājj, *al-Taqrīr wal-Taḥbīr: Sharḥ ʿalā Taḥrīr al-Imām al-Kamāl Ibn al-Humām*, 3 vols. (Cairo: al-Maṭbaʿa al-Kubrā al-Amīriyya, 1317/1899), III, 348, and in Shawkānī, *Irshād*, 270.

although in later commentaries (*shurūḥ*) the controversy seems to have become more complex. In these works, four distinct views are recorded with regard to this issue. According to the first, a *muqallid* is permitted to issue legal opinions provided he has mastered the teachings of his school and is able to reason correctly. The second allows him to act as a jurisconsult if and only if a *mujtahid* is nowhere to be found in the town where the questioner (*mustaftī*) resides or in its vicinity. The third permits a *muqallid* to sit for *iftāʾ*, whatever his professional qualifications. The fourth view is that of the early theorists who insisted that no *muqallid* should occupy the office of *iftāʾ*. In time the controversy was to gain an additional element. Many of those who allowed a *muqallid* to issue *fatwā*s maintained that the *muqallid* should not follow the teachings of a dead *mujtahid*. Others, however, rejected this view and argued that in actual practice there was a general agreement upon the validity of following the doctrines of a dead *mujtahid*.[49]

Thus, within a span of less than three centuries, the discourse about the jurisconsult's qualifications changed dramatically. In the middle of the fifth/eleventh century, the requirement was one dimensional – the jurisconsult had to be a *mujtahid*. By the end of the seventh/thirteenth century, however, four positions had evolved, reflecting not only the variety in the discourse relating to this issue, but also the concessions legal theory had to make in order to accommodate judicial practice in the mundane world. The reality in which *muqallid*s, not *mujtahid*s, were the vehicles of the legal system was undeniable, and theory was compelled to respond to these changes.

The evolution of this discourse also reflects the emergence of another significant feature in the history of legal theory: the role of commentaries in the later development of this theory, a role that modern scholarship has thus far ignored, with the grave consequence that commentaries have been completely dismissed as dull, unoriginal and thus unworthy of our attention. In the foregoing discussion of the relationship between *ijtihād* and the jurisconsult's qualifications, we have taken note of the fact that the later commentaries constituted a principal medium of doctrinal change. A detailed study of these writings makes it clear that the commentators often managed to deviate from or modify the doctrines of the early authorities upon whose works they were commenting. Consider, for instance ʿAbbādī, who commented on Juwaynī's short work *al-Waraqāt*. In this work, Juwaynī, like all his contemporaries and predecessors, equates the *mujtahid* with the

[49] See, for instance, ʿAbd Allāh b. ʿUmar al-Bayḍāwī, *Minhāj al-Wuṣūl ilā ʿIlm al-Uṣūl*, 3 vols. (Cairo: al-Maṭbaʿa al-Kubrā al-Amīriyya, 1317/1899), III, 331.

jurisconsult. ʿAbbādī remarks that Juwaynī's statement "the jurisconsult, namely, the *mujtahid* . . ." means either that the jurisconsult must be a *mujtahid*, or that a jurisconsult may be a *mujtahid* whenever it is possible for him to be one. Immediately thereafter, however, ʿAbbādī adds that the second interpretation is more likely. It turns out that his view of the matter, expounded at some length, is entirely consonant with, and in fact is a defense of, this second interpretation. The first he relegates to oblivion.[50]

Interpreting away the earlier doctrines to accommodate new theoretical and mundane realities was but one way in which the commentators refined legal theory and contributed to its gradual but ongoing change. The reliance on later works which had already brought about some change was another method through which the commentators carried this process further. A detailed study of the jurisconsult's qualifications as discussed in these commentaries shows that in order to justify their departure from older doctrines the commentators drew heavily upon those later authors who had already made inroads toward adapting theory to the new realities.[51] This reliance of the commentators on later doctrines was a hallmark of the change that was brought about.

The commentaries may thus be characterized as a major component of the variables in legal theory, and they hold much potential for future research. But we must be careful to distinguish among several types of commentaries, for each commentary had a particular reason for which it was written. It is possible to distinguish no less than five types of commentary on works of legal theory. The first type annotates the lexical connotations of terms and technical concepts employed by the original author, or if it is a super-commentary, by the first commentator. Although this type shows little creativity, its function for the theorists themselves was of crucial importance. Throughout the Muslim world, the Arabic language was by no means uniform; each region developed not only its own vernacular but also its local version of classical (*fuṣḥā*) technical Arabic. An Andalusian or Moroccan jurist did not always readily understand the legal language of the eastern jurists. And the passage of time had the same effect as did geographical disparity; thus, for a tenth/sixteenth century legist from Baghdad the legal language of a third/ninth century legist from Fez was less than lucid and felicitous. The role of this type of commentary was to make difficult texts lexically accessible to students and scholars alike.

The second type of commentary explicates undeveloped concepts and expands on issues raised in the original text. It is often the case that these

[50] See his *Sharḥ ʿalā Sharḥ al-Maḥallī ʿalā al-Waraqāt*, printed on the margins of Shawkānī's *Irshād*, 230. [51] See Hallaq, "*Iftā'* and *Ijtihād* in Sunnī Legal Theory."

are commentaries on short works or on abridgments of larger works authored by the commentator himself. What is significant in this process of abridging and commenting is the end-product embodied in the final commentary. A theorist may abridge a longer work, and in so doing may take liberties in selecting certain materials and in rearranging them. In writing his commentary on such an abridgment he might take further liberties in determining what is important or less important, thus emphasizing or deemphasizing issues as he sees fit. The result of this process was that the original, unabridged text had little in common with the final commentary; the latter, having passed through an abridgment, and more importantly, through the "ideological" screen of the abridger and commentator, would reflect the doctrine of this commentator and only minimally that of the original author.

The declared purpose of the third and fourth types of commentary is, respectively, to defend or criticize a particular doctrine. Some commentaries were especially written – as their authors would at times openly admit – with a view to rebutting criticism directed at a particular theory or refuting a doctrine with which they disagreed.

Finally, the fifth type has as its main concern the synthesis of theories expounded by authors belonging to different legal schools, or sometimes the divergent doctrines of a number of theorists belonging to the same school.

Most of these commentaries exhibit a certain measure of originality and creativity, not unlike the originality and creativity manifested by the authors upon whose works these commentaries were written. Like these authors, the commentators, in writing their works, were subject to influences brought about by the new realities of juridical practice as well as by the intellectual environment and scholarly traditions in which they flourished. In sum, their abridgments, and especially their commentaries, constituted the medium as well as the vehicle of doctrinal growth and change in legal theory.

But the change and growth reflected in the commentaries, and to which they indeed contributed, were gradual and seem always to have grown out of the traditional and widely accepted discourses of legal theory. Commentaries were never the medium of expressing dramatic shifts either in the constitutive structure of legal theory or, as a consequence, in substantive legal doctrines. In fact, such shifts, by their nature, required specialized treatises whose exclusive concern was to expound theories attempting to introduce these shifts. Here we shall discuss only two theories, leaving the third, which is far more complex, to the following chapter.

The first of these theories was elaborated by the Mālikite Qarāfī, the second by the Ḥanbalite Ṭūfī. Both theories were unique, and both had, perhaps because of their revolutionary nature, little effect on the constructs of other theorists. This is especially true of Qarāfī, whose innovative thought attracted no attention. Ṭūfī's theory met with the same fate, although it has been rejuvenated in recent times due to its relevance to the discourse of modernist reformers. It can safely be assumed that the failure of these two theories to gain ground in the medieval context had to do with the dramatic changes in the super- and infra-structure which their implementation would have entailed. Their implementation would have, in effect, required altering not only the face of the then existing legal system but also the basic assumptions and founding principles governing legal theory throughout its history.

Before we discuss the substance of these theories, we must say a word about *how* these should be taken as theories, for both appear, in formal terms, as parts of larger works whose purpose is not necessarily the exposition of this theory. Qarāfī's theory constitutes part of a treatise concerned, *inter alia*, with the distinctions that should be made between the jurisconsult's legal opinion (*fatwā*) and the judge's decision (*ḥukm*).[52] Ṭūfī's theory, on the other hand, is expounded as part of a work of commentary on Prophetic reports.[53] Although both of these theoretical constructs represent parts of larger sets of ideas, they contain sufficiently fundamental principles and general precepts to stand on their own as initial guidelines for a comprehensive theory of law.

Qarāfī's innovative ideas were developed around Prophetic reports, which, by the admission of many major jurists, provided the greatest bulk of raw material in elaborating the body of substantive law. We recall that the juristic "science of Prophetic reports" drew distinctions among the types of *ḥadīth* on two levels, the first of which is the mode in which a report came into being. The Prophet either utters a statement, or performs a particular act, or tacitly approves a statement uttered, or an act committed, in his presence. The second level is epistemological; reports are distinguished, in degrees of probability and certainty, according to the manner in which they were transmitted. With this in mind, a report may be put to the service of the law like any other text; its epistemological status and textual clarity (or equivocality) are the two chief hermeneutical considerations.

52 The treatise is entitled *al-Iḥkām fī Tamyīz al-Fatāwī ʿan al-Aḥkām wa-Taṣarrufāt al-Qāḍī wal-Imām*, ed. ʿIzzat al-ʿAṭṭār (Cairo: Maṭbaʿat al-Anwār, 1938), 22–29 (Question 25).

53 His theory is advanced in *Sharḥ al-Arbaʿīn al-Nawawiyya*, in the commentary on the thirty-second of forty Prophetic reports cataloged by the Shafiʿite jurist and traditionist Nawawī. The text of the commentary on this tradition is printed in Muṣṭafā Zayd, ed., *al-Maṣlaḥa fī al-Tashrīʿ al-Islāmī*, 2nd edn. (Cairo: Dār al-Fikr al-ʿArabī, 1348/1964), 206–40.

Qarāfī, however, introduces another typology of Prophetic reports, one which has far-reaching implications.[54] According to him, the Prophet functioned in four capacities: as a prophet, a jurisconsult, a judge and a head of state. After his death, the jurisconsults took up the function of the Prophet as a jurisconsult, the judges assumed his function as a judge, and the Caliph took up the Prophet's function as a head of state. Now, the legal effect of any particular report depends on the manner in which it came into being, namely, as a legal opinion, as a judicial decision or as a political act. If a Prophetic report containing a prohibition to perform an act is brought to bear upon a case of law, the question that poses itself in light of Qarāfī's classification is whether the prohibition is binding or not. For if the report turns out to be a product of the Prophet's function as a jurisconsult, then the prohibition may not be binding, since it is only an "opinion." It will, however, be binding if the report came into being as a judicial decision decreed by the Prophet in his capacity as a judge. Thus, an attempt at applying this basic conception of Prophetic reports to the existing substantive law is bound to lead to major changes in this law. What was previously deemed binding may become less so in light of the report on the basis of which the rule was derived. Conversely, what is normally understood to be a private transaction may now be considered subject to the courts' injunction and thus to state supervision.[55]

Equally important is the implication of this approach for the textually oriented legal theory. Qarāfī brings to center stage a non-textual and contextual method of interpreting the Sunna, a method that stands in sharp contrast to the prevalent hermeneutical attitude of the theorists toward this source of law. In the opinion of those theorists, the Prophetic reports, like all other revealed texts, are to be interpreted as independent, linguistic units, whose meaning is determined by the text itself and does not transgress, or permit transgression by, elements external to the text. Qarāfī's contribution to what may be seen as a limited and perhaps narrow conception of legal language lies in adding to this conception a new hermeneutical principle according to which a significant part of meaning is embedded not only in the very words subject to interpretation but also in the objective reality that gave rise to these words. In the history of legal theory, Qarāfī's conception was as unique and as innovative as it was ephemeral.

Less ephemeral was Ṭūfī's theory of *maṣlaḥa*, which he expounded as part of his commentary on the solitary Prophetic report "Do not inflict

[54] See Sherman Jackson, "From Prophetic Actions to Constitutional Theory: A Novel Chapter in Medieval Muslim Jurisprudence," *International Journal of Middle East Studies*, 25, 1 (1993): 71–90. [55] Ibid., 79.

injury or repay one injury with another." The crux of Ṭūfī's theory is the supremacy of public good and public interest among the sources of the law. *Maṣlaḥa* is defined as the means by which the intent of the Lawgiver is fulfilled either through religious and ritual worship or through mundane transactions. The former are rights owed to God by man, whereas the latter are mutual rights and obligations among people. This notion of public interest and its supremacy are anchored, according to Ṭūfī, in the aforestated report. But the epistemic status of the report raises the question of whether or not such a claim can be made on the basis of textual evidence that enjoys a degree of probability but not certainty. How, in other words, can the theory of *maṣlaḥa* be held to be superior to the Quran, the Sunna and consensus, if it is supported by nothing more than a solitary (probable) Prophetic report? Ṭūfī seems to give two interconnected answers. First, the report, when taken in isolation is indeed solitary and leads only to probability; but this report has been bolstered by other textual pieces of evidence which render it "strong" (*qawiya bil-shawāhid*). Second, all the indicants in the Quran, the Sunna and consensus attest to the truth and validity of the principle embodied in the report. If there is any practice or rule contrary to the principles of public interest, then this is nothing but an exception which aims at protecting these principles. Executing the murderer in and of itself appears to contravene the notion of protecting life, which is one of the essential ingredients of *maṣlaḥa*. But executing criminals is in fact intended to protect the lives of all members of society, first by punishing the murderer himself for what he has committed, and second by setting an example that will serve as a deterrent to others.

Since the Sharīʿa has been given to Muslims with the purpose of protecting their interests, there should be no real contradiction between *maṣlaḥa*, on the one hand, and the Quran, the Sunna and consensus, on the other. However, if there appears to be a contradiction, then the dictates of *maṣlaḥa* must be made to supersede the other sources through particularization (*takhṣīṣ*), not by setting them aside altogether. Ṭūfī does not explain how the principle of particularization may operate in solving the seeming contradiction, but he alludes to the principles of linguistic particularization[56] as well as to the particularizing and explicatory role the Prophetic reports play vis-à-vis the Quran.

It remains clear, however, that the disparity between the concept of *maṣlaḥa*, on the one hand, and the spirit and word of the law as embodied in the Quran, the Sunna and consensus, on the other, is too obvious to bypass it with such a vague solution. Ṭūfī dwells on the likely situation in

[56] On particularization, see pp. 45 ff. above.

which *maṣlaḥa* might stand in stark contrast to the dictates of the three textual sources. In such a situation *maṣlaḥa* must override the imperatives of these sources, because it is superior to the most powerful of these sources, namely, consensus. Ṭūfī reasons that if he can demonstrate that *maṣlaḥa* is superior to consensus, then he can prove that *maṣlaḥa* reigns supreme among all the sources of the law. He thus proceeds to a discussion of the authoritativeness of consensus and, by emphasizing arguments voiced by the critics of consensus, he attempts to show that the authoritative basis of this sanctioning instrument is questionable.[57]

Furthermore, Ṭūfī adduces at least three arguments in support of the proposition that *maṣlaḥa* overrides consensus as well as the two other primary sources, the Quran and the Sunna. First, he maintains, critics as well as supporters of consensus are all in agreement concerning the centrality of *maṣlaḥa*. That is to say, *maṣlaḥa* is the focus of unanimous agreement, whereas consensus and its authoritativeness are subject to disagreement. Second, textual evidence in the Quran, the Sunna and consensus is varied and at times contradictory, leading to severe disagreements among the jurists. *Maṣlaḥa*, however, is subject to no disagreement and it has thus been conducive to unity among Muslims, a unity which God has enjoined in a number of verses. Third, history has shown that a large number of influential personalities in Islam, from the Companions onwards, abandoned the evidence of the texts in favor of decisions and opinions arrived at on the basis of *maṣlaḥa*.

Against those who might argue that adopting *maṣlaḥa* as the exclusive source of the law necessarily means that the other primary sources have been entirely set aside, Ṭūfī maintains that his theory principally operates according to the universally accepted doctrine of preponderance (*tarjīḥ*), where one piece of evidence is chosen over and against another because it is superior to it. Indeed, this is one of the doctrines upon which consensus has been reached. Yes, abandoning the revealed texts unconditionally is categorically prohibited, but abandoning them in favor of other, stronger textual evidence is not. And this is what implementing *maṣlaḥa* means.

It is noteworthy that Ṭūfī nowhere defines in any detail his concept of *maṣlaḥa* and its scope. Nor do available historical sources allow us to investigate his biography in order to shed light on the possible reasons that prompted him to elaborate his novel theory. But whatever definition *maṣlaḥa* receives, it must supersede the dictates of the Quran, the Sunna and consensus. The basis of this theory of public good rests in effect on the authority of a solitary Prophetic report, but one that is corroborated by

[57] See pp. 75 ff. above.

various texts and principles to the effect that the Sharīʿa's main goal is the aversion of harm and the promotion of the community's general good. By the standards of Ṭūfī's predecessors, contemporaries and successors his theory was, epistemologically, inferior to the average theoretical discourse. And this may be another reason for the oblivion into which it sank for centuries, until it was rejuvenated again in the twentieth century, when *maṣlaḥa* became a main axis around which legal reform revolves.

LEGAL THEORY AND SUBSTANTIVE LAW

The corpus of substantive or positive law, which in fact also included procedural law, is to be found articulated in standard manuals and lengthy treatises known as "the books of *furūʿ*." Literally signifying "branches," the term *furūʿ* eloquently expresses the relationship between legal theory and substantive law. Ghazālī, we recall, conceived of law metaphorically as a tree, legal theory being the stem and the roots, and substantive law the fruits. Similarly, in the common usage and perception of the jurists throughout the centuries, *furūʿ* works, embodying substantive law, represented the growth in the tree that is neither the roots nor the stem; without the latter, the former can have no existence.

Works on substantive law were intended to render a crucial service to the jurist, be he a judge or a jurisconsult. They provided a collection of all conceivable cases so that the jurist might draw on the established doctrine of the school, and they included the most recent as well as the oldest cases of law that arose in that school. At times, they incorporated court decisions, but mostly they aimed, and succeeded, at integrating all significant and relevant *fatwā*s issued by the acknowledged, and not only the leading, jurisconsults of a particular school. In fact, the "science of *fatwā*" was often equated with the "science of substantive law," for the jurisconsult's legal opinion formed the main source from which substantive and procedural law was first constructed and later elaborated.

Although the role of court decisions in the evolution of a substantive body of law is not to be underestimated – especially during the formative period – it was the jurisconsult who seems to have provided the legal system, gradually and piecemeal, with a comprehensive *corpus juris*. Many of the court decisions incorporated into the body of positive law were deemed fit for inclusion not necessarily by virtue of the fact that they were court decisions, but rather because they underwent the juristic scrutiny of a jurisconsult before or during trial. This explains the unilateral dependence of the judge upon the jurisconsult, which was the prevailing norm: in difficult cases, judges commonly had recourse to the jurisconsults whose task it was to provide the court with a solution and (upon the special request of the judge) with a legal analysis of the case. Thus, it seems that after the formative period the body of substantive and procedural law was chiefly drawn from the contribution of the jurisconsults, and from the judges' decisions when these were either sanctioned or, alternatively, provided *in toto*, by the jurisconsult.

The fundamental role of the jurisconsult in constructing and replenishing the body of substantive and procedural law is underscored by the fact that the legal theorists were insistent throughout the centuries upon equating the *mujtahid* with the jurisconsult, not with the judge. True, unlike the magistrate's decision, the jurisconsult's legal opinion was not binding, but his opinion, by virtue of its having emanated from a highly qualified authority, became part of, and indeed defined, the law. It was the common perception in the legal profession that the judge's decision is particular (*juzʾī*) and that its import does not transcend the interests of the parties to the dispute, whereas the jurisconsults' *fatwā* is universal (*kullī*), and applicable to *all* similar cases that may arise in the future.[58]

Whether in his capacity as a private legal expert (which was commonly the case), or as an advisor to the court, the jurisconsult determined the law. When his opinion was solicited by a layman and put forth as part of the court's proceedings, it was the responsibility of the judge to establish the facts of the case. The jurisconsult's opinion was, as a rule, based upon the facts as submitted to him by the questioner (*sāʾil*).

Be that as it may, the jurisconsult had to find new solutions for those cases that had not yet occurred in his school (*madhhab*), and for those that had occurred, he had either to "transmit" the established doctrine or, when more than one opinion had been formulated, he had to give preponderance to one over the other(s). Thus, the first type of case required *ijtihād*, whereas the second required what came to be known as *al-iftāʾ bil-ḥifẓ* (merely citing the opinion of an authority, normally deceased). Preponderance was known as *tarjīḥ*.

It was the function of legal theory to provide the jurisconsult with the tools to perform his task, mainly with regard to *ijtihād* and *tarjīḥ*. Both of these constituted the desideratum behind the methodology of legal theory. Much of the energy of theorists was expended on elaborating methods and formulating principles which would be of service to the jurisconsult in the domains of *ijtihād* and *tarjīḥ*. It was not without good reason that some jurists explicitly linked their substantive law works with their treatises on

[58] For a discussion of the role played by the jurisconsult and the judge, see W. B. Hallaq, "From *Fatwās* to *Furūʿ*: Growth and Change in Islamic Substantive Law," *Islamic Law and Society*, 1 (1994), 24 ff.

legal theory. The Ḥanafite jurist Sarakhsī, for instance, declares that the theory he expounds in his work *al-Uṣūl* is intended to explain the methodology of law and legal reasoning on the basis of which he elaborated the substantive law in *al-Mabsūṭ*.[59] Qarāfī also links his substantive law as expounded in *al-Dhakhīra* with his theory of law which he laid down in *Tanqīḥ al-Fuṣūl*, making the latter the methodological prolegomenon to the former.[60]

But legal theory was in fact more than a methodology of juridical reasoning and interpretation, for some of its doctrines functioned in a double-edged manner. On the one hand, they fulfilled the immediate purpose for which they were intended, while on the other, they played, obliquely, a role in actual judicial practice. The theory of legal prepositions (*ḥurūf*), for instance, was first and foremost intended to aid in the interpretation and explication of the revealed texts so that the jurisconsult could reach, on the basis of the explicated text, a legal ruling for a new case. At the same time, however, the theory of prepositions was employed in a different domain altogether, namely, in defining the language of a disputed contract or a deed. In fact, in their efforts to settle judicial disputes concerning deeds, the jurists seem to have frequently exploited the full range of linguistic principles expounded in legal theory. What the theorist applied to the language of the Quran and the Sunna, they used to define the language of legal instruments.[61]

Other principles of legal theory played a fundamental role in developing and shaping judicial practice. The notion that *ijtihād* is wholly confined to the region of probability is one that legal theory was careful to nurture and promote. In fact, this notion was the linchpin of legal theory. But it was not the task of this theory to carry the ramifications of this notion into the field of legal practice, for this was not perceived to be within its province. A central doctrine deriving from this notion was, however, developed within the realm of judicial practice, and it had to do with judicial review or appeal. It is well known that Islam never knew an appellate structure such as that which exists in other legal systems, notably the common law and continental legal systems. But the question of whether or not one legal decision can be repealed by another was certainly raised, and the answer was, as a matter of general principle, in the negative. No ruling directly and explicitly stipulated in the revealed texts can be abrogated. And since one

59 Sarakhsī, *Uṣūl*, I, 10. 60 See his *Sharḥ Tanqīḥ al-Fuṣūl*, 2.

61 See, for example, Jalāl al-Dīn ʿAbd al-Raḥmān al-Suyūṭī, *al-Ashbāh wal-Naẓā'ir* (Beirut: Dār al-Kutub al-ʿIlmiyya, 1979), 105; David Powers, "*Fatwā*s as Sources for Legal and Social History: A Dispute over Endowment Revenues from Fourteenth-Century Fez," *al-Qanṭara*, 11 (1990): 324 ff.

ijtihād is as probable as any other, no conclusion reached on the basis of *ijtihād* can repeal another (this being expressed in the maxim *al-ijtihād lā yunqaḍ bil-ijtihād*).

Allowing for judicial review or appeal would have meant allowing one legal decision to repeal another decision of the same epistemological status – a proposition universally and categorically rejected in Sunnī (and for that matter Shīʿī) jurisprudence. Instituting judicial review as an integral part of normative judicial practice would result, in the perception of jurists, in a situation in which legal consistency and the stability of legal decisions are undermined. If one decision is made to supersede another, then this latter decision can be overridden by another *ad infinitum* – an inconceivable thought.[62] Accordingly, if a judge discovers that his decision concerning a particular case was erroneous, and he reaches, after promulgating his decision, another one, he cannot abrogate the earlier decision in favor of the later one. If an identical case is presented to the same judge at a later time, then he must pronounce the outcome of the subsequent, revised *ijtihād.*

All this is in perfect accord with the epistemological principles laid down in the chapters treating of *ijtihād* in works of legal theory. Also in accord is the doctrine that proclaims judicial review and outright repeal of an existing legal decision to be valid when it can be proven that the decision stands in violation of the dictates of scripture and/or of consensus.[63] This is not surprising. It seems that the only other ground for repealing an earlier decision is discovering that a mistake has occurred in determining the evidence on the basis of which the decision was reached. For example, if it can be determined that a written testimony, central in the case, was forged, then the decision may be rescinded. Barring evidential forgery and barring contradiction of the explicit decrees of the Quran, the Sunna and consensus, there would otherwise be no ground whatsoever for rescinding a standing decision.

Thus far we have discussed one side of the double-edged function of legal theory, namely, the effects the latter had on determining, directing and shaping judicial doctrine and practice. The other function was that for which the theory was created, that is, arriving at what the jurisconsult conceives to be the law as it exists in the mind of God. In the remainder of this chapter, we shall look at one case of law from its genesis down to the stage in which it became an integral part of the substantive law recorded in the standard legal manuals. The case illustrates not only the implementation of

[62] On this particular perception, and on judicial review in general, see Suyūṭī, *al-Ashbāh wal-Naẓāʾir*, 101–05.

[63] See David Powers, "On Judicial Review in Islamic Law," *Law and Society Review*, 26 (1992): 315–41.

legal theory in judicial practice but also the transformations that take place in the legal process, carrying a case from its moment of birth in mundane reality to its final and textual form as represented in the highest authoritative legal discourse of *furūʿ* works.

The case involves an intentional homicide which took place in the Andalusian city of Cordoba in 516/1122.[64] The victim left behind three children – the oldest of whom reached the age of four at the time of the incident – and one brother who had two adult sons. The case was adjudicated in the Mālikite school, according to a *fatwā* issued by Ibn al-Ḥājj (d. 529/1134) and a number of other jurisconsults. The murderer, having admitted his guilt, was executed at the instigation of the victim's brother and his sons. The fact that the murderer was inebriated at the time he committed the crime was judged to be entirely irrelevant. The death-penalty verdict was perfectly in conformity with the established, authoritative Mālikite doctrine according to which the children of the murder victim, should they be minors, must waive the right to demand punishment in favor of other agnates, in this case their paternal uncle and his sons.[65]

The leading Mālikite judge and jurisconsult Ibn Rushd categorically rejected the *fatwā*s of his contemporaries, however. In a *fatwā* which he issued with regard to the same case, he asserted that the victim's children must be allowed to reach the age of majority before any sentence should be passed, whereupon they may seek the murderer's punishment, monetary compensation or a pardon without compensation. He also insisted that the traditionally held doctrine was inconsistent with the general legal and hermeneutical principles of the Mālikite school since it was derived by means of the method of juristic preference and not through the commonly accepted method of *qiyās*. The latter method – which, he insisted, must be followed – dictates a departure from the authoritative doctrine of the school.

In reasoning according to *qiyās*, Ibn Rushd first cites Q. 17:33: "Whoso is slain unjustly, We have given power unto his heir, but let him [the heir] not commit excess in slaying [the murderer]." While this verse clearly assigns to the "heir" the right to demand punishment, it does not determine who the "heir" is. Another relevant verse (2:178) compounds the ambiguity: "And for him who is forgiven somewhat by his murdered brother, prosecution according to established custom and payment unto

[64] On intentional homicide, see p. 86 above.

[65] Ibn Rushd, *Fatāwā*, II, 1196–97; Aḥmad b. Yaḥyā al-Wansharīsī, *al-Miʿyār al-Mughrib wal-Jāmiʿ al-Muʿrib ʿan Fatāwī ʿUlamāʾ Ifrīqiyya wal-Andalus wal-Maghrib*, 13 vols. (Beirut: Dār al-Maghrib al-Islāmī, 1401/1981), II, 319; Muḥammad al-Ḥaṭṭāb, *Mawāhib al-Jalīl li-Sharḥ Mukhtaṣar Khalīl*, 6 vols. (Tripoli: Maktabat al-Najāḥ, 1969), VI, 252.

him in kindness." The referent of "him who is forgiven" is equivocal, for it may be the agnates of the victim or the murderer himself. In other words, the verse does not clearly establish whether or not the murderer (or his agnates) has the right to refuse the payment of blood-money and to insist, contrary to the wishes of the victim's agnates, on the death-penalty. In clarification of this ambiguity, Ibn Rushd cites a Prophetic report which states: "The victim's kin may opt for the death penalty or may pardon the murderer and receive blood-money." From this, Ibn Rushd took the murderer's consent to be immaterial, since what is at stake is only the wishes of the victim's agnates.

Thus far, Ibn Rushd has shown us the basic lines of reasoning and the textual basis on which the case rests. The central question remains, however: Who is entitled to demand the murderer's punishment – or, alternatively, payment of blood-money – the children of the victim or his brother? In support of the children's right, Ibn Rushd refers to analogous cases in other areas of the law where the children's right is protected until they reach majority. One such area is preemption, defined as the right of a person to take the place of the purchaser in acquiring ownership of real property, by virtue of his interest as a co-owner, a sharer in right of way, or an adjoining neighbor.[66] Nearly all jurists hold that upon reaching the age of majority, the children of the deceased are fully entitled to exercise their right of preemption. Thus, if the immediate neighbor sold his property to a third party while they were minors, the third party must, on pain of violating the law, resell the property to them if they so wish upon their reaching the age of majority. The same principle applies to other cases involving the destruction or usurpation of a minor's property; the minor is entitled to full compensation when he or she becomes of age. Ibn Rushd maintains that precluding the agnates from acting on behalf of the minors in these cases must, by analogy, also apply to the case of homicide at hand, especially in light of the fact that a consensus, based on *qiyās*, has been reached concerning the preservation of minors' rights until they reach the age of majority.

But the conclusions of *qiyās* in this case were in fact set aside in favor of juristic preference, which would have entitled the children to exercise their rights if they were reasonably close to the age of majority at the time of the murder. As this was not the case, it was the uncle and his sons who exercised the right to have the murderer punished. The reasoning appears to have taken the following form: since the consent of the murderer to pay

66 Mālikite law, however, does not recognize the right of an adjoining neighbour to preemption. See Farhat Ziadeh, "Shufʿah: Origins and Modern Doctrine," *Cleveland State Law Review*, 34 (1985–86): 35.

blood-money was required, and since such a payment was in no way contingent upon the wishes of the "heirs," the only unimpeded right these "heirs" may have had was to demand either the murderer's punishment or his pardon without any monetary compensation. The presumption seems to be that the potential refusal of the murderer to pay blood-money *a fortiori* precluded the right of the agnates to such a payment. Theoretically, therefore, the agnates were left with the choice of either seeking to inflict the death penalty or pardoning without monetary compensation. An integral part of this *istiḥsān* argument is that punishment (which amounts to avenging the blood of the victim) and not forgiveness should be the only resort, for the Quran stipulates that "there is life for you in retaliation" (2:179). Ibn Rushd argues that in giving effect to this verse, the jurists who reasoned on the basis of *istiḥsān* intended the death penalty to act as a deterrent against murder. And since no monetary compensation was involved, they further reasoned that the right to demand punishment could be assigned to the uncle and his sons without this being in any way detrimental to the children.

But the fundamental assumption that retaliation must override compensation or forgiveness – which in fact predetermines the rule in the case – is challenged by Ibn Rushd on Quranic grounds. Against the aforementioned verse (2:179), he enlists three verses, all to the effect that God recommends forgiveness over retaliation. In support of the theme expressed in these verses, he adduces, among other things, a report in which the Prophet also recommends pardoning. Thus, if pardoning is a right and an option which is as valid as retaliation, then it is the children who must decide in the matter when they attain the age of majority. At that time, they may demand the murderer's execution, or they may instead pardon him.

Add to all this the fact that the murderer was intoxicated when he committed the crime, a fact which, Ibn Rushd argues, brings to the fore the flaws involved in reasoning by *istiḥsān*. Although intoxication does not constitute a ground for total vindication, it must be considered, he maintains, a mitigating factor. Taking into consideration this fact brings into sharper focus the contrast between the *istiḥsān*-based verdict of execution and the *qiyās*-based conclusion which insists on the less severe penalty of monetary compensation or even an unconditional pardon. Ibn Rushd claims that a consensus has been reached concerning the mitigated punishment of an inebriated murderer. This consensus further dictates that the children must be allowed to reach the age of majority before making their decision, for they might well opt for pardoning.

Now, this *fatwā* presents us, in the context of legal theory, with two noteworthy features. First, in arguing his case, Ibn Rushd has drawn extensively on the principles of legal theory. In accordance with this theory, he marshals all relevant Quranic verses, then Prophetic reports, followed by the pertinent issues upon which consensus has been reached. Within the realm of consensus, he adduces a number of what may be called subsidiary arguments to bolster his legal reasoning, including cases of substantive law relating to preemption and damages. Ibn Rushd's *fatwā* thus represents one instance in which legal theory is brought to bear upon actual cases of substantive law, cases that originated in a concrete social reality.

Second, Ibn Rushd felt free to challenge a legal doctrine that was not only unquestioned in his school but also had no competing counterpart. This indicates the room allotted to the exercise of *ijtihād* in Islamic law, despite the fact that this *ijtihād* is conducted against an established doctrine. In other words, not only was his *ijtihād*, *ipso facto*, an innovation, but in advancing it he challenged what was considered to be an unrivaled doctrine of Mālikism. Ibn Rushd's contribution can by no means be considered an exception, and when considered alongside many of the other jurisconsults' *fatwā*s in which *ijtihād* was practiced, it becomes only too easy to dismiss the claim that the "gate of *ijtihād*" was closed.[67]

The significance of Ibn Rushd's contribution becomes more pronounced in light of the fact that it was later incorporated into the standard law manuals of the Mālikite school. It is only to be expected that, in a legal system that sought the highest degree of comprehensiveness, *fatwā*s that contained *ijtihād* were, as a rule, included in the manuals of substantive law (*furūʿ*) as well as in commentaries and super-commentaries on such manuals. A study of some of the more highly reputable manuals that were written during the few centuries after Ibn Rushd reveals that this *fatwā*, along with many others, was assimilated – after having been stripped of its particular characteristics[68] – into these manuals to become part and parcel of the standard doctrine of substantive law.

With the incorporation of *fatwā*s into the standard manuals of substantive law the circle of the legal process is closed. A new case provokes a new rule based on textual evidence, a set of hermeneutical principles and various methods of reasoning. The rule is applied to the case, which occurs in a highly particularized circumstance. The case along with the rule, having been validated by the jurists, is then abstracted and transplanted into the

[67] For a revision of this claim, see Hallaq, "Was the Gate of Ijtihād Closed?" 3–41; Hallaq, "The Controversy about the Existence of Mujtahids," 129–41.

[68] Such as the actual names of persons involved, and other details irrelevant to the law. For a detailed account of the modalities of incorporating this *fatwā*, and for the controversy surrounding it in substantive legal doctrine, see W. B. Hallaq, "Murder in Cordoba: *Ijtihād*, *Iftā'* and the Evolution of Substantive Law in Medieval Islam," *Acta Orientalia*, 55 (1994): 67–74. For the modalities of incorporating *fatwā*s in general, see Hallaq, "From *Fatwā*s to *Furūʿ*," 42–52.

substantive legal corpus, where, by virtue of its having been admitted therein, it becomes part of the jurisconsults' reference (or library, if you will). Any new case that arises thereafter must first be checked against those relevant cases contained in that corpus. If no "precedent" is found, then *ijtihād* must be exercised. But if a case in the legal corpus proves to be identical or so similar to it as to justify treating it as that case, then the jurisconsult must apply the rule in the "precedent" to the new case. This is where legal consistency becomes most evident; a legal doctrine that has been established must not be abandoned or ignored unless there is good reason to do so. This is a requirement insisted upon by both the legal theorists and the specialists of substantive law.

5

SOCIAL REALITY AND THE RESPONSE OF THEORY

INTRODUCTION

IN the foregoing chapter, the main variables to be found in the body of legal theory were highlighted with a view to demonstrating the variety of factors that exercised influence in shaping this theory throughout the centuries. In the present chapter I shall expand on the theme of relationships between legal theory as abstracted discourse and the worldly and mundane elements that contributed to the form, substance and direction of this discourse. We shall concentrate on Abū Isḥāq al-Shāṭibī's (d. 790/1388) legal theory not only in order to illustrate these significant relationships, but also because his was a theory that represented the culmination of an intellectual development that started as early as the fourth/tenth century. By his time, legal theory had reached such a high level of maturity that it was capable of being entirely remolded – as it indeed was – while maintaining its traditional function of discovering the law and regulating its continual creation and, to some extent, functioning. But the choice of Shāṭibī here has more than meets the eye. While his theory exemplifies a distinctive reaction to a particular worldly and social reality, it has also played an important role in modern legal reform. In this respect, it will be interesting to see, on the one hand, how Shāṭibī's theory was understood and put to use by modern legal reformists (the concern of the next and final chapter), and, on the other, the actual historical circumstances that gave rise to it, and which, ultimately, endowed it with its defining characteristics.

The uniqueness of Shāṭibī's theory, some scholars have argued, stems from the fact that Shāṭibī, realizing the failure of law in meeting the challenges of socio-economic change in eighth-/fourteenth-century Andalusia, tried in his theory to answer the particular needs of his time by showing how it was possible to adapt law to the new social conditions.[1] In this chapter, I shall maintain that while it is true to argue for an intimate connection between Shāṭibī's theory and the juridico-social practices prevailing at his time, the causes that gave rise to his theory were by no means embedded in a desire to create a theoretical apparatus which would provide for flexibility and adaptability in positive law. Rather, we shall insist that Shāṭibī's theory, for all its ingenuity and novel character, aimed at restoring what its author perceived to be the true law of Islam, a law which he thought was adulterated by two extreme practices in his day, namely, the lax attitudes of the jurisconsults and, far more importantly, the excessive legal demands imposed by what seems to have been the majority of contemporary Ṣūfīs, in whose ranks there must have been a certain population of legal scholars. A careful reading of his work on legal theory, *al-Muwāfaqāt*,[2] especially in conjunction with his other quasi-juridical work *al-Iʿtiṣām*,[3] reveals beyond any shadow of doubt that the main thrust of his theoretical exposition is directed at the mystics of his time, who, judging from his subtle references and allusions, were a powerful force advocating, *inter alia*, what he thought to be a rigid and unduly demanding application of the law.[4]

In his *Iʿtiṣām*, which he wrote in refutation of the charge that he had deviated from the true religious path and that he was a religious innovator (*mubdiʿ*), he lists six positions which he is accused of having maintained. The first three consist of charges that he held certain subversive views. But more relevant for our concerns are the fourth, fifth and sixth charges. In the fourth, which clearly emanates from the jurists' camp, he is said to have been stringent in his legal views, demanding the application of laws that lead to hardship. "What caused them to charge me with this," Shāṭibī replies, "is my commitment to issue legal opinions in conformity with the dominant and widely accepted (*mashhūr*) doctrines in our [Mālikite] school . . . But they do transgress the limits of the school's doctrines by issuing legal opinions that deviate from the *mashhūr*, opinions agreeable to the people and their pleasures."[5] The fifth is the accusation that he adopted an inimical attitude toward the Ṣūfīs and publicly preached against their

1 Khalid Masud, *Islamic Legal Philosophy: A Study of Abū Isḥāq al-Shāṭibī's Life and Thought* (Islamabad: Islamic Research Institute, 1977), v, 35, 101.

2 *al-Muwāfaqāt fī Uṣūl al-Aḥkām*, ed. M. Muḥyī al-Dīn ʿAbd al-Ḥamīd, 4 vols. (Cairo: Maṭbaʿat Muḥammad ʿAlī Ṣubayḥ, 1970).

3 Ed. Muḥammad Rashīd Riḍā, 2 vols. (repr.; Riyadh: Maktabat al-Riyāḍ al-Ḥadītha, n.d.).

4 See *Muwāfaqāt*, I, 208, 241 ff.; II, 181 ff., and throughout. It must be emphasized that Shāṭibī, apparently fearing the Ṣūfī backlash, frequently refers to the mystics he criticizes as pseudo-Ṣūfīs. In his *Iʿtiṣām* (I, 89–90), he states that the genuine Ṣūfīs, such as Abū al-Qāsim al-Qushayrī and Sahl al-Tustarī, did not consider themselves above observing the law as stipulated by the legal specialists.

5 *Iʿtiṣām*, I, 11–12.

"heretical" practices. Finally, he is accused of deviating from the religious community (*jamāʿa*). "This accusation," he argues, "is based on the assumption that the community, which must be followed, is [defined as] that of the majority. They [his accusers] do not realize, however, that the upright community is that which follows the example of the Prophet, his Companions and their followers."[6] In other words, it is not the size or sheer number that counts, but rather the quality of the practices prevailing in a society. In this society Shāṭibī observed many innovations, increments and flaws, and he chose, at the risk of being persecuted, to oppose them.[7]

Viewing Shāṭibī's theory as a response to these practices explains the emphasis and deemphasis he placed on the topics with which he dealt, and accounts for his choice in including or excluding certain topics. Most of all, it accounts for his novel epistemology which became necessary in order to sustain the demands of his theory, i.e., to restore the law to what he deemed to be its pristine form. This form was presented by Shāṭibī as a middle-of-the-road position between two objectionable extremes; on the one hand stood fanatic and unduly excessive application of the law, and on the other, unwarranted leniency, if not virtual neglect, in applying the paradigmatic doctrine (*madhhab*) of substantive law.

If we take Shāṭibī's *Muwāfaqāt* to constitute a field of discourse as well as a legal polemic (as we shall show in due course to be the case) it becomes easier to understand the role he intended his epistemology to play in his theory. His aim was not only to criticize but also, and perhaps primarily, to persuade. And persuasion not only dictated a measure of repetition and reaffirmation of his arguments throughout his work; it also required him to have systematic recourse to the epistemological category of certainty which he considered to be his greatest weapon against his adversaries. Epistemology, then, formed both the cornerstone of Shāṭibī's theory and the linchpin of his persuasive discourse.

EPISTEMOLOGY REFASHIONED

Like all other legal theorists, Shātibī posits certitude as the epistemic foundation of the sources of the law.[8] Conversely, these sources do not partake in probability, for if they are to be tainted with anything less than certainty, the entire legal edifice would become questionable and, indeed, doubtful. If probability is to be predicated of the sources of law, which include among other things the Quran and the Sunna, then probability may be

[6] Ibid., I, 12. [7] Ibid., I, 10.

[8] Shāṭibī discusses the epistemological principles in a number of places in his *Muwāfaqāt*, but the main ideas may be found in vol. I, 10 ff.; II, 4 ff.

predicated of the fundamentals of theology (*uṣūl al-dīn*) which prove the existence of God and the truthfulness of Muhammad's prophethood; and this is utterly unthinkable.

Shāṭibī posits another postulate, namely, that all the fundamental premises (*muqaddimāt*) of legal theory are certain. These premises may be rational, conventional or revelational. In the mind, things fall into three categories – the necessary, the possible and the impossible. The same is true of the conventional premises. The habitual course of events, or convention, dictates that it is impossible for gold to become copper. And reason dictates that the number two, when multiplied by itself, must, as a matter of necessity, yield the number four. Whatever the case, these premises are certain. The revelational premises are also certain because their meaning is unequivocal and because they have been multiply transmitted, either through recurrent thematic reports (*tawātur maʿnawī*) or through recurrent verbal reports (*tawātur lafẓī*),[9] or, furthermore, through a fairly exhaustive inductive survey of the entirety of Sharʿī material.

From this point on, Shāṭibī parts company with the other theorists. The epistemic foundations of his theory turn out to be anchored not in any multiply transmitted report or Quranic verse, but rather in comprehensive inductive surveys of all relevant evidence, be it textual or otherwise. The probability of solitary reports is quite obvious and universally acknowledged, and the certainty of *tawātur lafẓī* (through which the Quran itself is transmitted) hinges upon premises, most, if not all, of which cannot be known for certain to be true. The transmission of language from person to person, over a long period of time, is an uncertain affair, especially if the language is, as is most often the case, laden with complicated structures – metaphors, homonyms, etc. – which are not readily transmittable without some sort of distortion. Therefore, the truly reliable premises, according to Shāṭibī, are those that have been culled through a broad inductive survey of a large number of probable pieces of evidence all sharing one theme, so large in fact that in their totality they yield certitude. It is through such means, for instance, that the five pillars of Islam, such as prayer and fasting, are known with certainty to be mandatory.

This method of evidential corroboration clearly resembles multiply transmitted Prophetic reports of the thematic kind (*tawātur maʿnawī*). But the quality of the contents generated by Shāṭibī's method is vastly more diverse than that of the latter. The material from which *al-tawātur al-maʿnawī* derives is limited to Prophetic reports, whereas inductive corroboration as Shāṭibī defines it draws on a wide variety of evidential support, ranging

9 See pp. 60–65 above.

from the Quran and the Sunna to consensus, *qiyās* and contextual evidence (*qarā'in al-aḥwāl*).[10] When a large or sufficient number of pieces of evidence converge to confirm one idea, notion, or principle, the knowledge of that idea or principle becomes engendered in the mind with certainty because the confluence of the evidence has the effect of a virtually complete, if not perfect, inductive corroboration.[11] Shāṭibī forthrightly declares, and this is significant, that this mode of cultivating evidence lies at the foundations of his own method in constructing his theory and arguments in *al-Muwāfaqāt.*

For example, the five fundamental universals for the protection of which the Sharīʿa was instated – namely, the preservation of life, property, progeny, mind and religion – do not find attestation in any particular piece of conclusive evidence, either in the Quran or the Sunna. Yet, the knowledge of these universals is enshrined with certainty in the collective mind of the Muslim community as well as in the minds of Muslim individuals. This certainty is engendered by virtue of the fact that these principles have been attested to by a wide variety of pieces of evidence, which, in their totality, lead to certitude, although when taken individually they do not rise above the level of probability.

It is precisely this method of inductive corroboration on a large scale that draws the line between legal theory – dealing with what has been characterized as "the roots of the law" – and substantive law, the latter depicted, in accordance with the same metaphor, as the branches of that law (*furūʿ*). These individual substantive rules are based on particular pieces of evidence, such as a Prophetic report or a Quranic verse. And most of these are probable, thus resulting in rules that are by and large removed from certainty. The theory of the "roots," on the other hand, is grounded in such an extensive body of evidence that, although the particular pieces of this evidence may be probable, they result, due to their mutual corroboration, in certainty. Consensus, juristic preference and public interest are but three constituent parts of this theory whose authoritativeness (*ḥujjiyya*) is justified by this method of corroboration. For example, there exists no Quranic verse or highly reliable Prophetic report that explicitly states the infallibility of the Muslim community. And yet, the authoritativeness of consensus can be demonstrated on the basis of verses, reports and other circumstantial pieces of evidence which have *in common* the indubitable theme of the inerrancy of the Muslim community.

Seen from a different angle, the major constituents of legal theory, such

[10] On *qarā'in al-aḥwāl*, see W. B. Hallaq, "Notes on the Term *Qarīna* in Islamic Legal Discourse," *Journal of the American Oriental Society*, 108 (1988): 475–80.

[11] See Hallaq, "Inductive Corroboration," 24–29.

as consensus and public interest, are made up of universal principles, or simply universals (*kulliyyāt*), as Shāṭibī calls them. "These universals constitute the foundations of the Sharīʿa,"[12] and each of them is formed on the basis of a multiplicity of particulars (*juzʾiyyāt*; sing. *juzʾī*), all of which attest to one meaning or theme embodying that universal. On the other hand, a particular must necessarily be subsumed under one universal or another, for if it stands in solitude it cannot be of service in legal theory. A universal is thus nothing without the particulars of which it consists; it enters the realm of existence only by virtue of the particulars that give it its form and content. Here, Shāṭibī joins the company of many a Muslim theologian in adopting a nominalist stance, advocating the view that no universal exists extra-mentally; only particulars do. Adopting a universal that lacks substantiation by particulars amounts therefore to adopting an unfounded thesis.

The particular is by definition a part of the universal, for to utter the term "particular" is to imply an entity of which the particular forms a part, and this entity is the universal. The same applies to the term "universal," which implies the subsumption of particulars. This dialectical relationship between the universal and its particulars dictates that the setting aside of a particular is detrimental to the cognate universal; conversely, considering a universal while neglecting to consider its constituent particulars would undermine that universal.

Since a conclusive universal cannot be reached without the enumeration of all the particulars belonging to its class, there can be no particular instance that is relevant, yet at the same time contrary, to the universal. For if it were relevant and were not taken into consideration in inductive enumeration, then the universal would merely be a pseudo-universal, and therefore revocable. But what if a diverging particular surfaces only after a universal has been established on the basis of a multitude of other supporting particulars? Arguably, in legal matters, it is normative to establish general principles on the basis of the great majority, but not the consummate totality, of the extractable evidence. Thus, once the five fundamental universals – of protecting life, property, progeny, etc. – are established, law must be interpreted according to them, and any particular, hitherto not considered, must be either subsumed under these universals or, if it is a non-conforming particular, it must be left out. Still, such particulars must be accounted for, since they could not have been decreed purposelessly. But explaining how Shāṭibī accounts for non-conforming particulars presupposes certain assumptions and propositions relating to what he calls the aims or intentions of the law (*maqāṣid al-Sharīʿa*).

[12] *Muwāfaqāt*, III, 4.

THE AIMS OF THE LAW

Following very closely Ghazālī's taxonomy,[13] Shāṭibī perceives the existential purpose of the Sharīʿa to be the protection and promotion of three legal categories, which he calls *ḍarūriyyāt*, *ḥājiyyāt*, and *taḥsīniyyāt*.[14] The aim of these in turn is to ensure that the interests (*maṣāliḥ*) of Muslims are preserved in the best of fashions in this world and in the hereafter, for God, Shāṭibī insists (treading in the footsteps of the Muʿtazilites) acts according to the best interests of His subjects. "The Sharīʿa was instituted for [the promotion of] the good of believers" (*al-Sharīʿa . . . wuḍiʿat li-maṣāliḥ al-ʿibād*).[15]

The *ḍarūriyyāt* (lit. necessities), which comprise the five aforementioned universals, signify those aspects of the law that are absolutely necessary for the proper functioning of religious and mundane affairs. Any rupture in these will necessarily result in disorder and chaos in this world, and in a less than happy state in the life to come. The *ḍarūriyyāt* are maintained by two means: on the one hand, they are enhanced and strengthened, while on the other, all harm that may be about to affect them is averted. Religious worship, for instance, aims to promote religion and law insofar as faith and its ritual aspects, such as prayer, fasting and pilgrimage, are concerned. Customary and daily practices regulated by law are also intended to preserve life and mind insofar as mundane existence is concerned, such as taking food, shelter, clothing, etc. Contractual, commercial and other transactions aim at perpetuating progeny and safeguarding property. On the other hand, any harm that might threaten the *ḍarūriyyāt* may be averted by means of penal law as well as other types of punishment, damages and compensation, which ensure the orderly functioning of the five universals subsumed under the *ḍarūriyyāt*.

The *ḥājiyyāt* (lit. needs) signify those aspects of the law that are needed in order to alleviate hardship so that the law can be followed without causing distress or predicament. The admission of the *ʿarāyā* contract which involves risk,[16] and the abridgment of ritual obligations under circumstances of hardship and illness, are two examples of relaxing the law when the need to accommodate the exigencies of daily life arises. These mitigated laws are *needed* in order to make the life and legal practice of Muslims tolerable.

13 See pp. 88 ff. above. 14 *Muwāfaqāt*, II, 4 ff. 15 Ibid., II, 3.

16 *ʿArāyā* is a type of contract in which unripe dates on the palm tree are bartered against their value calculated in terms of edible dried dates. Although Islamic law does not allow the element of risk in contractual transactions, the *ʿarāyā* contract was recognized despite the risk and uncertainty it involves. See Subkī, *Takmilat al-Majmūʿ*, XI, 2 ff.

The *taḥsīniyyāt* (lit. improvements) refer to those aspects of the law such as the recommendations to free slaves, to perform ablution before prayer, to be charitable to the poor, etc. These are not needed to such an extent that without them the law becomes inoperable or deficient, and relinquishing them is not detrimental to the *ḍarūriyyāt* or the *taḥsīniyyāt*, but they certainly *improve* the general character of the Sharīʿa.

In light of this taxonomy of interests (*maṣāliḥ*) placed in the service of the aims of the law (*maqāṣid*), we can turn back to the epistemic problem of how to account for a particular that does not conform to a universal. Let us take as an illustration the *ʿarāyā* contract, which stands in sharp contrast to the standard contractual principles of the Sharīʿa, and yet is deemed a valid contract. This exception, one of a great many, belongs in fact to that category of universals known as *ḥājiyyāt*. For, after all, the function of this last category is to mitigate the stiff demands of the category known as *ḍarūriyyāt*. The emergence of a universal, it will be noted, is the result of the existence of a number of exceptions *sufficient* to produce another universal. Accordingly, failure to account for exceptions will ultimately lead to the undermining of the second and third categories, namely, the *ḥājiyyāt* and the *taḥsīniyyāt*. Setting aside non-conforming particulars will neither serve the interests of man, nor be faithful to the intent of the law, for the Lawgiver could not have decreed them in vain. However, if a particular continues to contradict any of the three categories, Shāṭibī maintains, then it must be set aside.

But how does this assertion square with his previous statement that non-conforming particulars should be accounted for? The three categories, he argues, represent, as noted earlier, the *raison d'être* of the law and there should therefore be no particular that stands in opposition to them. If there appears to be a particular contravening a given universal, then the said particular must have been revealed to protect another universal principle or to undergird another aspect of the same universal. Capital punishment, a particular, surely contradicts the subcategory of *ḍarūriyyāt* which calls for the protection and preservation of human life. Although killing the murderer is in and of itself an act violating this principle, it is absolutely necessary to maintain that very principle; one life is taken to protect another (by the logic of deterrence). Shāṭibī insists that a non-conforming particular can never undermine a universal, much less the three categories. "In Sharīʿa," he says, "the great majority of particulars [constituting a universal] are considered tantamount to a conclusive general, since the instances diverging from a universal cannot constitute another universal which can then compete with the first established universal."[17] They cannot

[17] *Muwāfaqāt*, II, 37.

constitute another universal because they can only be isolated exceptions. Thus, only universals count, for they are conclusive and as such they are in no way subject to revocation.

As the five universals subsumed under the highest-ranking category of *ḍarūriyyāt* are epistemologically certain, they may not be set aside or violated. In fact, any violation affecting this category produces far-reaching consequences that go beyond the five universals. The two other categories, being structurally subservient and substantively complementary to the *ḍarūriyyāt*, will be adversely affected, although any damage affecting the *taḥsīniyyāt* will only partially affect the *ḥājiyyāt*. The same applies to the relationship between this latter and the highest category: any deficiency in the *ḥājiyyāt* will result only in a minor disturbance in the *ḍarūriyyāt*. Accordingly, in order to ensure the integrity of the law and the purposes for which it was revealed, it is essential to preserve the three categories in the order of their importance; that is to say, beginning with the *ḍarūriyyāt* and ending with the *taḥsīniyyāt*.

An essential part of protecting and promoting the purposes of the law is the willing acceptance of the fact that the benefits accruing to man in this world and the hereafter must be understood to be relative, not absolute. Put differently, no benefit can be attained without it being faintly marred by some sort of hardship. For instance, all the benefits regulated by the law concerning livelihood – such as securing food, clothing and shelter – entail hardship, albeit tolerable. So are harmful deeds which are preeminently injurious, but which may also result in some good. Thus, the crux of the matter is that benefit and harm are relative, being distinguished from each other by the amount of harm embodied in each act producing them. The purpose of the law is the protection and promotion of those acts that are predominantly beneficial, and the discouragement and prohibition of those overshadowed by harm and undue hardship.

Benefit and harm, on the other hand, are not absolutely relative. Their promotion and prohibition, respectively, are predicated upon an established and fixed paradigm where benefit and harm are in no way determined by considerations of secular public good. Rather, the overriding consideration in determining benefit and harm, together with the legal value that should be attached to each act falling under either heading, is the construction of a legally sound system of behavior in this life, thereby preparing one for life in the hereafter. Bringing individuals in line with the commands of the law as prescribed by God, and curbing their personal desires and whims, are precisely the reasons for which the Sharīʿa was decreed. It follows, therefore, that any act resulting from a purely personal consideration and violating the letter and spirit of the law is utterly forbidden.

At this juncture, Shāṭibī directs his attention to legal knowledge (*ʿilm sharʿī*) and to those who consider themselves to have some command of it. He asserts, with a great deal of force, that lawful *ʿilm* is that which leads to action (*ʿamal*) in accordance with the Sharīʿa. This proposition allows him to launch an attack (which he will follow by another, much later in the book) on what he calls "evil religious scholars" who preach the ideal of the law but themselves act, and advise others to act, according to considerations of personal desire and interest.[18] The knowledge these scholars possess is nothing but pseudo-knowledge, to be sharply distinguished from real legal knowledge – this latter encompassing all actions and behavior that stand in perfect accord with the law. Between these two, a third type of knowledge is posited, namely, abused knowledge. Fanatic and intolerant preaching of religious and legal knowledge, excessive scrutiny in the science of authenticating Prophetic reports, and the extreme practices of the Ṣūfīs (whose demands make it impossible for the average person to adhere to the law) are all examples he gives of this type of knowledge.

In countering all these practices, Shāṭibī offers a fundamental proposition on the basis of which he continues to elaborate his critical theory. The Sharīʿa, like the Prophet who transmitted it, is not "lettered" (*ummiyya*), this carrying the clear implication that it was revealed in a language that the unlettered Arabs could readily understand. Thus, Shāṭibī asserts, for us to understand the true meaning of the Quran we should always take into consideration how the Arabs of the Prophet's Arabia would have understood the text. Any notion contrary or alien to the familiar ways in which the Arabs communicated among themselves at that time ought to be discarded and must not be employed in interpreting the language of the revealed texts. Words should be assigned meanings within the bounds of Arab linguistic conventions, thus utterly avoiding idiosyncratic and odd interpretations.

The unlettered nature of revelation also means that the association of the Quran with "foreign" rational sciences, such as logic, physics and metaphysics, has no justification whatsoever. Subjecting the Quran to interpretations in accordance with the governing principles of these sciences leads to conceptions at variance with those originally intended by God when He revealed it through the Prophet. Add to that the alien nature of such interpretations. Consider, for instance, the difference between the unlettered and the excessively complicated (here philosophical) definition of such a word as "angel," definitions which are thought necessary in order to form a conception (*taṣawwur*) of things. Whereas the unlettered definition is

[18] On these practices in his own days, see *Iʿtiṣām*, II, 353 ff.

simply "that which is created by God and which acts in obedience to Him," the philosophical definition is that it is "a quiddity abstracted from matter." This latter definition represents the undue complexity that might encroach upon the law and which causes its alienation from the ordinary individual for whom, after all, the law was intended. Therefore, it is essential that law must be elucidated in a way that makes it possible for the ordinary folk to readily understand all their obligations in the areas of both worship and mundane transactions. Excessively elaborate and technical exposition of the law will prevent such understanding, and will alienate a major segment of the public from proper legal practice.

Alienating any part of the community due to excessive profundity is thus forbidden, and must be avoided at any expense. For universality in the application of the law is a fundamental feature of the Sharīʿa: it is universal in the sense that *all* Muslims are *equally* subject to *all* its decrees in the same way. No adult Muslim who possesses a sound mind (*mukallaf*) is exempt from any of its ordinances. Exceptions, Shāṭibī insists, simply do not exist.

What is the significance of this assertion? Shāṭibī is only too willing and able to provide an explanation. Those who do not understand the aims or intentions of the Law think that the Ṣūfīs are entitled to follow sets of laws different from, and in fact superior to, those applicable to the ordinary members of the community. This faulty perception of the special status accorded to the Ṣūfīs led some to argue for the existence of a duality in the law. It is said, Shāṭibī reports, that when a Ṣūfī shaykh was asked a question with regard to the alms-tax, he gave two different answers, one in accordance with the teachings of the Ṣūfī "school" (*madhhab*), the other with the legal school of the questioner.[19] But this is not all. These Ṣūfīs, perceiving themselves to be superior to the masses, consider themselves subject to a distinct law which absolves them from prohibitions otherwise applicable to non-Ṣūfīs. An example in point, says Shāṭibī, is the common Ṣūfī practice of chanting (*ghināʾ*) which "we [i.e., the jurists] have declared to be prohibited."[20]

Just as legal rules are equally applicable to, and binding upon, all Muslims, so are the Prophet's own virtues and characteristics which he, as part of his Sunna, bequeathed to the entirety of his community, without any preference for one group of Muslims over another. Here, Shāṭibī enumerates thirty types of such Prophetic virtues and traits, including mercy, wisdom and immunity against heretical errors – an immunity which, we may recall, formed the authoritative basis of consensus in the writings of

19 *Muwāfaqāt*, II, 181. 20 Ibid.; Shāṭibī, *Iʿtiṣām*, I, 264 f.; II, 348 f.

legal theorists. But one particular characteristic emerges as central, namely, Prophetic miracles. After devoting a lengthy section to discussing the legitimacy of the miraculous acts performed by Ṣūfī saints,[21] Shāṭibī arrives at the expected conclusion that no act, miraculous or otherwise, is deemed legitimate unless it has a precedential basis (*aṣl*) in the Sunna of the Prophet. If the alleged saintly miracle finds a parallel in Prophetic miracles, then it is lawful and should be accepted. Whatever the case, Shāṭibī emphatically states, the Sharīʿa must be and is the final criterion for judging the validity and legality of all human acts, including saintly miracles.[22] In short, Ṣūfīs or not, all Muslims are subject to one and the same Sharīʿa.

Having dispensed with the Ṣūfīs, Shāṭibī immediately turns his attention to what seems to have been a segment of the community of jurists and jurisconsults whom he thought to be far too lenient in the application of the law. Many of his contemporary jurisconsults, he claims, issued *fatwā*s with the view of satisfying, not the requirements of the law, but rather personal interests and greed. In conceding to greed and earthly personal interests and desires, they allowed laymen to combine, in an unlawful manner, the most convenient doctrines from amongst the various schools (*tatabbuʿ rukhaṣ al-madhāhib*) with the view of achieving legal results otherwise impossible within the boundaries of one school.[23] Furthermore, it appears that recourse to legal stratagems (*ḥiyal*; sing. *ḥīla*) was taken beyond lawful limits, a phenomenon which may explain why Shāṭibī allocates numerous pages to discussing the difference between lawful and unlawful types of stratagems. Stratagems constitute legal means by which one can arrive at juridical results otherwise prohibited by the law.[24] Unlawful stratagems are those that lead to avoiding obligatory acts, or to rendering permissible what is not. The Sharīʿa, argues Shāṭibī, was revealed for the purpose of regulating benefits which are universally applicable. Resorting to unlawful stratagems or combining the doctrines of more than one school in an arbitrary manner defeats this purpose and wreaks havoc with the universals of the law.

It is clear that by insisting on the universals of the law as an epistemologically conclusive category, Shāṭibī was attempting to establish, once and for all, that the true Sharīʿa aims at steering a middle course between attitudes guided by personal interests, on the one hand, and those that are religiously over-zealous and excessively demanding on the other. This is why he states time and again throughout the book, and in a variety of contexts,

[21] On the difference between Prophetic and saintly miracles, see *Encyclopaedia of Islam*, New Edition (Leiden: E. J. Brill, 1960–), s.v. "Karāma" (by L. Gardet), IV, 615–16.

[22] *Muwāfaqāt*, II, 182–205. [23] Ibid., IV, 85–86.

[24] See *Encyclopaedia of Islam*, s.v. "*Ḥiyal*" (by J. Schacht), III, 510–13.

that the Sharīʿa represents nothing but a middle-of-the-road position (*al-ṭarīq al-wasaṭ*) between undue difficulty (*ʿusr*) and extreme ease (*yusr*). There is little doubt that in the mind of Shāṭibī the former attitude represents that of the Ṣūfīs, and the latter that of the legists. Subtle, and at times not so subtle, references to the two extreme positions regularly surface in the text of *al-Muwāfaqāt*, thus pointing to the socio-religious forces that gave rise to Shāṭibī's discourse.

THE LEGAL NORMS

Of the five norms constituting the entire range of legal deontology, Shāṭibī concentrates primarily on the category of permissible (*mubāḥ*) acts whose commission or omission is equally legitimate. In neither case is there a reward or punishment. Whereas this category normally receives little more than a succinct definition in works by other theorists, it is the focus in Shāṭibī's discourse of a highly elaborate and at times intense discussion. He goes to great lengths to assert and adduce textual evidence in support of the doctrine that since the permissible is a strictly neutral category, neither the commission nor the omission of a permissible act can be praiseworthy or blameworthy. Again, it turns out that his assertions are principally directed toward the Ṣūfīs who seem to have persistently argued that performing permissible acts leads a man to indulge himself in the pleasures of life, when he must instead be preoccupied with performing good deeds in this world in preparation for the hereafter. The upright mystical path thus requires the omission of permissible acts.[25]

In response to such views, Shāṭibī advances an elaborate and novel taxonomy of the permissible. The category of the permissible consists of two divisions, each of which comprises in turn two sub-categories. The first division is the permissible act insofar as it is permissible in its particulars but whose performance is necessary on the universal level, either in a recommended or obligatory fashion. The second division represents the permissible act insofar as it is permissible in its particulars, but whose performance is prohibited on the universal level, it being classified as either reprehensible or outrightly forbidden. Within each of these two divisions are thus included four sub-categories. The first is that which is permissible in part although in its consummate totality it is recommended (*mandūb*). Food, clothing and shelter, for instance, may be abandoned in part for a certain period of time. But if they are abandoned categorically and for ever, then such acts would be in violation of what the law prescribes as recom-

[25] *Muwāfaqāt*, I, 63–73.

mended. The second is that which is permissible in part, although in its totality it is obligatory (*wājib*). For example, a man may choose not to have sexual intercourse with his wife for a period of time, a choice which is permissible. But if all men decide to abstain from sexual intercourse at all times, then the act of abstention will cease to be permissible for it would be detrimental to the universal category of *ḍarūriyyāt* in which procreation and progeny are not only encouraged but necessarily required. The third is that which is permissible in part but in its totality it is reprehensible (*makrūh*). Legitimate forms of singing and chanting are, for instance, permissible if performed on one particular day or on a special occasion. But singing as a habitual, constant practice is considered reprehensible (note the allusion to Ṣūfī practices). Finally, there is that which is permissible in part although in its totality it is utterly forbidden (*mamnūʿ*, *ḥarām*). Here, Shāṭibī does not provide examples, but it is clear that persistence in performing some permissible acts will render these acts prohibited. Thus the dividing line between the permissible and the impermissible (i.e., the recommended, obligatory, reprehensible and forbidden) is the degree of frequency and repetition in the performance of the act. A person's testimony in a court of law would be deemed admissible, though he may be found to chant or play chess occasionally. But if he regularly practices chanting or avidly plays chess, then his acts will undermine his own uprightness and rectitude, and will accordingly disqualify him as a court witness. The permissibility of acts is therefore relative and always contingent upon their sporadic performance. Once they are regularly and repeatedly performed or, alternatively, abandoned, then their commission or omission becomes, respectively, obligatory.

The recommended and reprehensible acts can be analyzed according to a similar taxonomy. A recommended act performed occasionally retains its status as recommended, but in its totality – that is, as an act universally and constantly practiced – it is obligatory. For instance, the law enjoins men and women to enter into matrimony. Since engaging in marriage is only a recommendation, some men or women may choose to remain single. But if all members of society abstain from marriage, then recommendation becomes detrimental to the five universals subsumed under the category of the *ḍarūriyyāt*. Likewise, an act that is deemed reprehensible if occasionally performed becomes forbidden when frequently repeated. Thus the recommended complements the obligatory, just as the reprehensible complements the forbidden. And it appears that the permissible, pursuant to Shāṭibī's analysis, also complements all the other four norms.[26]

[26] Ibid., I, 79–80, 92.

The interrelatedness of the norms as exemplified in this taxonomy demonstrates that the permissible (as well as the two other intermediate norms of recommendation and reprehensibility) cannot be set aside categorically. The Ṣūfīs' insistence that the permissible allows man excessive luxuries and distracts him from pure forms of worship is shown by Shāṭibī to amount, in the final analysis, to nothing short of a violation of the principles of the law and the purposes for which it was revealed. Moreover, the Ṣūfī enthusiasm for the harsher and less lenient aspects of the law does not guarantee them, or so we gather from Shāṭibī's writings, a better reward in the hereafter. They seem to have argued that performing the obligatory and recommended acts sooner than later, or in any case sooner than the law stipulates, is more pious and thus more faithful to God's decree. But Shāṭibī firmly rejects this argument and holds that whatever the law stipulates to be the time for performing the act is the right time, whether it is sooner or later. God has a purpose in every rule or decree which He reveals, and if his purpose would be better served in delaying the performance of an act, then He would command that it be performed later than sooner. Insisting on performing such an act sooner than legally required would then stand in opposition to God's will and intention. And when the law allows for a certain latitude in timing the performance of acts, then the believer will be rewarded irrespective of when he performed the act, as long as he has done so within the time frame stipulated by the law. Those required to pay penance (*kaffāra*), for instance, have the choice between feeding the poor or freeing a slave. Although one of the two options may be more costly or more troublesome than the other, the reward in either form of penance would be the same, for the law gave the individual the freedom to choose either of the two means with no conditions or qualifications attached and without placing more weight on one option than on the other.

Shāṭibī carves out what seems to be a sixth legal norm which – though strictly not one of the commonly accepted norms – he considers integral to the law. It enhances the two other norms of the recommended and the permissible, and allows for some latitude and tolerance in legal practice. Shāṭibī labels this norm as *ʿafw*, a concept signifying a case that has been either undecided or decided, but, if decided, the individual who commits the act does not know or forgets what the rule is. The notion of *ʿafw* has a long history in Islamic law, a history which is thought to begin with a Prophetic report that states: "The most sinful of Muslims is he who enquires about a matter which has not been prohibited, but becomes prohibited when he asks about its legal status."[27] The idea behind the report

[27] Ibid., I, 100.

is that as long as an act has not been decided by the law to fall into one of the five norms, then it belongs to what may be described as the "undecided." If a case is undecided, the Muslim individual, as long as he or she does not seek a professional legal opinion about it, can do as he or she wishes, with neither punishment nor reward being attached to the act. This is why the Prophet reportedly disliked enquiries about legal matters, for enquiries may lead to prohibition whereas, before the enquiry, the status would simply be undecided. Undecided cases do not entail violation of the law, since there is no legal norm to breach. And if no breach occurs, then punishment is not in order. This is precisely what *ʿafw* means in undecided cases.

In cases where the legal norm has been decided, however, *ʿafw* signifies waiving the punishment, whatever it may be, on the grounds that there is a good reason to do so. Committing a forbidden act due to forgetfulness (*nisyān*) does not entail punishment. If someone forgets that he or she is fasting during Ramadan, and they eat, then no punishment is entailed. Cases of mistake (*khaṭaʾ*) are treated by the law in a quite similar fashion.

Belonging to this category also are cases involving undue hardship. But in these cases it is not the punishment that is waived; rather, the original rule, known as *ʿazīma*, is substituted by a more lenient one, technically known as *rukhṣa*. Before we proceed further with our discussion of this dichotomy, we must stress its significance in Shāṭibī's theory. His expanded discussion of this dichotomy is another extensive variation on the themes he elaborated in his response to the Ṣūfīs who argued that the permissible norm diverts believers from adequate worship and devoted piety. In emphasizing *rukhṣa*, Shāṭibī was reaffirming, in the face of Ṣūfī "over-zealousness," that leniency is inherently embodied in, and prescribed by, the law and that dismissing the legal norm of permissibility, together with such notions as *ʿafw* and *rukhṣa*, as both earthly and impious indulgence, amounts to violating the most fundamental principles of the law.

Turning to the notion of mitigating hardship, Shāṭibī begins by explaining *ʿazīma* which represents the general rule to which *rukhṣa* is an exception. *ʿAzīma* is the original state of legal rules when they are equally applicable to all situations and persons, original in the sense that they have been neither modified on the basis of, nor preceded by, any previously stipulated legal rules. *Rukhṣa*, on the other hand, characterizes those original rules that have been mitigated due to excessive hardship. But modifying the rules on these grounds is not the same as modifying them on the basis of dire needs, such as in the case of the *salam* contract. This type of contract, involving the ordering of (usually fungible) goods to be delivered in the future for a price paid in the present and upon concluding the contract, is deemed valid although it involves risk and usury.[28] It is allowed because of the fundamental need for it in the continuing operation of economic and mercantile life. *Rukhṣa*, however, in order to qualify as such, must arise out of undue hardship, not only of need. For instance, an *ʿazīma* rule is that in order for a Muslim to perform a valid prayer, she must pray while standing up. But if she falls ill, then she is allowed to pray while sitting down. Undue hardship here has given rise to *rukhṣa*. The difference between dire need and *rukhṣa* is ultimately drawn by the permanency of the legal condition: dire need, such as that found in the *salam* contract, is permanent, whereas *rukhṣa* is limited to such a point of time when the cause giving rise to mitigation disappears. The Muslim who has fallen ill shall be permitted to pray while sitting down for as long as she is ill. Upon recovery, however, this license is no longer permissible.

In the context of Shāṭibī's theory of universals and particulars, the *ʿazīma* represents a universal, whereas the license is the exceptive particular. Thus, *rukhṣa* may belong to any of the three categories of universals – the *ḍarūriyyāt*, *ḥājiyyāt* or *taḥsīniyyāt* – depending on the cause that gives rise to that license. When Muslims, congregating on Friday, pray while sitting down in emulation of their *imām* who, for health reasons, is incapable of standing up, their sitting down is considered a *taḥsīnī* license. They are granted that license not because they are themselves physically incapacitated but because it is more appropriate and agreeable to conduct themselves after the example of their *imām*.

Be that as it may, the rights and duties embedded in the dichotomy of *ʿazīma* and *rukhṣa* represent the respective distinction between man's duty toward God and God's benevolence toward man. In this sense, the category of license and the legal norm of the permissible share a common denominator, namely, both are deliberately designed, within the confines of the divine law, to facilitate man's life.

Shāṭibī claims that the Ṣūfīs consider many rules of the Sharīʿa to be licentious, and therefore to be avoided. They practice only those aspects of the law that come under *ʿazīma*. In his view, the Ṣūfīs' stern and diehard attitude runs counter to the aims and intention of the Lawgiver, for legal license, as attested by more than a dozen Quranic verses and Prophetic reports, is granted to man in accordance with divine wisdom and decree, not purposelessly. Promoting human welfare is the aim and intention of the law, and if license becomes necessary to achieve this end, then the law must, and does, allow it. But license is relative, and each individual must

[28] On the *salam* contract, see Joseph Schacht, *An Introduction to Islamic Law* (Oxford: Clarendon Press, 1964), 153; Shams al-Dīn b. Shihāb al-Dīn al-Ramlī, *Nihāyat al-Muḥtāj ilā Sharḥ al-Minhāj*, 8 vols. (Cairo: Muṣṭafā Bābī al-Ḥalabī, 1357/1938), IV, 178 ff.

decide for himself or herself the point at which a matter becomes intolerably hard, thus justifying the adoption of license. For instance, the bedouin who is used to hunger, and can properly function in daily life while being subject to it, is not permitted the license of eating the flesh of animals that have died (*mayta*), because they are ritually impure. However, others, such as city folk, are not normally accustomed to hunger, and if they starve, they will cease to function normally. Accordingly, if they run out of provisions while traveling in the desert, they would be within the boundaries of the law if they were to resort to license, and thus consume the meat of dead animals.[29]

Shāṭibī goes so far as to argue that *ʿazīma* in effect does not have priority over license, and he advances a number of arguments in support of his claim. First, epistemologically, the principle of license is in no way inferior to *ʿazīma*; both enjoy certitude. For even if we assume that the principle of license is not known with certainty, the claim for the absolute certainty of *ʿazīma* is not, after all, warranted since license, its contrary, is epistemically sustained, at the very least, by a high degree of probability. In other words, it cannot be maintained that resorting to *ʿazīma* remains certain when it is believed with high probability that resort should be made to license, its normative opposite. Second, alleviating hardship (*rafʿ al-ḥaraj*) is a legal principle that enjoys certitude by virtue of the support from multiple Quranic verses and Prophetic reports. Accordingly, license, an efficient means to alleviate hardship, has precedence over *ʿazīma* since it combines both obedience to God – albeit in a mitigated form – and a consideration of man's welfare. *ʿAzīma*, on the other hand, takes no cognizance of man's welfare, for it is single-mindedly directed to achieve obedience to God. Third, numerous pieces of textual evidence, inductively gathered from the texts, point to the law's abhorrence of exaggerated conduct and stringency, whose instrument is *ʿazīma*. Finally, the excessive demands dictated by *ʿazīma* are counterproductive, leading believers away from legal obligation and discouraging them from voluntary, benevolent conduct.[30]

By adopting this doctrine of license, Shāṭibī was in effect advancing a two-pronged argument against the Ṣūfīs. On the one hand, by insisting that license is an integral part of the law, he demonstrated the extremist and stringent Ṣūfī legal demands to be contrary to the letter and spirit of the law. On the other hand, by emphasizing the relativity of license, he was countering what appears to have been a Ṣūfī demand that all Muslims, and not only the Ṣūfīs, should resort neither to license nor to the legal category of the permissible.

[29] *Muwāfaqāt*, I, 208–13. [30] Ibid., I, 230–34.

It is obvious from Shāṭibī's writings that he was acutely aware of the Ṣūfī view that the heavenly reward for living a life of hardship is greater than that received for a life lived in comfort or even mitigated hardship. No doubt, he argues, legal obligation generally entails some hardship. But this hardship, as inductively attested by the revealed sources, is not meant by God to be beyond the normal tolerance of humans. Most, if not all, efforts aimed at earning a living involve some sort of hardship. Whatever this hardship may be, it is tolerable, normal and ordinary (*mashaqqa ʿādiyya*).[31] This is the case because divine wisdom realizes the consequences of imposing on believers obligations and duties that amount to intolerable, absolute hardship. Worship would become detestable, and fulfillment of legal obligations would be neglected, particularly in light of the fact that each legally capacitated person (*mukallaf*) already has a number of other obligations imposed upon him by the requirements of daily life. The imposition of hardship would result in people's ignoring worship and legal obligation, and this would mean that not only would the person's own daily affairs be adversely affected, but his obligations toward other members of society, including his own family, would be neglected as well. And this is neither the aim nor the intention of the Lawgiver (*qaṣd al-Shāriʿ*).[32]

That the Lawgiver did not intend to impose hardship on His subjects does not mean that He permits them to do as they like and arbitrarily choose what they find easy and convenient. This qualification to his anti-Ṣūfī argumentation Shāṭibī found necessary in order to criticize, on another front, the practice of some Andalusian legists whom he thought to be too lax in their prescription and application of the law. *ʿAzīma* is relinquished only when it entails excessive difficulty and undue hardship; if the legal obligation entails hardship that is ordinary and well within the limit of human tolerance, then it shall be prescribed and performed without modification or mitigation. The Sharīʿa, Shāṭibī insists, steers a middle course (*ṭarīq wasaṭ*) between the two extremes of excessive hardship and permissiveness.[33]

THE CONSTITUENT ELEMENTS OF THE LAW'S AIMS

Shāṭibī's doctrine of hardship forms an integral part of his theory of *maqāṣid*, the aims and intentions of the law, a theory for the elaboration of which he devotes the entirety of the second volume of *Muwāfaqāt*. The centrality of this theory is manifested by the fact that throughout the other three volumes Shāṭibī not only makes constant reference to the discussions

[31] Ibid., II, 84 ff. [32] Ibid., II, 96–102. [33] Ibid., II, 111–19.

of *maqāṣid*, but also frequently states that these discussions constitute the basis of the other doctrines he elaborated in the *Muwāfaqāt*. Space does not permit a detailed description, much less a thorough analysis, of the *maqāṣid* theory here. But it is necessary to give a brief account of the elements making up this theory.

Generally, the aims of the law may be divided into two broad categories: those related to the intention of the Lawgiver and those pertaining to the intention of the *mukallaf*, the individual who is legally capacitated and who is charged with fulfilling the requirements of the law. The first category is in turn divided into four sub-categories, each dealing from a different angle with the intention of the Lawgiver. Under the first sub-category, Shāṭibī discusses the original intention of God in revealing the law, i.e., to protect the interests of man (both mundane and religious) insofar as the universals of *ḍarūriyyāt*, *ḥājiyyāt*, and *taḥsīniyyāt* are concerned. Here, he advances his own legal epistemology, which we have expounded earlier.[34] Alongside these issues, another theme runs throughout, namely, that in revealing a law which is anchored in the concept of *maṣāliḥ*, God intended to provide for humans a life that prepares them for the hereafter, and not to let them lead a life according to their own whims and pleasures. Ultimately, the Sharīʿa has been revealed for the purpose of ridding Muslims of their base desires and predilections.[35]

In the second sub-category, Shāṭibī deals with the intention of the Lawgiver in making the Sharīʿa linguistically intelligible to those for whom it was revealed. Here, he deals briefly with the Quranic language, and argues that for all intents and purposes the Holy Book was revealed in Arabic, untainted by foreign vocabulary, and that its style, idiom, syntax and structure have been made to conform to the linguistic conventions of the Arabs. From this it follows that the Quran and the Sharīʿa are unlettered, so that they can be intelligible to the Arabs who are themselves unlettered (*ummiyyūn*).[36] Both the Quran and the Sharīʿa can be understood only with reference to the linguistic conventions prevalent among the Arabs. And if there is no convention to inform the Quran, then whatever interpretation is adopted, it shall neither be contradictory to any convention nor even unfamiliar to the ways of the Arabs. The Sharīʿa must thus be intelligible to the commoner and layman, and must avoid being elitist. The purpose, after all, is to bring the believer into the domain of divine law, for if he cannot comprehend the language of the law, then the law would be defeating its own purposes.[37]

[34] See pp. 164–67 above. [35] *Muwāfaqāt*, II, 3–44.
[36] Ibid., II, 48. For a useful study on the *ummī*, see Norman Calder, "The *Ummī* in Early Islamic Juristic Literature," *Der Islam*, 67 (1990): 111–23. [37] *Muwāfaqāt*, II, 44–75.

The third sub-category is relatively straightforward, and for the most part asserts that in revealing his law, the Lawgiver intended to ensure the complete adherence of Muslims to his decree. But adherence would not be possible unless the divine demands were commensurate with the capabilities of the believers. Excessive demands ultimately frustrate all attempts at conforming to, and implementing, the law. If the law, say, forbids Muslims to eat and drink, then how could they be expected to adhere to that law? It follows, therefore, that none of the attributes with which man is born may be subject to a legal ruling that might adversely affect it. Indeed, the Lawgiver intended no excessive hardship whatsoever to be imposed. Here, Shāṭibī discusses at some length what constitutes undue hardship, which he links to the concepts of *ʿazīma* and *rukhṣa*; for, as we have seen, it is through the latter that excessive hardship can be mitigated.[38] We have also seen that his doctrine of *rukhṣa*, which is highly developed, is directed at the Ṣūfīs of his time.

Countering the excessive requirements of the Ṣūfīs, on the one hand, and the lax attitudes of some legists, on the other, seems to be the main reason behind the fourth, and final, sub-category. On the basis of Quranic citations and Prophetic reports, as well as arguments deriving from what may be characterized as the natural course of events (*majārī al-ʿādāt*),[39] Shāṭibī asserts that the good life cannot be attained by indulging in personal whims and pleasures, which the Sharīʿa clearly was not revealed to accommodate.

At this point, Shāṭibī enters into a dialogue with a hypothetical interlocutor whose claims are an eloquent expression of the position to which Shāṭibī was opposed. The interlocutor asserts that the law was not revealed in vain (*ʿabathan*), but rather for a reason dictated by divine wisdom (*ḥikma*). This reason is the promotion and protection of public good (*maṣlaḥa*), a good, the interlocutor continues, that is predicated either of God or His subjects. And since God is omnipotent and entirely self-sufficient, it follows – and this is established in the science of Kalām – that only His subjects are in need of *maṣlaḥa*. Hence, the Sharīʿa came to guarantee *maṣlaḥa*, a proposition which amounts to the argument that the Sharīʿa is designed to respect the needs and even personal pleasures of God's subjects. In reply to this, Shāṭibī asserts that *maṣlaḥa* was indeed intended to work for the benefit of man, but in a way that is determined by God, not by man's own predilections. This explains why legal obligation is known to be demanding, though in a fair and reasonable manner. For while *maṣlaḥa*

[38] Ibid., II, 76 ff.

[39] See Harry Wolfson, *The Philosophy of the Kalam* (Cambridge, Mass.: Harvard University Press, 1976), 544–51; Hallaq "Authoritativeness," 437.

is aimed at promoting the interest of man in this world and the hereafter, it is defined by the revealed law, not by the "secular," or utilitarian needs of man.

The law, having been determined by God, comprises two types of obligations, one of which relates to financial, contractual and other mundane matters, and the other to worship. The former is conducted among individuals, the latter between man and his Lord. Now, the obligations in the former type are divided in turn into two sorts, one capable of representation, the other not. Those capable of representation may be disposed of by proxy. Empowering legal agents to sell, buy or rent on one's behalf are but a few examples in point. Examples of those obligations incapable of being disposed of by proxy are sexual relations in matrimony and receiving penalties; no one should represent another in fulfilling these obligations.

For a different reason altogether, matters of worship do not lend themselves to representation. Obviously, the purpose behind their imposition upon humans is to create a relationship in which man submits to God with humility. Delegating these obligations to others negates this submission. Besides, if representation in matters of worship were to be accepted, then it would be equally accepted in matters of faith, which is absurd. The interlocutor raises an objection and argues that representation in worship is valid, for the Prophet is reported to have said "He who dies without completing his fast, let his next of kin complete it on his behalf." Furthermore, a consensus has been reached with regard to the validity of paying the alms-tax on behalf of those who are not possessed of financial means. Similarly, it is lawful for the male agnates of the murderer to pay blood-money on his behalf. But Shāṭibī flatly dismisses all these examples as irrelevant, pertaining to matters financial and having nothing to do with worshipping God and drawing closer to Him.[40]

It is difficult to determine the reasons that precipitated this discussion in *al-Muwāfaqāt*, but it is likely that Shāṭibī was addressing the Ṣūfis who held the view that certain obligations of religious ritual and worship may be disposed of by the Ṣūfī Master on behalf of his followers.

The stringency of the Ṣūfis, Shāṭibī contends, caused some to believe that their excessive legal demands had led them to uphold a system of law dictated by their specifically mystical thought, which seemed at variance with, or even loftier than, the system operative in society at large. This, he argues, is exemplified by the reaction of an anonymous leading mystic who, when asked about alms-tax, enquired whether the questioner wished to receive an answer in accordance with the Ṣūfī or non-Ṣūfī law. Others,

[40] *Muwāfaqāt*, II, 166 ff.

Shāṭibī adds, believe that the Ṣūfīs have declared certain things permissible for themselves, when they are in fact prohibited by law. A case in point is chanting, which the Ṣūfīs deem permissible for themselves, though prohibited by the community of jurists. All this leads Shāṭibī to the assertion, which he lays down as a matter of principle, that all believers come under the law as equals, and that none has special privileges or exemptions.[41]

Equality before the law does not mean that the law is blind to specific social needs that arise in certain contexts. Law does recognize two types of custom; one legal, meaning that it is subject to one of the five legal norms, the other not, i.e., it is subject to none of these norms. The former type is invariable, and takes cognizance of no particular demand or view. What is permissible under this category can never become impermissible, however much the Muslims' tastes or sets of value undergo change. The prohibition on revealing sexual organs was, is and will continue to be imposed, whether or not Muslims change their views or values with regard to this matter.

The second type of custom may either be permanent or mutable. If permanent, it may be lawfully considered in the elaboration of rulings. Eating, drinking, speaking and sexual relations are immutable, instinctive habits, and they are always to be taken into consideration in legal reasoning without a change in their status. If the custom is mutable, however, then law must change as the custom changes from time to time or from place to place. In a country where it is customary not to wear headgear, the law pertaining to the dress code would be different from that of another country in which it is conventional to cover the head. Laws concerning a number of financial transactions and contracts may be expected to change from one place to another due to changes in the attitudes and customs of peoples in different regions. But these changing features should not be attributed to double standards in the law. Rather, they must be seen as indicative of flexibility in accommodating human exigencies and cultural differences. If the law were not to take into account these mutable elements, then legal obligation would be intolerable (*taklīf mā lā yuṭāq*), and this is not admitted in the Sharīʿa.[42]

We have noted earlier that Shāṭibī perceived the aims of the law as being divided into two broad categories: the first, which we have been discussing, is related to the intentions (*maqāṣid*) of the Lawgiver in revealing His law, while the second pertains to the intentions of the *mukallaf*, the individual who is legally capacitated and who is charged with fulfilling the requirements of the law. In this respect, the intentions of the *mukallaf* in carrying out any legal command must correspond to the intentions of the Lawgiver

[41] Ibid., II, 179 ff. [42] Ibid., II, 209 ff.

in decreeing that command. Thus, God's intentions behind promoting and maintaining the three universals – the *ḍarūriyyāt*, *ḥājiyyāt*, and *taḥsīniyyāt* – must be identical to the individual's intentions in implementing the law as grounded in these universals. The individual is then God's deputy on earth in that he represents, or ought to represent, God in promoting social welfare through adopting the same intentions that God had adopted when He decreed the law. He who seeks to use the law in ways other than those intended by the Lawgiver would, in Shāṭibī's view, be violating the Sharīʿa.[43]

The hypothetical interlocutor is made to argue that intending to achieve ends otherwise unintended in the law is not necessarily illicit. Legal stratagems (*ḥiyal*) provide many examples, one of which is the device of marrying off a divorcée to a man (*muḥallil*) other than her former husband, then having immediately obtained a divorce from that man, she is allowed to remarry her first husband. The "middle" marriage and divorce are intended to circumvent the prohibition imposed upon husbands against remarrying the women they have divorced, without first being married and divorced by other husbands, a prohibition intended to restrain the freedom of husbands to divorce their wives. In reply to this, Shāṭibī argues – though not very convincingly – that those who admit the validity of such legal stratagems believe that the validity of the *muḥallil* marriage is justified by virtue of the benefits that may accrue to the spouses and the harm that may be averted. (It may be noted in passing that Shāṭibī's argument here is distinctly reminiscent of Ṭūfī's theory of *maṣlaḥa*, a theory that finds its ultimate support not in any particular textual citation, or set of citations, but rather in a general notion of public good based upon a "universally" inductive understanding of what the Sharīʿa aims to achieve.)

Be that as it may, it is clear that violating the law with intent to do so is punishable to the extent and gravity of that violation. But what about a case in which the legal act is in conformity with the stipulations of the law but the intention of the act's performer is to violate the law? In this case, the performer either knows or does not know that his act constitutes a violation. An instance of the absence of such knowledge is when a person drinks grape-juice thinking it is wine. Here, he is conforming to the law in practice but violating it in intention. This amounts to saying that insofar as the rights of his fellow men are concerned he has abided by the law; but he has sinned (*āthim*) insofar as the rights of God are concerned. On the other hand, he may perform an act while knowing that he is doing so in conformity with the intention of the Lawgiver, but intends nonetheless to violate the law. Praying in public solely for the sake of showing off one's piety and

[43] Ibid., II, 238 ff.

thus for gaining a good image and higher standing in the eyes of society is a case in point. This, Shāṭibī asserts, represents a violation of the law more severe than that which involves the intention to break the law without in practice doing so, as in the case of drinking the grape-juice.

It is also conceivable that the act may be in violation of the law whereas the intention is not. Adding, out of piety, a new religious obligation or ritual to what has already been stipulated by the law would belong to this category. As in the previous set of examples, the performer may or may not know that his act constitutes a violation. If he knows, then the act would be a religious innovation that is deemed reprehensible, if not outrightly forbidden (note the oblique reference here to Ṣūfī practices). If he does not know that the act is in breach of the Lawgiver's intention, then he would not be deemed blameworthy in the eyes of the law – the governing principle here being that acts are judged by the intentions behind them (*innamā al-aʿmāl bil-niyyāt*).

It appears that Shāṭibī's discourse about human intention is thus far elaborated with the Ṣūfīs in mind. At this point, however, he moves on to discuss legal stratagems (*ḥiyal*) in light of the correspondence, or lack of it, between divine and human intentions. And it is clear that his target shifts from the Ṣūfīs to the group of jurists whom he considers to adopt excessive leniency in legal matters, probably by resorting, *inter alia*, to *ḥiyal*. In criticizing these jurists, he argues that the main purpose of *ḥiyal* is to circumvent an existing rule or to alter it so as to arrive at a result that the law did not intend to achieve. It is in this sense, he insists, that *ḥiyal* are generally deemed unlawful. Conversely, and as an exception, any legal stratagem that does not contravene an established legal principle or a principle of public good is valid and may well be admissible in the law.[44]

We have here an admission that Shāṭibī accepts *ḥiyal* in at least some cases, as he explicitly states.[45] He defends his position by maintaining that such qualified and partial acceptance does not amount to any legal infringement, for admitting the validity of some *ḥiyal* is based upon the investigated conclusion that they are in perfect harmony with the intention of the Lawgiver. In illustration of his point, he calls upon the case of the *muḥallil* marriage which constitutes a device, or properly so-called a *ḥīla*, by which the wife can remarry her first husband. This *ḥīla* is seen to be in perfect agreement with the law, for the Prophet stated: "If he divorces her [i.e., his wife], then she will no more be lawful unto him until such time when she marries [and obtains a divorce from] a man other than him." The point of the second marriage is to make the woman enter into a sexual relationship

[44] Ibid., II, 281–85. [45] Ibid., II, 285 ff.

with another man so as to deter the husband from rushing into divorcing his wife if he does not indeed wish to do so. Arranging a second marriage and divorce for the purpose of "returning" the woman to her first husband stands, Shāṭibī argues, in consonance with both the letter and intention of the law.

Defending the legitimacy of certain types of *ḥiyal* has no doubt to do with the fact that those *ḥiyal* were admitted into the authoritative substantive doctrine of the Mālikite school. Shāṭibī's aim was to defend enough of the *ḥiyal* doctrine as to steer a middle course between the uncompromisingly strict and excessively lenient approaches to the law. The strict approach tends to exaggerate legal obligation and curb licentious legal behavior to an extent that, he thought, God never intended in the law. By the same token, the lenient approach violates the sense of obligation intended to be both the symbol and force commanding submission to the Lord. It is thus the intention of the Lawgiver that must be the ultimate measure against which all rules, laws and principles must be determined. The divine intention emerges as a type of rationale or wisdom (*ḥikma*) that is not always transparent to the human mind, but cognizance of which must nonetheless always be taken. In matters pertaining to mundane life, it is relatively easy to speculate on, if not disclose, the nature of that intention. The determination of the *ratio legis*, indispensable for any case, presents no more difficulty than those entailed in defining the rationale and thus the intention. In matters of ritual and worship, the intention is nearly impossible to determine. Here, the stipulation of the Lawgiver must be abided by to the letter, with the understanding that God commands submission through certain religious obligations, obligations that we are at no liberty whatsoever to abridge or expand. This is because, as Shāṭibī might have said, God knows *exactly* what He wants for and from us.

LEGAL INDICANTS AND LEGAL LANGUAGE

It is obvious by now that Shāṭibī uses and twists what is otherwise the traditional subject matter of legal theory to achieve his own ends. This is no less obvious in those chapters in *al-Muwāfaqāt* where he treats of legal indicants (*adilla sharʿiyya*), namely, the textual evidence adduced in justification of legal rules. The uses to which Shāṭibī puts his discussion of indicants reveal yet another feature of the practices and ideas he sets out to refute and criticize. In these chapters, though, the main focus of his discourse is the community of jurists who, he thought, had deviated from the straight path. The Ṣūfīs, for a change, seem to stand largely on the margins of this discourse.

Shāṭibī begins his discussion by distinguishing two types of complementary indicants, one rational, the other revelational. Revealed indicants require rational thought in order to be meaningful, and reason can by no means be acceptable in matters legal unless it is grounded in revelation. It is not reason therefore that sanctions revelation, but rather the other way round, this carrying the distinctly clear implication that legal indicants are, in the final analysis, reduced to the body of revelation. Revelation, then, is the source of all law, of both the general principles and particular rules.

Having established this basic premise, Shāṭibī moves on to draw a distinction between two types of legal indicants. The first type is that which was adopted by all or most of the early authorities in the vast majority of cases. The substantial support this type receives from the community and its leaders throughout time makes recourse to it by later generations most desirable. The difficulty lies with the second type which time has shown to have either little or no place in the reasoning of legists. The fact that this type received less attention from the community of jurists must be due, Shāṭibī argues, either to a lawful or unlawful reason. Since the community of jurists, representing the Muslim community at large, cannot err, the preference for the first type over the second must be due to a perfectly legitimate and convincing reason – the implication here being that legal indicants that have little or no support among the preceding generations of jurists lack legitimacy and must thus be set aside in legal reasoning. Adopting such legal indicants entails not only abandoning the righteous, majoritarian path of the forefathers and aiding in the destruction of their exemplary practices but also entails spreading that which is antithetical to the spirit and word of the ideal law they followed. It is of particularly grave consequence, Shāṭibī stresses, if those who participate in the propagation of those fallacies are leaders in, and thus the model for, the community.[46]

It is of course possible that a genuine *mujtahid* might fall into error with regard to a case, but this is not the sort of fallacy of which Shāṭibī is speaking here. Such a *mujtahid* deserves a reward in the hereafter even if he is mistaken, this being the common doctrine held by the Sunnī theorists. What Shāṭibī is concerned with here is another type of legist who is not in possession of the necessary tools to conduct *ijtihād*, and who deceptively pretends, without the professional approval of fellow jurists, to have attained this lofty rank. Diverging from the authoritative doctrines of the predecessors occurs most often, if not always, among such legists, for genuine *mujtahids* do not, as a rule, swerve from precedent. The end result of this departure from the predecessors' authoritative doctrines is the creation of

[46] Ibid., III, 24–45.

a body of law that is self-contradictory. Pseudo-*mujtahid*s tend to resort to a legal indicant which appears to be relevant to the case, when in fact it is not. It is clear that Shāṭibī does not mean to attribute this anomaly to sheer ignorance, for he strongly insinuates that the manipulation of indicants is a conscious act, motivated by personal, utilitarian interests.

Having made these cautionary remarks concerning the misuse of legal indicants, Shāṭibī turns his attention to the standard topics normally discussed under the general heading of *al-adilla al-sharʿiyya.* It is noticeable at once, however, that he is not concerned with the issues that usually occupy the legal theorists. Rather, he takes for granted much of their doctrines, and what little he appears to introduce in line with the established tradition he introduces with a distinct twist. Nothing is said or argued without an agenda, however hidden it may be. We shall now discuss in outline the five major topics subsumed under this heading.

Ambiguous and univocal language[47]

The main argument of this section is that while there are ambiguous (*mutashābih*) verses in the Quran, they are relatively few. The received notion that the number of such verses is large is due to the fact that some unqualified, impious scholars misunderstood the texts and attributed to them the quality of ambiguity because, Shāṭibī seems to say, they were attempting to explain away, and thus discard, those texts that are otherwise relevant to the cases in hand. Again, the motivation of those pseudo-*mujtahid*s who claim the existence of ambiguity in the texts is serving one sort of personal interest or another.

In a subsidiary argument, Shāṭibī maintains that ambiguity does not occur in the language pertaining to the universal principles of the law, but rather in that pertaining to the particulars, namely, the individual legal rulings. An inductive survey of the law readily demonstrates this fact, let alone the contradiction that ensues if this were to be true; for if the language stipulating the universals were ambiguous, then the Sharīʿa would be on the whole ambiguous, and this clearly is not the case.

Abrogation[48]

Central to Shāṭibī's theory is the doctrine that the universal principles of the law were laid down in the Meccan phase of revelation, and that what followed in the Medinese period were either specific legal rules or supplements

[47] Ibid., III, 56–65. [48] Ibid., III, 70–79.

to the Meccan principles. Thus, the Meccan period resulted in revealing only a small number of particular legal rules. Put differently, the *ḍarūriyyāt* universals were by and large revealed in Mecca, whereas the *ḥājiyyāt* and *taḥsīniyyāt* were almost entirely decreed in Medina.

An inductive survey of the Sharīʿa reveals that abrogation (*naskh*) was not applied to the Meccan universals but rather to some of the Medinese specific rules. The reason behind abrogation in the Medinese phase was to appeal to new converts and ease their path into Islam. Increasing the number of prayers from two to five, changing the direction of prayer (*qibla*) from Jerusalem to the Kaʿba, and permitting, then finally prohibiting, the temporary (*mutʿa*) marriage, are but three cases in point. Now, given that abrogation never applied to the Meccan universals and only infrequently did it apply to the specific rules revealed in Mecca, it follows that abrogation is not common in the Sharīʿa as a whole, and in fact is far less common, Shāṭibī argues, than is generally believed. This is due to the fact that there is no agreement among legal scholars as to whether abrogation occurs in many of the instances in which it is argued that one verse abrogates another; often there is no conclusive proof to establish cases of abrogation. Here, Shāṭibī refers to Ibn ʿArabī who dismissed a large number of what was said by some scholars to be cases of abrogation. Furthermore, the belief that abrogation is common in the law is due to misunderstanding of the usage of the early religious scholars (*mutaqaddimūn*) who, in fact, applied the term "abrogation" too liberally. They employed the term, *inter alia*, to the qualification (*taqyīd*) of unrestricted language (*muṭlaq*), and to the particularization (*takhsīs*) of general (*ʿumūm*) words. In our age, Shāṭibī argues, these conventions do not obtain; the term "abrogation" is used in a much more restricted sense.

Commands and prohibitions[49]

Charging believers to commit an act is known, properly speaking, as *amr*. It is differentiated from *nahy* (prohibition) in that the latter signifies charging believers to omit the performance of an act. In one sense, then, both the *amr* and *nahy* are commands, but one is intended to effect the performance of an act whereas the other is designed to effect non-performance. The command to perform, or to omit performance of, an act may be graded from a strict to a rather mild form. Whatever is integral to natural human behavior and conduct (e.g., eating, drinking, having sex) God did not insist upon by means of strict commands and prohibitions. Rather, omitting or

[49] Ibid., III, 81–165.

performing such conduct was stipulated in the forms of recommendation or permission. On the other hand, religious obligation and rituals (such as fasting and prayer) are not integral to human nature, and thus were regulated by means of strict forms of command and prohibition. Here, stern divine intervention was deemed necessary.

Commands and prohibitions may be found expressed in the texts in either of two forms, explicit or implicit. The former are directly stated, whether or not the rationale or *ratio legis* behind them can be known. In matters of ritual, for instance, we do not know the reason why God commanded the performance of ablution and the omission of any act causing so-called impurity. But we have no doubt that the command and prohibition in these matters are explicitly stated. Similarly, we know that God explicitly prohibited Muslims from conducting business during certain hours on Friday, and commanded them instead to worship Him, although we do not know precisely the rationale behind these particular commands and prohibitions. The implicit forms, on the other hand, only suggest the command to perform or to omit an act. When the texts state that "God does not like those who are extravagant," we can, strictly speaking, define such a statement as neither a command nor a prohibition. In it is implicit the notion and argument that if God does not like extravagance, then we should take it to mean that extravagance is objectionable, if not altogether prohibited.

Whether they are explicit or implicit, commands and prohibitions, when perceived to be so, are each translated into two possible legal norms. Commands may be taken to mean either obligation (*wujūb*) or recommendation (*nadb*). In the same vein, prohibitions may be seen as leading either to impermissibility (*taḥrīm*) or reprehensibility (*karāha*). Whatever the case, the four subdivisions share the common quality of being a requirement (*iqtiḍā*ʾ), a requirement to commit or omit an act. From this vantage point, then, there exists no difference between obligation and recommendation, or between impermissibility and reprehensibility. It is the obviation of differences among these categories that led the Ṣūfīs to recognize only the stringent forms deriving from command and prohibition, namely, obligation and impermissibility, respectively. Shāṭibī argues that they held obligation and impermissibility to be what the law normally requires (*ʿazīma)*, while recommendation and reprehensibility were regarded by them to be licentious (*rukhṣa*). This in turn led them to consider minor sins as equal to grave sins, and this, he insists, is unwarranted exaggeration and excessive piety. God had a purpose behind decreeing licenses and making them part of the law, and would not have done so in vain. Yet again, we sense here Shāṭibī's censure of stringent Ṣūfism.

General and particular[50]

In line with the epistemological foundations of his theory, Shāṭibī declares himself interested not in the linguistic forms of the general expression (*ʿumūm*) conventionally explicated by the legal theorists, but rather in the general expression insofar as it is inductively culled from an array of sources. The obligation to pray, for instance, is a general rule garnered from a large number of indicants, and not only from a single linguistic formulation (*ṣīghat al-ʿumūm*). When the contexts relevant to prayer are inductively surveyed, it becomes clear that prayer is a general obligation. The epistemological strength of this obligation is in no way inferior to that which is known through a single textual statement to that effect. Just as the statement may enjoy certainty or less than certainty, the inductive method may lead to the knowledge that a matter is general either with certitude or with probability, depending on the strength and comprehensiveness of the inductive survey. That is to say, if induction is complete, then it is deemed certain, but if a limited number of instances in the law are surveyed, then knowledge of the generality of the statement remains probable. An example of certainty is the principle of alleviating hardship in religion (*rafʿ al-ḥaraj*). Assuming that no one statement in the texts declares that excessive hardship is averted in legal obligation, we undertake an inductive survey of the law and find that there are numerous specific statements, embedded in a variety of sources, to the common effect that legal obligation is mitigated when excessive hardship is involved in the performance of a duty. Cleansing with sand (*tayammum*) in the absence of water; praying while sitting down when standing up is difficult; waiving the obligation to fast when traveling; combining two prayers in one when falling ill, traveling, or passing through a rain storm; allowing the consumption of the flesh of dead animals when starving in the desert or other forsaken places; praying in any direction when the location of the *qibla* cannot be known: all these, and many more, lead the jurist to derive the general principle that the presence of undue hardship is concomitant with mitigated rulings. This general principle then becomes the governing precept whenever the issue of hardship arises in legal reasoning. It acquires the same strength as if it were directly deduced from a single statement in the revealed texts. Thus, even in the absence of any direct statement, the *mujtahid* must treat the derived principle or precept as if it were derived from such a statement.

Once a general principle is derived through the inductive method with certainty, no diverging particular can refute or falsify it. This is in line with

[50] Ibid., III, 166–94.

the epistemology Shāṭibī had already delineated. Particulars are always probable, incapable of refuting a certain universal that was attested by a large number of supporting cases and contextual indications (*qarāʾin*). But when the inductive support is incomplete, the universal remains of course probable, and subject to falsification. In such a case, the *mujtahid* must continue to weigh the probable universal against those relevant particulars until that universal is either fully corroborated or refuted. If full corroboration is not possible, the *mujtahid* must suspend judgment (*tawaqquf*) as to its being certain, and must tentatively treat it as merely probable or highly probable.

But completeness in induction must not be understood in the modern, scientific sense. While Shāṭibī does not, of course, put it in these terms, it is quite clear that he does not expect law to meet the exact and strict standards of logic and philosophy. In enacting law, he asserts, God did not impose such standards, for if the great majority of the members of a class share a common feature (namely, generality), then the majority becomes the rule. This is the convention of God (*sunnat Allāh*) in promulgating His law. For instance, full mental capacity in legal matters is concomitant with attaining the age of majority. No one can be recognized as having full mental capacity until such time as he or she reaches this age, although it is well known that some people possess this capacity before attaining that age. The law simply cannot acknowledge or account for dissenting particulars.

It appears here that Shāṭibī is speaking of two levels of incomplete induction, for he acknowledges, as we have seen, that one type of incomplete induction remains probable, and that the *mujtahid* is entrusted with pursuing his investigation until he confirms or refutes the alleged universal at hand. Nowhere does Shāṭibī explain the difference, but we may safely state that he distinguishes between a high and a low level of corroboration. A low level is tentative, and is susceptible to falsification. A high level, though incomplete, engenders certainty, and is impervious to refutation by what Shāṭibī seems to consider a marginal number of dissenting particulars.[51]

Lucidity and obscurity[52]

Shāṭibī's fundamental assertion here is that the legists are the heirs of the Prophet, an assertion that is intended to serve a purpose which is in other respects outside the compass of the topics of lucidity (*mubayyan*) and obscurity (*mujmal*) as normally elaborated by the legal theorists. Indeed, it would seem that the heading of this section is used merely as a pretext for pursuing his critique of the Ṣūfis.

[51] See pp. 164–67 above. [52] *Muwāfaqāt*, III, 196–223.

The Prophet, in his sayings (*aqwāl*) and deeds (*afʿāl*), had clarified in a lucid manner (*bayyana*) the thrust of legal obligations, and since the legists are his heirs, they are bound by the same duty not only to clarify the legal subject matter in their professional discourse but also to confirm it in their own personal actions. Just as the Prophet's deeds and tacit approval (*iqrār*) of legal issues were taken by later generations to be his binding Sunna, the legists must, in their own deeds, comply with their own preachings. For when a jurist informs the public of a legal obligation, and then himself behaves in complete accord with his own declaration, the public will then be more convinced of the validity and strength of the obligation. On the other hand, if he says one thing concerning a legal matter and then practices another, then public faith in the authoritative character of that matter would be significantly diminished. In sum, the jurists are the model of their respective communities, just as the Prophet had been the archetypal model of the community of Muslims at large.

At this point, Shāṭibī abruptly moves on to discuss what he calls the connection between lucid expressions and legal norms. In doing so he reverts to the assertion he made earlier to the effect that the recommended act must not be equated with the obligatory, but now adds that this should occur neither in discourse nor in actions. The same applies to the categories of the recommended/permissible and the reprehensible/forbidden. Treating the recommended as obligatory would render superfluous the legal norm of recommendation, this being tantamount to setting aside, and thus obliterating, a universal principle of the law. Religious scholars, including jurists, must practice those acts that are recommended so that the populace and laymen can learn from them. If the religious elite, the leading example of the community, consistently practice the recommended acts, then the populace will be led to think that such acts are obligatory. Such is also the case with reprehensible acts; if the populace observes that the elite avoid these acts, then it will think they are forbidden. The elite must at times avoid practicing the recommended and must at times practice the reprehensible in order to maintain the distinctions between the five legal norms in the eyes of the populace. Here, Shāṭibī clearly subsumes the Ṣūfīs, or at least their leadership, under the general term "elite" which includes the religious scholars (*ʿulamāʾ*). He finds blameworthy their assimilation of the recommended with the obligatory, the reprehensible with the forbidden, and their total avoidance of legal licenses (*rukhaṣ*).

But in one instance at least,[53] he appears somewhat empathetic, saying that they are justified in their secrecy about their stringent legal behavior,

[53] Ibid., III, 216 (lines 6–15).

since they do not wish to be misunderstood by the general public. Immediately thereafter, however, he returns to his earlier assertion that the law neither allows nor tolerates obliterating the distinctions between the legal categories. In the final analysis, the fleeting moment of empathy with the Ṣūfīs seems, I think, no more than a carefully calculated move to appease them. From this and other contexts, it would not be far fetched to conclude that the Ṣūfīs were a powerful factor in the socio-religious configuration of Shāṭibī's milieu, a factor with which he had to contend. That he wrote *al-Iʿtiṣām* in his own defense against their charges, and, at least partly, in vindication of the views he expressed in *al-Muwāfaqāt*, constitutes substantial evidence of their power.

THE QURAN AND SUNNA

Going beyond the conventional, atomic view of the Quran, Shāṭibī presents us with a unique theory in which the text is seen as an integral whole. No verse or part can be properly understood without reference to other parts, as well as to the particular and general circumstances in which the text was revealed (*asbāb al-nuzūl*).[54] Without such a referential approach, the meanings of the verses and God's intentions in revealing them would be unintelligible to the human mind. All this, however, presupposes a thorough knowledge of the linguistic conventions prevalent among the Arabs during the time of revelation. God addresses the Arabs in the language they understand with reference to a reality that was specifically theirs, and since both language and reality may – and Shāṭibī implies that they do – differ from later usages and realities, the jurist must thoroughly ground himself in them.

Thus adequate knowledge of the Arabic language and of the circumstances of revelation, coupled with a wholistic reading of the text may guarantee what Shāṭibī deems a reasonable, moderate, and middle-of-the-road interpretation. To be properly understood, a Quranic verse must be viewed in light of the verses that preceded it in time. The later parts in the text must therefore be explained in terms of the earlier ones, just as the entire Medinese revelation must be viewed in light of the Quran's Meccan phase. And within each of the Medinese and Meccan phases the later verses are to be interpreted only after a full consideration of what was revealed earlier. An example of this general principle is the Meccan Sūra "the Cattle," which embodies a wholistic view of the universal principles (*uṣūl*

[54] Ibid., III, 224 ff. For a more detailed study of the function of the Quran in Shāṭibī's theory, see W. B. Hallaq, "The Primacy of the Qur'ān in Shātibī's Legal Theory," in W. B. Hallaq and D. P. Little, eds., *Islamic Studies Presented to Charles J. Adams* (Leiden: E. J. Brill, 1991), 69–90.

kulliyya) of the law. Casting aside any part of it will lead to blighting the legal system. When the Prophet emigrated to Medina, the Sūra of the Cow was revealed in order to explain the general principles in the Sūra of the Cattle. Though some of these details appear elsewhere, here are found specific laws relating to ritual, diet, crime, commercial transactions, marriage, etc. The universal principles established in the Cattle concerning the preservation of one's religion, life, mind, offspring and property are all confirmed in the Cow. Thus what is revealed in Medina subsequent to the Cow must be viewed in its light. The significance of chronology here can hardly be exaggerated.

That the later Sūras and verses explain what was revealed prior to them in time leads to a certain hierarchy in the Quran with the very early Sūras being the most comprehensive. Even if a Medinese verse appears general in scope, there must always be a more general verse revealed earlier, the later verses always supplementing the earlier ones. The Meccan revelation thus constitutes the ultimate reference, particularly those parts of it revealed at the outset of the Prophet's career. They establish the most general and universal principles, namely, the protection of the right to religion, life, mind, progeny and property. Later revelation, particularly the Medinese, may complement these principles, but in the main they provide explanations and details relative to these universals.

Whether or not the Quran contains all the details of the law, God perfected for Muslims their religion by the time the last verse of the text was revealed. Citing Q. 5:3, "Today I have perfected your religion for you," Shāṭibī argues that the Quran contains all the fundaments of faith, spiritual and practical; it treats of all things, and, conversely, nothing needed in religion and life stands outside its compass.

The logical consequence of this argument represents no less than a complete relegation of the Prophetic Sunna to a secondary status, and Shāṭibī, to be sure, does reach this very conclusion. But though the Quran lays down the foundations of the law and religion, no rulings ought to be extracted from it without consulting the Sunna, because the latter, just like the Medinese revelation, provides explanations and details for the Quran. Nevertheless, Shāṭibī affirms the completeness and self-sufficiency of the latter and, in consequence, rejects the view that the Sunna offers any substantive addition to the Quran.

Shāṭibī's position here is no doubt novel, signaling a total departure from the conventional view propounded in legal theory. He asserts that in the *mujtahid*'s legal reasoning about individual legal cases the Quran merits attention before the Sunna. That the latter should be demoted to a secondary role is the result of the higher degree of certitude the Quran enjoys.

While both sources as a whole are certain, the individual verses possess a degree of certitude higher than that enjoyed by individual Prophetic reports.

The traditional doctrine of legal theory affirms that when the Quran is ambiguous on a particular matter, the Sunna intervenes to determine the specific intent of the Lawgiver. Similarly, the Sunna functions in the same manner whenever the Quran fails to address any problem with exactitude and clarity. A case in point is the Quranic injunction to cut off the hand of a thief. The Sunna delimited the Quranic command by decreeing that this punishment must be meted out only when there is a break and entry and the value of the stolen goods exceeds a certain prescribed amount. In the same vein, the unconditional Quranic permission for matrimony was narrowed down in scope by precluding marriage to the maternal or paternal aunts of one's wife. Shāṭibī does accept the authority of the Sunna in such cases, but only insofar as it complements the Quran. The Sunna, in his view, merely brings out and articulates the intention of the Quran. If a jurist establishes the exact meaning of a verse, we cannot say, Shāṭibī analogically argues, that the ruling based on that verse stems from the authority of the jurist himself. He, like the Sunna, functions only as an interpreter of what is ultimately the very word of God.

When the *mujtahid* is presented with two different or contradictory pieces of evidence, both of which enjoy the same degree of certainty – thus precluding the possibility of one superseding the other – the common practice was to choose the evidence that was more suitable to the particular case at hand, even though it might not be Quranic. In this practice Shāṭibī sees no problem, because the evidence in the Sunna represents, in the final analysis, an explanation or reformulation of a general Quranic text. Put differently, the evidential competition is not between the Quran and the Sunna, but ultimately between two different or seemingly contradictory statements within the Quran. The latter, Shāṭibī reaffirms, contains the essence of the Sharīʿa, and anything else represents, so to speak, footnotes to the self-sufficient Book. But the hypothetical interlocutor replies by citing a number of Quranic verses (such as 4:59, 5:92, 59:7) to the effect that the Prophet must be obeyed and that his Sunna constitutes a source of authority equal to that of the Quran. The specific directive to bow to the Prophet's authority clearly indicates that he did introduce injunctions unspecified in the Quran. Furthermore, they cite a number of reports to the same effect, adding the Prophetic condemnation of those who make the Quran their sole reference.

But Shāṭibī does not see how this evidence confutes his position. When the Sunna renders clear a verse pertaining to a particular legal ruling, the said ruling would be ultimately grounded in the Quran, not the Sunna. Both God and the Prophet presumably bestow on the case a certain authority. Distinguishing between the two sanctioning authorities does not entail differentiating between two different rulings. In other words, when the Quran calls, as it does, upon believers to obey God and the Prophet, it is understood that the Prophet's authority derives, in the final analysis, from that of God. And since no distinction is made between two different rulings belonging to a single case, then there is no proof that the Sunna contains material not within the compass of the Quran.

A major role that the Sunna plays vis-à-vis the Quran is to prefer one verse over another concerning a particular case of law. For instance, the Quran generally permitted the consumption of good foods and forbade that of putrid ones, without, however, defining the status of many specific types. The Sunna then intervened to decide each kind in accordance with the principles regulated in the Quran, by subsuming certain foods under one legal norm or another. Among these were the prohibitions with regard to the flesh of donkeys and certain predatory animals. Similarly, God prohibited inebriants but permitted non-alcoholic beverages. The rationale behind the prohibition was the effect of alcohol on the mind, for, in addition to its negative social effects, it distracts the Muslim from worshipping his Lord. The Sunna interfered here to determine to which of the two categories date-wine and semi-intoxicating beverages belong. On the basis of Quranic data, the Sunna articulated the classic dictum that any beverage that inebriates when consumed in large quantities is prohibited even in small quantities (*mā askara kathīruhu fa-qalīluhu ḥarām*).

But all this, Shāṭibī maintains, does not change the fact that the Sunna is ultimately rooted in the Book. Indeed, the Sunna may contain some legal subject matter which is found neither in a laconic Quranic statement nor even in an ambiguous or indirect one. But such subject matter still has its origins in the Quran. It is Shāṭibī's fundamental assumption that each Quranic verse or statement possesses multifaceted meanings, some direct and others oblique. While a verse may exist in its own particular context and may appear to have an immediate, obvious meaning, this very verse may, at the same time, manifest another meaning which is identical to those found in other verses. To put it differently, a group of verses may all have in common one theme which happens to be subsidiary to the main meaning in each verse. The inductive corroboration of one verse by the others lends the common theme a certain authority which could reach the degree of certitude. Whereas this theme remains hidden in the linguistic terrain of the Quran, the Sunna unfolds it in the form of a Prophetic report. The result of one such case of corroboration in the Quran is the well-known and all-important Prophetic report "No injury and counter injury in Islam."

The Quran, however, does provide what Shāṭibī characterizes as the most important foundation of the law, namely, the principle governing the interests of people. For after all, the entire enterprise of the Sharīʿa was instituted in the interests of Muslims, whether these interests pertain to this life or to the hereafter. In order to safeguard these interests, the Sharīʿa seeks to implement the principles embodied in the three universals of *ḍarūriyyāt*, *ḥājiyyāt* and *taḥsīniyyāt*. The Sunna, in its detailing of particular cases, represents nothing but an extension of the all-embracing Quranic principles. The contrast here is between the Quranic *taʾṣīl*, laying down the foundations, and *tafṣīl*, the explication of the foundations by extending their law to particular cases. All five sub-categories of the *ḍarūriyyāt* are prescribed by the Quran and then further expounded by the Sunna. In the same vein, the principles governing the other two categories of the *ḥājiyyāt* and *taḥsīniyyāt* and their sub-categories are essentially stated in the Quran, with the minute details provided in the Sunna.

By relegating the Sunna to a status subsidiary to the Quran, and by hierarchically and chronologically structuring Quranic material, Shāṭibī was aiming at achieving a result that he nowhere alludes to in the dozens of pages he allocates to the discussion of the two sources and their relationship to each other. The significance of his novel approach becomes obvious only in the last chapter of his book, where he treats of *ijtihād* and *mujtahid*s. It is to the exposition of this chapter that we shall now turn.

IJTIHĀD, *MUJTAHID*S AND *MUFTĪ*S

The enumeration of the sciences the *mujtahid* must master had become by Shāṭibī's time a commonplace in works of legal theory. In order to qualify for this rank, the jurist must possess, *inter alia*, a thorough knowledge of the Arabic language, consensus and disagreement, abrogating and abrogated verses, the Prophetic Sunna, and the methods of legal reasoning and causation.[55] All these, Shāṭibī appears to say, constitute the second set of credentials required to attain this rank. First and foremost, the *mujtahid* must fully understand the doctrine of intentions (*maqāṣid*), a doctrine that Shāṭibī elaborates and defines in the second volume of his work. The second set of requirements, he asserts, is subservient to the first, for without understanding the doctrine of *maqāṣid*, the knowledge encompassed by the second set cannot be utilized adequately.[56]

[55] Shīrāzī, *Lumaʿ*, 85–86. [56] *Muwāfaqāt*, IV, 67.

At the same time, the jurist who encounters a new case of law is not necessarily required to possess the comprehensive knowledge of subjects deemed necessary for the full-fledged *mujtahid* (*mujtahid muṭlaq*). All he needs to know are those aspects necessary for him to solve the case. Even the great *mujtahid*s, the founding fathers of the schools, were not all fully equipped with all the tools needed for *ijtihād*. For instance, neither Abū Ḥanīfa nor Shāfiʿī was sufficiently expert in the science of Prophetic reports, yet both are considered not only *mujtahid*s but also the founders of legal schools. Thus, a "partial" *mujtahid*[57] may adopt legal premises already proven by an earlier *mujtahid* in order to solve a particular case.

Naturally, the requirements in each situation vary. If the case requires the derivation of a rule from the primary texts, then knowledge of the Arabic language is indispensable. Any other requirement may be compensated for through a reliance on the efforts of other legal experts. But if the texts have no bearing upon the case, then recourse is made to general themes in the law, and these require no particularly deep knowledge of Arabic. What is needed instead is a genuine and complete understanding of the intentions of the law.

Thus far, Shāṭibī discussed the *ijtihād* that involves a direct confrontation with the revealed texts. But he classifies the general category of *ijtihād* into two major types: that which may not come to an end and that which may. The first type, known as *taḥqīq al-manāṭ*, has never been subject to dispute and all judges and jurisconsults practice it in their respective professions. It signifies the investigation and then confirmation of the locus of the legal rule. For instance, from the textual injunction "Let those of just character amongst you be witnesses," the jurist establishes that being just is a requisite for witnessing. *Taḥqīq al-manāṭ* involves the process of determining whether or not a person is deemed admissible as a witness on the basis of the quality of rectitude prescribed in the texts. It is not the quality as such that is the object of *taḥqīq al-manāṭ*, but rather its locus in the case at hand. People range from those who are abundantly just to those whose rectitude can hardly be spoken of. The wide spectrum in between presents the range open to the *mujtahid*, a range from which to select those who meet the criterion. Another example of this type of *ijtihād* is the evaluation of damages, such as the determination of the compensatory price of domestic animals or goods. Now, the reason why this type of *ijtihād* can never come to a halt is that without it legal ordinances remain nothing more than theoretical and mental constructs, having virtually nothing to

[57] Shāṭibī's "partial *mujtahid*" is defined by the following statement: "*lā yalzamu al-mujtahid fī al-aḥkām al-sharʿiyya an yakūna mujtahidan fī kulli ʿilm yataʿallaq bihi al-ijtihād ʿalā al-jumla.*" Ibid., IV, 68.

do with practical application without which the law becomes a non-entity. *Taḥqīq al-manāṭ* represents the process of individuating cases and realizing them in the external world.

The second type of *ijtihād* that may come to an end Shāṭibī divides into three categories, the first of which is termed *tanqīḥ al-manāṭ*, that is, the identification of the *ratio legis* insofar as it is isolated from attributes that are conjoined with it in the texts. The second category, known either as *takhrīj al-manāṭ* or *al-ijtihād al-qiyāsī*, involves investigating the texts in order to extract what is otherwise an unspecified *ratio legis*. These two categories of *ijtihād* we have discussed earlier.[58] The third category, Shāṭibī maintains, is a variation on the theme of *taḥqīq al-manāṭ*, the first major type discussed above. Whereas this category subsumed under the first type relates to the genus or class of things, such as the quality of being just or the price of sheep or camels, the third category of the second type is confined to the particular individuals to whom the rule is applicable. This is a more exact and subtle form of *ijtihād*. More specifically, it is applicable to each believer insofar as he or she is subject to the rule of law in accordance with the highly particular and contextualized circumstances relevant to that single believer. The *mujtahid*'s function here is to investigate these special circumstances and to apply to them the law that is most suitable.

It seems that this third category is novel, making no appearance in other works of legal theory. The novelty of this category is suggested by the fact that Shāṭibī advances in its vindication a rather lengthy discussion, citing, among other things, the example of the Prophet, who gave a variety of answers to the same questions he was asked because the questioners came from different backgrounds. Why Shāṭibī introduced this category into the typology of *ijtihād* is a question we will attempt to answer in due course. Why he declared this category, along with the other two categories of the second type, to belong to the *ijtihād* that may come to an end is a question that is far more difficult to answer. It may be speculated that the first two categories subsumed under this type – representing the *mujtahid*'s direct confrontation with the revealed texts to solve completely new cases – may come to an end either because the *mujtahid*s of high calibre, who are fully capable of dealing with such cases, may become defunct or because such cases may not arise. That they may not arise is, in the view of classical and medieval theoreticians, a possibility that is almost inconceivable. It was commonly held that cases not covered by the texts will continue to "befall" the Muslim community until the Day of Judgment. That the *mujtahid*s of high calibre may become defunct is a theoretical possibility that was a topic

58 See pp. 88 ff. above.

of debate among most later legal theorists. Many Mālikites, like Shāṭibī himself, espoused that possibility.[59]

At this point we should turn to another central issue with which Shāṭibī deals, namely, that the Sharīʿa revolves around a unity of opinion (*qawl wāḥid*) despite the juristic disagreements (*khilāf*) by which it is engulfed. Here, Shāṭibī adduces a lengthy argument to prove his point, an argument the details of which are not of particular interest to us. Rather, what is of interest is the question, Why does he put forth this argument? By "unity of opinion" in the Sharīʿa, Shāṭibī means that in the final analysis each case has one true legal solution, whereas the other solutions are not. This is why no *mujtahid* is allowed to hold two contradictory or varying opinions with regard to one case at the same time. If he encounters two differing pieces of evidence pertaining to a single case, the *mujtahid* must weigh them against each other, adopting the preponderant view. If only one opinion is valid for each *mujtahid*, then, *a fortiori*, the *muqallid* must not follow any opinion that suits him or which is agreeable to his needs, interests or desires. Rather, he should adopt the opinion that he deems, in the footsteps of the *mujtahid*, to be juristically preponderant. Some have thought, Shāṭibī charges, that the *muqallid* is free to choose whichever view he regards as of service in achieving his personal goals. His choice, they mistakenly held, is no different from the choice proffered by the *kaffāra* penance, whereby the believer is entirely free either to manumit a slave or feed the poor. In short, the *muqallid* must exercise his thought (*bil-aʿlamiyya*) in resorting to the more weighty view of a *mujtahid*. It is noteworthy here that Shāṭibī applies the term "*muqallid*" equally to both the jurist-imitator and the layman.

In a revealing passage, Shāṭibī explicitly speaks of the reason that prompted him to put forth his lengthy argument. He remarks that

> Neglecting to observe this principle [of choosing the weighty view; *rājiḥ*] has led many jurist-imitators to issue for their friends and relatives *fatwā*s which they would not otherwise issue for others, and this they did to satisfy those relatives' and friends' desires and personal predilections. This practice may be found in times past, as well as in our own times. Nowadays, we also find the practice of arbitrarily combining the most convenient opinions from amongst the various schools (*tatabbuʿ rukhaṣ al-madhāhib*) with the purpose of fulfilling base desires and achieving personal ends.[60]

That the arbitrary choice of opinions is impermissible is attested by the fact that the judge should attain the rank of *ijtihād*, so he can judiciously choose

[59] For a detailed discussion of this matter, see Hallaq, "Was the Gate of Ijtihād Closed?," 3–41; Hallaq, "The Controversy about the Existence of Mujtahids," 129–41.
[60] *Muwāfaqāt*, IV, 85.

the legally valid opinion. Failing the attainment of this rank, the judge would be ordinarily bound by the political will of the sovereign to follow a particular *mujtahid*, and in the absence of an opinion from that *mujtahid* with regard to a particular case, he would follow that of another *mujtahid*, also designated by the sovereign. This alone can not only guarantee consistency (*inḍibāṭ*) in the legal system but also curb arbitrary practices which have detrimental effects on the law.[61]

It also appears that Shāṭibī was responding to two extreme camps in the legal culture he knew. The first, apparently dominated by the Ṣūfīs, claimed that free movement for the individual between various schools of legal thought, within and without the *madhhab*, must be and is allowed in order to enable him to choose the most demanding and rigorous of legal obligations, in fulfillment of his strict (presumably Ṣūfī) religious tenets. The other camp is that which seems to have consisted of the more earthly legal scholars who advocated the same view but with the option of choosing the more lenient view. It also appears that Shāṭibī here concerns himself more with the latter camp, which indeed becomes his main preoccupation in the later parts of his book. He mentions the claims of the first camp only in passing, whereas he gives a more detailed account of the arguments adduced by the second camp, arguments which included Quranic verses and Prophetic reports cited in support of their own position. He reminds these legists of his earlier discussion concerning the principles governing hardship (*mashaqqa*), where he dwelled on the theme that religious obligation cannot be devoid of burdensome duties and responsibilities, although they are generally tolerable. The Sharīʿa, he had already emphasized, is virtually synonymous with steering an ideally middle course between agreeable pleasure and intolerable hardship.

Those jurists who pretend to the rank of *ijtihād* should also follow the example of the true *mujtahid*s insofar as the latter take into consideration, through tremendous foresight, the far-reaching consequences of the rulings they declare. For it is often the case that a benefit embedded in a legal ruling might lead to abuse of the law. Certain types of sale, for instance, are rendered lawful because they facilitate commercial and financial transactions. But the fact is that these sales contain elements of risk and usury, both being prohibited by the law. Thus, allowing them initially on a limited scale might lead, in the long run, to their widespread practice, with the attendant consequence that risk and usury may become rampant. The *mujtahid* must then calculate not only the immediate effects of the rulings they reach, but also their ultimate consequences in law and society.[62]

[61] Ibid., IV, 90–96. [62] Ibid., IV, 128–31.

It is also to this second camp, or at least some elements in it, that he addresses himself at length when he speaks of a warped form of *ijtihād* that seems to have existed in his legal environment.[63] This *ijtihād* emanates from jurists who have not equipped themselves with the tools necessary for valid ways of legal reasoning. Being dictated by personal desires (*tashahhī*), this *ijtihād* leads to illegitimate results which have no place in the legal system. But despite Shāṭibī's scathing criticism, he was unwilling to excommunicate them from the community. No one, in his opinion, can demonstrate conclusively that they have committed a grave sin, and since we can judge them only with probability, they should be considered part of the community.

Shāṭibī next turns his attention briefly to the Ṣūfīs, and here he reintroduces the hierarchical and diachronic constitution of the Quranic text, with the view of bringing out its significance within the context of his discourse about the *mujtahid* as a jurisconsult. Now he remarks that the Meccan revelation, with all its characteristic universality, is general and simplified in nature, intended for an unlettered audience. It is addressed to the community at large, the legal expert and layman alike. Every Muslim, hailing from any walk of life, can comprehend it, and can thus heed its injunctions without any intermediary. The Medinese revelation, on the other hand, came down to explain, in some technical detail, the universal principles laid down earlier. Hence, only the legal experts are equipped to deal with, and understand, the Medinese text. The complexity of its subject matter simply precludes the layman from confronting it directly.

We are now told that the universality and generality of the Meccan revelation *ipso facto* means that it is devoid of mitigation and juridical licenses (*tarakhkhuṣ*). The Medinese texts were thus revealed in order to modify and qualify the rigor that was communicated earlier in point of time. We are also told that the Ṣūfīs set aside the Medinese licenses, and adhered solely to the stringent demands of the Meccan Sūras. Shāṭibī strongly insinuates that the Ṣūfīs attempted to impose their view of the law upon the lay public. By insisting on the intellectual simplicity of the Meccan revelation, Shāṭibī was in effect arguing that laymen should be able to understand, and comply with, this revelation without intermediary. He seems to say that if the Ṣūfīs choose to subject themselves to rigorous piety, so be it. But it is not within their legitimate right to impose their will and perception of the law on the community of laymen. In these terms, he equally addresses himself to the jurisconsults (whether or not they are also Ṣūfīs, we do not know) who, he advises, must not make evident to the public any of their practices that are unusually strict. For if they do, they will cause those who take them as a

[63] Ibid., IV, 108–27.

model to imitate them, thus leading some members of the public to suffer extreme, unjustified hardship. If a jurisconsult finds himself misleading, in this manner, the laymen surrounding him, he must at once abandon his over-zealous behavior, lest harm befall them.

The exemplary role the jurisconsults play in society is explained in terms of Prophetic legacy. Muhammad was the first jurisconsult of the Muslim community, and later jurisconsults have continued to play the very role he played. Just as his utterances and deeds were taken as examples to be emulated, so are the utterances (=opinions) and deeds of later jurisconsults. The importance of their utterances to the legal system, Shāṭibī avers, can hardly be overemphasized. And their deeds are in no way less significant. If a jurisconsult's personal behavior stands in accord with what he preaches, this behavior can only strengthen the conviction of the truth and authority of the law he propounds in society. If, on the other hand, his actions and legal pronouncements are at variance, then not only will the belief of the populace in the authority of the law be undermined but it will become necessary that his legal opinions should not be followed. Conversely, the jurisconsult who deserves to be followed is one whose deeds are in complete conformity with his expert utterances.[64] It is fairly safe to assume that Shāṭibī here was militating against the jurisconsults, probably of his own time, who preached an ideal of law but did not themselves adhere to the very law they were proclaiming.

CONCLUSION

Shāṭibī's *Muwāfaqāt* represents one instance of legal theory that is brought to bear upon a particular legal culture and the problems the author perceived to permeate certain segments of it. The specificity of his theory as a response to the challenges created by these problems accounts for the emphasis, deemphasis and omissions of topics that are otherwise treated by other legal theorists. We note the distinct absence in the *Muwāfaqāt* of any treatment of consensus, *qiyās,* legal causation (*taʿlīl*), and a host of other subjects. These omissions, we conclude, appear to be due to the fact that on these subjects Shāṭibī had no particular message to convey to the Ṣūfīs and jurists he was addressing and criticizing. On the other hand, his unusually expanded discussions of, and vigorous assertions concerning, such topics as the legal norms and licenses bespeak the space within these topics that allowed him to articulate his critique. But his discourse was not merely critical, or simply aimed at pointing to distortions and abuses of the

[64] Ibid., IV, 162–82.

law. It would be equally true to view it as a discourse of persuasion, aiming at rectification and reedification. In a religious science that abhorred digression and repetition, Shāṭibī's style and method of discourse clearly exhibit his persuasive bent, the landmark of which was precisely the attributes of repetition and digression. Digression, it must be noted, was necessary and subservient to repetition.

For Shāṭibī to achieve his dual purpose, namely, criticizing and persuading, he could not have merely reiterated the corpus of legal theory as it had been conventionally laid down by earlier theorists. His arguments had each to be charged with specific agendas, grounded ultimately in an epistemological framework that would be immune to the rebuttals of his powerful opponents. A marriage of the concepts of intention (*maqāṣid*) and induction provided him with the weapons he needed to achieve his purpose, namely, to criticize and persuade. In the creative wedding of these two concepts he found an instrument which allowed him to carve out a legal philosophy that mediates between two extreme approaches to, and practices of, the law, namely, those adopted by (at least some) Ṣūfīs on the one hand, and an unidentifiable group of legists, on the other. We must stress that much of the practices adopted by the latter group, which Shāṭibī criticized, later came to be known as the Mālikite *ʿamal*.[65]

The logical method of induction no doubt reached maturity before Shāṭibī's time, but Shāṭibī was the only legal theorist we know to have utilized this method on such a sophisticated level and to achieve such formidable ends. The significance of induction as he put it to use in the service of legal theory does not seem to have been appreciated by posterity. We detect no influence by his theory on later generations. But Shāṭibī's induction, which appealed to a variety of sources within the Sharīʿa, and which depended on scanning the intention and spirit of the law – without limiting itself to specific textual statements (the common characteristic of other theories) – has made it attractive to a group of modern thinkers whose primary occupation is to free the Muslim mind from the fetters created by the immediate, and perhaps shackling, meanings of the revealed texts. These thinkers, who have to contend with a shrinking world in which western, secularized values overshadow their own lives, are the modern legal reformers, the modernists, to whose ideas and intellectual frustrations we shall now turn.

65 On Mālikite *ʿamal*, see *Encyclopaedia of Islam*, s.v. "*ʿAmal*" (by J. Berque), I, 427–28; H. Toledano, *Judicial Practice and Family Law in Morocco* (Boulder: Social Science Monographs, 1981), 9–24.

6

CRISES OF MODERNITY: TOWARD A NEW THEORY OF LAW?

THE BACKGROUND

AS we have seen in chapters 2 and 3, a salient characteristic of pre-modern legal theory is the great attention it accords to the literal interpretation of the Quran and the Sunna. The language of these two sources was construed to have a direct and literal effect on law cases that required solutions. No amount of interpretation in this theory could have changed, for instance, the legal effect of the Quranic verse that allots the male heir twice the share of the female.[1] Furthermore, the theological postulate that sustained most legal theories, of Ashʿarite inspiration, states that man's intellectual capabilities are thought to be insufficient to determine the rationale behind God's revelation. God's wisdom, deeply embedded in His Sharīʿa, is simply incomprehensible for humans. Thus, the rationales of rules in the revealed texts were to be sought solely in the inner structures of these texts: only what God chose to declare explicitly to be the *ratio legis* of a case was to be taken thus, and what He decided merely to allude to was to be subjected to an interpretive enquiry that was deemed to result in a probable judgment. But nothing more was to be attributed to God's motives and rationale.

Even Shāṭibī could not free himself (assuming that he wished to do so) from the literal grip of the hermeneutic that so thoroughly permeated Muslim juristic thinking. Although he did not subscribe to the Ashʿarite theological postulate, and although he advocated an inductive, not a literal, understanding of the divine sources, he remained, as attested in his *fatwās*,[2]

[1] Further on this point, see the conclusion below.

[2] Shāṭibī's *fatwās* have been collected by Wansharīsī, *al-Miʿyār al-Mughrib*, I, 26, 29, 278, 327; II, 292, 468, 511; IV, 140, 205; V, 23, 26, 59, 60, 201, 213, 219, 387; VI, 71, 327, 387, 389; VII, 101, 105, 109, 111, 125; VIII, 133, 284; IX, 227, 252, 633; X, 102; XI, 39, 42, 103, 112, 123, 131, 132, 139; XII, 10, 12, 14, 18, 25, 29, 30, 35, 42, 293.

obdurately loyal to the positive legal doctrines of his school. The grip that positive legal doctrines had on the minds of Muslim jurists and judges was sufficiently tight to marginalize completely, if not to silence, any hermeneutic that attempted a change or restatement of the law. One of the victims of this state of affairs was the Ḥanbalite jurist al-Ṭūfī.

There is good reason to believe that the commitment (*taqlīd*) to substantive legal rulings as well as the conservatism of the pre-modern legal profession were not exclusively an outcome of the nature of legal theory, for the latter described – and less frequently prescribed – juridical reality, and often responded to and sanctioned the changes that took place in the world of real practice. True, legal theory as a whole never created, or attempted to create, an alternative hermeneutical possibility, for this would have amounted to nothing less than an act of self-negation. And true, it perpetuated the status quo by insisting on its own, well-preserved hermeneutic. But legal theory was also no more than a super-structure that was itself a product of a larger and more powerful structure.

The reasons for this trenchant commitment and conservatism lay elsewhere; namely, in the overall structure of the judicial system in Islam.[3] It is well known that the legal profession in classical and medieval Islam, on all levels, was generally independent of any state regulation. Muslim states and governments throughout the centuries had no hand in the training and certification of jurists and jurisconsults whose task it was to formulate the law. True, the state exercised some influence on the court system, but it did not interfere in the processes through which the law was determined. This was exclusively the province of the jurists and jurisconsults who were largely independent in their practice of the law. The institution of *iftāʾ*, which played a crucial role in developing legal doctrine, was not, strictly speaking, formally regulated; that is to say, anyone who considered himself to have a sufficient level of legal learning could sit for *iftāʾ*. There simply was no such thing as a Bar Association to control the qualifications, and entry into the profession, of jurisconsults. The medieval literature is replete with evidence that points to the problem of an institutionalized system coping with inadequately qualified persons. In fact, a sizable body of religio-legal discourse burgeoned in response to this problem. And in order to maintain the integrity and the diachronically consistent application of legal doctrine – a feature essential and common to all legal systems – the establishment was compelled to develop a normative mechanism whereby abuse and manipulation of the system could be prevented or at least minimized.[4]

[3] For a more detailed statement of this matter, see Hallaq, "From *Fatwās* to *Furūʿ*," 59 f.

[4] One case of curbing such abuse and manipulation is analyzed by Nissreen Haram, "Use and Abuse of the Law: A Muftī's Response," in Khalid Masud, Brink Messick and David Powers,

The most efficient method developed and effectively harnessed in regulating the profession from within was a self-imposed criterion of what type of legal doctrine was deemed admissible and what was not. Each school of law came to recognize a set of canonical works produced by, or attributed to, its founding fathers. With the passage of time, and with the cumulative evolution of legal doctrine, some works by later authors acquired a canonical status, though in theory they were never equal in prestige to those of the founding fathers. The works of Rāfiʿī (d. 623/1226) and Nawawī (d. 676/1277) in the Shāfiʿite school, and that of Marghīnānī (d. 593/1196) in the Ḥanafite school, represent such authoritative works.[5] In practice, however, such later works generally supplanted the works of the early masters. Be that as it may, the function of this insistence on the application of rulings as formulated in these canonical works was, *inter alia*, to exclude the possibility of an unqualified person issuing a *fatwā* or a legal judgment inconsistent with the system of law as it has normatively and consensually operated. In the literature of all the four schools of law, for instance, it is tirelessly reiterated that he who wishes to serve as a jurisconsult must abide in his practice by a certain authoritative hierarchy of the sources, and any departure from the legal doctrine (*madhhab*) as stated in these sources renders his opinion suspicious if not altogether void. It is rendered void because it is accorded no weight whatsoever in the court system which is the ultimate authority in deciding admissible and inadmissible "arguments."

Preserving this system of control was positively crucial for the efficiency, to say nothing of the survival, of the pre-modern legal structure. Simply put, without it no law could be properly administered. And because the system worked remarkably well, the legal structure remained intact for over twelve centuries. In fact, law has been so successfully developed in Islam that it would not be an exaggeration to characterize Islamic culture as a legal culture. But this very blessing of the pre-modern culture turned out to be an obstacle in the face of modernization. The system that had served Muslims so well in the past now stood in the way of change – a change that proved to be so needed in a twentieth-century culture vulnerable to an endless variety of western influences and pressures.

While the insistence upon the authoritative substantive doctrines may

eds., *Islamic Legal Interpretation: Muftīs and their Fatwās* (Cambridge, Mass.: Harvard University Press, 1996), 72–86.

[5] Abū al-Qāsim ʿAbd al-Karīm b. Muḥammad al-Rāfiʿī, *Fatḥ al-ʿAzīz fī Sharḥ al-Wajīz*, printed with Yaḥyā b. Muḥyī al-Dīn Sharaf al-Dīn al-Nawawī, *al-Majmūʿ: Sharḥ al-Muhadhdhab*, 12 vols. (Cairo: Maṭbaʿat al-Taḍāmun, 1344/1925); Abū al-Ḥasan ʿAlī b. Abī Bakr al-Marghīnānī, *al-Hidāya: Sharḥ Bidāyat al-Mubtadī*, 4 vols. (Cairo: Maṭbaʿat Muṣṭafā Bābī al-Ḥalabī, 1400/1980).

have had a highly justifiable function in the past, it no longer serves the purposes of the present. The fact, however, remains that the authority and prestige attached to the founding fathers and the later distinguished jurists is still significantly maintained and even defended by many modern Muslims. This is nowhere more obvious than in the methods (if they can be called that at all) adopted for reforming the Islamic legal system in matters of personal status. When it became apparent that the traditional law could no longer serve Muslim society in the modern world, there were several attempts at introducing European codes lock, stock and barrel. These codes were variably French, German and Swiss. However, it was soon discovered that such codes were largely inadequate for a society that was fundamentally different from those western societies for which these codes were originally drafted. The modern Muslim states then turned to other devices that were inspired by the traditional Islamic doctrines.

Acknowledging that the doctrine of a single school no longer served the purposes of the reformers, recourse was made to a device according to which law could be formulated by an amalgamated selection (*takhayyur*) from several traditional doctrines held by a variety of schools. Even weaker doctrines within an individual school, inadmissible in the traditional system, have been rejuvenated and bestowed with a legitimacy equal to that enjoyed by the "sound" (*ṣaḥīḥ*) doctrines. The Ottoman Law of Family Rights (1917) represents the first major attempt in this direction. Later codes in Arab countries expanded this device to include Shīʿite doctrines, a step previously unthinkable. Moreover, the reformers resorted to the so-called *talfīq* according to which part of a doctrine of one school is combined with a part from another. An example in point may be found in the Egyptian Law of Testamentary Disposition (1946) and the Sudanese Judicial Circular No. 53. The background of this law is the Sunnī traditional doctrine which was subject to an entrenched consensus and which stipulated that no bequest whatsoever may be made to an heir. Bequests amounting to no more than one-third of the estate can, however, be made, but only to persons who are not sharers in the inheritance, and who would not otherwise inherit. Now, in attempting to expand the rights of a person to dispose of his wealth, the Egyptian and Sudanese legislators declared, basing themselves on Shīʿite law, that a testator's bequest to one of his legal heirs, provided it does not exceed one-third of his net estate, is valid without this being, in any way, dependent upon the consent of his other heirs.[6]

[6] For this and other examples, see J. N. D. Anderson, *Law Reform in the Muslim World* (London: Athlone Press, 1976): 52 ff.

In addition to this method of selection and amalgamation, which was the main device through which the legal systems of Middle Eastern countries were modernized, the reformers exercised their own version of interpretation, *ijtihād* – this in no way being akin, for reasons I will presently discuss, to the traditional form of *ijtihād*. A classic and well-known example of this interpretation is provided by the Tunisian Law of Personal Status of 1956, which addressed, among other things, the problem of polygamy. The traditional law permitting a man to marry up to four wives was increasingly viewed by many Muslim governments as offensive, and the Tunisian legislators opted to abolish this law in its entirety. Their justification revolved around the Quranic verse 4:3, which sanctioned marriage to four wives in the first place: "Marry of the women, who seem good to you, two or three or four; and if ye fear that ye cannot do justice then one only . . . It is more likely that ye will not do justice." The Tunisian reformers, emphasizing the latter part of the verse, argued that in both history and recent times no one, besides the Prophet himself, could treat two or more wives with complete equality and justice; hence, viewed realistically, the latter part of the verse supplants the permission to marry more than one wife.

It goes without saying that neither this quasi-*ijtihād* nor the device of selection and amalgamation are sustained by any type of cohesive legal methodology. In particular, the amalgamation of parts of divergent doctrines for the purpose of producing a doctrine suitable to modern needs suffers from a serious methodological flaw. For such an amalgamated doctrine would rest on a variety of lines of reasoning that are not necessarily compatible, and the rationale for the ruling in a case would be lost in the midst of the often contradictory lines of reasoning. The ramifications of this arbitrary device are grave, since further elaboration of the law on the basis of amalgamated cases can create problems of inconsistency in legal reasoning and hence in the legal system.

There is no doubt that the changes brought to bear upon the traditional legal system have been met by many Muslim intellectuals, be they traditional or modern, with disapproval and at times even opposition. In the second half of the nineteenth century, the opposition was mainly directed at the displacement of Islamic law by European codes, which was considered by many to be an affront to the time-honored Islamic values. In the twentieth century, however, criticism has revolved around the incoherent methods used by the ruling class to reform the law. There is little question that dissatisfaction with the means and results of legal reform permeates many levels of Muslim society, particularly the educated religious elite.

The search for an adequate and cohesive legal methodology was embarked upon during the second half of the nineteenth century. The Egyptian intellectual Muhammad ʿAbduh (d. 1905) is considered to have been the first major religious reformer to have laid the foundations for the modern ideas of reform. Strictly speaking, he did not articulate any proposal for a new legal methodology. Rather, his contribution lay in crafting – or perhaps more accurately reviving – a theology that was necessary for restructuring and rehabilitating legal ideas. A chief postulate of this theology, considerably influenced by the rationalist Muʿtazila, is that sound human reason is capable of distinguishing between good and bad, right and wrong. This is a tenet that occupied a minority position in medieval Islam, where the Ashʿarite majority held human reason to be utterly incapable of making such distinctions. But ʿAbduh, who consistently sought to remain within the traditional Sunnī mainstream, argued for harmony between sound reason and revelation, which he thought could never stand in conflict. If there appears to be a contradiction or conflict between the two, it is because one or the other has been misunderstood.

The dichotomy of reason and revelation, and the elevation of reason to a fairly independent position, has, to be sure, a pragmatic function in ʿAbduh's theory. It allows the individual to determine for himself what is good and what is bad behavior, and at the same time, it enables this rational capacity to make such distinctions in an organic relationship with the effects of revelation. Whereas reason dictates that a particular act is objectionable, revelation, for its part, demands avoidance of this act and provides penalty in the hereafter for him who commits it. The individual's avoidance of the act stems from religious faith, though the knowledge of its reprehensibility is attained by reason.

The value of this theology for the modern reformers lies in its emphasis on reason as a source of knowledge without severing reason from religious values. On the basis of this theology Muslims can decide what is best for them without violating the spirit of their religion. In fact ʿAbduh himself explicitly advocated the view that Muslims should not overly concern themselves with the hereafter to the detriment of their worldly life, for the best way to live as a Muslim is to pursue material progress.[7] This theology, which constituted a fundamental break with the traditionally accepted doctrines, paved the way for a wide variety of theories that ranged from the religiously conservative to the more or less secular.

The amount of twentieth-century writings on legal reform is staggering,

[7] See Malcolm Kerr, *Islamic Reform: The Political and Legal Theories of Muhammad ʿAbduh and Rashīd Riḍā* (Berkeley: University of California Press, 1966), 103–86.

to say the least. Any attempt at doing full justice to this massive discourse would run far beyond the limits of space allotted to this chapter. Therefore, I shall not even try to be exhaustive. All I can do here is to identify trends and discuss the main representatives of each trend, hoping, nonetheless, that no significant or influential contribution to the debate over legal methodology is overlooked.[8] It must be noted, however, that even within a single trend there exists a rich variety of theories that can be said to subscribe to a single major thesis or assumption.

At this point it must be noted that I shall not be concerned here with two groups. The first is the secular, whose advocates nowadays represent a rather marginal force, and who uphold the view that Islam should be altogether set aside. Powerful representatives of this group may be found among the Arab nationalists, in such figures as the Syrian Ṣādiq Jalāl al-ʿAẓm, and among a small number of more recent intellectuals, such as the Egyptian Faraj Fūda.[9] The second is the traditional group, represented, among others, by the official advocates of the Saudi regime, which aims at applying the Sharīʿa in its presumably intact, puritanist traditional form, notwithstanding the reformist spirit of Wahhābism. Together with these may be included the reformist ideologies of Sirhindī (d. 1034/1625), Shāh Walī Allāh of Delhi (d. 1176/1762) and the Sanūsī movement in Libya.[10] Despite their vigorous social and political reformist bent, and despite their unanimous proclamation of the right to exercise *ijtihād*, they mostly stressed the need to return to the pristine religious forms of the first

8 The omission of the theories of some reformers from the present discussion is dictated by the fact that their contributions are either obliquely related to legal theory or do not offer a real alternative to the traditional theory. To the latter type belongs Ḥasan Ḥanafī's discourse. In his *Les méthodes d'exégèse: essai sur la science des fondements de la comprehension "ʿilm uṣūl al-fiqh"* (Cairo: Le Conseil Supérieur des Arts, 1385/1965), he advances a detailed and comprehensive restatement of *uṣūl al-fiqh*, but the changes he introduces are mainly formal and barely alter the substance of traditional legal theory. See also the Arabic summary of his French work in *Dirāsāt Islāmiyya* (Beirut: Dār al-Tanwīr lil-Ṭibāʿa wal-Nashr, 1982), 55–82. In a number of works (see the References), Muhammad Arkoun puts forth an articulate methodology whereby he reinterprets several aspects of the traditional sciences, but legal theory, as an organic science, receives no special attention. This partial interest in legal theory is also characteritic of Abdullah An-Naʿim's *Toward an Islamic Reformation: Civil Liberties, Human Rights and International Law* (Syracuse: Syracuse University Press, 1990). As the title indicates, the focus of the work is highly specialized, and constitutes an area of discourse that was by no means integral to *uṣūl al-fiqh*. To the exception of the theories of these three reformers, whom we are justified in excluding from our discussion (especially in light of the restriction on space), there remain only marginal reformers that we will also exclude.

9 Al-ʿAẓm's secularist ideology has been expressed in a number of writings. See, in particular, his *Naqd al-Fikr al-Dīnī* (Beirut: Dār al-Ṭalīʿa, 1977); his *al-Naqd al-Dhātī baʿda al-Hazīma* (Beirut: Dār al-Ṭabīʿa lil-Ṭibāʿa wal-Nashr, 1970). On Faraj Fūda, see Aḥmad Jūda, *Ḥiwārāt ḥawl al-Sharīʿa* (Cairo: Dār Sīnā lil-Nashr, 1990), 13–19.

10 On their notions of renewal and *ijtihād*, see R. Peters, "*Ijtihād* and *Taqlīd* in 18th and 19th Century Islam," *Die Welt des Islams*, 20 (1980): 131–45.

Islamic generation, and yet were "able to make but little headway in the reformulation of the content of Islam."[11]

Aside from these, two trends that dominate the Muslim world today can be identified. I shall call these trends, for lack of better terms, religious utilitarianism and religious liberalism. Theologically, both take for granted the broad outlines of the doctrine espoused by Muhammad ʿAbduh. They also share the same goal, namely, the reformulation of legal theory in a manner that brings into successful synthesis the basic religious values of Islam, on the one hand, and a substantive law that is suitable to the needs of a modern and changing society, on the other. The methods they use to arrive at this end, however, differ significantly. The religious utilitarianists couch their theory chiefly in terms of public interest (*maṣlaḥa*), traditionally a principle of a rather limited application, but which they nonetheless have considerably expanded so as to make it the principal component of legal theory and methodology. These utilitarianists subscribe to a particular set of principles which were laid down by the early and medieval jurists of Islam. But they share these principles rather nominally, for they have drastically manipulated and indeed recast them to their own advantage. The religious liberalists, on the other hand, discard altogether the principles developed by the traditional jurists, and their hermeneutic, though far from being well developed, is a new phenomenon in Islam. But their substantive assumptions are not. They seem to have adopted the rationalist side of ʿAbduh's thesis together with the legacy it left behind, and it is in this sense that ʿAbduh may be claimed, paradoxically, as both the ideational father of the utilitarianists, and the distant intellectual ancestor of the liberalists. We shall begin with the former.

RELIGIOUS UTILITARIANISM

It was in the writings of Muhammad ʿAbduh that the seedling of religious utilitarianism was planted, and it was left for his disciple, Rashīd Riḍā (d. 1935), to give form and content to a potentially powerful idea. We have already noted that the cornerstone of the utilitarianist thesis was the concept of *maṣlaḥa*, which we have also seen to be somewhat controversial among the traditional jurists.[12] Riḍā was faced with a formidable task, for he not only had to recast the concept in such a way as to make it unqualifiedly palatable to the orthodox, but also to divest it of the fetters of the medieval theoretical discourse, of which the concept was an integral part.

[11] Fazlur Rahman, "Revival and Reform in Islam," *The Cambridge History of Islam*, vol. IIB, P. M. Holt et al., eds. *Islamic Society and Civilization* (Cambridge: Cambridge University Press, 1970), 640. See also Peters, "*Ijtihād* and *Taqlīd*." [12] See pp. 112–13 above.

This required nothing less than amplifying the concept of public interest to such an extent that it would stand on its own as a legal theory and philosophy. But for achieving any degree of success it was also necessary to abandon other jurisprudential concepts as well as traditional substantive law that were the products of legal theory and, more importantly, so close to the heart of his contemporaries.

Thus, the first step in this process required Riḍā to insist on what he characterized as the pure form of Islam, embodied in nothing more than the Quran, the Sunna of the Prophet and the consensus of doctrine arrived at by the Companions. All legal doctrines elaborated by the jurists, whether positive or theoretical, were to be completely set aside. The common Muslim individual, he argued, stands helpless before the formidable and intricate doctrines elaborated by these jurists, for their hair-splitting resulted in a highly technical law that is so difficult to comprehend as to render adherence to it a burdensome task. The contemporary phenomenon of setting aside the Sharīʿa in favor of a wholesale importation of foreign laws is but one consequence of the inherited legacy of legal complexities in the traditional system.[13]

The technically elaborate nature of traditional legal doctrine is further compounded by the immense detail generated by explaining specific and minute positive legal rulings. In reacting to this trend, Riḍā goes to some lengths in adducing a number of Quranic verses and Prophetic reports to the effect that enquiring about the legal status of matters unspecified in the revealed texts is abhorrent. He quotes, among others, Q. 5:101: "O you who believe! Ask not of things which, if they were made known to you, would be detrimental to you; but if you ask of them when the Quran is being revealed, they will be made known unto you." From such verses he concludes, and stresses time and again, that Muslims should not enquire about any issue that the Prophet did not touch upon, for this can only lead to the swelling of the body of legal obligations, thus making adherence to the law burdensome and arduous. And this is precisely what has happened in modern times: the law has lost its ability to remain moderate and tolerable.[14]

Resorting to legal speculation and an over-use of reasoning negates the essence of Islam, which is the reasonableness of religious obligation. In further illustration of this claim, Riḍā sets forth a number of what he calls "premises," not all of which, we must note, can be readily seen as relevant to his claim. First, it is known with certitude that God perfected His

[13] In this section I draw heavily on his *Yusr al-Islām wa-Uṣūl al-Tashrīʿ al-ʿĀmm* (Cairo: Maṭbaʿat Nahḍat Miṣr, 1956). [14] Ibid., 12–23.

religion. Second, the Quran is the cornerstone and foundation of Islam. Third, the Prophet's statements (to be taken here as encompassing the Quran and the Sunna) concerning matters of worship are infallible. But this is not so with regard to worldly, mundane matters. The Prophet is known to have erred, and those parts of his Sunna relative to these matters are fallible. Fourth, God entrusted Muslims, individually and collectively, to run their own worldly affairs based on the fundamental assumption that, all things being equal, these affairs are permitted, not prohibited to them (*"al-aṣl fī al-ashyā' al-ibāḥa"*). In political administration, too, the assumption is that the state is run pursuant to the principle of consultation (*shūrā*). Fifth, and this is particularly significant, God perfected, once and for all, all matters related to worship, since these do not change in time or place. But because worldly matters do change from time to time, and from place to place, God laid down only those broad and general principles according to which these matters should be treated. The obvious implication here is that the determination of details pertaining to the concrete legal status of these mundane matters remains within the province of man's discretion. Sixth, in accordance with the disdain with which excessive queries about legal matters are viewed in the revealed texts, the early forefathers condemned innovation (*ibtidāʿ*), the use of reasoning and rational thought. In citing the forefathers' position as an authoritative stance against rational thought and innovation, Riḍā's intention is to forewarn against those reformists who call for the total abolition of the Sharīʿa in favor of secular legislation. Seventh, after the generation of the Prophet's Companions, the Muslim community became divided upon itself due to the misuse of legal methods of inference. Riḍā seems to suggest that these communal divisions preempted the existence of consensus in later generations. The only conceivable and credible consensus is therefore that of the Companions.[15]

It is difficult to see the interrelationship of these premises, although they seem to prepare the way for Riḍā to steer a middle course between the conservative forces advocating the traditional status quo of the Sharīʿa, on the one hand, and the secularists who aimed to replace the religious law by non-religious state legislation, on the other. By attacking the many flaws and excessive complexities of the traditional legal system, and by sharply distancing himself from free thought and rationality, he was distinguishing himself as one of the middle-of-the-roaders, i.e., the "moderates who affirm that it is possible to revive Islam and to renew its true identity by following the Book, the sound Sunna, and the guidance of the pious forefathers."[16]

[15] Ibid., 24–28. [16] Ibid., 7.

Following in the footsteps of the *ʿulamāʾ*, Riḍā drew on earlier authorities in support of his position. But also in the tradition of the reformists, he was eclectic in his choice of historical antecedents that could lend authoritative backing to his arguments. Of all the medieval prodigies, he appeals, with much acclaim, to the Ẓāhirite Ibn Ḥazm and the Ḥanbalite Ibn Taymiyya – the former for his total rejection of *qiyās*, and the latter for the reservations he expressed concerning the frequent and common misuses of this method. At the same time, Riḍā called upon the teachings of Ibn Taymiyya's student, Ibn Qayyim al-Jawziyya (d. 751/1350), who criticized, in the footsteps of Sunnī tradition, the Ẓāhirite opposition to *qiyās* as an *a fortiori* argument. In God's statement "Do not say 'Fie' unto them [your parents],"[17] the Ẓāhirites were wrong to reject the implication that striking parents, among many other harmful acts, is also forbidden. This and other limited applications of *qiyās*, Riḍā argues, must be admitted as outrightly valid. Here, he details the admissible forms of *qiyās*, including one form practiced by the Companions, and another to which the jurists resorted in civil transactions (*muʿāmalāt*).[18] On the other hand, Ibn Qayyim is approvingly cited as a critic of those jurists who freely practiced *qiyās al-shabah* (analogy of resemblance) and who were thereby led to derive rulings contrary to the intention of the Lawgiver. By carving out a middle position between these jurists and the anti-*qiyās* Ẓāhirites, Riḍā was able to insist on revelation as the ultimate source of law but without the fetters of the traditionally comprehensive, but limiting, method of *qiyās*.

What Riḍā excluded from the domain of traditional *qiyās* he replaced by the concept of *maṣlaḥa*. Since the Quran and the Sunna have fallen short of supplying all the answers to problems of civil transactions – though they did provide a complete system of worship and belief – it is necessary to consider worldly interests (*maṣāliḥ dunyawiyya*) in dealing with such problems so long as these considerations do not contradict religious tenets. Riḍā argues that it is a common misconception that the majority of traditional jurists considered *maṣlaḥa* as an extraneous, controversial source of law. In point of fact, he affirms, *maṣlaḥa* was a method integral to the processes of determining the *ratio legis* by means of suitability (*munāsaba*) or relevance (*mulāʾama*).[19]

As we have seen in our discussion of traditional legal theory, a suitable *ratio legis* is one that the jurist derives rationally. When the *ratio* finds support in the revealed texts, it is deemed admissible; but when it contradicts the texts, it must be rejected. In between these two extremes stands a third category, namely, a *ratio* that neither contradicts nor agrees with a particular

[17] Quran 17:23. [18] *Yusr*, 44–45. [19] See pp. 88 ff. above.

verse or Prophetic report but one that finds corroboration in the general spirit and intention of the law (*maqāṣid al-sharʿ*). This, Riḍā vigorously asserts, is reasoning according to *maṣlaḥa*, reasoning that all classical and medieval jurists utilized in the construction of the legal corpus. Again, he makes recourse to the early authorities, such as Zarkashī (d. 794/1392) and others, who argued that *maṣlaḥa* is utilized by all jurists and all schools. Furthermore, he expounds Ṭūfī's theory which, we have seen,[20] revolved around this concept and which he characterizes as based on convincing proofs.[21] In fact, he goes so far as to imply that classical and medieval law elaborated by the jurists through *qiyās* represents a roundabout way of arriving at the same conclusions that could be reached through *maṣlaḥa*. This notion he advances with Shāṭibī's theory in mind. Citing several cases considered by Shāṭibī to have been reached by means of *istiṣlāḥ*, Riḍā argues that the same conclusions could be obtained by the *qiyās* method from the Quran and the Sunna.[22]

Having established, through a heavy reliance on Ṭūfī and Shāṭibī, that *maṣlaḥa* is a principle that derives its strength from the revealed sources, Riḍā is now ready to derive some conclusions. All matters of worship and belief must be directly subject to the dictates of the revealed texts. Anything else, such as political, judicial and civil matters, should be determined by one of five different types of evidence. First, revealed texts bearing conclusive evidence in both content and transmission (*qaṭʿī al-dalāla wal-riwāya*) are not only binding but allow, due to their unambiguity, no room for *ijtihād*. No other evidence may override these texts unless the counter evidence is a more weighty text (*arjaḥ*) or a principle derived from a general survey of the Sharīʿa, such as the principle of necessity (*ḍarūra*). In another work, however, Riḍā further elaborates his position on this point. He argues that in the absence of textual evidence "necessity alone would suffice as a legal source to justify the process of deduction known today as *tashrīʿ*"[23] by which he means the state legislation described at the outset of this chapter. It is to be noted that here we have an expanded use of necessity which, being nearly synonymous with *maṣlaḥa*, is capable of creating new rules on the basis of human needs. Kerr aptly observes that "this equation of interest and necessity, put forth in such a manner as to make formal deductions from the revealed sources only a secondary confirmation of what the law should be, amounts to an affirmation of natural law."[24]

Second, cases attested by a sound, unambiguous text on the validity of

[20] See pp. 150–53, above. [21] *Yusr*, 70–71. [22] Kerr, *Islamic Reform*, 194–95; *Yusr*, 72–74.
[23] Cited from *al-Khilāfa aw al-Imāma al-ʿUẓmā*, 158/94, in Kerr, *Islamic Reform*, 201.
[24] Kerr, *Islamic Reform*, 201–02.

which the first generation of Muslims reached a consensus are binding. But it is distinctly implied that this evidence is also subject to the same exceptions of necessity and interest articulated in the first type. Third, texts that are not altogether clear (*qaṭʿī al-dalāla*) or Prophetic reports that are less than highly sound, and on the interpretation of which scholars disagreed, are not necessarily binding. Such texts are open for discussion and if found, after investigation and analysis, capable of verification and authentication, then they will be subsumed under the two previous types, with necessity and interest being two overriding principles. If these texts prove unverifiable, then cases that come under their purview will be considered to lack any textual support. Again, the implication here is that these cases will directly fall under the umbrella of necessity and interest. Fourth, other texts pertaining to the personal attitudes and habits of Muslims – such as dress, food and drink – ought to be binding unless personal or public interest dictates otherwise. It emerges that even these texts, in the final analysis, may be superseded if need dictates abandoning them. Fifth, and finally, cases that lack attestation in the revealed texts must be left for human discretion. Whatever rules are created on the basis of interest and necessity would be legitimate, for, after all, interest and necessity are in no way contradictory to revelation but rather dictated by it.[25]

Riḍā's doctrine amounts to a total negation of traditional legal theory. What is interesting about the way in which he achieves this task is that he draws extensively on a highly limited and minor concept in that theory in order to suppress the rest of it. The concepts of necessity and interest (the latter known to traditional theorists as textually unregulated benefits)[26] were traditionally of a limited use, and only a small minority of theoreticians gave these concepts prominence in their writings. The ideas of this minority, consisting mainly of Ṭūfī and Shāṭibī, became in Riḍā's theory the standing paradigm. Thus, aside from matters of worship and religious ritual, which were to remain within the purview of revelation, Riḍā upheld a legal theory strictly anchored in natural law, where considerations of human need, interest and necessity would reign supreme in elaborating a legal corpus. Any revealed text, however epistemologically evincive it may be, could be set aside if it contravened such considerations. It would seem that Riḍā was preparing the ground for the total dissociation of religion from strictly non-religious, mundane matters. But his was a theory that constituted a radical shift from the religious values of the law, values that the Muslim world found difficult to abandon. It found it difficult because the alternative that Riḍā provided lacked both true religious foundation and a

[25] *Yusr*, 76 ff. [26] See pp. 112–13 above.

theoretical depth that could successfully compete with, and match, the impressive intellectual achievements of traditional legal theory.

The ambivalence created by the tenacious grip of traditional legal theory and the attractiveness of what amounts to pseudo-religious ideas expressed in the concepts of necessity and interest is eloquently reflected in the writings of some more recent scholars who saw in the ʿAbduh–Riḍā thesis an appealing option. But it is precisely because of this ambivalence that these writings remained mere academic discussions, failing to affect the world of practice. Yet despite their failure, they were seen by some as a synthesis between the legacy of traditional theory and the theoretical needs of modern times. This attempt at a synthesis bestowed upon the writings of these scholars a certain popularity which was enjoyed from as far west as Egypt to as far east as Indonesia. We may take the Egyptian scholar ʿAbd al-Wahhāb Khallāf (d. 1956) as a representative example of an author who, in one sense, drifted aimlessly between traditional theory and Riḍā's reformist proposals.

In what is perhaps one of the most influential of his works,[27] Khallāf aims to show that the sources of the law, "if properly understood," "are flexible, rich and fit for responding to the interests of man and to developing conditions."[28] Yet, he excludes from the purview of modern *ijtihād* any case that comes under the jurisdiction of clear and authentic revealed texts, and on which the legists of any particular generation reached a consensus. Thus, for instance, the Quranic stipulations concerning inheritance are *ab initio* excluded from the domain of *ijtihād*. The flexibility of the texts is then confined to those cases regarding which no revealed text or consensus is to be found. And this, we are told, constitutes the great majority of the corpus of substantive law elaborated by the early and medieval jurists who dealt with the law in terms relevant to their own environment. Just as the requirements and conditions of their age were taken into consideration in legal reasoning, thus yielding rules appropriate to their needs, so succeeding generations may reconsider these rules in light of the changing times and conditions. Therefore, provided that no clear text or consensus exists, a former *ijtihād* with regard to the textually unregulated cases may be supplanted by a fresh *ijtihād* based upon an investigation that is dictated by the imperatives of the prevailing conditions in any specific time and place. For after all, Khallāf anachronistically observes, *qiyās* and *maṣlaḥa*, the two chief methods of reasoning, promote the interest and good of man. More specifically, the aims of *maṣlaḥa* and *qiyās* are to sustain

[27] *Maṣādir al-Tashrīʿ al-Islāmī fīmā lā Naṣṣa fīh* (Cairo: Dār al-Kitāb al-ʿArabī, 1955).
[28] Ibid., 5.

benefit and avert harm, and benefit and harm are subjective values, mutable under differing circumstances and changing times.[29]

It is remarkable that *qiyās* in Khallāf's mind becomes virtually indistinguishable from *istiṣlāḥ* in that the primary consideration in both is the interest of man, including averting any harm that may befall him. In discussing the nature of legal causation under *qiyās*, he remarks that if the Lawgiver forbade a certain substance or a transaction, it is not because He intended to constrain his subjects or deprive them of their individual freedoms; rather, there exists a rationale (*ḥikma*) behind His prohibitions and permissions, and it is through these that He promotes his subjects' interests by bestowing upon them certain benefits and by protecting them from harm.[30] In other words, God has in mind nothing other than human welfare. When Khallāf comes to discuss *maṣlaḥa*, his language concerning legal causation does not change, except for the obvious fact that *qiyās* is ultimately grounded in the texts, whereas *maṣlaḥa* is not. It is noteworthy that he characterizes *istiṣlāḥ* as a superior means by which law can be adapted to changing times and conditions. It is also significant that here he calls upon the theories of both Shāṭibī and Ṭūfī to enhance his discourse about *maṣlaḥa*.[31]

Khallāf's vacillation between the tenacious authority of the revealed texts and the imperatives of legal change is even more evident in his discussion of customary practices (*ʿurf*) and of their relation to the law. At first, he seems certain that those practices that conform to the law are to be accepted as valid, whereas those that contradict the law must be deemed null and void. This certainty, however, does not last; a custom that contravenes the dictates of the revealed texts may, after all, be legalized. If an unlawful contract or transaction has become widespread in a particular society, such as insurance, then need and necessity will override the textual norms. Seeking the support of religious authority, he cites the Azharite Muḥammad Khaḍr Ḥusayn who also advocated the legalization of any customary practice that proves necessary for the welfare and ongoing needs of society, however much this practice contradicts the revealed sources and the law that derives therefrom. In doing so, Ḥusayn argues, the legislator does nothing different from the earlier legists who resorted to licenses (*rukhaṣ*).[32] But Khallāf goes further and argues that since customary practices do change over time, the law that governs them must change accordingly, it being understood that legal change here is effected exclusively in consonance with the principles of need and necessity.

It is significant that Khallāf ends his work with a chapter he entitles "The

[29] Ibid., 8–11. [30] Ibid., 40–42. [31] Ibid., 70–80. [32] Ibid., 124–25.

Sources of Islamic Legislation are Flexible and Take Cognizance of People's Interests and their Development."[33] The title is significant not only because it includes the word "legislation" – by which he stresses modern modes of enacting law and avoids the notion of Islamic law in its traditional sense – but also because in this chapter he attempts to restrict the scope and bindingness of the revealed sources, one by one. He begins with the Quran which, he argues, provided general, not specific, guidance to the community. In the footsteps of Riḍā, he sharply distinguishes between those parts of the Book that deal with matters of worship and ritual, on the one hand, and those that treat of civil, constitutional, criminal and economic matters, on the other. With regard to the latter, the Quran provided no more than general principles. For instance, of the more than one hundred articles pertaining to contracts in the Egyptian code only four are Quranic. Similarly, in criminal law the Quran provided for only five violations. Thus, Khallāf takes these facts to mean that the Quran intentionally left unregulated numerous spheres of the law in order to allow for legislation that takes into account the changing social environment. Moreover, the Quran must not be understood strictly according to its letter, but rather according to its spirit. By espousing this view, it is clear that Khallāf was aiming to free the law from the constraints of a literal interpretation, especially in light of the understanding that the law does not aim at subjecting people to merciless religious obligations in order to affirm their obedience to God, but rather at promoting their well-being and interests. This latter is underscored by the various principles the legal sources proffered, such as the principle that states that "Things are assumed to be permissible until the contrary is proven," and the principle of alleviating hardship and promoting human welfare.

By confining the scope of the Quran to a few, general, principles and rules, Khallaf was clearly attempting to circumscribe its legislative function significantly. However, nowhere does he explain how the few Quranic rules he accepts as binding should be interpreted to accommodate social change. This remains a moot point. On the other hand, no difficulty arises concerning what he perceives as the Quranic principles, for these, as we have seen, promote the notion of legal change in the face of a changing world.

The Prophetic Sunna is disposed of with less difficulty. The Prophet either duplicated and explained some of the Quranic contents or introduced new material that conflicted in no way with the Quran. The duplicated and explained materials pose no problem, for they should be treated in the same manner in which the Quranic text is treated. But the non-

[33] Ibid., 131 ff.

Quranic Sunnaic subject matter must be analyzed in terms of relevance; if conclusive evidence (*qarīna qāṭiʿa*) exists to the effect that that Sunnaic subject matter was intended to treat an issue exclusively relative to the time of revelation, then it is not binding upon the succeeding generations. If, on the other hand, evidence shows that it was intended to apply to one and all situations, then it must be taken as binding during and after the Prophet's time. Khallâf does not articulate this point, but he seems to imply, albeit faintly, that the bindingness of this Sunnaic subject matter is contingent upon the continued concomitance (*wujūdan wa-ʿadaman*) of the Prophetic rules with the existence of *maṣlaḥa*. Put differently, when the *maṣlaḥa* is not served, these rules do not apply.[34]

When he comes to discuss consensus, Khallāf is more explicit in his total rejection of it in its classical and medieval forms. He acknowledges that consensus and mutual consultation (*shūrā*) are required by the Quran and the Sunna, but he rejects the method by which the occurrence of conventional consensus was established. Khallāf's consensus is collective, where the *mujtahid*s as a collectivity advise the sovereign on matters of law. Here, he appeals to the Quran as well as to the Prophet and his Companions to show that during the first generation of Islam collective consultation was the normative practice. Consensus based on the individual opinions of jurists is not only ineffective and nearly impossible to determine but also leads to legal disagreement and the fragmentation and stagnation of the law. And this is precisely what transpired in pre-modern times, for Muslim rulers left legislation in the hands of individual jurists. Khallāf does not explain how the conventional consensus led to stagnation, nor does he show how the modern, collective consensus contributes to flexibility in the law, a proposition of which he seems certain.[35]

We have already seen that Khallāf virtually equates *qiyās* with *istiṣlāḥ*, both having the primary purpose of serving the interests, welfare and needs of society. But now he adds to these *istiḥsān*, juristic preference, which he perceives as sharing, with the other two methods, in the promotion of these same ends.

True, by severely limiting the legislative scope of the revealed texts, and by altering the methodological functions of the processes of legal reasoning (*qiyās*, *istiṣlāḥ*, *istiḥsān*) so as to render them sensitive to social needs and necessities – at the expense of the conventional hermeneutic which is bound by the literal dictates of revelation – Khallāf freed himself from the firm grip of medieval legal tradition. But his success, at the same time, is severely marred for two reasons. First, he failed to account, in any specific

[34] Ibid., 139. [35] Ibid., 140–42.

and exact way, for those textual stipulations with unambiguous legal effects that run counter to the exigencies of modern society, such as the shares of women in inheritance, polygamy, usury, and so on. A theory that aims to lay down the principles of legislation remains deficient without addressing these issues. Second, Khallāf's theory, like that of Riḍā, has recourse to such principles as need, necessity and interest without defining in any precise or convincing manner how such principles derive from the religious tradition. To accept, on the one hand, the revealed texts' affirmation of the cause of welfare, interest and necessity, and, on the other, to reject nearly all other stipulations of rules and precepts, without proper theoretical justification, amounts to nothing less than sheer arbitrariness. If law is to remain Islamic in the religious, and not only cultural, sense, departures from the texts such as those advocated by Khallāf must be justified. As it stands in both his and Riḍā's theories, law derived on the basis of necessity, interest and need remains only nominally Islamic and dominantly utilitarian.

This utilitarianism may be found in an emasculated form among a group of reformers who advocated what is in essence a concept of natural law that is paradoxically constrained by the intervention of both the revealed texts and medieval legal methodologies. A representative of this trend may be found in the figure of the Moroccan intellectual ʿAllāl al-Fāsī (d. 1973)[36] who, in the footsteps of ʿAbduh, upheld a Muʿtazilite notion of legal causality. In his work *Maqāṣid al-Sharīʿa al-Islāmiyya wa-Makārimuhā*, he argues, against the Ashʿarites, that religious law lends itself to analysis in terms of the causes and motives attributable to the intention of the Lawgiver, and these causes are in turn necessarily explicable in terms of man's welfare and interest which God had in mind when He revealed the law. Thus the purpose of the law is to promote the good life on earth, a life in which order, justice and welfare are the prevailing norms.[37] The attribute of justice (under which, we understand, Fāsī subsumes public interest and human welfare) is, after all, essential to, and inseparable from, God.[38] As universal and general norms, these are immutable, for no amount of interpretation or textual manipulation can affect or diminish their pervasive presence in the Sharīʿa. But the specific and individual rules that bring about the realization of these norms in society are mutable according to changing circumstances, locales and times. They are not

[36] For a biographical account, see the *Oxford Encyclopedia of the Modern Islamic World*, ed.-in-chief, John L. Esposito, 4 vols. (New York/Oxford: Oxford University Press, 1995) (by L. Michalak), IV, 4–5.

[37] See his *Maqāṣid al-Sharīʿa al-Islāmiyya wa-Makārimuhā* (Casablanca: Maktabat al-Waḥda al-ʿArabiyya, 1963), 3–7, 41–2. [38] Ibid., 62.

meant to exist for their own sake, but are rather intended as instruments to achieve the higher goals of justice and human welfare. The very existence of abrogating and abrogated verses (*nāsikh* and *mansūkh*) in the Quran represents an eloquent testimony to the ephemeral nature of the individual rules (*aḥkām*) in substantive law. Once a rule or a legal verse was deemed outmoded or irrelevant to social needs, it was repealed by another that served these needs.

Since the rationale behind God's law lies within the bounds of human comprehension, man is capable of perceiving the divine intention and thus its rationale. For revelation cannot be understood without the intervention of human reason, just as human reason cannot, without the aid of revelation, comprehend the divine intention. Reason and revelation perfectly complement each other.[39]

Having brought the revealed texts under the tempered control of human reason, Fāsī marshals a number of arguments to the effect that law is intended for the layman, and must therefore be intelligible to the non-specialist. Here, he summons the support of Shāṭibī who, we recall, insisted upon the unlettered nature of the law. Shāṭibī is also quoted as saying that the Sharīʿa by definition can do no less and no more than steer a middle course (*ṭarīq wasaṭ*) between intolerable religious obligations and a lax attitude toward the law, an attitude which Fāsī anachronistically views in the modern context as a renunciation of God's decree. He also calls upon Riḍā and ʿAbduh to support the notion of the primacy of *maṣlaḥa* in legislation. Yet Fāsī distinguishes himself from the ranks of Riḍā and his followers who saw in Ṭūfī's theory a legacy upon which they could draw. He does discuss Ṭūfī, but only to disagree with him, particularly with regard to the supremacy of *maṣlaḥa* over the clear texts.[40] In an explicit statement, he sides with traditional theory in confining *maṣlaḥa* to those cases in the law that revelation does not sanction as either valid or invalid.[41] Fāsī's traditionalism is further betrayed by his unqualified acceptance of *qiyās* and *istiḥsān* as elaborated by the medieval theorists. But on consensus he parts company with these theorists, and adopts a view quite similar to that espoused by Khallāf.[42]

It is difficult to make sense of Fāsī's thought in light of his hesitant and selective appropriations from traditional legal theory. He clearly appreciates the necessity to remold legal theory so as to render it responsive to modern exigencies. Yet, he is reluctant to abandon the conventional hermeneutic as expressed in *qiyās*, *istiḥsān* and the literalist approach to legal language. More important, while he hovers over a renewed notion of *istiṣlāḥ*

[39] Ibid., 63–64. [40] Ibid., 143 ff. [41] Ibid., 180–81. [42] Ibid., 115–19.

to justify, if nothing else, the modern reforms in the law,[43] he proves himself unable to embrace a legal philosophy that relegates the texts of revelation to a place subservient to the imperatives of modern social change. The rationalistic characterization of legal causation seems to have been undertaken in vain, and its full implications he completely fails to tease out. It would be safe to state that in Fāsī's discourse a concept of natural law has been entirely frustrated; at the same time, his reproduction of conventional legal theory was rendered deficient by the constraints and qualifications he imposed on it due to his realization of the need to adapt this theory to the dramatic changes of modernity. In short, Fāsī could neither accept nor reject the structures of conventional legal theory, with the attendant consequence that he was never able to make any advance toward pinning down a modern theory of law.

Even over half a century after Riḍā, the failure to articulate a theory of law anchored in the concept of *maṣlaḥa* still persists. One of the last reformers who trod Riḍā's path and whose jurisprudential thought remains in the realm of generalities is the influential Sudanese intellectual and politician Ḥasan Turābī. In a short monograph published in 1980, and significantly entitled *The Renewal of Islamic Legal Theory*, Turābī admits the rudimentary nature of his attempt to refashion a theory of law,[44] a theory he perceives to be an integral part of his discourse on "renewal" (*tajdīd*). He goes on to express his intention to articulate a detailed theory sometime in the future, but thus far he does not seem to have done so.[45] Nevertheless, Turābī's ideas, despite their preliminary and ambiguous character, are worth sketching here if only to show their intrinsic inability to yield a systematic and pragmatic proposal for a legal theory that goes beyond, or even matches, those theories advocated by Riḍā and Khallāf.

Nonetheless, Turābī distinguishes himself from all the thinkers we have thus far discussed in one important respect: he is the first categorically to renounce conventional legal theory, which he views as obsolete and as having nothing to do with the realities of modern life and its problems. This theory is conceived as narrow and bound by strictures of formal logic

[43] In the case of abolishing polygamy, he advanced *istiṣlāḥ* over both the texts and consensus. See ʿAbd al-Majīd Sharafī, *al-Islām wal-Ḥadātha* (Tunis: al-Dār al-Tūnisiyya lil-Nashr, 1991), 174 (n. 34).

[44] *Tajdīd Uṣūl al-Fiqh al-Islāmī* (Beirut and Khartoum: Dar al-Fikr, 1980), 46. For a brief biographical profile of Turābī, see ibid., 47; *Oxford Encyclopedia of the Modern Islamic World*, "Turābī, Ḥasan al-" (by Peter Woodward), IV, 240–41.

[45] In his much later work *Tajdīd al-Fikr al-Islāmī* (Rabat: Dār al-Qarāfī lil-Nashr wal-Tawzīʿ, 1993), Turābī essentially reiterates the ideas he expressed in *Tajdīd Uṣūl al-Fiqh*. In fact, nearly all the sections treating of legal theory in the former work are nothing more than a reproduction of the latter work. Cf. pp. 5–47 of *Tajdīd Uṣūl al-Fiqh*, which are virtually identical to pp. 34–53 of *Tajdīd al-Fikr*.

that rob it of any ability to deal with the dynamics of a changing society. While conventional theory may have served the purposes of classical and medieval Muslim societies, it has now become irrelevant because it tends to treat law as an aggregate of specific rules each resulting from a consideration of limited factors entering into the narrow lines of legal reasoning. The challenges of modern society, however, require a wholistic approach to legal issues, and conventional theory lacks the mechanism to accommodate such an approach. The eclectic method adopted in modern legal reform has severed its ties with conventional theory but itself lacks an articulated theoretical foundation. Thus, insofar as legal identity is concerned, Turābī is acutely aware of the obsoleteness of conventional theory as well as of the need to articulate an alternative theory that can successfully sustain the structure of substantive law, whatever this structure may be.[46]

Conjoined with this realization is the perception that earlier Muslim generations, from that of the Companions onward, do not necessarily impose upon modern Muslims an exemplary model that must in any way be followed. Constant change and permutation are the quintessence of history, which means that religion, being inextricably connected with the historical process, is ever-changing. The religious model provided by the Companions neither constituted the only model that Islam offered nor was it itself immutable. It too changed, as did all other succeeding models. Now, this perception of history allows Turābī to dissociate modern Islamic realities from the grip of the past. In particular, it liberates his agenda from the shackles of both the tradition as a social construct and conventional theory as its attendant legal manifestation.

The grip of the past is further loosened by positing a gap between conventional law and traditional society. In fact, we have an admission that, after all, communal Islamic life in the past swerved from the true dictates of the divine law, and *fiqh*, the regulating instrument of that life, also swerved with it. This deviation was responsible, at the least, for the total neglect of the public areas of the law, such as national economy, the political process, government, foreign relations, etc. And it is these areas that have become for today's Muslims most in need of immediate attention. Such areas of the law as personal status also require updating, but these are not of an urgent nature, for in the meantime there is no harm in drawing on traditional law.[47] On the other hand, areas of public law need extensive *ijtihād*, and in order to construct such a set of laws the need arises to formulate a fresh legal theory and methodology. Here, hermeneutic – heavily drawn upon by traditional theory – becomes an insufficient and inadequate

[46] Turābī, *Tajdīd Uṣūl al-Fiqh*, 7–11. [47] Ibid., 20, 42.

tool due to the sparseness of revealed texts bearing upon these laws and, consequently, the virtual absence of these laws from traditional jurisprudence. Furthermore, traditional *qiyās* remains incapable of addressing these areas of the law, having been hampered by the limiting effects of formal logic. If traditional legal hermeneutic and *qiyās* fail to respond to a modern vision of public law, then what is the alternative?

Turābī introduces two concepts, both of which find their roots in traditional legal theory. He calls these *al-qiyās al-ijmālī al-wāsiʿ* (wholistic, expansive *qiyās*) and *al-istiṣḥāb al-wāsiʿ* (expansive *istiṣḥāb*). The former he equates, quite interestingly, with what he labels as *qiyās al-maṣlaḥa al-mursala.*[48] Nowhere, however, does he define in any precise manner the meaning of this *qiyās*, and the reader is left to her own devices to assess its nature. But he is more clear about expansive *istiṣḥāb*, which he acknowledges to have derived from traditional theory – but this he does with a twist. Religions, he argues, never intend to abrogate all that has preceded them. The Prophet, for instance, did not rescind all practices and laws that existed prior to Islam; rather, he aimed to rectify those aspects of life that had gone wrong and which contradicted the principles and tenets of the new religion.

Without being in any way specific and without providing any scriptural citation, Turābī insists that there exists an abundance of textual evidence to demonstrate the validity of the principle of *istiṣḥāb.* But by qualifying *istiṣḥāb* as expansive, Turābī removes the principle from its narrow limits in traditional theory to a new, broader dimension. In traditional law, *istiṣḥāb* was mainly conceived as applicable to specific cases, such as that involving missing husbands. A man who has not returned from a journey is assumed to be alive until evidence shows otherwise, or until such time has elapsed that he can no longer be thought to have escaped natural death. As long as these two conditions are not met, his wife cannot be assumed to be a widow, and thus she is not permitted to remarry. But this is not the type of *istiṣḥāb* of which Turābī is thinking, for the qualification "expansive" is intended to raise the concept from the domain of particular cases of substantive law to that of general principles of legal methodology. Turābī's *istiṣḥāb* then becomes applicable to those traditional principles of legal theory that must continue to operate in modern legislation; and their continued operation, we assume, becomes mandatory so long as no evidence exists to render them irrelevant or obsolete. But the choice of those principles is quite revealing. They do not include the traditional hermeneutic, be it linguistic, *qiyās*- or *istiḥsān*-based. Rather, the choice falls upon the principle that, unless otherwise stipulated in binding revelation, all things,

48 Ibid., 24–26.

including acts, are presumed to be permitted; that legal obligation is not mandatory; that whatever the Muslim does in his or her life is an acceptable form of expressing obedience to God; and that whatever benefit he or she derives from worldly life is legally neutral, to be considered neither praiseworthy nor blameworthy.[49] Now, if we combine these principles with the expansive *maṣlaḥa* (which we take to be virtually synonymous with expansive *qiyās*), then what we will have, Turābī asserts, is a broad-ranging legal methodology which can successfully deal with issues in the public areas of modern Islamic life.

What processes are involved in this new methodology is a question that Turābī never attempts to answer. We can only infer a partial and sketchy answer from the few comments he makes with regard to what he characterizes as the "order the *mujtahid*'s reasoning should follow." Having a legal problem at hand, the *mujtahid* must, of course, begin with the revealed texts, the Quran and the Sunna. Employing exegetical and hermeneutical methods (which Turābī never cares to describe), the *mujtahid* subjects the results of his interpretive effort to the dictates of expansive *istiṣḥāb* and expansive *istiṣlāḥ*. In typical fashion, no specific legal cases are provided to illustrate this process. We understand, however, that subjecting the hermeneutic to expansive principles means taking into consideration the concrete realities of mundane life. No revealed text should be approached without considering the social and mundane realities involved in the issue at hand. The relation between the texts and reality is then emphatically dialectical: in no way should revelation be severed from reason, or reality from law. Here comes the crucial question: What if the dictates of the revealed texts result in a less than pragmatic and reasonable law? Turābī provides an answer, though a vague one: if reasoning on the basis of the texts leads to extreme hardship (*ḥaraj ʿaẓīm*), then it is necessary to consider the *maṣāliḥ*, and the purely hermeneutical outcome cannot stand alone. What this means in precise terms, and what the nature of the textual–*maṣāliḥ* relationship is in the case of a conflict between the two, are questions that, again, receive no answer.

Whatever the nature of legal reasoning, it must be controlled by means that Turābī explains in less than exact terms. The need for this control arises because of the expansive scope of the methods and principles proposed, for they could lead to rampant and obdurate disagreements. The instrument of control in matters of crucial importance to the community is mutual consultation (*shūrā*) in the widest public sense, consultation which continues until such time as a consensus emerges or when a decision

49 Ibid., 27.

is taken by the great majority of Muslims. On issues of lesser importance, the decision is left to the political sovereign or to the state's officials, depending on their area of competence and jurisdiction.

Yet, it is not necessary that disagreement be kept at an absolute minimum. Reasonable diversity of opinion concerning both the legal sources and individual cases of substantive law is much needed in order to provide a wide range of material from which the community and its leaders can choose. Individual *ijtihād* is thus permitted, and even encouraged, so long as it provides a diversity of constructive proposals finally contributing to an informed communal decision.[50] Turābī's *mujtahid*, however, is not identical with his traditional counterpart. While the latter has to fulfill a number of conditions reflecting high standards of legal scholarship,[51] the former may be any educated person (*mutaʿallim*) who possesses adequate knowledge of the law, the Arabic language and a sound understanding of his or her own culture and social reality. If the issue under *ijtihād* falls within an area of specialization, such as economics or medicine, then it is expected that the *mujtahid* must also have proper grounding in that area.[52] But Turābī does not insist that all *mujtahid*s be of equal rank and thoroughly educated in order to undertake this task. Since the outcome of *ijtihād* remains nothing more than a proposal – subject to approval or rejection – any individual can contribute to the discussion. The final choice remains in the hands of the community and the body politic representing it. After arriving at a consensus or an agreement of the majority, the state drafts the rules into a binding code. All other proposals will be discarded.[53]

At best, Turābī's reformation (*tajdīd*) of legal theory remains general and vague. The crucial issue of the role that the revealed texts should play in legislation is not adequately clarified. That the principles of expansive *maṣlaḥa* and expansive *istiṣḥāb* are indispensable and that they cannot be superseded by the stipulations of the revealed texts bespeak their central role in legal reasoning. But how the texts should be explained away when they stand in contradiction to the dictates of *istiṣḥāb* and *istiṣlāḥ* remains an unsolved question. To say, as he does, that the texts cannot be the only criterion in the case of such a contradiction is not a satisfactory solution. It is in providing an answer to this question that the real test of Turābī's inventiveness lies. Without articulating an elaborate and detailed theory that addresses these concerns, Turābī cannot be said to have offered an adequate legal program to sustain what has been called "Turābī's Revolution."[54]

[50] Ibid., 29–30; Turābī, *Tajdīd al-Fikr*, 23 ff. [51] See pp. 117 ff., 199 ff. above.
[52] *Tajdīd Uṣūl al-Fiqh*, 31–32, 33; Turābī, *Tajdīd al-Fikr*, 46–47.
[53] *Tajdīd Uṣūl al-Fiqh*, 35, 37; Turābī, *Tajdīd al-Fikr*, 47–48.
[54] As evidenced in Abdelwahab El-Effendi's *Turabi's Revolution* (London: Grey Seal, 1991).

Ultimately, reliance on the concepts of *istiṣlāḥ* and necessity, the two major ingredients in the theories espoused by the school of religious utilitarianism, amounts to nothing short of subjectivism, a feature that has been noted, and rightly so, by some reformers who have opposed this school.[55] To speak of these concepts without a methodology that can control the premises, conclusions and the lines of reasoning these concepts require is a highly relativistic venture. It is not the idea of a humanistic law that these latter reformers have found objectionable, for they, in the final analysis, also want to bring about a law that fully meets the needs of modern Muslim society. Rather, these reformers – whom we have labeled the religious liberalists – differ from the utilitarianists in that they insist on disclosing a *methodology*, not mere juristic devices, which can bring into a dialectical relationship the imperatives of the revealed texts and the realities of the modern world.

RELIGIOUS LIBERALISM

The main thrust of the liberalist approach consists of understanding revelation as both text and context. The connection between the revealed text and modern society does not turn upon a literalist hermeneutic, but rather upon an interpretation of the spirit and broad intention behind the specific language of the texts. (And it is in this sense that we have labeled this approach as liberalist.) Nor does it turn upon such utilitarian principles as need and necessity, principles seen by the liberalists as narrow and only deceptively Islamic. Although relatively few reformers adopted the liberalist approach, their methodologies significantly differ from each other. Admittedly, the minimal denominator that brings them together is essentially a negative one, rather than a positive one; namely, their insistence that the traditional literalist interpretation is neither faithful to religion nor capable of adapting law to ever-changing situations.

On the moderate side of liberalism stands a significantly pragmatic and progressive proposal for reformulating legal theory, a proposal advocated by the Egyptian jurist Muḥammad Saʿīd ʿAshmāwī,[56] whose distinguished career spans the academic as well as legal professions. In addition to having served as a Counsellor of the Court of Appeal and a member of the State Commission for Legislation, he has served as the Chief Justice of the Criminal Court and as Professor of Islamic and comparative law in the University of Cairo.

[55] Fazlur Rahman, "Towards Reformulating the Methodology of Islamic Law: Sheikh Yamani on 'Public Interest' in Islamic Law," *New York University Journal of International Law and Politics*, 12 (1979): 223. [56] *Uṣūl al-Sharīʿa* (Beirut: Dār Iqra', 1983).

The linchpin of ʿAshmāwī's theory is the crucial distinction between religion as a pure idea and religious thought as an elaboration of that idea. Religion is suprahuman; it is an idea lodged in the mind of God and transmitted in an unadulterated form to the prophets, from Adam down to Muhammad. In Islam, religion as a pure idea finds expression in the Quran and the Sunna of the Prophet. The exegesis and interpretation of these two texts, as well as the entire system of Islamic hermeneutics constructed on the basis of these texts throughout the centuries, are nothing but systems of religious thought that are merely human, and thus susceptible to error. Here, a potent assumption is at work: Religion *qua* religion is endowed with objectivity, unaffected by either variation or permutation. Conversely, all human commentary on, and understanding of, religion can never hope to attain the degree of purity with which the latter is endowed, let alone the involved weaknesses of human subjectivity and fallibility. Thus, religion as an idea, or a system of ideas and beliefs, is divine and cannot be located in a human context; hence its purity. On the other hand, religious thought is thoroughly human, and, being so connected to society, can never be isolated from the particular reality and history of that society.[57]

Apart from this historical consciousness, ʿAshmāwī's distinction between religion and religious thought seems, in and by itself, only little removed from the medieval latent perception of the separation between law as a divine entity and law as a human, even fallible construction of that entity. But ʿAshmāwī, with the advantage of historical hindsight, puts his own distinction to a completely different use, as we shall see later on.

With this understanding of the difference between religion and religious thought, ʿAshmāwī has taken the first step in divesting the traditional law from its idealistic religious features. The complete stripping of these features is performed in a gradual process in which he unfolds what he calls the "general principles of Sharīʿa." These represent founding principles, and they are mostly justified either by the Quran or by the circumstances under which it was revealed. The first principle, strikingly general and idealistic in nature, declares the Sharīʿa to be more than a magnificent totality of rules and penalties; first and foremost, the Sharīʿa is a state of mind – a *Weltanschauung*, if you will. It presumes the existence of a generous and loving spirit that pervades society, for without such a spirit the rule of law would not be sustained by a genuine desire to conform to both the letter and lofty aspirations of the law. Society must thus be thoroughly permeated by this spirit in order to be ready for a proper application of the Sharīʿa.[58]

[57] Ibid., 52–53. [58] Ibid., 55, 59 ff.

The second principle paves the way for what ʿAshmāwī regards as the correct interpretation of the Sharīʿa, which was revealed for particular reasons that have to do with a particular human reality. ʿAshmāwī takes issue with the medieval scholars who propounded the view that the divine texts were pre-existent and that they were revealed within the context of a human reality that was deliberately created with the purpose of serving as a *post eventum* justification for revealing these texts. This notion, he argues, is inextricably connected with the theological doctrine of the eternity of the Quran, upheld by the majority of Muslims since the third/ninth century. The notion that the Quran is an eternal speech, coexisting with God, has led to the faulty view that the mission of Muhammad constituted not a reason for, but an occasion of, revelation. Such misapprehensions have had serious consequences, for they have led Muslim scholars to interpret the texts in isolation from the particular human reality in which they were revealed. And this in turn has resulted in a deficient interpretation of the texts and in applying the effects of interpretation to later realities that were vastly at variance from those social contexts in which the texts were originally revealed. An example in point, ʿAshmāwī argues, is Q. 5:3 ("This day I have perfected your religion for you and completed My favor unto you, and have chosen for you Islam as religion") which was interpreted to mean that religion has been completed, and that the Quran contained all that Muslims need in order to live by the dictates of their religion. Furthermore, the verse was taken as a categorical statement applicable to all situations and times. But an enquiry into the actual circumstances under which the verse was revealed unfolds a different interpretation of its meaning. The verse was revealed at a time when the Prophet and his Companions were in Mecca on pilgrimage, and the thrust of its meaning is that, with the performance of this pilgrimage, all the ritual practices required for the perfection of Islam as a religion were at last completed. Therefore, the dialectical relationship between revelation as a text and the human reality that gives rise to it is indispensable for a proper interpretation of the Quran. This holy Book, ʿAshmāwī maintains, is nothing less than a "living creature" which dynamically interacted with daily existence and the social fabric throughout the Prophet's lifetime. It is the basis not of abstract formulations but rather of human conduct in actual reality.[59]

The third principle requires that the Sharīʿa be viewed as intended to serve the public interest, and that the abrogation of one verse by another has no function other than serving that interest. The Quran represents a *process* of revelation inextricably connected with the constant changes that

[59] Ibid., 70.

took place during the Prophet's lifetime. In support of this principle, ʿAshmāwī adduces the many verses revealed in connection with the legal status of intoxicants. Q. 2:219 states that in the consumption of wine there is "a great sin, and some utility for men; but the sin of them is greater than their usefulness." In 4:43, however, the Quran takes a slightly different position on the matter: "O you who believe, do not come to pray when you are drunken, till you know what you utter." Thereafter, it is reported, Ḥamza, the uncle of the Prophet, became intoxicated, and, having lost control over his faculties, he vilified both the Prophet and ʿAlī b. Abī Ṭālib. Thereupon, Q. 5:90 was revealed and in it a categorical prohibition was finally placed on the consumption of intoxicants. Such cases, in which revelation was modified according to changing situations, are many, and ʿAshmāwī discusses at least one more case pertaining to inheritance. All this goes to show, ʿAshmāwī argues, that the Sharīʿa, as inspired by the Quran, is intimately connected with the reality it came to regulate; revelation changed and progressed with the changes and progress of society. ʿAshmāwī maintains that some medieval jurists, such as Qarāfī, have understood this phenomenon, and has argued that the rules of Sharīʿa related to social customs undergo changes in consonance with the changes in these customs.

The fourth principle has to do with the Quranic discourse pertaining, in one way or another, to the Prophet, which ʿAshmāwī divides, in the manner of classical and medieval jurists, into discourse that has universal import and discourse whose relevance is strictly confined to the person of the Prophet. The former is considered legally binding upon Muslims, whereas the latter is not. Although most of the verses clearly belong to one or the other category, there are those that do not readily lend themselves to classification. Such verses can be determined to fall into one of the two categories only by interpreting their meaning and significance. The question that arises here is: Who should be entrusted with this interpretation? In attempting an answer, ʿAshmāwī refers us to a later chapter in his book where he discusses the principles of government in Islam. Turning to that chapter, one is at pains to find an answer – at least a direct one. It seems that ʿAshmāwī assumes that the democratically elected government he propounds, through one of its agencies, has the power to decide in such matters. Beyond this vague reference, nothing is said of the mechanics of such interpretation.

Nor is the significance of this principle entirely clear. It might be tempting, in light of ʿAshmāwī's liberal agenda, to think that he introduced this principle in order to undermine the medieval doctrine according to which the verses relevant to the Prophet, which lack universal applicability, are quantitatively marginal. By expanding the volume of verses limited in their legal relevance to the Prophet and his personal life, it might be thought that ʿAshmāwī wished to reduce the number of the verses and thus minimize the immediate legal bearing of the Quran upon contemporary positive law. But this does not seem sufficiently obvious in his writings.

Somewhat related to the second principle, the fifth aims to establish a close link between the Quran and Sharīʿa on the one hand and the realities of the pre-Islamic world on the other. Just as Islam came into existence on the heel, and as a confirmation, of other monotheistic religions, it also emerged out of a particular society with which it had a certain relationship and from which it derived some of its norms. Cutting off a thief's hand was a pre-Islamic Arab penalty which the Quran adopted as part of the divine law. The Quran adopted whatever it found good, and left out whatever was discordant with its spirit. Thus, if this principle proves anything, it is that the Sharīʿa derives some of its laws from pre-existing social customs and values, and that its rulings are neither impositions from above nor of foreign origin, but a genuine expression of indigenous social values and customs. It is one of ʿAshmāwī's cardinal beliefs that a constant attention to the organic relationship between the Sharīʿa and the historical and social framework from which it emerged is the best guarantee for maintaining a legal system that will keep pace with the constant changes of social values and structures.

Finally, in his sixth principle ʿAshmāwī postulates that perfecting the Sharīʿa can be attained only by bringing it to bear, consistently and systematically, upon the social and human exigencies which are in a continuous state of flux. Here, he reverts to the distinction between religion as a pure, divine idea and the religious system as a human creation based on that idea. The Sharīʿa is nothing but a way or a method of conduct (*minhāj*) that expresses belief in God, and each nation or group conceives of a particular way that suits its needs, to express its own belief in the one and only God. This is why religion is but one, emanating from one God, but the *sharāʾiʿ* (pl. of *sharīʿa*) governing societies commensurately differ in accordance with the differences existing among these societies. This explains Q. 5:48: "For each of you [Jews, Christians, and Muslims], we have appointed a divine law, and a way of conduct (*minhāj*)." The divine act of bestowing different systems of law on different societies has no reason to justify it other than the will to give each society a law that corresponds to its particular character and needs. And if God, in all His glory, has taken into account the needs of each society at the time of revelation, then each society ought to follow this divine wisdom by attending to its own law in relation to its own worldly exigencies. Accordingly, ʿAshmāwī concludes that the Sharīʿa is completely compatible with progress and with the ever-changing requirements of life.

The elaboration of these principles, ʿAshmāwī hastens to add, is not intended to serve as a mere theoretical construct, but rather – and this is its chief goal – to lay down the foundations for a positive legal system whose function is to deal in an effective manner with the actual realities of society and the constant changes that occur within it. For a legal theory that confines itself to an idealistic vision of the world would ultimately become dissociated from such realities and would thus stand in flagrant contradiction with the spirit of Islam. Having said this, ʿAshmāwī moves on to demonstrate the ways in which these principles yield a fresh and flexible understanding of what positive law should be. It is here, in the concrete proposals for a new positive law, where ʿAshmāwī's contribution as well as shortcomings become most evident.

The first issue he deals with is international law, a law that the medieval jurists constructed in terms of the dichotomy in which Islam and Islamic lands stand in diametrical opposition to non-Muslim peoples and non-Muslim territories.[60] In theory, this law demanded that the World of Islam remain in a constant state of war with non-Muslim territories until all the inhabitants of these territories are subdued and brought under Muslim dominion. But ʿAshmāwī rejected this law altogether. He argues, and in this he seems to be a faithful disciple of ʿAlī ʿAbd al-Rāziq (d. 1966), that neither the Quran nor the Sunna has given any indications relative to the form of government in Islam. Islam was sent to people as a human, not a political, entity. Nothing in the Quran and the Sunna suggests that Islam was sent to a political community. On the contrary, the Quran is replete with such statements as "O you who believe. . ." and "O mankind. . .," an incontrovertible proof of Islam's disregard for any form of political regime. From this one may conclude, ʿAshmāwī insists, that Islamic international law must not be seen as concomitant with an Islamic body politic for the defense and promotion of which this law is constructed.[61]

Islamic international law is to be formulated on the basis of the Quranic verses that bear on the relationship between Muslims and non-Muslims. And these verses must be interpreted in accordance with the principles that have already been set forth, namely, the understanding that the circumstances of their revelation were ineluctably intertwined with the concrete realities of the early Muslims. Thus, when the Prophet and his followers, having been forced out of Mecca, migrated to Medina, they were attacked

[60] For classical and medieval Islamic international law, see Majid Khadduri, *War and Peace in the Law of Islam* (Baltimore: Johns Hopkins University Press, 1955).
[61] *Uṣūl al-Sharīʿa*, 88, 93–95.

by non-Muslims. Under these circumstances, Q. 22:39 was revealed: "Sanction is given unto those who fight because they have been wronged." Thereafter, the Quran defined more precisely the enemy against whom war is to be launched; Q. 2:91–2 reads:

> Fight in the way of God against those who fight against you, but do not begin hostilities, for God does not love aggression. And slay them wherever you find them, and drive them out of their places whence they drove you out, for persecution is worse than slaughter. And fight not with them in the Inviolable Place of Worship until they attack you, then slay them. Such is the reward of disbelievers.

Accordingly, ʿAshmāwī argues, fighting in the Sharīʿa must be understood to be confined to belligerent disbelievers who attacked the Prophet and forced him out of his city. Nowhere does the Quran enjoin fighting those who believe in other scriptures, unless these first attack the Muslims.

Nor does the Quran command Muslims to launch war against non-Muslims with the view of converting them to Islam, for if God's plan were to convert all people to Islam, He would have created them Muslims *ab initio*. This is attested in a number of verses; e.g., Q. 6:35 and 2:256 state, respectively: "Had God willed He could have made you one community" and "There is no compulsion in religion." So do Q. 2:62 and 5:96 declare. "Those who believe, and those who are Jews, Christians and Sabaeans – whoever believed in God and the Last Day and doeth right – surely their reward is with their Lord, and there shall no fear come upon them neither shall they grieve."

Those who misunderstood the Sharīʿa, ʿAshmāwī maintains, misinterpreted Q. 9:29 and 9:123 as categorical commands enjoining Muslims to fight the people of scriptures: "Fight against those who have been given the Scripture as believe not in God nor the Last Day, and forbid not which God had forbidden by His messenger, and follow not the religion of truth, until they pay the tribute readily, being brought low," and "O you who believe, fight those disbelievers who come close to you." ʿAshmāwī holds that there is nothing in the first verse to indicate that non-Muslims should be fought until they convert to Islam. All that this verse commands is that fighting must be initiated only against those among the scripturalists who do not believe in God and the Last Judgment. And one surely cannot conclude from this verse that the scripturalists must be fought until they convert to Islam. The tribute, known as *jizya*, is to be paid only by those disbelievers among the scripturalists, and this must be taken as a sign of goodwill on their part toward Muslims. By the same token, there is nothing in the second verse that indicates that all scripturalists must be fought and converted. All it says is that those who follow on the heels of Muslims for the purpose of attacking them must be fought back. The Sharīʿa then commands fighting only when Muslims come under attack: the law calls for such drastic measures solely in self-defense. If anything, the Sharīʿa urges peace, as attested in a number of verses, e.g., Q. 8:61: "If they incline to peace, incline thou also to it."

ʿAshmāwī argues that the traditional interpretation of these verses, which led to a law that requires an unwavering war against non-Muslims until they die or convert, was the result partly of the dogmatic attitude of the medieval scholars, and partly of the realities under which Muslims lived in the first few centuries of Islam. But by discerning the specific circumstances under which the Quran was revealed, as well as the reasons and rationale behind its language, one comes to the understanding that the commands to launch war against non-Muslims were relevant to the time of the Prophet, and their interpretation in modern times must not be taken beyond self-defense.

With the same approach adopted for the interpretation of the Quran in matters of international law, ʿAshmāwī discusses a number of issues ranging from personal status to fiscal and criminal law. In the interest of economy, I shall deal with only two issues here; namely, the fiscal law of interest (*ribā*) and intoxication. The choice of these two is deliberate, for it is largely in the reinterpretation of such matters that any attempt at reform reveals the extent to which it departs from the traditional substantive law.

It becomes immediately clear that ʿAshmāwī supports the provisions in the Egyptian law currently in effect, a law which regulates the levying of interest at the rate of 4 percent in civil transactions and 5 percent in commercial dealings. The question that arises here is: How does ʿAshmāwī justify his position in light of the Quranic verses (2:275–79) that categorically prohibit the levying of interest? Again, the second and third principles, which ʿAshmāwī has already postulated, are brought to bear upon the solution to this problem. The Quranic provisions relative to usury were revealed to a society in which the common practice was to charge the debtor exorbitant amounts of interest, with the result that the amount owed to the lender would become with the lapse of time far larger than that of the principal. Thus, in the Arabian society the Quran addressed, usurious transactions amounted to a flagrant exploitation of the debtor. And the Quran intended to put an end, not to commercial and profitable transactions, but to exploitation. It is for this reason alone, ʿAshmāwī holds, that interest was prohibited.

In a modern economy, on the other hand, no exploitation of this sort exists. The function of interest is not the undue enrichment of those persons with capital, but rather the protection of the value of money. The frequent fluctuation of monetary value in today's economy requires that the lender be allowed to levy such interest on his capital as to ensure that when the loan is paid back the actual value of the principal would not be less than that he had originally lent. Under the conditions of a modern economy, if the lender is not allowed to levy interest, he may be on the losing side, and this will surely result in a situation in which no one would be willing to make his money available for borrowing. The economic consequences of such a situation would then be grave.

Furthermore, while in Arabian society the activities of borrowing and lending were limited to individuals, the greatest part of such activities are nowadays conducted between corporate entities, not private individuals. Borrowing in a corporate economy is not a matter of personal need but rather amounts to a business enterprise; corporations borrow in order to invest, and investment yields more profit than the amount of interest owed on the loan. Thus by borrowing, corporate entities manage to increase their shares of profit. Interest in such an economy can hardly be characterized as exploitative.

The same can be said of the interest paid by financial institutions to those who invest or bank with them. Such institutions cannot be said to suffer from exploitation, because they in turn invest the capital entrusted to them and make sufficient profit to pay back the principal and interest to the investor after having accumulated certain profits for themselves. Similarly, when an individual invests with a financial institution – in the form of cash, bonds, or otherwise – she would be able to do so even if the principal invested is small. Without such possibilities provided by financial institutions, minor investors would not be able to make any profit on their capital. But by pooling a sufficient number of small capital, these institutions manage to invest them and bring a profitable return to themselves as well as to the minor investors.

The only problematic of such a system of banking and financing is a situation in which an individual borrows from another or from a financial institution as a matter of genuine need. But in today's complex social and financial structure, it is extremely difficult to determine who has a genuine need for financial assistance and who has not. Setting a reasonable rate of interest on non-commercial loans would be as justified as setting a minimum age for marriage, which is twenty-one years according to the Egyptian law. However imperfect ʿAshmāwī's analogy here may be, his point is that in view of the fluctuating value of currency, setting a reasonable rate of interest for those in need does not amount to exploitation of the needy individual on the part of financial institutions, but rather a device by means of which the actual monetary value of the loan is maintained. ʿAshmāwī proposes that the state might consider establishing a system of lending whereby the needy could borrow, in accordance with their needs, certain amounts free of interest. Thus loans for marriages, funerals, etc., would be commensurate with the needs in each situation and their size would not exceed a certain percentage of the annual income of the borrower.

Be that as it may, ʿAshmāwī maintains, eliminating interest from the economy is unfeasible if not altogether impossible. For local economies are now tied to a global economy and are deeply affected by any changes in it; and since interest constitutes the nerve of global economy, eliminating it in a local economy would have severe adverse effects. But this obviously is a tangential argument. ʿAshmāwī's main point about charging interest in a modern economy is that it does not involve exploitation, and thus it should not be prohibited by the Sharīʿa.[62]

On the matter of intoxication, ʿAshmāwī succeeds only partially in interpreting away the provisions in the traditional texts. Having cited the verses (by now well known to the reader) dealing with grape-wine, ʿAshmāwī remarks that these verses raise three questions: First, is wine prohibited or must it only be avoided? The implication of this question seems to call for a distinction between prohibition as a strictly legal norm and prohibition as a merely moral value. That it is to be avoided is abundantly clear from the verses. But that it is outrightly forbidden is not so clear, because in 6:146 the Quran in effect states that, with the exception of carrion, blood and swine flesh, no food or drink was prohibited by God. Now, the fact that this verse was among the very last to be revealed places the previous verses relative to date-wine in a less secure position, and at least calls for reevaluating the legal effect of these verses. ʿAshmāwī, however, does not develop his argument further, and stops at the insinuation that textual evidence on this issue is less than decisive.

The second question that ʿAshmāwī raises is: What does the term *khamr* mean in the Quran? The Muslim legists, he rightly argues, understood the term to refer to any beverage that inebriates, thus causing the person who consumes it to lose control over his own proper conduct. Some jurists, however, took *khamr* to refer only to fermented grape-juice, and it is only this, ʿAshmāwī insists, that the Quran meant, and it is the consumption of this drink that it prohibited. The implication of this hermeneutic is clear and is inconsistent with ʿAshmāwī's own principles which he already set forth: the Quranic verses are to be taken (following the tradition of the

[62] Ibid., 110–16.

Ẓāhirites) in their literal sense, and they are not to transcend their immediate meaning. The rationale behind the prohibition of wine is wholly ignored in favor of a restrictive understanding of the Quranic language. But this interpretive stance not only undermines the second principle ʿAshmāwī has advocated, but its adoption heralds a hermeneutical approach that his theory cannot, as it stands, sustain.

The third question pertains to the penalty of inebriation. The Quran and the Prophet, ʿAshmāwī remarks, did not set a penalty for intoxication. But when the second Caliph, ʿUmar, was asked about the matter, he prescribed eighty lashes, by analogy with the penalty for falsely accusing a person of fornication. "If a man becomes inebriated," ʿUmar is reported to have said, "he will utter nonsense, and if he utters nonsense, then he will slander others" – the reasoning being that both persons, the false accuser and the drunkard, utter language that offends and defames. ʿAshmāwī rejects this line of reasoning, *inter alia*, on the ground that the drunkard, unlike the false accuser, does not necessarily defame people. ʿAshmāwī concludes his discussion of the matter by saying that the penalty, whatever it is, must be inflicted upon a person who consumes alcohol with the deliberate purpose of getting drunk. But he who drinks as a consequence of a "calamity that befell him" is not subject to punishment – in accordance with Q. 2:173: "He who is driven by necessity, neither craving nor transgressing, it is no sin for him. Lo! God is forgiving, merciful."[63]

ʿAshmāwī's attempted solution to the problem of inebriation nicely demonstrates the absence of an adequate methodological mechanism which can be brought to bear upon any problem, whatever its nature or characteristics. Resorting to a narrow and literalist interpretation of the meaning of *khamr* further illustrates the failure to provide for a hermeneutical scheme by which the immediate import of the texts can be transcended. As long as the tension between text and context remains, ʿAshmāwī's legal methodology is not likely to stand the test of practice. Furthermore, the intense opposition to his views in Egypt makes it unlikely that his proposal for a legal methodology, even if drastically improved, will find approval.

A more reasoned and convincing methodology, and one that strikes an almost perfect balance between text and context, is advocated by the Pakistani scholar and reformer Fazlur Rahman (d. 1988). Rahman takes strong exception to the traditional theory and its authors, blaming them for a fragmented view of the revealed sources. In his opinion, both the traditional legal theorists and the exegetes treated the Quran and the Sunna

[63] Ibid., 125.

verse by verse, and the Sunna report by report. The lack of cross-reference to the textual sources was thus responsible for the absence of an effective *Weltanschauung* "that is cohesive and meaningful for life as a whole."[64] A central ingredient of the task to understand the Quranic and Prophetic message as a unity is to analyze it against a background, and that background is the Arabian society in which Islam first arose. Thus a thorough understanding of the Meccan social, economic and tribal institutions becomes necessary in order to understand the import of revelation for the purpose of universalizing it beyond the context of the Prophet's career.

In an attempt to explain the significance of understanding the Quran as a whole and within a situational context, Rahman takes the case of alcoholic beverages, declared prohibited by the traditional jurists. As we have already seen, the Quran initially considered alcohol among the blessings of God, along with milk and honey (Q. 16:66–69). Later, when Muslims moved to Medina, some of the Companions urged the Prophet to ban alcohol. Consequently, Q. 2:219 was revealed, stating that "They question you about alcohol and games of chance; tell them in both there is great harm but there is also certain utility for people in them. But their harm outweighs their utility." Still later, a group of people belonging to the Ansar consumed alcohol and became inebriated, and one member of the group misread the Quran. Immediately thereafter, another verse was revealed (4:43), stating "Do not approach prayer while intoxicated, so that you know what you utter." On the occasion of yet another drinking party, a brawl was started and caused severe discord among the Prophet's followers. Again, immediately thereafter a verse was revealed (Q. 5:90–91): "Alcohol . . . [is] an abomination and the handiwork of the devil . . . The devil seeks only to sow discord and rancor amongst you by means of alcohol and games of chance, and to turn you from the remembrance of God and from [His] worship. Are you then going to desist?"

From this gradual prohibition of alcohol, the jurists concluded that the last verse abrogates those that have preceded it, and in an attempt to rationalize this abrogation they resorted to what he terms the Law of Graduation according to which the Quran sought to wean Muslims from certain ingrained habits in a piecemeal fashion, instead of commanding a sudden prohibition. Hence, it was necessary to support this Law of Graduation by other considerations in order to make the contradiction between the various verses intelligible. In the Meccan period, the Muslims were a small minority, constituting an informal community, not a society. It appears, Rahman says, that alcohol consumption in the midst of this com-

[64] "Interpreting the Qur'an," *Inquiry*, 3 (May 1986): 45.

munity was in no way a common practice. But when the prominent Meccans converted to Islam at a later stage, there were many who were in the habit of drinking. The evolution of this minority into a community and then into an informal state coincided with the growing problem of alcohol consumption; hence the final Quranic prohibition imposed on all inebriating substances.

> Therefore we see how the background of all these verses makes intelligible to us even a case which is extremely difficult to explain either on the principle of Naskh [abrogation] or on the principle of graduation alone. This is what we mean by taking the context into account. The net conclusion, so far as our present case is concerned, is of course that when human beings become a society, alcohol becomes harmful in a way that its consumption cannot be allowed.[65]

It is thus necessary to draw from the isolated verses and Prophetic reports, which are particular and fragmented in nature, a general principle which embodies the rationale behind a certain ruling. The failure of the traditional jurists to elicit such principles, Rahman argues, has led to chaos. A telling example of this failure may be found in the case of polygamous marriage. In 4:2, the Quran complains of the guardians' abuse and unlawful seizure of the property of orphaned children with whom they were entrusted. In 4:126, the Quran says that these guardians should marry the orphaned girls when they come of age rather than return their properties to them. Accordingly, in 4:3 the Quran says that if the guardians cannot do justice to the children's properties and if they insist on marrying them, then they may marry up to four provided that they treat them justly. If they cannot afford them such a treatment, then they must marry only one. On the other hand, 4:127 stipulates that it is impossible to do justice among a plurality of wives. As in the case of alcohol, the Quran is seemingly contradictory here: while it permits marriage to four wives if they can be treated with justice, it declares that justice can never be done in a polygamous marriage. But it must not be forgotten, Rahman asserts, that the whole Quranic discussion occurred in the limited context of orphaned women, not in unconditional terms. The traditional jurists deemed the permission to marry up to four wives as carrying a legal force, whereas the demand to do justice to them was considered to be a mere recommendation, devoid of any binding effect. By so doing, the traditional jurists turned the issue of polygamy right on its head, taking a specific verse to be binding, and the general principle to be a recommendation. In "eliciting general principles of different order from the Qur'an . . . the most general becomes the most basic and the most

[65] Ibid., 47.

deserving of implementation, while the specific rulings will be subsumed under them."[66] In accordance with this principle, Rahman argues, the justice verse in polygamous marriages should have been accorded a superior status over the specific verse of permission to marry up to four. The priority given to the justice verse in this case is further supported by the recurrent and persistent Quranic theme of the need to do justice.

The task of eliciting general principles from specific rulings in the Quran and the Sunna must be undertaken then with full consideration of the sociological forces that produced these rulings. Since the Quran gives, be it directly or obliquely, the reasons for certain ethical and legal rulings, an understanding of these reasons becomes essential for drawing general principles. The multi-faceted ingredients making up the revealed texts, along with those ingredients making up the background of revelation, must therefore "be brought together to yield a unified and comprehensive socio-moral theory squarely based upon the Quran and its *sunna* counterparts."[67] But it may be objected that the process of eliciting general principles in this manner is excessively subjective. In refuting this claim, Rahman invokes the fact that the Quran speaks of its own purposes and objectives, a fact that should contribute to minimizing subjectivity. Furthermore, whatever difference of opinion results from the existing subjectivity should be of great value provided that each opinion is seriously and carefully considered.

This process of eliciting general principles represents the first step toward implementing a new methodology of the law. This methodology consists of two movements of juristic thought, one proceeding from the particular to the general (i.e., eliciting general principles from specific cases), the other from the general to the particular. Hence the designation of Rahman's methodology as "the Double Movement Theory." In the second movement, the general principles elicited from the revealed sources are brought to bear upon the present conditions of Muslim society. This presupposes a thorough understanding of these conditions, equal in magnitude to that required to understand the revealed texts with their background. But since the present situation can never be identical to the Prophetic past, and since it could differ from it "in certain important respects," it is required that "we apply those general principles of the Quran (as well as those of the Sunna)[68] to the current situation espousing

[66] Ibid., 49. [67] Rahman, "Towards Reformulating the Methodology of Islamic Law," 221.

[68] Although Rahman speaks, more often than not, of the Quran to the exception of the Sunna, it is clear that in his discourse the latter is always subsumed under the former. See his *Islamic Methodology in History* (Karachi: Central Institute of Islamic Research, 1965), 178; and his "Towards Reformulating the Methodology of Islamic Law," 221.

that which is worthy of espousing and rejecting that which must be rejected."[69] Just what the criteria are for rejecting certain "important respects" and not others is a crucial question that Rahman does not seem to answer decisively. For if these respects are important and may nevertheless be neutralized, then there is no guarantee that essential Quranic and Sunnaic elements or even principles will not be set aside. In a vague attempt to address the subjectivity involved, Rahman remarks:

> One may ask whether the contemporary situation influences contemporary legislation and thus deflects the law from the standards of justice and purity required by the teaching of the Quran and the *sunna*. Yet this process is precisely what the application of principles to a new situation means. It does not mean that Quranic principles fall short of meeting the requirements of the present world; nor, on the other hand, does it mean that they fail to control the present situation. In fact, the successful meeting point of the normative principles of Islam and the assessment of the new situation will be a sure proof that both tasks have been performed currently. In the case of failure, either the normative study of Islam or the study of the new situation – or both – has been faulty.[70]

The weakness of Rahman's methodology thus lies in the not altogether clear mechanics of the second movement, that is, the application of the systematic principles derived from the revealed texts and their contexts to the present situations. Furthermore, the relatively few cases he repeatedly advances in his writings on the subject do not represent the full spectrum of cases in the law, with the result that his methodology may be thought to be incapable of providing an outline sufficiently comprehensive to afford modern Muslims the methodological means of solving problems different in nature from those he so frequently cites. What of those cases in which only a textual statement is to be found without information about the backdrop against which the statement was revealed? Or, still, how do modern Muslims address fundamental problems facing their societies when no Quranic or Sunnaic text is to be found? That Rahman does not seem to provide answers for such questions may be the function of his interest in elaborating a methodology confined in outlook to the revealed texts rather than a methodology of law proper.

These questions and many more do find thoughtful answers in the revolutionary and innovative theory of the Syrian engineer Muḥammad Shaḥrūr, whose recent work *al-Kitāb wal-Qur'ān*[71] advances some of the

[69] "Interpreting the Qur'an," 49.
[70] "Towards Reformulating the Methodology of Islamic Law," 223.
[71] *al-Kitāb wal-Qur'ān: Qirā'a Mu'āṣira* (Cairo and Damascus: Sīnā lil-Nashr, 1992).

most controversial ideas in the Middle East today. It is not difficult to see that his formal training as an engineer had great impact on his mode of analysis, in that in "re-reading" the Quran and the Sunna he draws heavily on the natural sciences, particularly mathematics and physics. His, then, is a unique contribution to the reinterpretation of the Quran and the Sunna in particular, and to law as a comprehensive system in general. Although Shaḥrūr modestly claims that his work represents no more than a "contemporary reading" of the Quran, being in no way an exegetical or a legal work,[72] it is impressive in that it offers both depth and range, virtually unparalleled in modern writings on the subject.

On the basis of Q. 15:9 ("Indeed, We have revealed the Remembrance, and lo, we verily are its Preservers"), Shaḥrūr maintains that the Quran, having been constantly "preserved" by divine power, is as much the property of later generations as that of earlier or even the earliest generations. Since each generation bestows on the Quran an interpretation emanating from the particular reality in which it lives, we, in the twentieth century, are entitled to confer on the "Remembrance" an interpretation that reflects the conditions of this age. In this sense, modern Muslims are more qualified to understand the Quran for their own purposes and exigencies than earlier generations were. Thus, traditional interpretations of the Quran must not be taken as binding upon modern Muslim societies. But Shaḥrūr goes further: modern Muslims are better equipped to understand the meaning of revelation than their classical and medieval counterparts because they are far more "cultured." The Quran speaks of the bedouins as having been "more hard in disbelief and hypocrisy" than the other Arabs who possessed higher culture and civilization, and "likely to be ignorant of the limits which God revealed to His Messenger" (9:97). The Quranic criterion of a proper comprehension of the revealed texts is thus a level of high culture which the bedouins were thought to have lacked. Since Muslims in the twentieth century enjoy a higher level of culture and scientific knowledge than their predecessors, then they are better equipped to understand revelation than these predecessors were.[73]

Having arrogated to his generation the superior right to interpret (=re-read) the "Remembrance," Shaḥrūr goes on to draw a crucial distinction between what he calls the Quran and the Book (these two words constituting the title of his work). This distinction directly emanates from yet another distinction, namely, between the function of Muhammad as Messenger (*rasūl*) and as Prophet (*nabī*). As Prophet, Muhammad received a body of information having to do with prophecy, religion and the like. As

[72] Ibid., 45. [73] Ibid., 44, 472.

Messenger, he was the recipient of a corpus of legal instructions, *in addition to* that information he received as a Prophet. The function of the Prophet, then, is religious, whereas that of the Messenger is legal. Now, prophetic information is textually ambiguous, capable of varying interpretations. This is the Quran. On the other hand, the legal subject matter is univocal, but nevertheless capable of being subjected to *ijtihād*. This is the Book. It must be clear, however, that Shaḥrūr clearly distinguishes between *ijtihād* and interpretation. Interpretation involves changing the meaning of ambiguous speech, thus creating two or more varied perceptions of the same language. *Ijtihād*, on the other hand, does not involve interpretation in the strictly linguistic sense. It is a process whereby legal language is taken to yield a particular legal effect suitable to a particular place and time, when it may, in another place and time, yield another effect.[74]

In order to understand the legal Message, it is necessary to draw another fundamental distinction between two contradictory, yet complementary, attributes found in the Book. These are straightness (*istiqāma*) and curvature (*ḥanīfiyya*). It is to be noted here that our English rendering of these two Arabic terms does not represent their immediate meaning as they have been traditionally understood but rather as Shaḥrūr perceives them by means of his own linguistic derivation. Listing numerous Quranic verses in which these two terms occur, he concludes that the meaning of *ḥanīfiyya* is deviation from a straight path or from a linearity. The opposite of *ḥanīfiyya* is *istiqāma*, the latter being the quality of being straight or of following a linear path.[75]

Both of these attributes are integral to the Message, coexisting in a symbiotic relationship. Curvature is a natural quality, meaning that it is intrinsic to human nature as it exists in the material, objective world. Physical laws show that things do not occur in a linear, but rather in a non-linear, fashion. Motion in the natural world, for instance, is characterized by curves. All things, from minute electrons to the colossal galaxies, move in curves. In line with this perception of nature, curvature in law is seen as representing the quality of non-linear movement, where customs, habits and social traditions tend to exist in harmony with the needs of particular societies, needs that tend to change from one society to another and, diachronically, within a society. It is for the purpose of controlling and restraining this change that "straightness" becomes indispensable for maintaining a legal order. But unlike curvature, straightness is not a natural quality. Rather, it is divinely ordained in order for it to coexist with curvature and to partake in the ordering of human societies. Thus, curvature

[74] Ibid., 37. [75] Ibid., 448.

stands in need of straightness, as attested in Q. 1:5, where man is represented as seeking the guidance of God by imploring Him to "show us the straight path." On the other hand, there exists no Quranic verse, Shaḥrūr maintains, in which man is portrayed as seeking curvature (*ḥanīfiyya*), because curvature is pre-existing in the natural order.[76]

The relationship between curvature and straightness is thus wholly dialectical, where constants and permutations are intertwined. This dialectic is significant because it indicates that the law is adaptable to all times and places (*ṣāliḥ li-kulli zamān wa-makān*). But what is the form of straightness that God revealed in order to complement curvature? Here Shaḥrūr advances the crux of his theory, which we may call the Theory of Limits (*ḥudūd*). Ultimately, then, man moves in curvature *within* these Limits which represent straightness.

The Theory of Limits may be described as follows: it is the divine decree, expressed in the Book and the Sunna, which sets a Lower and an Upper Limit for all human actions; the Lower Limit represents the minimum required by the law in a particular case, and the Upper Limit the maximum. Just as nothing short of the minimum is legally admissible, so nothing above the maximum may be deemed lawful. Once these Limits are transcended, penalties become warrantable, in proportion to the violation committed.

Shaḥrūr distinguishes six types of Limits, the first of which is the Lower Limit when it stands alone. An example of this Limit is the Quranic prohibition imposed on marrying one's mother, daughters, maternal and paternal aunts, etc. Once these relations are excluded, marriage to other relations and non-relations becomes permitted. Second is the Upper Limit when it stands alone. An example of this limit may be found in Q. 5:38: "As for the thief, both male and female, cut off their hands." Here, the stipulated penalty represents the Upper Limit that should not be exceeded. However, the penalty may be mitigated, according to the objective conditions prevailing in a particular society. It is the responsibility of the *mujtahid*s to determine what type of theft requires the cutting off of hands, and what type does not. But what about grand theft, which may lead to grave consequences such as stealing intelligence through espionage or stealing or embezzling money on the corporate and state levels? In these cases, where national security and economy are at stake, Q. 5:38 does not apply. Instead, recourse to Q. 5:33 must be had: "The only reward of those who make war upon God and His messenger and strive after corruption in the land will be that they should be killed or crucified, or have their hands and feet on alternate sides cut off, or be expelled out of the land." Again, the *mujtahid*s

[76] Ibid., 449–50.

must decide, in light of the requirements of their society, which penalty is commensurate with the particular crime committed.[77]

The third type consists of the Lower and Upper Limits when they are conjoined. In illustration of this type, the Quranic verse related to inheritance (4:11) is cited. The general tenor of this verse is that the male receives "the equivalent of the portion of two females, and if there be women more than two, then theirs is two-thirds of the inheritance, and if there be only one then the half." What we have here, Shaḥrūr argues, is a determination of the Upper Limit for men and the Lower Limit for women, irrespective of whether the woman was a bread-winner. At any rate, the woman's share can never be less than 33.3 percent whereas the man's can never reach more than 66.6 percent of the estate. If the woman is given 40 percent and the man 60 percent, then both the Upper and Lower Limits cannot be said to have been violated. The percentage allocated to each is determined in accordance with the objective conditions existing in a particular society at a particular time. This example, Shaḥrūr argues, amply demonstrates the freedom of movement (=curvature) within the Limits (=straightness) stipulated by the law, Limits determined by each society according to its specific needs. Law, he contends, must not be perceived as the literal application to a modern condition of a text revealed centuries ago. Should this application be accepted, then Islam would loose its *ḥanīfī* character.

Fourth is the meeting of the Upper and Lower Limits together. It is interesting here that in all of the Book and the Sunna, only one Quranic verse is of this type, namely 24:2, which states: "The adulterer and the adulteress, scourge ye each one of them with a hundred lashes. And let not pity for the twain withhold you from obedience to God, if ye believe in God and the Last Day. And let a party of the believers witness their punishment." Here, both the Upper and Lower Limits are set at one meeting point, namely, one hundred lashes. God's insistence that the adulterers should not be pitied signifies that the punishment must not be mitigated. It should neither be less nor more than one hundred stripes.[78]

Fifth is the type in which the curvature moves between the Lower and the Upper Limit but touches neither. The sexual relations between men and women exemplify this type. Beginning with a point above the Lower Limit, where the sexes are not to touch each other, the curvature moves upward in the direction of the Upper Limit where they come close to committing adultery but do not. Finally, in the sixth type the curvature moves between a positive Upper Limit and a negative Lower Limit. Fiscal transactions illustrate the consistency of this type: the Upper Limit is represented by the

[77] Ibid., 455. [78] Ibid., 463.

levying of interest and the Lower Limit by the payment of alms-tax (*zakāt*). Since these Limits are positive and negative, then there exists in between them a stage that is equivalent to zero. An example of this middle stage is an interest-free loan. Thus, there exist three major categories for imparting money: (1) payment of a tax; (2) giving an interest-free loan; and (3) giving a loan with interest.[79]

In his discussion of the sixth type, Shaḥrūr introduces a fairly detailed discourse on interest. Having cited more than half a dozen Quranic verses that touch upon the question of usury, and having explained that the meaning of usury in Arabic (*ribā*) is "growth or increase" of wealth, Shaḥrūr asserts that the prohibition on interest is not conclusive in Islam. In support of this assertion, he calls upon ʿUmar b. al-Khaṭṭāb who is reported to have wished that the Prophet had clarified in explicit terms the legal status of interest.[80] All this is, of course, intended to pave the way for the argument that economic activities involving interest must be considered lawful in Islamic law. According to Q. 9:60, "The alms are only for the poor and the needy"; in Shaḥrūr's interpretation, the poor and needy in modern societies are those who cannot repay their debts. It is precisely for this impoverished segment of society that Q. 2:276 was revealed: "God has blighted usury and made alms-giving fruitful." Hence, society must support its poor and needy without expecting any return. However, there are others who can repay their debts but without any accumulation of interest. In their case, they only owe the sum borrowed, with no payment of interest (this being the midmost point between the positive Upper Limit and the negative Lower Limit). The Quranic basis of this financial policy is 2:280 which states that "if the debtor is in straitened circumstances, then [let there be] postponement to [the time of] ease; and that ye remit the debt as alms-giving would be better for you if ye did but know."

The remaining sections of society, the great majority, do not qualify for these exemptions, for they are sufficiently prosperous. The backbone of the economy is the merchants, industrialists, farmers, skilled professionals and their like who, if they happen to need to borrow money, can repay it with interest and without any harm coming to them. But in no case shall the debtor pay an amount of interest that is larger than the principal he borrowed. In other words, the cumulative interest owed shall in no case exceed 100 percent of the original loan, irrespective of the debt's duration. This represents the positive Upper Limit, defined by the following Quranic terms: "O you who believe! Devour not usury, doubling and quadrupling [the sum lent]" (3:130).[81]

[79] Ibid., 464. [80] Ibid., 468. [81] Ibid., 468–70.

Through the application of the Theory of Limits, Shaḥrūr addresses another thorny issue in modern Islam, namely, polygamy. But before he does so, he makes a number of remarks to the effect that the doctrines of the traditional legal schools are not binding upon modern Muslims because they are based upon certain misconceptions. First, the traditional jurists did not distinguish between the verses and Prophetic reports that express the Limits of God and those that do not, and embody mere instructions (as in Q. 33:59). But these jurists are not to be blamed, for they were articulating the *Weltanschauung* of the age in which they lived. Second, classical and medieval Muslim scholars thought that by the end of the Prophet's career the process by which women were liberated had reached completion. Thus, if during that time women did not hold judicial and political offices, such as judgeships or ministerial positions in government, then it was concluded that they are barred from these offices. The fact, however, is that the new religion was introducing gradual changes, whereby ruptures in social, economic and other structures were avoided. The liberation of women started during the Prophet's lifetime, and was supposed to continue thereafter. It did not, however; the Sunna was not seen as an ongoing process but rather as a complete model, a model that was to remain frozen in time.

But with the Theory of Limits, the concept of polygamy may be explained in historical terms which can transform its image from a backward to a noble practice. The two verses treating of polygamy are 4:2–3: "Give unto orphans (*yatāmā*) their wealth. Exchange not the good for the bad [in your management thereof] nor absorb their wealth into your own wealth . . . And if ye fear that ye will not deal fairly with the orphans, marry of the women, who seem good to you, two, three or four; and if ye fear that ye cannot do justice then one only . . . It is more likely that ye will not do justice." Now the Limits revealed in these verses are of two types: quantitative and qualitative. Quantitatively, the Lower Limit is marriage to a single wife, whereas the Upper Limit is to four wives. This has been the understanding prevailing among Muslims thus far. But the qualitative aspect of these verses is just as important to a complete understanding of the verses' import. The traditional jurists never asked, for instance, what sort of women are meant in these verses. They took "women" to refer to the whole class of women, without qualification. But the text of the verse does not allow for this generalization, for the phrase "if ye fear that ye will not deal fairly with the orphans" is inextricably connected with what follows it, namely, "marry of the women. " That God did, in this context, allow a second, a third and a fourth wife, and that He did not mention the first, suggests that the first wife is qualitatively, not quantitatively, excluded from this permission. Shaḥrūr is here referring to the fact, inferred from the texts, that the women associated with the orphans are widowed mothers. Earlier in his work, he defines in some detail the meaning of "orphan" (*yatīm*) as one whose father, not mother, has died when he or she is at a young age.[82] The implication of this definition is that the widow, the orphans' mother, is a relatively young woman. Thus, the permission to marry a second, a third and a fourth wife amounts in effect to a permission to marry young widows who will bring with them to marriage their young children. This is the whole point behind the permission.

In addition to the first wife – who may not be a widow – and her children, the other co-wives along with their children too are the responsibility of the husband. The Quranic reference to "doing justice" must be seen, Shaḥrūr argues, as bearing upon the husband's treatment of his children from the first wife on the one hand, and of the widows' children brought to the marriage with them, on the other. In other words, the Book enjoins men not to marry more than one wife if they cannot treat with complete equality and impartiality the young orphans who come to marriage with their widowed mothers. The last words of Q. 4:3 confirm the notion that it is difficult to do justice, economic or otherwise, when there are so many children in a single household. At the same time, the Book does encourage men of financial means to marry widows who have young children, for this was deemed to be an effective way to provide care for orphaned families. The high value attached to this humane act is corroborated by a report in which the Prophet is reported to have said, while pointing to his two intertwined fingers, "Those who provide for the orphans and I will be like that in Paradise." Furthermore, Shaḥrūr stresses that the Book exempts men from paying dowry to their wives as long as they adequately provide for their orphaned children (4:127) who come to the marriage with their widowed mothers. Likewise, the Book (4:129–30) does not insist that these wives should be treated with full justice because marrying them is done not for their sake but rather for the sake of their fatherless children. Since, therefore, the crucial issue in the Book is justice toward orphans, the whole import of the "polygamy verse" is in no way relevant to the wives themselves. It is precisely here where the traditional jurists went wrong.[83]

The early and medieval legists went wrong because they did not understand the significance of the Theory of Limits; what is more, they even did not realize its existence. Shaḥrūr borrows the metaphor of a soccer match, where the teams play *within* and *between* the borders of the field not *at* the borders. The traditional jurists played, so to speak, at the borders and left the entire field intact.[84]

[82] Ibid., 512. [83] Ibid., 598–600. [84] Ibid., 579.

We have already noted that Shaḥrūr's Theory of Limits draws as much upon the Sunna as the Book. The former, in his view, represents a methodological model for legislation. Put differently, like the Book, it does not necessarily provide for specific and concrete cases of legislation but rather it furnishes the methodological path (*minhāj*) for constructing a system of law. Those parts of the Sunna that are conducive to creating the methodology and Theory of Limits will be taken as highly relevant. Those that do not will be taken as exclusive to the private life of the Prophet and as binding upon no one but those who lived in his age.

Aside from the Book and those provisions from the Sunna relevant to the Theory of Limits, Shaḥrūr rejects as obsolete and oppressive all the other traditional "sources" of the law. He also describes *qiyās* as oppressive, for, he asks, how could an analogy be drawn between the seventh and the twentieth centuries? Indeed, it is a credit to Shaḥrūr that he was able to dispense of *qiyās* by providing a substitute to it in the Theory of Limits. Similarly, he was able to render superfluous the notion of consensus because his epistemology does not, by definition, require the element of certainty. Law, in his view, is ever changing, as long as it moves between the Limits and not beyond them. The only concept of consensus he admits is one where the majority of citizens vote on a proposed law, and once the proposal passes for law, they become committed to its implementation. The traditional notion of consensus, Shaḥrūr insists, is imaginary (*wahmī*) and is in no way binding upon the Muslims of the modern age.[85]

Finally, an essential question poses itself: How does Shaḥrūr propose to deal with those cases in the law that do not come within the purview of the revealed texts? Shaḥrūr's answer is simple: if God wanted to regulate these cases He would have done so. That He did not means that He intended to leave it to us to determine these laws for ourselves. All those cases that the traditional jurists subsumed under *maṣāliḥ mursala*, such as income tax, tariffs, etc., must be determined by one government agency or another. It is the state and the people who decide on those textually unregulated matters. In the case of taxes, for instance, the Lower Limit would be zero, whereas the Upper Limit would be determined by the social and economic conditions prevailing at a particular place and time.[86]

CONCLUDING REMARKS

Of all the attempts to reformulate legal theory, Shaḥrūr's seems thus far the most convincing, though Rahman's does not lag far behind. However, the

[85] Ibid., 579–82. [86] Ibid., 474–75.

ultimate success of any legal methodology hinges not only upon its intellectual integrity and a sophisticated level of theorization but also upon its feasibility in a social context. It is here where another distinction may be made between what we termed the religious utilitarianists and their liberalist counterparts. The former's ideas (and we should not call them theories or methodologies) have been more or less implemented in the legal systems of most Islamic countries. In fact, it was ʿAbduh's school that played a central role in bringing about the sort of reforms we have described at the outset of this chapter. And it was the later utilitarianists, such as ʿAllāl al-Fāsī and Khallāf, who were rationalizing the status quo, rather than prescribing a new legal theory or a reformulated methodology. On the other hand, the liberalists remained, and continue to stand, outside the current mainstream of legislation. It is no coincidence that all of the thinkers we have discussed under the category of religious liberalists – ʿAshmāwī, Rahman and Shaḥrūr – have met with stiff resistance from a large and powerful segment of native Islamicist movements. All of them, especially Rahman and Shaḥrūr, offer new conceptions of law and legal methodology that have proved thus far alien to the majority of Muslims.

What is curious and ironic about this scene is that the rejected liberalists offer not only a more cohesive and respectable methodology of law but also, and clearly, a more Islamically committed system of thought. We have seen that the religious utilitarianists – Riḍā, Khallāf and others – pay no more than lip service to Islamic legal values; for their ultimate frame of reference remains confined to the concepts of interest, need and necessity. The revealed texts become, in the final analysis, subservient to the imperatives of these concepts. Rahman's and Shahrūr's methodologies, on the other hand, refuse to succumb to such concepts, employing instead structured notions of textual/contextual analysis where emphasis is placed upon a humanistic law that is suggestively and generally guided, and not literally and textually dictated, by the divine intention.

7

CONCLUSION

THE search for a legal identity in twentieth-century Islam and the crises that are associated with reformulating both a legal theory and a general concept of law represent the latest historical stage in which humanistic and positivist tendencies have collided with the imperatives of revelation. True, this collision is unprecedented in the profound impact and the havoc it wreaked upon the intellectual and structural make-up of the traditional Islamic legal systems. But the tension between reason and revelation – that is, between human considerations of man's own welfare in this life, on the one hand, and divine intervention and decree, on the other – has been consistently present since Muhammad migrated to Medina. The very fact that the Quran untiringly called upon the Arabs to obey God and His Prophet, and to abandon their old ways in favor of a new "path" prescribed by the Deity, constitutes the practical equivalent of a higher will dictating to man modes of thinking and living that are often at variance with his normative ways. This divine interference, with its own internal dynamic, was on the increase with the passage of time. Obviously, the Quran could not provide on its own the basis for this intervention in mundane affairs. A second agency was required, and this was the Prophetic Sunna which emerged some decades after the Prophet's death. The later massive growth of the body of traditions signaled, dialectically, both the cause and the outcome of a gradually prevailing religious movement within which rationalist tendencies were competing with, but slowly losing ground in favor of, the traditionalists.

Once the subject matter of the revealed sources stabilized, the competition between reason and revelation moved to another front where issues of methodology became central. Shāfiʿī's stricter and narrower definition of *qiyās*, and his total rejection of *istiḥsān* as a method of human legislation, signaled yet another victory against the rationalists. But the victory was not to be absolute and unqualified, for by the end of the third/ninth century a balance between reason and revelation was struck: revelation, too, had to concede to reason a certain role in the process of discovering God's law, a process declared to be the chief *raison d'être* of legal theory. It is notable that those groups that significantly strayed from the rationalist–traditionalist synthesis were doomed to extinction, and those that represented ultra-rationalist or ultra-traditionalist tendencies had, in order to survive, to concede to the dictates of that synthesis. The early Ḥanbalites, on the traditionalist side, and certain Muʿtazilites, on the rationalist side, are only two cases in point.

Having achieved a certain balance between reason and revelation, legal theory continued to flourish while attempting to maintain that balance. Insofar as substantive law was concerned, the revealed texts were ever-present; just as legal theory itself and the authority behind it were sustained by an interpretation of the texts, so was the corpus of positive law anchored in the same hermeneutic. From a different perspective, and as a logical consequence of its fundamental reliance on revelation, legal theory had to anchor itself in a larger theological structure from which it was to derive both its overall religious authority and operative epistemology. In other words, legal theory, logically and substantively, presupposed theology, for the foundational premises upon which it was squarely based – existence, unity and the attributes of God, etc. – were strictly theological.

The organic relationship between legal theory and theology, on the one hand, and legal theory and substantive law, on the other, bestowed upon the literature of *uṣūl al-fiqh* a dualistic character. Although some theorists tend to pay more attention to the theological dimension of the discipline, there is little doubt that the genre as a whole was thoroughly and equally engulfed by both theological and positive legal questions. This, however, should not obscure the fact that the essential subject matter of the discipline is overwhelmingly juridical and not theological. Those issues that were of pure theological provenance were no more than a few, and their comparative weight in the overall body of theory was relatively marginal. It was the cumulative commentary on the otherwise legal and juridical issues that was imbued with theological underpinnings. Thus, if the woof of legal theory was theological, its constitutive warp was heavily juridical.

The theological concerns permeating legal theory affected two major features that became integral to that theory. Despite the general theological bent of legal theory, it did not escape the theoreticians that the theological issues raised were, in the final analysis, alien to the main themes of *uṣūl al-fiqh*. But the two said features, namely, epistemology and logic, became part of the discipline – the former being the product of indigenous Islamic soil, the latter an importation from Greece. The more fundamental of the two is undoubtedly epistemology, for it constituted, both structurally and substantively, the backbone of the discipline. In fact, it is difficult to conceive of *uṣūl al-fiqh* without the epistemological thread that runs through the entire gamut of its constitutive subject matter. Since the whole purpose of the law is to bring man to worship God in all aspects of life, and since the complete and perfect knowledge of how to worship Him lies in His mind alone, and is expounded only in part by revelation, the main epistemological issue that arises is this: How certain or probable is the jurist's conjecture of what God's law in a particular case is? For after all, the jurist's province is not legislation, but merely the interpretation of the texts with a view only to discover, not enact, the ruling. The juristic determination of a ruling as enjoying certainty amounted to a universal, consensual acknowledgment that the ruling that obtains in a social, human context is identical to the one lodged in the mind of God. Thus the distinction between what is probable and what is certain acquires immediate significance as a theological issue and has, simultaneously, far-reaching consequences in the world of judicial practice. Among many other consequences, a judge's decision grounded in a ruling deemed to be certain is irrevocable and thus unsusceptible to judicial review or reversal.

Logic, on the other hand, made an entry to legal theory at a later stage of that theory's life, mainly after the fifth/eleventh century. Unlike epistemology, which was richly woven into the fabric of methodology since its early formation, logic remained structurally somewhat external, and its acceptance was not always unqualified. Apart from a minority of legal theoreticians who rejected it *in toto*, there were many who incorporated into their writings either a modified or a partial theory of Aristotelian logic. But if the majority of Muslim jurists were unable to dispose of this logic altogether, it was for a good reason: they could not divorce their discipline from the theological discourse that dominated the world of intellectual enquiry, a discourse which was permeated by logic to the same extent that legal theory was permeated by theology itself. The traditional theory of knowledge (*ʿilm*) that dominated the scene until Ghazālī's lifetime lost its grip and influence with the introduction of the Aristotelian theory of definition (*ḥadd*) which normally constituted the first part of logic. The theory of definition, the *conceptio/verificatio* dichotomy, as well as the theory of syllogism became, theoretically, necessary as categories of analysis. But it is difficult to see how these new ideas influenced, on the practical plane, the substantive contents of *uṣūl al-fiqh*. In contrast with epistemology – which evolved over time hand-in-hand with the constitutive ingredients of legal theory and thus affected the judicial process – logic made an entry into this theory only after it had already reached a high level of crystallization and articulation.

The introduction of logic into legal theory at a later stage in its life is but one instance of the process whereby a new subject matter is introduced to inform one segment of theoretical discourse or another. In fact, the history of *uṣūl al-fiqh* may be said to consist of a massive body of *questions* (*masā'il*) which infiltrated the growing corpus of that theory throughout the centuries. Entirely new questions and questions stemming from older issues continued to arise and to demand theoretical attention. There is very little doubt then that the number and sheer content of the issues discussed continued to grow with the passage of time. The tradition was cumulative in the truest sense of the word.

While as a collective entity legal theory may have been cumulative, individual theorists were rather selective in their choice of the particular topics (=*questions*) that made up their respective theories. The choice of certain topics in preference to others was combined with another feature which added to the individualized character of each theory, namely, the emphasis and deemphasis placed upon the issues discussed. The very inclusion of one issue rather than another is quite significant and telling; but more telling is the generality or intensity of detail with which each issue is treated. Not entirely representative, but certainly an illustrative example, is the case of Shāṭibī. With every omission, expansion and digression, Shāṭibī was attempting to serve his own purpose, a purpose latently dictated by a clearly envisioned agenda. It is also in Shāṭibī that we observe how social and other factors determine both the form and content of legal discourse.

Now, all this means that both diachronically and synchronically legal theory was far from monolithic. Indeed, the synchronic and diachronic variations are so profound and prominent that in making terminological choices we ought to refer to the individual theories as independent and distinct contributions, although they must be considered thus within the purview of a tradition, that is, the collective and cumulative product of *uṣūl al-fiqh*. Acknowledging the distinctness of each theorist's ideas is an obvious methodological necessity. No longer can one afford to speak of a fifth-/eleventh-century Juwaynī and a seventh-/thirteenth-century Āmidī interchangeably; nor can one afford to treat as identical the theories of contemporary authors writing in different environments.

Obviously, the most salient feature of the tradition within which all theories have been expounded is the divine source that binds them together. Yet, concomitant with this source there emerged a particular hermeneutic – constituting a common denominator in all these theories – which remained the single force that bestowed on theoretical discourse a certain unity within which interpretative variations could and did exist. No doubt this hermeneutic, which persistently defined the general character of Sunnī *uṣūl al-fiqh*, was a product of the sociological structure of classical and medieval Muslim societies. More precisely, this hermeneutic represented the descriptive (and later prescriptive) methodology that was dictated by the imperatives of the positive legal system in existence. When we say that no amount of interpretation could have altered the legal effects of the Quranic verse that allots the male in inheritance twice the share of the female,[1] we mean in effect that the social structure as well as the positive legal system that was built to cater to its needs could not have allowed a different interpretation, say, an interpretation similar to that proffered by the modernists, Shaḥrūr or Rahman. The divine source, the combination of the Quran and Sunna, was textually and hermeneutically bound, ineluctably, with the sociological and, consequently, juridical realities of classical and medieval Muslim societies. Thus, in the final analysis, the source becomes subservient to the imperatives of the social and legal structures, that is to say, subservient to the imperatives of a particular, historically dictated, hermeneutic.

It is precisely this relationship between *uṣūl al-fiqh* and the particular sociological and juridical backgrounds against which it had developed and was finely elaborated that became the locus of the modern reformist critique. Except for a minority of secularists, the great majority of modern Muslim thinkers and intellectuals insist upon the need to maintain the connection between law and the divine command. At the same time, they reject the specifically traditional connection, defined by the classical and medieval hermeneutic, as irrelevant to the modern age. Their rejection stems from two factors that are inextricably linked to each other. First, there is the wave of fundamental social, technological, economic and political changes that accompanied the military and cultural domination of the West over the Orient. With these changes, a new reality, on virtually all levels, emerged, thereby rendering the traditional legal system largely obsolete. The need for a substitute to the traditional system had already become obvious by the first half of the nineteenth century, when European codes were introduced to the Ottoman Empire lock, stock and barrel.

The second factor that dictated and still dictates the shape of new reformist ideas is the movement of codification (based on indigenous and foreign laws) which has gained momentum in the Muslim world since the middle of the nineteenth century. With the introduction of these codes there arose the need to modify the infrastructure of the existing legal

[1] See the opening paragraph of chapter 6, p. 207 above.

system in order to sustain these codes. In addition to the introduction of a western-styled hierarchy of courts, a new legal profession emerged. The training of modern lawyers who staffed these courts required the institutionalization of modern colleges of law, a fact which had a fundamental structural impact upon the traditional class of legal scholars. The role these scholars played in the judicial system was gradually phased out, with the concomitant result that they could no longer be conceived as an integral part of the legal system. Their traditional colleges of law lost the financial support of both the state and private individuals, and the prestige of the social status of the traditional *faqīh* thus gave way to the emerging class of modern lawyers.

The transference of "law-making" from the hands of the traditional jurists to those of the state constituted a major shift in legal theoretical discourse. The *mujtahid–muqallid* dichotomy, which was the backbone of both the judicial system and the legal theory that accompanied it, was forced to disappear, thus creating new imperatives in the reformulation of legal theory. Individual *ijtihād* became, for all purposes and intents, extinct, having been replaced by state legislation committees staffed mainly by modern lawyers.

With the virtual disappearance of the traditional class of legists, and with the emergence of codification as an answer to the new social realities imposed by western cultural and technological domination, there emerged a new legal *Weltanschauung* that entirely rejected some of the elements of traditional theory, and which demanded that whatever was retained had to be drastically modified. Needless to say, the Quran and the Sunna were by and large left untouched for the obvious reason that they constituted the connection between the believers and their God. Law can never be deemed Islamic without it being somehow anchored in these two sources. But aside from this basic, and at times symbolic, concession to the primacy of these two sources, little else of hermeneutics associated with these sources was admitted as pertinent. The details and even the broad outlines of the theory of legal language were set aside in favor of a variety of new ways (not, strictly speaking, methods) of interpretation. The traditional rules governing ambiguous, univocal, restricted, particular and general language were largely abandoned. So were the theories of abrogation and consensus. It is particularly this sanctioning instrument of consensus that met with the stiffest resistance on the part of modern reformers. Having traditionally depended upon the backward projection of the agreement of legal scholars, consensus was no longer relevant to a legal culture whose mainstay became state legislation rather than the collective voice of what was otherwise the independent opinions of individual *mujtahid*s. As attested in the theories of Riḍā, Khallāf, Fāsī, Turābī and others, consensus has acquired the wholly new connotation of a consultative assembly (*shūrā*), advising any particular Muslim state on matters of legislation and policy-making.

Perhaps the most central element that underwent a fundamental structural change in modern times is the set of methodological rules governing legal reasoning. It is here, more than anywhere else in legal theory, where the crises facing modern theoreticians are most evident. The traditional methodology of *qiyās*, the mainstay of legal reasoning in *uṣūl al-fiqh* and traditional law in general, has largely been abandoned. The atomistic nature of this methodology and its particularized reliance upon the narrow effects of single legal texts have rendered it irrelevant to the endeavor of refashioning a modern Islamic law. Such is also the case with juristic preference (*istiḥsān*), which has been deemed by the reformers to be too confined to the narrow considerations of a legal cause, however modified it may be. It appears that no modern reformer can pretend to formulate a twentieth-century legal theory while still maintaining the methodological elements of traditional *qiyās* and *istiḥsān*. Whenever a modern reference is made to these two methods, it is one that entails significantly modified connotations of legal reasoning.

Interestingly, the burden of legal reasoning in many a modern reformulation fell upon what was otherwise a marginal concept in traditional legal theory, namely, *istiṣlāḥ*. Through this significantly redefined concept, a new legal system, chaotically grounded in such devices as *takhayyur* and *talfiq*, was justified. It is also through this concept that lip service was paid to the imperatives of the divine sources. The notions of need and necessity, justified by *maṣlaḥa*, became paramount and were readily allowed to supersede the imperatives of the religious texts. The results to which *istiṣlāḥ* led were found objectionable by a number of influential reformers, who also thought that the concept of *maṣlaḥa* is arbitrary and lacks the intellectual and methodological rigor that must be maintained if a successful and modern methodology is to be elaborated. Their answer to the problem, which constitutes a fresh and highly promising theoretical construct, represents a new wholistic and contextual approach to legal language and legal interpretation. Shaḥrūr and Rahman are only two names associated with this trend.

Of the two trends of modern reform we have identified, it is the religious utilitarianists who succeeded in having their ideas implemented on the practical level, albeit only partially. This success may be explained by the fact that the reformist ideas espoused by this trend represented more a justification of what was already taking place on the legal scene than a prescription of what ought to take place. On the other hand, the religious liberalists remain entirely marginal, this being a function of the foreignness of their theories to the existing legal systems and of their isolation from the centers of political power which is indispensable for the practical implementation of any idea. It is not a coincidence that ʿAshmāwī, Rahman and Shaḥrūr met and continue to meet with a good deal of opposition from a variety of circles around the Muslim world. This opposition symbolizes the crises engulfing modern attempts at reformulating a legal theory. Whereas the strained and unsystematic ideas of the utilitarianists enjoy the popular, essential support of the state legislative agencies, the liberalists, whose theories are legally and intellectually far more rigorous and convincing, have yet to find a sympathetic ear.

REFERENCES

THE following list contains four categories of sources, the first of which are general, primary works in Arabic essential for the study of treatises of legal theory. Of prime importance in this category are technical dictionaries and bio-bibliographical works. The former are necessary for unraveling the technical meanings of terms used in legal discourse, whereas the latter for reconstructing a history of legal theory. Here are also included, among other things, those works of substantive law that tend to indicate the lines of reasoning employed by some jurists. The second category encompasses Arabic works of legal theory, beginning with the quasi-theoretical work of Shāfiʿī and ending with the writings of early nineteenth-century authors. Since a rupture exists between traditional works of legal theory and the modern expositions of it, the third category includes, *inter alia*, those works that simply recount what is assumed by their authors to be a theory of law in the tradition of *uṣūl al-fiqh*, as well as those works aiming at a reformulation of traditional legal theory. The final category encompasses specialized as well as general secondary works, mostly in European languages, treating of one aspect or another of traditional legal theory and of modern attempts at reforming that theory.

In the fourth category, numbers printed in bold at the ends of some entries indicate recommended readings for particular chapters or sections within chapters. The first number refers to the chapter, whereas the second, separated by a dot, to the section. Thus, for instance, 3.4 refers to chapter 3, section 4. When only one number appears after an entry, it means that the entry is a recommended reading for the entire chapter. Two numbers separated by a dash (e.g. 4–5) indicate that the marked reference is a recommended reading for the whole chapters whose numbers are specified.

In classifying entries no account is taken of the letter *ʿayn* and the Arabic definite article *al-*.

General Primary Sources

ʿAbbādī, Abū ʿĀṣim Muḥammad b. Aḥmad. *Ṭabaqāt al-Fuqahāʾ al-Shāfiʿiyya*, ed. Gosta Vitestam (Leiden: E. J. Brill, 1964).

ʿAbd al-Bāqī, Fu'ād. *al-Muʿjam al-Mufahris li-Alfāẓ al-Qur'ān al-Karīm*(Cairo: Dār al-Kutub al-Miṣriyya, 1945).

Aḥmadnagarī, ʿAbd al-Nabī b. ʿAbd al-Rasūl. *Jāmiʿ al-ʿUlūm fī Iṣṭilāḥāt al-Funūn al-Mulaqqab bi-Dustūr al-ʿUlamā'*, 4 vols. (repr.; Beirut: Mu'assasat al-Aʿlamī lil-Maṭbūʿāt, 1975).

ʿAlā'ī, Khalīl b. Kanīkaldhī Ṣalāḥ al-Dīn. *Ijmāl al-Iṣāba fī Aqwāl al-Ṣaḥāba*, ed. Muḥammad Sulaymān al-Ashqar (Kuwait: Manshūrāt Markaz al-Makhṭūṭāt wal-Turāth, 1407/1987).

Āmidī, Abū al-Ḥasan ʿAlī Sayf al-Dīn. *al-Mubīn*, ed. ʿAbd al-Amīr al-Aʿṣam(Beirut: Dār al-Manhal, 1987).

Anbārī, Kamāl al-Dīn. *Lumaʿ al-Adilla fī Uṣūl al-Naḥw*, ed. Attiya Amer (Stockholm: Almqvist & Wiksell, 1963).

Asnawī, Jamāl al-Dīn ʿAbd al-Raḥmān. *Ṭabaqāt al-Shāfiʿiyya*, ed. ʿAbd Allāh al-Jubūrī, 2 vols. (Baghdad: Ri'āsat Dīwān al-Awqāf, 1970–71).

al-Tamhīd fī Takhrīj al-Furūʿ ʿalā al-Uṣūl, ed. Muḥammad Ḥasan Haytū (Beirut: Mu'assasat al-Risāla, 1984).

ʿAsqalānī, Aḥmad b. ʿAlī Ibn Ḥajar. *al-Durar al-Kāmina fī Aʿyān al-Mā'a al-Thāmina*, 4 vols. (Hyderabad: Dā'irat al-Maʿārif, 1350/1931).

Lisān al-Mīzān, 7 vols. (Beirut: Mu'assasat al-Aʿlamī lil-Maṭbūʿāt, 1390/1971).

Baghdādī, ʿAbd al-Qāhir. *Uṣūl al-Dīn* (repr.; Beirut: Dār al-Kutub al-ʿIlmiyya, 1981).

Baghdādī, al-Khaṭīb. *al-Faqīh wal-Mutafaqqih*, 2 vols. (Beirut: Dār al-Kutub al-ʿIlmiyya, 1975).

Bājī, Abū al-Walīd b. Khalaf. *Kitāb al-Ḥudūd fī al-Uṣūl*, ed. Nazīh Ḥammād (Beirut: Mu'assasat al-Zuʿbī lil-Ṭibāʿa wal-Nashr, 1973).

al-Minhāj fī Tartīb al-Ḥijāj, ed. ʿAbd al-Majīd Turkī (Paris: Paul Geuthner, 1976).

Bayhaqī, Abū Bakr Aḥmad Ibn al-Ḥusayn. *Aḥkām al-Qur'ān*, 2 vols. (Beirut: Dār al-Kutub al-ʿIlmiyya, 1975).

Manāqib al-Shāfiʿī, ed. Aḥmad Ṣaqr, 2 vols. (Cairo: Maktabat Dār al-Turāth, 1971).

Bazdawī, ʿAlī b. Muḥammad. *See* Pazdawī.

Bukhārī, Abū ʿAbd Allāh Muḥammad. *Kitāb al-Jāmiʿ al-Ṣaḥīḥ*, ed. M. L. Krehl and T. W. Juynboll, 4 vols. (Leiden: E. J. Brill, 1908). Trans. O. Houdas and W. Marçais, *Les traditions islamiques*, 4 vols. (Paris: Leroux, 1903–14).

Daylamī, Shīrawayh b. Shahridār. *Kitāb Firdaws al-Akhbār*, 5 vols. (Beirut: Dār al-Kitāb al-ʿArabī, 1407/1987).

Fārisī, Abū ʿAlī. *Jawāhir al-Uṣūl fī ʿIlm Ḥadīth al-Rasūl* (Medina: al-Maktaba al-ʿIlmiyya, 1969).

Farrā', Muḥammad b. Abī Yaʿlā. *See* Ibn al-Farrā'.

Fāsī, Muḥammad b. al-Ḥasan al-Ḥujawī al-Thaʿālabī, *al-Fikr al-Sāmī fī Tārīkh al-Fiqh al-Islāmī*, 2 vols. (Medina: al-Maktaba al-ʿIlmiyya, 1397/1977).

Ghazālī, Abū Ḥāmid. *Iḥyā' ʿUlūm al-Dīn*, 6 vols. (Beirut: Dār al-Khayr, 1990).

Miʿyār al-ʿIlm fī Fann al-Manṭiq, ed. Sulaymān Dunyā (Cairo: Dār al-Maʿārif, 1961).

Ḥājjī Khalīfa (Katip Celebi). *Kashf al-Ẓunūn ʿan Asāmī al-Kutub wal-Funūn*, 2 vols.

(Istanbul: Maṭbaʿat Wakālat al-Maʿārif al-Jalīla, 1941–43).
Hāshimī, Sayyid Aḥmad. *Jawāhir al-Adab fī Adabiyyāt wa-Inshāʾ Lughat al-ʿArab*, 2 vols. (Beirut: Muʾassasat al-Risāla, n.d.).
Ḥaṭṭāb, Muḥammad. *Mawāhib al-Jalīl li-Sharḥ Mukhtaṣar Khalīl*, 6 vols. (Tripoli: Maktabat al-Najāḥ, 1969).
Haytamī, Ibn Ḥajar. *al-Fatāwā al-Kubrā al-Fiqhiyya*, 4 vols. (Cairo: ʿAbd al-Ḥamīd Aḥmad al-Ḥanafī, 1938).
Ḥusaynī, Abū Bakr Hidāyat Allāh. *Ṭabaqāt al-Shāfiʿiyya*, ed. ʿĀdil Nuwayhiḍ (Beirut: Dār al-Āfāq al-Jadīda, 1979).
Ibn ʿAbd al-Salām, ʿIzz al-Dīn. *Qawāʿid al-Aḥkām fī Maṣāliḥ al-Anām*, 2 vols. (Cairo: Maṭbaʿat al-Istiqāma, n.d.).
Ibn Abī Shāma, Shihāb al-Dīn b. Ismāʿīl. *Mukhtaṣar Kitāb al-Muʾammal lil-Radd ilā al-Amr al-Awwal*, in *Majmūʿat al-Rasāʾil al-Munīriyya*, vol. III (Cairo: Idārat al-Ṭibāʿa al-Munīriyya, 1346/1927), 19–39.
Ibn Abī al-Wafāʾ, ʿAbd al-Qādir al-Qurashī. *al-Jawāhir al-Muḍīʾa fī Ṭabaqāt al-Ḥanafiyya*, 2 vols. (Hyderabad: Maṭbaʿat Majlis Dāʾirat al-Maʿārif al-Niẓāmiyya, 1332/1914).
Ibn ʿAqīl, Abū al-Wafāʾ ʿAlī. *Kitāb al-Jadal*, ed. George Makdisi, "Le livre de la dialectique d'Ibn ʿAqīl," *Bulletin d'études orientales*, 20 (1967): 119–205.
Ibn Daqīq al-ʿĪd, Taqī al-Dīn. *Iḥkām al-Aḥkām: Sharḥ ʿUmdat al-Aḥkām*, ed. M. Fiqqī, 2 vols. (Cairo: Maṭbaʿat al-Sunna al-Muḥammadiyya, 1372/1953).
Ibn Farḥūn, Shams al-Dīn Muḥammad. *al-Dībāj al-Mudhahhab fī Maʿrifat Aʿyān al-Madhhab* (Cairo: Maṭbaʿat al-Maʿāhid, 1351/1932).
Ibn al-Farrāʾ, Muḥammad b. Abī Yaʿlā al-Baghdādī. *Ṭabaqāt al-Ḥanābila*, ed. M. Ḥ. al-Fiqī, 2 vols. (Cairo: Maṭbaʿat al-Sunna al-Muḥammadiyya, 1952).
Ibn Ḥazm, Muḥammad. *Muʿjam al-Fiqh*, 2 vols. (Damascus: Maṭbaʿat Jāmiʿat Dimashq, 1966).
Ibn al-ʿImād, Abū al-Falāḥ ʿAbd al-Ḥayy. *Shadharāt al-Dhahab fī Akhbār man Dhahab*, 8 vols. (Cairo: Maktabat al-Quds, 1350–51/1931–32).
Ibn Khaldūn, ʿAbd al-Raḥmān. *The Muqaddima*, trans. Fr. Rosenthal, 3 vols. (New York: Pantheon Books, 1958).
Ibn Khallikān, Abū al-ʿAbbās Shams al-Dīn. *Wafayāt al-Aʿyān wa-Anbāʾ Abnāʾ al-Zamān*, 8 vols. (Beirut: Dār Ṣādir, 1977–78).
Ibn al-Muwaqqiʿ, Abū ʿAbd Allāh Shuʿla al-Mūṣilī. *Ṣafwat al-Rāsikh fī ʿIlm al-Mansūkh wal-Nāsikh*, ed. Ramaḍān ʿAbd al-Thawwāb (Cairo: Dār al-Manāhil, 1995).
Ibn al-Nadīm. *al-Fihrist* (Beirut: Dār al-Maʿrifa lil-Ṭibāʿa wal-Nashr, 1398/1978). Trans. B. Dodge, *The Fihrist of al-Nadim: A Tenth-Century Survey of Muslim Culture* (New York: Columbia University Press, 1970).
Ibn Naqīb al-Miṣrī, Aḥmad. *ʿUmdat al-Sālik wa-ʿUddat al-Nāsik*, ed. and trans. N. H. Keller, *The Reliance of the Traveller* (Evanston: Sunna Books, 1991).
Ibn Qāḍī Shuhba, Taqī al-Dīn b. Aḥmad. *Ṭabaqāt al-Shāfiʿiyya*, ed. ʿAbd al-ʿAlīm Khān, 4 vols. (Hyderabad: Maṭbaʿat Majlis Dāʾirat al-Maʿārif al-ʿUthmāniyya, 1398/1978).

Ibn Qayyim al-Jawziyya, Shams al-Dīn Muḥammad b. Abī Bakr. *Iʿlām al-Muwaqqiʿīn ʿan Rabb al-ʿĀlamīn*, ed. Muḥammad ʿAbd al-Ḥamīd, 4 vols. (Beirut: al-Maṭbaʿa al-ʿAṣriyya, 1407/1987).

Ibn Qutayba, Abū Muḥammad ʿAbd Allāh b. Muslim. *al-Maʿārif*, ed. Muḥammad al-Sāwī (Karachi: Nūr Muḥammad, 1396/1976).

Ibn Quṭlūbughā, Zayn al-Dīn Qāsim. *Tāj al-Tarājim fī Ṭabaqāt al-Ḥanafiyya* (Baghdad: Maktabat al-Muthannā, 1962).

Ibn Rajab, ʿAbd al-Raḥmān Shihāb al-Dīn. *Kitāb al-Dhayl ʿalā Ṭabaqāt al-Ḥanābila*, 2 vols. (Cairo: Maṭbaʿat al-Sunna al-Muḥammadiyya, 1952–53).

Ibn Rushd, Muḥammad b. Aḥmad (al-Ḥafīd). *Bidāyat al-Mujtahid wa-Nihāyat al-Muqtaṣid*, 2 vols. (Beirut: Dār al-Maʿrifa, 1986). Trans. Imran A. K. Nyazee, *The Distinguished Jurist's Primer*, 2 vols. (Reading: Garnet Publishing, 1994).

Ibn Rushd, Muḥammad b. Aḥmad. *Fatāwā Ibn Rushd*, ed. al-Mukhtār b. Ṭāhir al-Talīlī, 3 vols. (Beirut: Dār al-Gharb al-Islāmī, 1978).

Ibn Taymiyya, Taqī al-Dīn. *Ibn Taymiyya against the Greek Logicians*, trans. Wael B. Hallaq (Oxford: Clarendon Press, 1993).

al-Radd ʿalā al-Manṭiqiyyīn, ed. ʿAbd al-Ṣamad al-Kutubī (Bombay: al-Maṭbaʿa al-Qayyima, 1368/1949).

Imām Shuʿla. *See* Ibn al-Muwaqqiʿ.

Isnawī, Jamāl al-Dīn ʿAbd al-Raḥmān. *See* Asnawī.

Jamāʿīlī, ʿAbd al-Ghanī ʿAbd al-Wāḥid. *al-ʿUmda fī al-Aḥkām fī Maʿālim al-Ḥalāl wal-Ḥarām*, ed. Muṣṭafā ʿAṭā (Beirut: Dār al-Kutub al-ʿIlmiyya, 1986).

Jurjānī, al-Sayyid Sharīf ʿAlī b. Muḥammad. *al-Taʿrīfāt* (Cairo: Maṭbaʿat Muṣṭafā Bābī al-Ḥalabī, 1938).

Juwaynī, Imām al-Ḥaramayn. ʿAbd al-Malik Abū al-Maʿālī. *al-Kāfiya fī al-Jadal*, ed. Fawqiyya Ḥusayn Maḥmūd (Cairo: Maṭbaʿat ʿĪsā Bābī al-Ḥalabī, 1399/1979).

Kaḥḥāla, ʿUmar. *Muʿjam al-Muʾallifīn*, 15 vols. (Damascus: Maṭbaʿat al-Taraqqī, 1957–61).

Kāsānī, ʿAlāʾ al-Dīn Abū Bakr Ibn Masʿūd. *Badāʾiʿ al-Ṣanāʾiʿ fī Tartīb al-Sharāʾiʿ*, 7 vols. (Beirut: Dār al-Kitāb al-ʿArabī, 1982).

Khuwārizmī, Muḥammad b. Aḥmad b. Yūsuf. *Mafātīḥ al-ʿUlūm*, ed. G. van Vloten (Leiden: E. J. Brill, 1968).

Laknawī, ʿAbd al-Ḥayy. *al-Fawāʾid al-Bahiyya fī Tarājim al-Ḥanafiyya* (Benares: Maktabat Nadvat al-Maʿārif, 1967).

Makhlūf, Muḥammad b. Muḥammad. *Shajarat al-Nūr al-Zakiyya fī Ṭabaqāt al-Mālikiyya*, 2 vols. (Cairo: al-Maṭbaʿa al-Salafiyya,1950).

Marāghī, ʿAbd Allāh Muṣṭafā. *al-Fatḥ al-Mubīn fī Ṭabaqāt al-Uṣūliyyīn*, 3 vols. (repr.; Beirut: Dār al-Kutub al-ʿIlmiyya, 1974).

Marghīnānī, Abū al-Ḥasan ʿAlī b. Abī Bakr. *al-Hidāya: Sharḥ Bidāyat al-Mubtadī*, 4 vols. (Cairo: Maṭbaʿat Muṣṭafā Bābī al-Ḥalabī, 1400/1980).

Muqātil b. Sulaymān. *Tafsīr al-Khams Māʾat Āya*, ed. I. Goldfeld (Shafāʿamr: Dār al-Mashriq, 1980).

Muslim, Abū al-Ḥasan b. al-Ḥajjāj al-Qushayrī. *Ṣaḥīḥ*, ed. Muḥammad Fuʾād ʿAbd al-Bāqī, 5 vols. (Cairo: ʿĪsā Bābī al-Ḥalabī, 1374–75/1955–56).

Nasafī, Najm al-Dīn Ibn Ḥafṣ. *Ṭalibat al-Ṭalaba fī al-Iṣṭilāḥāt al-Fiqhiyya* (Baghdad: Maṭbaʿat al-Muthannā, 1311/1900).

Nawawī, Muḥyī al-Dīn Sharaf al-Dīn. *al-Majmūʿ: Sharḥ al-Muhadhdhab*, 12 vols. (Cairo: Maṭbaʿat al-Taḍāmun, 1344/1925).

Nuʿmān, al-Qāḍī. *Kitāb Ikhtilāf Uṣūl al-Madhāhib*, ed. S. T. Lokhandwalla (Simla: Indian Institute of Advanced Study, 1972).

Qarāfī, Shihāb al-Dīn. *al-Furūq*, 4 vols. (Cairo: Dār Iḥyā' al-Kitāb al-ʿArabī, 1925–27).

al-Iḥkām fī Tamyīz al-Fatāwī ʿan al-Aḥkām wa-Taṣarrufāt al-Qāḍī wal-Imām, ed. ʿIzzat al-ʿAṭṭār (Cairo: Maṭbaʿat al-Anwār, 1938).

Qāsim b. Sallām, Abū ʿUbayd. *Kitāb al-Nāsikh wal-Mansūkh*, ed. John Burton (Bury St Edmunds: St Edmundsburgh Press, 1987).

Al-Qur'ān al-Karīm (Kuwait: Wizārat al-Awqāf wal-Shu'ūn al-Islāmiyya, 1402/1981). Trans. (1) Arthur J. Arberry, *The Koran Interpreted*, 2 vols. (London and New York: George Allen & Unwin Ltd., 1955); (2) Mohammed Marmaduke Pickthall, *The Meanings of the Glorious Koran* (New York: Mentor, n.d.).

Rāfiʿī, Abū al-Qāsim ʿAbd al-Karīm b. Muḥammad. *Fatḥ al-ʿAzīz fī Sharḥ al-Wajīz*, printed with Yaḥyā b. Muḥyī al-Dīn Sharaf al-Dīn al-Nawawī, *al-Majmūʿ: Sharḥ al-Muhadhdhab*, 12 vols. (Cairo: Maṭbaʿat al-Taḍāmun, 1344/1925).

Ramlī, Shams al-Dīn b. Shihāb al-Dīn. *Nihāyat al-Muḥtāj ilā Sharḥ al-Minhāj*, 8 vols. (Cairo: Muṣṭafā Bābī al-Ḥalabī, 1357/1938).

Raṣṣāʿ, Abū ʿAbd Allāh Muḥammad al-Anṣārī. *Sharḥ Ḥudūd Ibn ʿArafa al-Mawsūm al-Hidāya al-Kāfiya al-Shāfiya*, ed. Muḥammad Abū al-Ajfān and al-Ṭāhir al-Maʿmūrī, 2 vols. (Beirut: Dār al-Gharb al-Islāmī, 1993).

Rāzī, Fakhr al-Dīn. *Munāẓarāt Fakhr al-Dīn al-Rāzī fī Bilād mā Warā' al-Nahr*, in F. Kholeif, ed. and trans., *A Study on Fakhr al-Dīn al-Rāzī and his Controversies in Central Asia* (Beirut: Dar el-Machreq, 1966).

al-Tafsīr al-Kabīr, 32 vols. (Beirut: Dār Iḥyā' al-Turāth al-ʿArabī, 1980).

Sakkākī, Muḥammad b. ʿAlī. *Miftāḥ al-ʿUlūm* (Cairo: al-Maṭbaʿa al-Adabiyya, 1317/1899).

Shāfiʿī, Muḥammad b. Idrīs. *Kitāb al-Umm*, 7 vols. (Cairo: al-Maṭbaʿa al-Kubrā al-Amīriyya, 1325/1907).

Shahrastānī, ʿAbd al-Karīm. *al-Milal wal-Niḥal*, ed. William Cureton (Leipzig: Otto Harrassowitz, 1923).

Shāṭibī, Abū Isḥāq Ibrāhīm. *al-Iʿtiṣām*, ed. Muḥammad Rashīd Riḍā, 2 vols. (repr.; Riyadh: Maktabat al-Riyāḍ al-Ḥadītha, n.d.).

Shawkānī, Muḥammad b. ʿAlī. *al-Badr al-Ṭāliʿ bi-Maḥāsin man baʿda al-Qarn al-Sābiʿ*, 3 vols. (Cairo: Maṭbaʿat al-Saʿāda, 1348/1929).

Shīrāzī, Abū Isḥāq Ibrāhīm b. ʿAlī. *al-Maʿūna fī al-Jadal* (Kuwait: Manshūrāt Markaz al-Makhṭūṭāt wal-Turāth, 1987).

Ṭabaqāt al-Fuqahā', ed. Iḥsān ʿAbbās (Beirut: Dār al-Rā'id al-ʿArabī, 1970).

Subkī, Tāj al-Dīn b. Taqī al-Dīn. *Ṭabaqāt al-Shāfiʿiyya al-Kubrā*, 6 vols. (Cairo: al-Maktaba al-Ḥusayniyya, 1906).

Subkī, Taqī al-Dīn ʿAlī. *Fatāwā al-Subkī*, 2 vols. (Cairo: Maktabat al-Qudsī, 1937).

Takmilat al-Majmūʿ, 12 vols. (Cairo: Maṭbaʿat al-Taḍāmun, 1906).

Suyūṭī, Jalāl al-Dīn ʿAbd al-Raḥmān. *al-Ashbāh wal-Naẓāʾir* (Beirut: Dār al-Kutub al-ʿIlmiyya, 1979).

al-Radd ʿalā man Akhlada ilā al-Arḍ wa-Jahila anna al-Ijtihād fī Kulli ʿAṣrin Farḍ, ed. Khalīl al-Mays (Beirut: Dār al-Kutub al-ʿIlmiyya, 1983).

Tahānawī, Muḥammad b. ʿAlī. *Kashshāf Iṣṭilāḥāt al-Funūn*, 2 vols. (Calcutta: W. N. Leeds' Press, 1862).

Tamīmī, ʿAbd al-Qādir. *al-Ṭabaqāt al-Saniyya fī Tarājim al-Ḥanafiyya*, ed. ʿAbd al-Fattāḥ al-Ḥulw (Cairo: al-Majlis al-Aʿlā lil-Shuʾūn al-Islāmiyya, 1970).

Tirmidhī, Abū ʿĪsā. *Ṣaḥīḥ*, 2 vols. (Cairo: al-Maṭbaʿa al-ʿĀmira, 1292/1875).

Ṭūfī, Najm al-Dīn. *ʿAlam al-Jadhal fī ʿIlm al-Jadal*, ed. Wolfhart Heinrichs (Wiesbaden: Franz Steiner Verlag, 1987).

Wansharīsī, Aḥmad b. Yaḥyā. *al-Miʿyār al-Mughrib wal-Jāmiʿ al-Muʿrib ʿan Fatāwī ʿUlamāʾ Ifrīqiyya wal-Andalus wal-Maghrib*, 13 vols. (Beirut: Dār al-Gharb al-Islāmī, 1401/1981).

Zinjānī, Shihāb al-Dīn Maḥmūd. *Takhrīj al-Furūʿ ʿalā al-Uṣūl*, ed. Muḥammad Ṣāliḥ (Beirut: Muʾassasat al-Risāla, 1404/1984).

Traditional Primary Sources on Legal Theory

ʿAbbādī, Aḥmad b. Qāsim. *al-Āyāt al-Bayyināt ʿalā Sharḥ Jamʿ al-Jawāmiʿ*, 4 vols. (Cairo: n.p., 1289/1872).

Sharḥ ʿalā Sharḥ al-Maḥallī ʿalā al-Waraqāt, printed on the margins of Shawkānī, *Irshād al-Fuḥūl* (Surabaya: Sharikat Maktabat Aḥmad b. Saʿd b. Nabhān, n.d.).

ʿAbd al-Jabbār al-Asadabādī. *al-Mughnī fī Abwāb al-Tawḥīd wal-ʿAdl*, ed. Amīn al-Khūlī, XVII (Cairo: al-Dār al-Miṣriyya lil-Taʾlīf wal-Nashr, n.d.).

Āmidī, Abū al-Ḥasan ʿAlī Sayf al-Dīn. *al-Iḥkām fī Uṣūl al-Aḥkām*, 3 vols. (Cairo: Maṭbaʿat ʿAlī Ṣubayḥ, 1968).

Muntahā al-Sūl fī ʿIlm al-Uṣūl (Cairo: Maṭbaʿat Muḥammad ʿAlī Ṣubayḥ, n.d.).

Amīr Bādshāh, Muḥammad Amīn. *Taysīr al-Taḥrīr*, 4 vols. (Cairo: Muṣṭafā Bābī al-Ḥalabī, 1350–51/1930–31).

Anṣārī, Muḥammad b. Niẓām al-Dīn. *Fawātiḥ al-Raḥamūt*, 2 vols. (Cairo: al-Maṭbaʿa al-Amīriyya, 1324/1906).

Anṣārī, Zakariyyāʾ b. Muḥammad Zayn al-Dīn. *Ghāyat al-Wuṣūl: Sharḥ Lubb al-Uṣūl* (Cairo: Muṣṭafā Bābī al-Ḥalabī, 1941).

Aṣfahānī, Shams al-Dīn Maḥmūd. *Bayān al-Mukhtaṣar*, ed. Muḥammad Maẓharbaqā, 2 vols. (Jedda: Dār al-Madanī, 1406/1986).

Asnawī, Jamāl al-Dīn ʿAbd al-Raḥmān. *Nihāyat al-Sūl fī Sharḥ Minhāj al-Wuṣūl*, 3 vols. (Cairo: Muḥammad ʿAlī Ṣubayḥ, n.d.).

Badakhshī, Muḥammad b. Ḥasan. *Manāhij al-ʿUqūl fī Sharḥ Minhāj al-Uṣūl*, printed with Asnawī, *Nihāyat al-Sūl*, 3 vols. (Cairo: Muḥammad ʿAlī Ṣubayḥ, n.d.).

Baghdādī, Ṣafī al-Dīn b. ʿAbd Allāh. *Qawāʿid al-Uṣūl wa-Maʿāqid al-Fuṣūl: Mukhtaṣar Taḥqīq al-Amal fī ʿIlmay al-Uṣūl wal-Jadal*, in *Majmūʿat Mutūn Uṣūliyya* (Beirut: ʿĀlam al-Kutub, 1986).

Qawāʿid al-Uṣūl wa-Maʿāqid al-Fuṣūl: Mukhtaṣar Taḥqīq al-Amal fī ʿIlmay al-Uṣūl wal-Jadal, ed. Muḥammad Shākir (Beirut: ʿĀlam al-Kutub, 1986).

Bājī, Abū al-Walīd b. Khalaf. *Iḥkām al-Fuṣūl fī Aḥkām al-Uṣūl,* ed. ʿAbd al-Majīd Turkī (Beirut: Dār al-Gharb al-Islāmī, 1986).

al-Minhāj fī Tartīb al-Ḥijāj, ed. A. M. Turki (Paris: Maisonneuve et Larose, 1978).

Bannānī, ʿAbd al-Raḥmān. *Ḥāshiyat al-Bannānī ʿalā Jamʿ al-Jawāmiʿ*, 2 vols. (Bombay: Molavi Mohammed B. Gulamrasul Surtis, 1970).

Baṣrī, Abū al-Ḥusayn. *al-Muʿtamad fī Uṣūl al-Fiqh*, ed. Muhammad Hamidullah et al., 2 vols. (Damascus: Institut Français, 1964–65).

Bayḍāwī, ʿAbd Allāh b. ʿUmar. *Minhāj al-Wuṣūl ilā ʿIlm al-Uṣūl*, printed with Jamāl al-Dīn al-Asnawī, *Nihāyat al-Sūl fī Sharḥ Minhāj al-Wuṣūl ilā ʿIlm al-Uṣūl lil-Bayḍāwī*, 3 vols. (Cairo: al-Maṭbaʿa al-Kubrā al-Amīriyya, 1317/1899).

Bukhārī, ʿAlā' al-Dīn. *Kashf al-Asrār*, 4 vols. (repr.; Beirut: Dār al-Kitāb al-ʿArabī, 1394/1974).

Dabbūsī, Abū Zayd ʿUbayd Allāh b. ʿUmar. *Kitāb Ta'sīs al-Naẓar* (Cairo: al-Maṭbaʿa al-Adabiyya, n.d.).

Fawzān, ʿAbd Allāh b. Ṣāliḥ. *Sharḥ al-Waraqāt fī Uṣūl al-Fiqh* (Riyadh: Dār al-Muslim lil-Nashr, 1414/1993).

Ghazālī, Abū Ḥāmid Muḥammad b. Muḥammad. *al-Mankhūl min Taʿlīqāt al-Uṣūl*, ed. Muḥammad Ḥasan Haytū (Damascus: Dār al-Fikr, 1980).

al-Mustaṣfā min ʿIlm al-Uṣūl, 2 vols. (Cairo: al-Maṭbaʿa al-Amīriyya, 1324/1906).

Shifā' al-Ghalīl fī Bayān al-Shabah wal-Mukhīl wa-Masālik al-Taʿlīl, ed. Ḥamd al-Kabīsī (Baghdad: Maṭbaʿat al-Irshād, 1390/1971).

Harawī, Ḥasan. *Ḥāshiya ʿalā Ḥāshiyat al-Muḥaqqiq al-Sayyid al-Sharīf al-Jurjānī*, printed with al-Taftāzānī's *Ḥāshiya.*

Ibn ʿAbd al-Shakūr, Muḥibb Allāh. *Musallam al-Thubūt: Sharḥ Fawātiḥ al-Raḥamūt*, 2 vols. (Cairo: al-Maṭbaʿa al-Amīriyya, 1324/1906).

Ibn Amīr al-Ḥājj. *al-Taqrīr wal-Taḥbīr: Sharḥ ʿalā Taḥrīr al-Imām al-Kamāl Ibn al-Humām*, 3 vols. (Cairo: al-Maṭbaʿa al-Kubrā al-Amīriyya, 1317/1899).

Ibn al-ʿArabī, Muḥyī al-Dīn Muḥammad. *Risāla fī Uṣūl al-Fiqh*, in al-Qāsimī, ed., *Majmūʿ Rasā'il fī Uṣūl al-Fiqh,* 18–35.

Ibn Barhān, Aḥmad b. ʿAlī. *al-Wuṣūl ilā al-Uṣūl*, ed. ʿAbd al-Ḥamīd Abū Zunayd, 2 vols. (Riyadh: Maktabat al-Maʿārif, 1984).

Ibn al-Farrā', Abū Yaʿlā al-Baghdādī. *al-ʿUdda fī Uṣūl al-Fiqh*, ed. Aḥmad Mubārakī, 3 vols. (Beirut: Mu'assasat al-Risāla, 1980).

Ibn Fūrak, Abū Bakr Muḥammad b. al-Ḥusayn. *Muqaddima fī Nukat fī Uṣūl al-Fiqh*, in al-Qāsimī, ed., *Majmūʿ Rasā'il fī Uṣūl al-Fiqh,* 4–14.

Ibn al-Ḥājib, Jamāl al-Dīn Abū ʿAmr. *Mukhtaṣar al-Muntahā al-Uṣūlī* (Cairo: Maṭbaʿat Kurdistān al-ʿIlmiyya, 1326/1908).

Muntahā al-Wuṣūl wal-Amal fī ʿIlmayy al-Uṣūl wal-Jadal, ed. Muḥammad al-Naʿsānī (Cairo: Maṭbaʿat al-Saʿāda, 1326/1908).

Ibn Ḥalūlū, Aḥmad b. ʿAbd al-Raḥmān. *al-Ḍiyā' al-Lāmiʿ: Sharḥ Jamʿ al-Jawāmiʿ fī Uṣūl al-Fiqh*, ed. ʿAbd al-Karīm Muḥammad al-Namla, (Cairo: Dār al-Ḥaramayn lil-Ṭibāʿa, 1994).

Ibn Ḥazm, Muḥammad. *al-Iḥkām fī Uṣūl al-Aḥkām*, ed. Aḥmad Muḥammad Shākir, 8 vols. (Cairo: Maṭbaʿat al-Imtiyāz, 1398/1978).

Ibn al-Humām, Kamāl al-Dīn. *al-Taḥrīr fī Uṣūl al-Fiqh* (Cairo: Muṣṭafā Bābī al-Ḥalabī, 1351/1932).

al-Taḥrīr fī Uṣūl al-Fiqh, 3 vols. (Cairo: al-Maṭbaʿa al-Kubrā al-Amīriyya, 1317/1899).

Ibn al-Laḥḥām, ʿAlī b. ʿAbbās al-Baʿlī. *al-Qawāʿid wal-Fawāʾid al-Uṣūliyya*, ed. Muḥammad al-Fiqī (Beirut: Dār al-Kutub al-ʿIlmiyya, 1403/1983).

Ibn al-Najjār, Muḥammad b. Aḥmad al-Futūḥī. *Sharḥ al-Kawkab al-Munīr*, ed. M. Zuḥaylī and N. Ḥammād, 3 vols. (Damascus: Dār al-Fikr, 1400/1980).

Ibn Qudāma, Muwaffaq al-Dīn. *Rawḍat al-Nāẓir wa-Junnat al-Munāẓir*, ed. Sayf al-Dīn al-Kātib (Beirut: Dār al-Kitāb al-ʿArabī, 1401/1981).

Ibn Rushd, Muḥammad Abū al-Walīd. *al-Ḍarūra fī Uṣūl al-Fiqh aw Mukhtaṣar al-Mustaṣfā*, ed. Jamāl al-Dīn al-ʿAlawī (Beirut: Dār al-Gharb al-Islāmī, 1994).

Ibn Tāj al-Sharīʿa, ʿUbayd Allāh b. Masʿūd. *al-Tawḍīḥ fī Ḥall Ghawāmiḍ al-Tanqīḥ*, printed on the margins of Taftāzānī's *Talwīḥ*.

Ibn Taymiyya, Majd al-Dīn, Shihāb al-Dīn and Taqī al-Dīn, *Musawwada fī Uṣūl al-Fiqh* (Cairo: Maṭbaʿat al-Madanī, 1983).

Ibn Taymiyya, Taqī al-Dīn. *Fī Maʿnā al-Qiyās,* in *Majmūʿat al-Rasāʾil al-Kubrā*, II (Cairo: al-Maṭbaʿa al-ʿĀmira al-Sharafiyya, 1323/1905), 217–76.

Masʾalat al-Istiḥsān, ed. George Makdisi, "Ibn Taimīya's Autograph Manuscript on *Istiḥsān*: Materials for the Study of Islamic Legal Thought," in George Makdisi, ed., *Arabic and Islamic Studies in Honor of Hamilton A. R. Gibb*, (Cambridge, Mass.: Harvard University Press, 1965), 454–79.

al-Qiyās fī al-Sharʿ al-Islāmī, ed. Muḥibb al-Dīn al-Khaṭīb (Cairo: al-Maṭbaʿa al-Salafiyya, 1375/1955). Trans. H. Laoust, *Contribution à une étude de la méthodologie canonique de Takī-d-Dīn Aḥmad b. Taymiya* (Cairo: Imprimerie de l'Institut français d'archéologie orientale, 1939).

Ījī, ʿAḍud al-Dīn. *Sharḥ Mukhtaṣar Ibn al-Ḥājib*, ed. S. M. Ismāʿīl, 2 vols. (Cairo: Maktabat al-Kulliyyāt al-Azhariyya, 1973–74).

Sharḥ Mukhtaṣar al-Muntahā al-Uṣūlī, 2 vols. (Cairo: Maktabat al-Kulliyyāt al-Azhariyya, 1973).

Iṣfahānī, Shams al-Dīn Maḥmūd. *See* Aṣfahānī.

Isnawī, Jamāl al-Dīn. *Nihāyat al-Sūl fī Sharḥ Minhāj al-Wuṣūl ilā ʿIlm al-Uṣūl lil-Bayḍāwī*, printed on the margin of Ibn Amīr al-Ḥājj's *Nihāyat al-Sūl*, 3 vols. (Cairo: al-Maṭbaʿa al-Kubrā al-Amīriyya, 1317/1899).

Izmīrī, Muḥammad. *Ḥāshiya ʿalā Sharḥ Mukhtaṣar Mirʾāt al-Uṣūl fī Sharḥ Mirqāt al-Wuṣūl*, 2 vols. (Istanbul: n.p., 1302/1884).

Jaṣṣāṣ, Aḥmad b. ʿAlī al-Rāzī, *Uṣūl al-Fiqh al-Musammā al-Fuṣūl fī al-Uṣūl*, ed. ʿUjayl Jāsim al-Nashamī, I (Kuwait: Wizārat al-Awqāf wal-Shuʾūn al-Islāmiyya, 1985).

Jurjānī, al-Sayyid al-Sharīf. *Ḥāshiya ʿalā Sharḥ al-ʿAḍud al-Ījī*, printed with Saʿd al-Dīn al-Taftāzānī's *Ḥāshiya.*

Juwaynī, Imām al-Ḥaramayn ʿAbd al-Malik Abū al-Maʿālī. *al-Burhān fī Uṣūl al-Fiqh*, ed. ʿAbd al-ʿAẓīm Dīb, 2 vols. (Cairo: Dār al-Anṣār, 1400/1980).

Kitāb al-Ijtihād, ed. ʿAbd al-Ḥamīd Abū Zunayd (Damascus: Dār al-Qalam, 1408/1987).

al-Waraqāt fī ʿIlm Uṣūl al-Fiqh, printed with ʿAbbādī's *Sharḥ ʿalā Sharḥ al-Maḥallī ʿalā al-Waraqāt.*

Karāmāstī, Yūsuf b. al-Ḥusayn. *al-Wajīz fī Uṣūl al-Fiqh*, ed. A. Saqqā (Cairo: al-Maktab al-Thaqāfī, 1990).

Karkhī, ʿUbayd Allāh b. al-Ḥasan. *Risāla fī al-Uṣūl*, printed with Dabbūsī's, *Ta'sīs al-Naẓar.*

Maḥallāwī, Muḥammad b. ʿAbd al-Raḥmān. *Taḥṣīl al-Wuṣūl ilā ʿIlm al-Uṣūl* (Cairo: n.p., 1341/1922).

Maḥallī, Jalāl al-Dīn Muḥammad. *Sharḥ ʿalā Matn Jamʿ al-Jawāmiʿ*, printed with Bannānī's, *Ḥāshiyat al-Bannānī ʿalā Jamʿ al-Jawāmiʿ.*

Sharḥ al-Waraqāt (of Juwaynī) (Cairo: Maṭbaʿat Muḥammad ʿAlī Ṣubayḥ, n.d.).

Majmūʿat Mutūn Uṣūliyya (Beirut: ʿĀlam al-Kutub, 1986).

Mārdīnī, Shams al-Dīn Muḥammad b. ʿUthmān. *al-Anjum al-Zāhirāt ʿalā Ḥall Alfāẓ al-Waraqāt fī Uṣūl al-Fiqh*, ed. ʿAbd al-Karīm Muḥammad al-Namla (Cairo: Dār al-Ḥaramayn lil-Ṭibāʿa, 1415/1994).

Māwardī, ʿAlī Muḥammad b. Ḥabīb. *Adab al-Qāḍī*, ed. Muḥyī Hilāl Sarḥān, 2 vols. (Baghdad: Maṭbaʿat al-Irshād, 1391/ 1971).

Mullā Khusraw, Muḥammad b. ʿAlī. *Mirqāt al-Wuṣūl ilā ʿIlm al-Uṣūl* (Cairo: n.p., 1320/1902).

Mullā Zāda, Muḥammad Ḥalabī. *al-Maṣqūl fī ʿIlm al-Uṣūl*, ed. ʿAbd al-Razzāq Bīmār (Baghdad: Wizārat al-Awqāf wal-Shu'ūn al-Dīniyya, 1401/1981).

Muzanī, Ibrāhīm. *Kitāb al-Amr wal-Nahy*, in Robert Brunchvig, "Le livre de l'ordre et de la défense d'al-Muzani," *Bulletin d'études orientales*, 11 (1945–46): 145–94.

Nasafī, Abū al-Barakāt ʿAlī b. Aḥmad. *Kashf al-Asrār Sharḥ al-Manār fī Uṣūl al-Fiqh*, 2 vols. (Cairo: Maṭbaʿat Būlāq, 1316/1898).

Manār al-Anwār fī Uṣūl al-Fiqh (Diyuband: Maktabat Yūsufī, 1972).

Sharḥ al-Manār wa-Ḥawāshīhi min ʿIlm al-Uṣūl (Istanbul: al-Maṭbaʿa al-ʿUthmāniyya, 1315/1897).

Pazdawī, ʿAlī b. Muḥammad Ibn al-Ḥusayn. *Uṣūl*, printed with Bukhārī's *Kashf al-Asrār.*

Qarāfī, Shihāb al-Dīn. *Mukhtaṣar Tanqīḥ al-Fuṣūl fī al-Uṣūl* (Damascus: al-Maktaba al-Hāshimiyya, n.d.).

Sharḥ Tanqīḥ al-Fuṣūl fī Ikhtiṣār al-Maḥṣūl fī al-Uṣūl, ed. Ṭ. ʿAbd al-Ra'ūf Saʿd (Cairo: Maktabat al-Kulliyyāt al-Azhariyya, 1973).

Qāsimī, Jamāl al-Dīn, ed. *Majmūʿ Rasā'il fī Uṣūl al-Fiqh* (Beirut: al-Maktaba al-Ahliyya, 1324/1906).

Rāzī, Fakhr al-Dīn Muḥammad b. ʿUmar. *al-Maʿālim fī ʿIlm Uṣūl al-Fiqh*, ed. ʿĀdil Aḥmad ʿAbd al-Mawjūd and ʿAlī Muḥammad Muʿawwaḍ (Cairo: Mu'assasat Mukhtār, 1414/1994).

al-Maḥṣūl fī ʿIlm al-Uṣūl, ed. Ṭāhā J. ʿUlwānī, 2 vols., 6 parts (Riyadh: Lajnat al-Buḥūth wal-Ta'līf wal-Tarjama wal-Nashr, 1979–81).

al-Maḥṣūl fī ʿIlm Uṣūl al-Fiqh, 2 vols. (Beirut: Dār al-Kutub al-ʿIlmiyya, 1988).

Ṣanʿānī, Muḥammad b. Ismāʿīl. *Irshād al-Nuqqād ilā Taysīr al-Ijtihād*, in *Majmūʿat al-Rasā'il al-Munīriyya*, I (Cairo: Idārat al-Ṭibāʿa al-Munīriyya, 1346/1927), 1–47.

Sarakhsī, Muḥammad b. Aḥmad Abū Sahl. *al-Uṣūl*, ed. Abū al-Wafā al-Afghānī, 2 vols. (Cairo: Dār al-Maʿrifa, 1393/1973).

Shāfiʿī, Muḥammad b. Idrīs. *al-Risāla*, ed. Muḥammad Sayyid Kīlānī (Cairo: Muṣṭafā Bābī al-Ḥalabī, 1969).

al-Risāla, ed. Aḥmad Muḥammad Shākir (Cairo: Muṣṭafā Bābī al-Ḥalabī, 1940). Trans. Majid Khadduri, *al-Risāla fī Uṣūl al-Fiqh: Treatise on the Foundations of Islamic Jurisprudence*, 2nd edn (Cambridge: Islamic Texts Society, 1987).

Shāh Walī Allāh, Aḥmad b. ʿAbd al-Raḥmān. *ʿIqd al-Jīd fī Aḥkām al-Ijtihād wal-Taqlīd* (Cairo: al-Maṭbaʿa al-Salafiyya, 1385/1965).

Shāshī, Aḥmad b. Muḥammad. *Uṣūl al-Shāshī* (Beirut: Dār al-Kitāb al-ʿArabī, 1982).

Shāṭibī, Abū Isḥāq Ibrāhīm. *al-Muwāfaqāt fī Uṣūl al-Aḥkām*, ed. M. Muḥyī al-Dīn ʿAbd al-Ḥamīd, 4 vols. (Cairo: Maṭbaʿat Muḥammad ʿAlī Ṣubayḥ, 1970).

Shawkānī, Muḥammad b. ʿAlī. *Irshād al-Fuḥūl ilā Taḥqīq al-Ḥaqq min ʿIlm al-Uṣūl* (Surabaya: Sharikat Maktabat Aḥmad b. Saʿd b. Nabhān, n.d.).

al-Qawl al-Mufīd fī Adillat al-Ijtihād wal-Taqlīd (Cairo: Dār al-Maṭbaʿa al-Salafiyya, 1974).

Shīrāzī, Abū Isḥāq Ibrāhīm b. ʿAlī. *al-Lumaʿ fī Uṣūl al-Fiqh*, ed. Muḥammad al-Naʿsānī (Cairo: Maṭbaʿat al-Saʿāda, 1326/1908).

Sharḥ al-Lumaʿ, ed. ʿAbd al-Majīd Turkī, 2 vols. (Beirut: Dār al-Gharb al-Islāmī, 1988).

al-Tabṣira fī Uṣūl al-Fiqh, ed. Muḥammad Ḥasan Haytū (Damascus: Dār al-Fikr, 1980).

Ṣiddīq Ḥasan Khān, Muḥammad. *Ḥuṣūl al-Ma'mūl min ʿIlm al-Uṣūl* (Istanbul: Maktabat al-Jawā'ib, 1296/1878).

Sīnawānī, Ḥasan b. ʿUmar. *al-Aṣl al-Jāmiʿ fī Īḍāḥ al-Durar al-Manẓūma fī Silk Jamʿ al-Jawāmiʿ*, 2 vols. (Tunis: Maṭbaʿat al-Nahḍa, 1347/1928).

Subkī, Tāj al-Dīn b. Taqī al-Dīn. *Jamʿ al-Jawāmiʿ*, printed with al-Bannānī's, *Ḥāshiyat al-Bannānī ʿalā Jamʿ al-Jawāmiʿ*.

Taftāzānī, Saʿd al-Dīn. *Ḥāshiya ʿalā Sharḥ al-ʿAḍud al-Ījī*, 2 vols. (Cairo: Maktabat al-Kulliyyāt al-Azhariyya, 1973).

al-Talwīḥ fī Kashf Ḥaqā'iq al-Tanqīḥ, 2 vols. (Istanbul: Mekteb Sanayi Matbaasinde, 1310/1893).

Tilimsānī, Muḥammad b. Aḥmad al-Sharīf. *Miftāḥ al-Wuṣūl fī ʿIlm al-Uṣūl* (Cairo: Maktabat al-Kulliyyāt al-Azhariyya, n.d.).

Ṭūfī, Najm al-Dīn Sulaymān b. Saʿīd. *Sharḥ al-Arbaʿīn al-Nawawiyya*, in Zayd, ed., *al-Maṣlaḥa fī al-Tashrīʿ al-Islāmī*. Also printed as *Risālat al-Ṭūfī fī Riʿāyat al-Maṣāliḥ al-Mursala*, in ʿAbd al-Wahhāb Khallāf, *Maṣādir al-Tashrīʿ al-Islāmī fīmā lā Naṣṣa fīh* (Kuwait: Dār al-Qalam, 1390/1970).

Sharḥ Mukhtaṣar al-Rawḍa, ed. ʿAbd Allāh al-Turkī, 3 vols. (Beirut: Mu'assasat al-Risāla, 1407/1987).

Urmawī, Sirāj al-Dīn Maḥmūd. *al-Taḥṣīl min al-Maḥṣūl*, ed. ʿAbd al-Ḥamīd Abū Zunayd, 2 vols. (Beirut: Mu'assasat al-Risāla, 1988).

Modern primary sources on legal theory

ʿAbduh, Muḥammad. *al-Aʿmāl al-Kāmila lil-Imām Muḥammad ʿAbduh*, ed. M. ʿAmāra, 6 vols. (Beirut: al-Mu'assasa al-ʿArabiyya lil-Dirāsāt wal-Nashr, 1972–74).

al-Islām wal-Nuṣrāniyya maʿ al-ʿIlm wal-Madaniyya (Cairo: al-Mu'tamar al-Islāmī, 1955).

Risālat al-Tawḥīd (Cairo: al-Maṭbaʿa al-ʿĀmira al-Khayriyya, 1324/1906).

Abdul Hakim, Khalifa. "The Natural Law in the Muslim Tradition," E. F. Barrett, ed., in *University of Notre Dame Natural Law Institute Proceedings*, V (Notre Dame: University of Notre Dame Press, 1951), 29–65.

Adūnīs, Muḥammad Arkūn, Ḥalīm Barakāt, et al. *al-Islām wal-Ḥadātha* (London: Dar Al Saqi, 1990).

Amini, Mohammad Taqi. *Time Changes and Islamic Law* (Delhi: Idarah-i Adabiyat-i Delli, 1988).

Arkoun, Muhammad. *Essai sur la pensée islamique* (Paris: Maisonneuve et Larose, 1984).

al-Islām: al-Ams wal-Ghad (Beirut: Dār al-Tanwīr, 1983).

"al-Islām wal-Ḥadātha," in Adūnīs, Barakāt et al., *al-Islām wal-Ḥadātha,* 321–65.

Lectures du Coran (Paris: Maisonneuve et Larose, 1982).

Min Fayṣal al-Tafriqa ilā Faṣl al-Maqāl: Ayna Huwa al-Fikr al-Islāmī al-Muʿāṣir?, trans. Hāshim Ṣāliḥ (London: Dar Al Saqi, 1993).

Min al-Ijtihād ilā Naqd al-ʿAql al-Islāmī (London: Dar Al Saqi, 1993).

"Al-Naṣṣ al-Awwal/al-Naṣṣ al-Thānī," *Mawāqif*, 54 (1988): 4–12.

Pour une critique de la raison islamique (Paris: Maisonneuve et Larose, 1984).

ʿAshmāwī, Muḥammad Saʿīd. *Uṣūl al-Sharīʿa* (Beirut: Dār Iqra', 1983).

Ayyūbī, Muḥammad Hishām. *al-Ijtihād wa-Muqtaḍayāt al-ʿAṣr* (Amman: Dār al-Fikr, 1980).

ʿAẓm, Ṣādiq Jalāl. *al-Naqd al-Dhātī baʿda al-Hazīma* (Beirut: Dār al-Ṭabīʿa lil-Ṭibāʿa wal-Nashr, 1970).

Naqd al-Fikr al-Dīnī (Beirut: Dār al-Ṭalīʿa, 1977).

Falsafat al-Tashrīʿ al-Islāmī (Rabat: Akādīmiyyat al-Mamlaka al-Maghribiyya, 1987).

Faruki, Kemal. *The Constitutional and Legal Role of the Umma* (Karachi: Maʿaref, 1979).

Ijma and the Gate of Ijtihad (Karachi: Gateway Publications, 1954).

Islamic Jurisprudence (Karachi: Pakistan Publishing House, 1962).

"Legal Implications for Today of *al-Aḥkām al-Khamsa* (The Five Values)," in R. G. Hovannisian, ed., *Ethics in Islam* (Malibu: Undena Publications, 1985), 65–72.

Fāsī, ʿAllāl. *Maqāṣid al-Sharīʿa al-Islāmiyya wa-Makārimuhā* (Casablanca: Maktabat al-Waḥda al-ʿArabiyya, 1963).

Fawzān, ʿAbd Allāh b. Ṣāliḥ. *Sharḥ al-Waraqāt fī Uṣūl al-Fiqh* (Riyadh: Dār al-Muslim lil-Nashr, 1414/1993).

Fyzee, A. A. A. "The Reinterpretation of Islam," in John Donohue and J. Esposito, eds., *Islam in Transition* (Oxford: Oxford University Press, 1982): 181–87.

Haider, S. M. *Shariah and Legal Profession* (Lahore: Feroz Sons, 1985).
Ḥanafī, Ḥasan. *Dirāsāt Islāmiyya* (Beirut: Dār al-Tanwīr lil-Ṭibāʿa wal-Nashr, 1982).
Les méthodes d'exégèse: essai sur la science des fondements de la comprehension "ʿilm uṣūl al-fiqh" (Cairo: Le Conseil Supérieur des Arts, 1385/1965).
al-Turāth wal-Tajdīd (Beirut: al-Mu'assasa al-Jāmiʿiyya, 1992).
"al-Waḥy wal-Wāqiʿ: Dirāsa fī Asbāb al-Nuzūl," in Adūnīs, Barakāt et al., *al-Islām wal-Ḥadātha,* 133–75.
Hassan, Abdulkadir. *U-Shul Fiqh* (Surabaya: al-Muslimun Press, 1956).
Hassan, Ahmad. *al-Boerhan* (Bandung: Persatuan Islam, 1933).
Soal-Jawab Tentang Berbagai Masalah Agama, 4 vols. (Bandung: C. V. Diponegoro, 1968).
Ḥusayn, Muḥammad al-Khidr. "Uṣūl al-Fiqh: al-Sharīʿa al-Islāmiyya Ṣāliḥa li-Kulli Zamān wa-Makān," *Majallat al-Azhar*, 1 (1349/1931): 36–42, 139–46, 204–10, 278–83, 534–40.
Ibn ʿĀshūr, Muḥammad Ṭāhir. *Maqāṣid al-Sharīʿa al-Islāmiyya* (Tunis: al-Sharika al-Tūnisiyya lil-Tawzīʿ, 1978).
Ibn Ibrāhīm, Muḥammad. *al-Ijtihād wa-Qaḍāya al-ʿAṣr* (Tunis: Dār Turkī lil-Nashr, 1990).
Jābirī, Muḥammad ʿĀbid. *Bunyat al-ʿAql al-ʿArabī* (Beirut: Markaz Dirāsāt al-Waḥda al-ʿArabiyya, 1986).
Ishkāliyyāt al-Fikr al-ʿArabī al-Muʿāṣir (Beirut: Markaz al-Waḥda al-ʿArabiyya, 1989).
Takwīn al-ʿAql al-ʿArabī (Beirut: Dār al-Ṭalīʿa, 1985).
Jūda, Aḥmad. *Ḥiwārāt Ḥawl al-Sharīʿa* (Cairo: Dār Sīnā lil-Nashr, 1990).
Khallāf, ʿAbd al-Wahhāb. *ʿIlm Uṣūl al-Fiqh* (Cairo: Maṭbaʿat al-Naṣr, 1954).
Maṣādir al-Tashrīʿ al-Islāmī fīmā lā Naṣṣa Fīh (Cairo: Dār al-Kitāb al-ʿArabī, 1955).
Khaṭīb, Muḥammad Kāmil, ed. *al-Iṣlāḥ wal-Nahḍa* (Damascus: Manshūrāt Wizārat al-Thaqāfa, 1992).
Khuḍarī, Muḥammad. *Tārīkh al-Tashrīʿ al-Islāmī* (Cairo: Maṭbaʿat al-Istiqāma, 1353/1943).
Khūlī, Amīn. *Manāhij al-Tajdīd fī al-Naḥw wal-Balāgha wal-Tafsīr wal-Adab* (Cairo: Dār al-Maʿrifa, 1961)
Mahmaṣānī, Subḥī. "Adaptation of Islamic Jurisprudence to Modern Social Needs," in John Donohue and J. Esposito, eds., *Islam in Transition* (Oxford: Oxford University Press, 1982), 181–87.
Maududi, Abul Ala. *Islamic Law and Constitution* (Lahore: Islamic Publications, 1955).
Tafhīm al-Qur'ān, 6 vols. (Lahore: Maktabah-yi Tamir-i Insaniyyat, 1975–76). Trans. Zafar Ishaq Ansari, *Towards Understanding the Quran*, 4 vols. (London: The Islamic Foundation, 1988).
Muslehuddin, Mohammad. *Islamic Jurisprudence and the Rule of Necessity and Need* (Islamabad: Islamic Research Institute, 1975).
an-Na'im, Abdullah. *Toward an Islamic Reformation: Civil Liberties, Human Rights and International Law* (Syracuse: Syracuse University Press, 1990).

Al-Nowaihi, Mohamed. "Religion and Modernization: The General Problem and Islamic Responses," in Richard L. Rubenstein, ed., *Modernization: The Humanist Response to its Promise and Problems* (Washington: Paragon House, 1976), 309–40.

Rahman, Fazlur. "An Autobiographical Note," *Journal of Islamic Research*, 4 (1990): 227–31.

"Divine Revelation and Holy Prophet," *Pakistan Times*, 25 August, 1968: 2–5.

"Interpreting the Qur'an," *Inquiry*, 3 (May 1986): 45–49.

Islam and Modernity: Transformation of an Intellectual Tradition (Chicago: University of Chicago Press, 1982).

Islamic Methodology in History (Karachi: Central Institute of Islamic Research, 1965).

Major Themes of the Quran (Minneapolis: Bibliotheca Islamica, 1980).

"Some Key Ethical Concepts of the Qur'ān," *Journal of Religious Ethics*, 11 (1983): 170–85.

"Towards Reformulating the Methodology of Islamic Law: Sheikh Yamani on 'Public Interest' in Islamic Law," *New York University Journal of International Law and Politics*, 12 (1979): 219–24.

Riḍā, Rashīd. *al-Khilāfa aw al-Imāma al-ʿUẓmā* (Cairo: Maṭbaʿat al-Manār, 1341/1923).

Yusr al-Islām wa-Uṣūl al-Tashrīʿ al-ʿĀmm (Cairo: Maṭbaʿat Nahḍat Miṣr, 1375/1956).

Sardar, Ziauddin. *Islamic Futures: The Shape of Ideas to Come* (London and New York: Mansell Publishing Ltd., 1985).

Shaḥrūr, Muḥammad. *al-Kitāb wal-Qur'ān: Qirā'a Muʿāṣira* (Cairo and Damascus: Sīnā lil-Nashr, 1992).

Sunbuhlī, Muḥammad Burhān al-Dīn. *Qaḍāyā Fiqhiyya Muʿāṣira* (Damascus and Beirut: Dār al-Qalam, 1988).

Ṭāhā, Mahmoud Muhammed. *The Second Message of Islam*, trans. Abdullahi an-Naʿim (Syracuse: Syracuse University Press, 1987).

Ṭuʿayma, Ṣābir. *al-Sharīʿa al-Islāmiyya fī ʿAṣr al-ʿIlm* (Beirut: Dār al-Jīl, 1988).

Turābī, Ḥasan. "Principles of Governance, Freedom, and Responsibility in Islam," *American Journal of Islamic Social Sciences*, 4 (1987): 1–11.

Tajdīd al-Fikr al-Islāmī (Rabat: Dār al-Qarāfī lil-Nashr wal-Tawzīʿ, 1993).

Tajdīd Uṣūl al-Fiqh al-Islāmī (Beirut and Khartoum: Dar al-Fikr, 1980).

Turābī, Rashīd. "Ijtihad in Islam," *International Islamic Colloquium Papers* (Lahore: Panjab University Press, 1960): 107–09.

Secondary sources

Abbott, Nabia. *Studies in Arabic Literary Papyri*, II (Chicago: University of Chicago Press, 1967).

ʿAbd al-Karīm, Khalīl. *al-Judhūr al-Tārīkhiyya lil-Sharīʿa al-Islāmiyya* (Cairo: Sīnā lil-Nashr, 1990).

Abdel-Rahman, Hassan. "L'argument *a maiori* et l'argument par analogie dans la logique juridique musulmane," *Rivista internazionale di filosophia musulmane*, 48 (1971): 127–48.

"La place du syllogisme juridique dans la méthode exégétique chez Ġazali," in H. Hubien, ed., *Le raisonnement juridique* (Brussels: E. Bruylant, 1971).

Affendi, Abdelwahab. *See* El-Affendi.

Aghnides, Nicholas P. *Mohammedan Theories of Finance* (New York: Columbia University Press, 1916). Reprinted in part as *Introduction to Mohammedan Law* (Solo: Ab. Sitti Sjamsijah, 1955).

Ahmed, al-Haj Moinuddin. *The Urgency of Ijtihad* (New Delhi: Kitab Bhavan, 1992).

ʿAjūz, Aḥmad Muḥyī al-Dīn. *Manāhij al-Sharīʿa al-Islāmiyya*, 3 vols. (Beirut: Maktabat al-Maʿārif, 1983).

Alvi, Sajida. "The *Mujaddid* and *Tajdīd* Traditions in the Indian Subcontinent: An Historical Overview," *Journal of Turkish Studies*, 18 (1994): 1–15.

Amin, S. H. *Islamic Law and its Implications for (the) Modern World* (Glasgow: Royston Ltd., 1989).

Anderson, J. N. D. "Is the Sharīʿa Doomed to Immutability?" *Muslim World*, 56 (1966): 10–13.

"Islamic Law Today: The Background to Islamic Fundamentalism," *Arab Law Quarterly*, 2 (1987): 339–51.

Law Reform in the Muslim World (London: Athlone Press, 1976), **6.1**.

Ansari, Zafar Ishaq. "Islamic Juristic Terminology before Šāfiʿī: A Semantic Analysis with Special Reference to Kūfa," *Arabica*, 19 (1972): 255–300, **1.4**.

Arnaldez, Roger. *Grammaire et théologie chez Ibn Hazm de Cordoue* (Paris: J. Vrin, 1956).

"La place du Coran dans les *Uṣūl al-fiqh* d'après le *Muḥallā* d'Ibn Ḥazm," *Studia Islamica*, 32 (1970): 21–30.

Azami, M. M. *On Schacht's Origins of Muhammadan Jurisprudence* (New York: John Wiley, 1985), **1.3**.

Studies in Early Hadith Literature (Beirut: al-Maktab al-Islāmī, 1968), **1.3**.

Al-Azmeh, Aziz. "Islamic Legal Theory and the Appropriation of Reality," in Aziz al-Azmeh, ed., *Islamic Law: Social and Historical Contexts* (London: Routledge, 1988): 250–65.

Islams and Modernities (New York: Verso, 1993).

Bagby, Ihsan A. "The Issue of *Maṣlaḥa* in Classical Islamic Legal Theory," *International Journal of Islamic and Arabic Studies*, 2 (1985): 1–11.

Bāḥusayn, Yaʿqūb b. ʿAbd al-Wahhāb. *al-Takhrīj ʿInda al-Fuqahāʾ wal-Uṣūliyyīn* (Riyadh: Maktabat al-Rushd, 1414/1993).

Baljon, J. M. S. *The Reforms and Religious Ideas of Sir Sayyid Ahmad Khan* (Leiden: E. J. Brill, 1949), **6**.

Religion and Thought of Shāh Walī Allāh Dihlawī 1703–1762 (Leiden: E. J. Brill, 1968), **6**.

Ballantyne, William. "A Reassertion of the Sharīʿa: The Jurisprudence of the Gulf States," in Heer, ed., *Islamic Law and Jurisprudence,* 149–59.

Barrī, Zakariyyā. *Uṣūl al-Fiqh al-Islāmī* (Cairo: Dār al-Nahḍa al-ʿArabiyya, 1982).

Ben Choaib, Aboubekr Abdesselam. "L'argumentation juridique en droit musulman," *Revue de monde musulman*, 7 (1909): 70–86.

Bernand, Marie. *L'accord unanime de la communauté comme fondement des statuts légaux de l'Islam d'après Abū al-Ḥusayn al-Baṣrī* (Paris: J. Vrin, 1970), **2.7**.

"Bayān selon les uṣūliyyūn," *Arabica*, 42 (1995): 145–60.

"Ḥanafī *Uṣūl al-Fiqh* through a Manuscript of al-Ǧaṣṣāṣ," *Journal of the American Oriental Society*, 105 (1985): 623–35.

"L'iǧmāʿ chez ʿAbd al-Ǧabbār et l'objection d'an-Naẓẓām," *Studia Islamica*, 30 (1969): 27–38.

(-Baladi). "L'ijmāʿ, critère de validité juridique," in J.-P. Charnay, ed., *Normes et valeurs dans l'Islam contemporain* (Paris: Payot, 1966): 68–79.

"La notion de *ʿilm* chez les premiers muʿtazilites," *Studia Islamica*, 36 (1972): 23–45; 37 (1973): 27–56.

"Nouvelles remarques sur l'iǧmāʿ chez le qāḍī ʿAbd al-Ǧabbār," *Arabica*, 19 (1972): 78–85.

"Le probleme de l'*ašbāh* ou les implications ontologiques de la regle juridico-religieuse," *Arabica*, 37 (1990): 151–72.

"Les *uṣūl al-fiqh* de l'époque classique: Status quaestionis," *Arabica*, 39 (1992): 273–86.

Binsaʿīd, Saʿīd. *al-Aydulūjiyya wal-Ḥadātha* (Beirut: al-Markaz al-Thaqāfī al-ʿArabī, 1987).

Bousquet, G.-H. "Le mystère de la formation et des origines du *fiqh*," *Revue algerienne, tunisienne et marocaine de legislation et de jurisprudence*, 63 (1947): 66–81.

Bravmann, M. M. *The Spiritual Background of Early Islam* (Leiden: E. J. Brill, 1972), **1.3**.

Brock, S. P. "Syriac Views of Emergent Islam," in Juynboll, ed., *Studies on the First Century of Islamic Society*, 9–21.

Brockelmann, Carl. *Geschichte der arabischen Literatur*, 2 vols. (Leiden: E. J. Brill, 1943–49); 3 supplements (Leiden: E. J. Brill, 1937–42).

Brunschvig, Robert. "Considérations sociologiques sur le droit musulman ancien," *Studia Islamica*, 3 (1955): 61–73. Reprinted in *Études d'islamologie*, II, 119–31, **1**.

Études d'islamologie, ed. Abdel Maǧid Turki. 2 vols. (Paris: G.-P. Maisonneuve et Larose, 1976).

"Ǧāmiʿ Māniʿ," *Arabica*, 9 (1962): 74–76. Reprinted in Brunschvig, *Études d'islamologie*, I, 355–57.

"Le livre de l'ordre et de la défense d'al-Muzani," *Bulletin d'études orientales*, 11 (1945–46): 145–94.

"Logic and Law in Classical Islam," in G. E. von Grunebaum, ed., *Logic in Classical Islamic Culture*, (Wiesbaden: Otto Harrassowitz, 1970): 9–20.

"Logique et droit dans l'Islam classique," in Brunschvig, *Études d'Islamologie*, II, 347–61.

"Rationalité et tradition dans l'analogie juridico-religieuse chez le muʿtazilite ʿAbd al-Jabbār," *Arabica*, 19 (1972): 213–21. Reprinted in Brunschvig, *Études d'Islamologie*, II, 395–403.

"La théorie du *qiyās* juridique chez le Ḥanafite al-Dabūsī (Ve/XIe siècle)," in J. M. Barral, ed., *Orientalia hispanica: sive studia F. M. Pareja octogenario dicata*, I (Leiden: E. J. Brill, 1974): 150–54, **3.2**.

"Valeur et fondement de raisonnement juridique par analogie d'après al-Ġazālī," *Studia Islamica*, 34 (1971): 57–88. Reprinted in Brunschvig, *Études d'Islamologie*, II, 363–94.

Brunschvig, Robert and G. von Grunebaum, eds. *Classicisme et déclin culturel dans l'histoire de l'Islam* (Paris: G.-P. Maisonneuve, 1957).

Burton, John. *The Sources of Islamic Law: Islamic Theories of Abrogation* (Edinburgh: Edinburgh University Press, 1990).

Būṭī, Muḥammad Saʿīd. *Ḍawābiṭ al-Maṣlaḥa fī al-Sharīʿa al-Islāmiyya* (Beirut: Mu'assasat al-Risāla, 1977).

Calder, Norman. "Exploring God's Law: Muḥammad ibn Aḥmad ibn Abī Sahl al-Sarakhsī on *zakāt*," in Christopher Toll and J. Skovgaard-Petersen, eds., *Law and the Islamic World: Past and Present* (Copenhagen: Det Kongelige Danske Videnskabernes Selskab, 1995), 57–73.

"*Ikhtilāf* and *Ijmāʿ* in Shāfiʿī's *Risāla*," *Studia Islamica*, 58 (1984): 55–81, **1.5**.

"Al-Nawawī's Typology of *Muftī*s and its Significance for a General Theory of Islamic Law," *Islamic Law and Society*, 4 (1996): 137–64.

Studies in Early Muslim Jurisprudence (Oxford: Clarendon Press, 1993).

"The *Ummī* in Early Islamic Juristic Literature," *Der Islam*, 67 (1990): 111–23.

Chaumont, Eric. "Bāqillānī, théologien ashʿarite et usūliste mālikite, contre les légistes à propos de l'ijtihād et de l'accord unanime de la communauté," *Studia Islamica*, 79 (1994): 79–102.

"Tout chercheur qualifié dit-il juste?" in A. le Boulluec, ed., *La controverse religieuse et ses formes* (Paris: Les éditions du cerf, 1995), 11–27.

Chehata, C. "'L'équité' en tant que source du droit hanafite," *Studia Islamica*, 25 (1966): 123–38.

"Logique juridique et droit musulman," *Studia Islamica*, 23 (1965): 5–25.

"Nature, structure et divisions du droit musulmane," *Revue algerienne des sciences juridiques, economiques at politiques*, 10 (1973): 555–62.

"La religion et les fondements du droit en Islam," *Revue algerienne des sciences juridiques, economiques at politiques*, 10 (1973): 563–71.

Coulson, N. J. *Conflicts and Tensions in Islamic Jurisprudence* (Chicago: University of Chicago Press, 1969).

A History of Islamic Law (Edinburgh: Edinburgh University Press, 1964).

"The Islamic Legal System: Its Role in Contemporary Muslim Society," in *Veröffentlichungen der Kommission für Europarecht, Internationnales und Ausländisches Privatrecht*, Nr. 2, *Studien zum Islamischen Recht* (Vienna: Verlag der Österreichischen Akademie der Wissenschaften, 1983), 7–19.

Crone, Patricia and M. Cook. *Hagarism: The Making of the Muslim World* (Cambridge: Cambridge University Press, 1977).

Crone, Patricia and Martin Hinds. *God's Caliph: Religious Authority in the First Centuries of Islam* (Cambridge: Cambridge University Press, 1986).

Daniel, Raymond. "L'ijtihād chez Muwaffaq ad-Dīn B. Qudāma," *Revue des études islamiques*, 31 (1963): 33–47.

Denny, Frederick. "Fazlur Rahman: Muslim Intellectual," *Muslim World*, 79 (1989): 91–101.

Eaton, R. M. *General Logic* (New York: Longmans & Green, 1956).

Eickelman, Dale. "Islamic Liberalism Strikes Back," *Middle East Studies Association Bulletin*, 27 (1993): 163–68.

El-Affendi, Abdelwahab. *Turabi's Revolution* (London: Grey Seal, 1991).

Encyclopaedia of Islam, new (2nd) edition (Leiden: E. J. Brill, 1960–).

Encyclopedia of Islamic Law: A Compendium of the Major Schools, trans. Laleh Bakhtiar (Chicago: Library of Islam, 1995).

Ess, Joseph van. *Die Erkenntnislehre des ʿAḍud al-Dīn al-Ījī* (Wiesbaden: Akademie des Wissenschaften und der Literatur, 1966), **2.2**.

Fadel, Mohammad. *Adjudication in the Mālikī Madhhab: A Study of Legal Process in Medieval Islamic Law* (Ph.D. dissertation: University of Chicago, 1995).

"The Social Logic of *Taqlīd* and the Rise of the *Mukhtaṣar*," *Islamic Law and Society*, 4 (1996): 193–233.

Faḍl Allāh, Mahdī. *al-Ijtihād wal-Manṭiq al-Fiqhī fī al-Islām* (Beirut: Dār al-Ṭalīʿa, 1987).

Frank, Richard M. "Reason and Revealed Law: A Sample of Parallels and Divergences in Kalām and Falsafa," *Recherches d'islamologie* (Louvain: Peeters, 1977): 123–38.

Frantz-Murphy, Gladys. "A Comparison of the Arabic and Earlier Egyptian Contract Formularies, Part II: Terminology in the Arabic Warranty and the Idiom of Clearing/Cleaning," *Journal of Near Eastern Studies*, 44 (1985): 99–114.

Friedmann, Yohanan. *Shaykh Aḥmad Sirhindī* (Montreal: McGill–Queen's University Press, 1971).

Ghali, Riad. *De la tradition considerée comme source du droit musulman* (Paris: A. Rousseau, 1909).

Gibb, H. A. R. *Mohammedanism* (London: Oxford University Press, 1962).

Goitein, S. D. "The Birth-Hour of Muslim Law," *Muslim World*, 50, 1 (1960): 23–9. Reprinted in Goitein, *Studies in Islamic History and Institutions*, 126–34.

Studies in Islamic History and Institutions (Leiden: E. J. Brill, 1966).

Goldfeld, Yeshayahu. "The Development of Theory on Qur'ānic Exegesis in Islamic Scholarship," *Studia Islamica*, 67 (1988): 6–27.

Goldziher, I. *Introduction to Islamic Theology and Law*, trans. Andras and Ruth Hamori (Princeton: Princeton University Press, 1981).

Muslim Studies, ed. S. M. Stern, trans. C. R. Barber and S. M. Stern, 2 vols. (London: Allen & Unwin, 1967–71).

"Das Prinzip des istiṣḥāb in der muhammedanischen Gesetzwissenschaft," *Vienna Oriental Journal*, 1 (1887): 228–36.

"Über iğmāʿ," *Nachrichten von der königlichen Gesellschaft der Wissenschaften zu Göttingen, philologisch-historische Klasse* (Göttingen, 1916): 81–5.

The Ẓāhirīs: Their Doctrine and their History, trans. Wolfgang Behn (Leiden: E. J. Brill, 1971).

Guillaume, Alfred. *The Traditions of Islam: An Introduction to the Study of the Ḥadīth Literature* (Oxford: Clarendon Press, 1924).

Haarmann, Ulrich. "Religiöses Recht und Grammatik im Klassischen Islam," *Zeitschrift der Deutschen Morgenländischen Gesellschaft*, Suppl. II (1974): 149–69, **2.4**.

Halkin, A. S. "The Ḥashwiyya," *Journal of the American Oriental Society*, 54 (1934): 1–28.

Hallaq, Wael B. "On the Authoritativeness of Sunnī Consensus," *International Journal of Middle East Studies*, 18 (1986): 427–54. Reprinted in Hallaq, *Law and Legal Theory in Classical and Medieval Islam.*

"Considerations on the Function and Character of Sunnī Legal Theory," *Journal of the American Oriental Society*, 104 (1984): 679–89.

"The Development of Logical Structure in Islamic Legal Theory," *Der Islam*, 64 (1987): 42–67. Reprinted in Ian Edge, ed., *Islamic Law and Legal Theory* (*The International Library of Essays in Law and Legal Theory*, series editor Tom D. Campbell) (Hampshire: Dartmouth Publishing Co., 1993).

"From *Fatwā*s to *Furū*ʿ: Growth and Change in Islamic Substantive Law," *Islamic Law and Society*, 1 (February 1994): 17–56, **4**.

Ibn Taymiyya against the Greek Logicians, trans. Wael B. Hallaq (Oxford: Clarendon Press, 1993).

"*Iftā*ʾ and *Ijtihād* in Sunnī Legal Theory: A Developmental Account," in Khalid Masud, Brink Messick and David Powers, eds., *Islamic Legal Interpretation: Muftīs and their Fatwās* (Cambridge, Mass.: Harvard University Press, 1996), 33–43, **3.9**.

"On Inductive Corroboration, Probability and Certainty in Sunnī Legal Thought," in Heer, ed., *Islamic Law and Jurisprudence,* 3–31. Reprinted in Hallaq, *Law and Legal Theory in Classical and Medieval Islam.*

"Introduction: Issues and Problems," *Islamic Law and Society*, 4, 2 (1996): 127–36.

Law and Legal Theory in Classical and Medieval Islam (Aldershot: Variorum, 1995), **2–3**.

"Logic, Formal Arguments and Formalization of Arguments in Sunnī Jurisprudence," *Arabica*, 37 (1990): 315–58. Reprinted in Hallaq, *Law and Legal Theory in Classical and Medieval Islam.*

"The Logic of Legal Reasoning in Religious and Non-Religious Cultures: The Case of Islamic Law and the Common Law," *Cleveland State Law Review*, 34 (1985–86): 79–96. Reprinted in Csaba Varga, ed., *Comparative Legal Cultures* (*The International Library of Essays in Law and Legal Theory*, series editor Tom D. Campbell) (Hampshire: Dartmouth Publishing Co., 1992), 401–18; also reprinted in Hallaq, *Law and Legal Theory in Classical and Medieval Islam.*

"Murder in Cordoba: *Ijtihād*, *Iftā*ʾ and the Evolution of Substantive Law in Medieval Islam," *Acta Orientalia*, 55 (1994): 55–83.

"Non-Analogical Arguments in Sunnī Juridical *Qiyās*," *Arabica*, 36 (1989):

286–306. Reprinted in Hallaq, *Law and Legal Theory in Classical and Medieval Islam.*

"Notes on the Term *Qarīna* in Islamic Legal Discourse," *Journal of the American Oriental Society*, 108 (1988): 475–80. Reprinted in Hallaq, *Law and Legal Theory in Classical and Medieval Islam.*

"On the Origins of the Controversy about the Existence of Mujtahids and the Gate of Ijtihād," *Studia Islamica*, 63 (1986): 129–41. Reprinted in Hallaq, *Law and Legal Theory in Classical and Medieval Islam,* **3.7**.

"The Primacy of the Qur'ān in Shāṭibī's Legal Theory," in Wael B. Hallaq and Donald P. Little, eds., *Islamic Studies Presented to Charles J. Adams* (Leiden: E. J. Brill, 1991): 69–90. Reprinted in Hallaq, *Law and Legal Theory in Classical and Medieval Islam.*

Review of *The Search for God's Law: Islamic Jurisprudence in the Writings of Sayf al-Dīn al-Āmidī*, by Bernard Weiss, in *International Journal of Middle East Studies*, 26 (1994): 152–54.

"A Tenth–Eleventh Century Treatise on Juridical Dialectic," *Muslim World*, 77 (1987): 198–227.

"*Uṣūl al-Fiqh*: Beyond Tradition," *Journal of Islamic Studies*, 3 (1992): 172–202. Reprinted in Hallaq, *Law and Legal Theory in Classical and Medieval Islam.*

"Was the Gate of Ijtihād Closed?," *International Journal of Middle East Studies*, 16, 1 (1984): 3–41. Reprinted in Ian Edge, ed., *Islamic Law and Legal Theory* (*The International Library of Essays in Law and Legal Theory*, series editor Tom D. Campbell) (Hampshire: Dartmouth Publishing Co., 1993); also reprinted in Hallaq, *Law and Legal Theory in Classical and Medieval Islam,* **3.7**.

"Was al-Shafiʿi the Master Architect of Islamic Jurisprudence?," *International Journal of Middle East Studies*, 25 (1993): 587–605. Reprinted in Hallaq, *Law and Legal Theory in Classical and Medieval Islam.*

Haram, Nissreen. "Use and Abuse of the Law: A Muftī's Response," in Khalid Masud, Brink Messick, and David Powers, eds., *Islamic Legal Interpretation: Muftīs and their Fatwās* (Cambridge, Mass.: Harvard University Press, 1996), 72–86.

Ḥasan, Khalīfa Bābakr. *Manāhij al-Uṣūliyyīn fī Ṭuruq Dalālāt al-Alfāẓ ʿalā al-Aḥkām* (Cairo: Maktabat Wahba, 1989).

Heer, Nicholas L. ed., *Islamic Law and Jurisprudence: Studies in Honor of Farhat J. Ziadeh* (Seattle and London: University of Washington Press, 1990).

Heinrichs, Wolfhart. "On the Genesis of the *Ḥaqīqa-Majāz* Dichotomy," *Studia Islamica*, 59 (1984): 111–40.

Ḥifnāwī, Muḥammad Ibrāhīm. *Naẓarāt fī Uṣūl al-Fiqh* (Cairo: Dār al-Ḥadīth, 1980).

Hoebink, Michel. *Two Halves of the Same Truth: Schacht, Hallaq, and the Gate of* Ijtihad (Amsterdam: Middle East Research Associates, 1994).

Hourani, George. "The Basis of Authority of Consensus in Sunnite Islam," *Studia Islamica*, 21 (1964): 11–60.

Hurgronje, C. Snouck. *Selected Works*, ed. G.-H. Bousquet and Joseph Schacht (Leiden: E. J. Brill, 1975).

International Islamic Colloquium Papers (Lahore: Panjab University Press, 1960).

Ismāʿīl, Shaʿbān Muḥammad. *al-Imām al-Shawkānī wa-Manhajuhu fī Uṣūl al-Fiqh* (Dawḥa: Dār al-Thaqāfa, 1989).

Jackson, Sherman. "From Prophetic Actions to Constitutional Theory: A Novel Chapter in Medieval Muslim Jurisprudence," *International Journal of Middle East Studies*, 25, 1 (1993): 71–90.

"*Taqlīd*, Legal Scaffolding and the Scope of Legal Injunctions in Post-Formative Theory: *Muṭlaq* and *ʿĀmm* in the Jurisprudence of Shihāb al-Dīn al-Qarāfī," *Islamic Law and Society*, 4 (1996): 165–92.

Jāh, ʿUmar. "The Importance of Ijtihad in the Development of Islamic Law," *Journal of Islamic and Comparative Law*, 7 (1977): 31–40.

Johansen, Baber. "Legal Literature and the Problem of Change: The Case of the Land Rent," in Chibli Mallat, ed., *Islam and Public Law* (London: Graham & Trotman, 1993), 29–47.

Juynboll, G. H. A. *Muslim Tradition: Studies in Chronology, Provenance and Authorship of Early Ḥadīth* (Cambridge: Cambridge University Press, 1983), **1.3**.

"Some Notes on Islam's First *Fuqahā'* Distilled from Early *Ḥadīṯ* Literature," *Arabica*, 39 (1992): 287–314.

Juynboll, G. H. A., ed. *Studies on the First Century of Islamic Society* (Carbondale: Southern Illinois University Press, 1982).

Kamali, Mohammad Hashim. *Principles of Islamic Jurisprudence*, revised edn. (Cambridge: Islamic Texts Society, 1991).

Kerr, Malcolm. *Islamic Reform: The Political and Legal Theories of Muḥammad ʿAbduh and Rashīd Riḍā* (Berkeley: University of California Press, 1966), **6**.

Khadduri, Majid. "The *Maṣlaḥa* (Public Interest) and *ʿIlla* (Cause) in Islamic Law," *New York University Journal of International Law and Politics*, 12 (1979): 213–17.

"Nature and Sources of Islamic Law," *George Washington Law Review*, 22 (1953): 3–23.

War and Peace in the Law of Islam (Baltimore: Johns Hopkins University Press, 1955).

Khadduri, Majid and H. J. Liebesny, eds. *Law in the Middle East: Origins and Development of Islamic Law* (Washington, D.C.: Middle East Institute, 1955).

Khuḍarī, Muḥammad. *Tārīkh al-Tashrīʿ al-Islāmī* (Cairo: al-Maktaba al-Tijāriyya, 1967).

Kinberg, Leah. "*Muḥkamāt* and *Mutashābihāt* (Koran 3/7): Implication of a Koranic Pair of Terms in Medieval Exegesis," *Arabica*, 35 (1988): 143–72.

Kittānī, Muḥammad. *Jadal al-ʿAql wal-Naql fī Manāhij al-Fikr al-Qadīm* (Casablanca: Dār al-Thaqāfa, 1992).

Landau-Tasseron, Ella. "The 'Cyclical Reform': A Study of the *Mujaddid* Tradition," *Studia Islamica*, 70 (1989): 79–117.

Laoust, Henri. *Contribution à une étude de la méthodologie canonique de Taḳī-d-Dīn Aḥmad b. Taymiya* (Cairo: Imprimerie de l'Institut français d'archéologie orientale, 1939).

"La pédagogie d'al-Ġazālī dans le *Mustaṣfā*," *Revue des études Islamiques*, 44 (1976): 71–79.

"Le reformisme d'Ibn Taymiya," *Islamic Studies*, 1 (1962): 27–47.

Layish, Aharon. "The Contribution of the Modernists to the Secularization of Islamic Law," *Middle East Studies*, 14 (1978): 263–77.

Liebesny, H. J. *The Law of the Near and Middle East* (New York: State University of New York Press, 1975).

"Religious Law and Westernization in the Moslem Near East," *American Journal of Comparative Law*, 2 (1953): 492–504.

Linant de Bellefonds, Y. "The Formal Sources of Islamic Law," trans. M. Khalid Masʿud, *Islamic Studies*, 15 (1976): 187–94.

Lindholm, Tore and Kari Vogt, eds. *Islamic Law Reform and Human Rights: Challenges and Rejoinders* (Copenhagen: Nordic Human Rights Publications, 1993).

Mahmassani, S. *Falsafat al-Tashrīʿ fī al-Islām*, trans. F. Ziadeh, *The Philosophy of Jurisprudence in Islam* (Leiden: E. J. Brill, 1961).

Makdisi, George. "Ethics in Islamic Traditionalist Doctrine," in R. G. Hovannisian, ed., *Ethics in Islam* (Malibu: Undena Publications, 1985): 47–63.

"Freedom in Islamic Jurisprudence: *Ijtihad*, *Taqlid*, and Academic Freedom," in *La notion de liberté au moyen age: Islam, Byzance, Occident*, Penn–Paris–Dumbarton Oaks Colloquia (Paris: Société d'Edition des Belles Lettres, 1985): 79–88, **3.7**.

"The Juridical Theology of Shāfiʿī: Origins and Significance of *Uṣūl al-Fiqh*," *Studia Islamica*, 59 (1984): 5–47, **1.6**.

Religion, Law and Learning in Classical Islam (Aldershot: Variorum, 1991).

The Rise of Colleges (Edinburgh: Edinburgh University Press, 1981).

"The Scholastic Method in Medieval Education: An Enquiry into its Origins in Law and Theology," *Speculum*, 49 (1974): 640–61.

Makdisi, John. "Formal Rationality in Islamic Law and the Common Law," *Cleveland State Law Review*, 34 (1985–6): 97–112.

"Hard Cases and Human Judgment in Islamic and Common Law," *Indiana International and Comparative Review*, 2 (1991): 191–219.

"Legal Logic and Equity in Islamic Law," *American Journal of Comparative Law*, 33 (1985): 63–92, **3.3**.

Makdisi, John and Marianne Makdisi. "Islamic Law Bibliography: Revised and Updated List of Secondary Sources," *Law Library Journal*, 87 (1995): 69–191.

Mansour, Camille. *L'autorité dans la pensée musulmane* (Paris: J. Vrin, 1975), **2.7**.

Margoliouth, D. S. "Omar's Instructions to the Kadi," *Journal of the Royal Asiatic Society* (1910): 305–36, **1.3**.

Marmura, M. "Ghazālī and Demonstrative Science," *Journal of the History of Philosophy*, 3 (1965): 183–204.

Masud, Khalid. *Islamic Legal Philosophy: A Study of Abū Isḥāq al-Shāṭibī's Life and Thought* (Islamabad: Islamic Research Institute, 1977).

Mayer, Ann E. "Law and Religion in the Middle East," *American Journal of Comparative Law*, 35 (1987): 127–84.

"The Sharīʿa: A Methodology or a Body of Substantive Rules?" in Heer, ed., *Islamic Law and Jurisprudence*, 177–98, **6**.

Melchert, Christopher. *The Formation of the Sunnī Schools of Law: Ninth–Tenth Centuries C.E.* (Ph.D. dissertation: University of Pennsylvania, 1992), **1.6**.

Meron, Y. "The Development of Legal Thought in Hanafi Texts," *Studia Islamica*, 30 (1969): 73–118.

Messick, Brinkley. *The Calligraphic State: Textual Domination and History in a Muslim Society* (Berkeley: University of California Press, 1993).

Miller, Larry. *Islamic Disputation Theory: A Study of the Development of Dialectic in Islam From the Tenth Through the Thirteenth Centuries* (Ph.D. dissertation: Princeton University, 1984), **4.2**.

Modarressi, Hossein, "Some Recent Analyses of the Concept of *majāz* in Islamic Jurisprudence," *Journal of the Arabic Oriental Society*, 106 (1986): 787–91.

Motzki, Harald. "The *Muṣannaf* of ʿAbd al-Razzāq al-Ṣanʿānī as a Source of Authentic *Aḥādīth* of the First Century A.H.," *Journal of Near Eastern Studies*, 50 (1991): 1–21, **1.3–4**.

Mudzhar, Atho. *Fatwas of the Council of Indonesia ʿUlama': A Study of Islamic Legal Thought in Indonesia 1975–1988* (Jakarta: INIS, 1993).

Nashshār, ʿAlī Sāmī. *Manāhij al-Baḥth ʿinda Mufakkirī al-Islām* (Beirut: Dār al-Nahḍa al-ʿArabiyya, 1984).

Oxford Encyclopedia of the Modern Islamic World, ed.-in-chief, John L. Esposito, 4 vols. (New York/Oxford: Oxford University Press, 1995).

Paret, Rudi. "Problems of Legislation in Modern Islam," in *International Islamic Colloquium Papers* (Lahore: Panjab University Press, 1960): 104–06.

Perlmann, Moshe. "Ibn Hazm on the Equivalence of Proofs," *The Jewish Quarterly Review*, n.s. 40 (1949/50): 279–90.

Peters, Rudolph. "*Ijtihād* and *Taqlīd* in 18th and 19th Century Islam," *Die Welt des Islams*, 20 (1980): 131–45, **6.1**.

Powers, David S. "The Exegetical Genre *nāsikh al-Qur'ān wa-mansūkhuh*," in Andrew Rippin, ed., *Approaches to the History of the Interpretation of the Qur'ān* (Oxford: Clarendon Press, 1988): 117–38.

"*Fatwā*s as Sources for Legal and Social History: A Dispute over Endowment Revenues from Fourteenth-Century Fez," *al-Qanṭara*, 11 (1990): 295–340.

"On Judicial Review in Islamic Law," *Law and Society Review*, 26 (1992): 315–41.

Studies in Qur'an and Ḥadīth: The Formation of the Law of Inheritance (Berkeley: University of California Press, 1986), **1.2–4**.

"The Will of Saʿd b. Abī Waqqās: A Reassessment," *Studia Islamica*, 58 (1983): 33–53.

Qureshi, T. A. "Methodologies of Social Change and Islamic Law," *Hamdard Islamicus*, 10, 2 (1987): 3–34.

Rahman, Fazlur. "Functional Interdependence of Law and Theology," in G. E. von Grunebaum, ed., *Theology and Law in Islam*, (Wiesbaden: Otto Harrassowitz, 1971): 89–97.

"The Impact of Modernity on Islam," *Islamic Studies*, 5 (1966): 117–28.

Islam (Chicago: University of Chicago Press, 1979).

"Islamic Modernism: Its Scope, Method and Alternatives," *International Journal of Middle East Studies*, 1 (1970): 317–33.

"Law and Ethics in Islam," in R. G. Hovannisian, ed., *Ethics in Islam* (Malibu: Undena Publications, 1985): 3–15.

"Revival and Reform in Islam," in *The Cambridge History of Islam*, IIB, P. M. Holt, Ann K. S. Lambton, and B. Lewis, eds., *Islamic Society and Civilization*, (Cambridge: Cambridge University Press, 1970), 632–56, **6**.

Reinhart, A. Kevin. "Islamic Law as Islamic Ethics," *Journal of Religious Ethics*, 11 (1983): 186–203, **2**.

Rescher, Nicholas. "The Impact of Arabic Philosophy on the West," in N. Rescher, *Studies in Arabic Philosophy* (Hertford: University of Pittsburgh Press, 1966): 147–57.

Rippin, Andrew. "Al-Zuhrī, *Naskh al-Qur'ān* and the Problem of Early *Tafsīr* Texts," *Bulletin of the School of Oriental and African Studies*, 47 (1984): 22–43.

Rubin, Uri. "'Al-Walad lil-Firāsh' on the Islamic Campaign against 'Zinā'," *Studia Islamica*, 78 (1993): 5–26.

Salqīnī, Ibrāhīm Muḥammad. *al-Muyassar fī Uṣūl al-Fiqh al-Islāmī* (Beirut: Dār al-Fikr al-Muʿāṣir, 1991).

Schacht, Joseph. "Classicisme, traditionalisme et ankylose dans la loi religieuse de l'Islam," in Brunschvig and von Grunebaum, eds., *Classicisme et déclin culturel dans l'histoire de l'Islam*, 141–61.

"Foreign Elements in Ancient Islamic Law," *Journal of Comparative Legislation and International Law*, 32 (1950): 9–17, **1**.

An Introduction to Islamic Law (Oxford: Clarendon Press, 1964).

"Modernism and Traditionalism in a History of Islamic Law," *Middle Eastern Studies*, 1 (1965): 388–400.

The Origins of Muhammadan Jurisprudence (Oxford: Clarendon Press, 1950), **1**.

"Problems of Modern Islamic Legislation," *Studia Islamica*, 12 (1960): 99–129, **6**.

"Zur soziologischen Betrachtung des islamischen Rechts," *Der Islam*, 22 (1935): 207–38.

Serjeant, R. B. "The Caliph Umar's Letters to Abū Mūsā al-Ashʿarī," *Journal of Semitic Studies*, 29 (1984): 65–79, **1.3**.

"The 'Constitution of Medina'," *Islamic Quarterly*, 8 (1964): 3–16; reprinted in R. B. Serjeant, *Studies in Arabian History and Civilization* (London: Variorum, 1981).

Sezgin, Fuat. *Geschichte des arabischen Schrifttums* (Leiden: E. J. Brill, 1967–).

Shahid, Irfan. *Byzantium and the Arabs in the Fifth Century* (Washington, D.C.: Dumbarton Oaks Research Library and Collection, 1989).

Shalabī, Muḥammad M. *Uṣūl al-Fiqh al-Islāmī* (Beirut: Dār al-Nahḍa, 1406/1986).

Sharafī, ʿAbd al-Majīd. *al-Islām wal-Ḥadātha* (Tunis: al-Dār al-Tūnisiyya lil-Nashr, 1991).

Shehaby, Nabil. "*ʿIlla* and *Qiyās* in Early Islamic Legal Theory," *Journal of the American Oriental Society*, 102 (1982): 27–46.

"The Influence of Stoic Logic on al-Jaṣṣāṣ's Legal Theory," in John E. Murdoch and Edith D. Sylla, eds. *The Cultural Context of Medieval Learning* (Dordrecht–Boston: D. Reidel Publishing Co., 1975): 61–85.

Shorter Encylopaedia of Islam (Leiden: E. J. Brill, 1974).

Smith, Wilfred C. "Islamic Law: Its 'Sources' (*Uṣūl al-Fiqh*) and *Ijtihād*," in W. C. Smith, *On Understanding Islam: Selected Studies* (The Hague: Mouton Publishers, 1981).

"Law and Ijtihad in Islam," *International Islamic Colloquium Papers* (Lahore: Panjab University Press, 1960): 111–14.

Sonn, Tamara. "Fazlur Rahman's Islamic Methodology," *Muslim World*, 81 (1991): 212–30.

Spectorsky, Susan. "Aḥmad Ibn Ḥanbal's *Fiqh*," *Journal of the American Oriental Society*, 102 (1982): 461–65.

Tibi, Bassam. *The Crisis of Modern Islam*, trans. J. von Sivers (Salt Lake City: University of Utah Press, 1988).

Islam and the Cultural Accommodation of Social Change, trans. Clare Krojz (Oxford: Westview Press, 1991).

Toledano, Henry. *Judicial Practice and Family Law in Morocco* (Boulder: Social Science Monographs, 1981).

Turki, Abdel Magid. "Argument d'autorité, preuve rationelle et absence de preuve dans la méthodologie juridique musulmane," *Studia Islamica*, 42 (1975): 59–91.

"L'ijmāʿ Ummat al-Mu'minīn entre la doctrine et l'histoire," *Studia Islamica*, 59 (1984): 49–77.

"La logique juridique, des origines jusqu'a Shāfiʿī (réflexions d'ordre méthodologique)," *Studia Islamica*, 57 (1983): 31–45.

Tyan, Emile. *Histoire de l'organisation judiciaire en pays d'Islam* (Leiden: E. J. Brill, 1960).

"Méthodologie et sources du droit en Islam (*Istiḥsān*, *Istiṣlāḥ*, *Siyāsa Šarʿiyya*)," *Studia Islamica*, 10 (1959): 79–109.

Vesey-Fitzgerald, S. G. "The Alleged Debt of Islamic to Roman Law," *Law Quarterly Review*, 67 (1951): 81–102.

"Nature and Sources of the Sharīʿa," in Khadduri and Liebesny eds., *Law in the Middle East*, 85–112.

Vogel, Frank Edward. "The Closing of the Door of Ijtihād and the Application of the Law," *American Journal of Islamic Social Sciences*, 10 (1993): 396–401.

Islamic Law and Legal System: Studies of Saudi Arabia (Ph.D. dissertation: Harvard University, 1993).

Wakin, Jeanette. "Interpretation of the Divine Command in the Jurisprudence of Muwaffaq al-Dīn Ibn Qudāma," in Heer, ed., *Islamic Law and Jurisprudence*, 33–52, **2.4**.

Watt, W. M. "The Closing of the Door of Iğtihād," *Orientalia Hispanica*, I (Leiden: E. J. Brill, 1974): 675–78.

Islamic Fundamentalism and Modernity (London: Routledge, 1988).

Wegner, J. R. "Islamic and Talmudic Jurisprudence: The Four Roots of Islamic Law and their Talmudic Counterparts," *American Journal of Legal History*, 26 (1982): 25–71.

Weiss, Bernard. "Exotericism and Objectivity in Islamic Jurisprudence," in Heer, ed., *Islamic Law and Jurisprudence*, 53–71, **2.4**.

"Interpretation in Islamic Law: The Theory of *Ijtihād*," *American Journal of Comparative Law*, 26 (1978): 199–212, **2.2**.

"Knowledge of the Past: The Theory of *Tawātur* According to Ghazālī," *Studia Islamica*, 61 (1985): 81–105, **2.5**.

"Language and Law: The Linguistic Premises of Islamic Legal Science," in Arnold H. Green, ed., *In Quest of an Islamic Humanism: Arabic and Islamic Studies in Memory of Mohamed al-Nowaihi* (Cairo: American University of Cairo Press, 1986): 15–21, **2.4**.

"Language and Tradition in Medieval Islam: The Question of *al-Ṭarīq ilā Maʿrifat al-Lugha*," *Der Islam*, 61 (1984): 92–99.

"Law in Islam and in the West: Some Comparative Observations," in Wael B. Hallaq and Donald P. Little, eds., *Islamic Studies Presented to Charles J. Adams* (Leiden: E. J. Brill, 1991): 239–53.

"The Primacy of Revelation in Classical Islamic Legal Theory as Expounded by Sayf al-Dīn al-Āmidī," *Studia Islamica*, 59 (1984): 79–109, **2.7**.

The Search for God's Law: Islamic Jurisprudence in the Writings of Sayf al-Dīn al-Āmidī (Salt Lake City: University of Utah Press, 1992), **2.3**.

Wensinck, Arent Jan. *Concordance et indices de la tradition musulmane*, 8 vols. (Leiden: E. J. Brill, 1936–88).

Wiederhold, Lutz. "Legal Doctrines in Conflict: The Relevance of *Madhhab* Boundaries to Legal Reasoning in the Light of an Unpublished Treatise on *Taqlīd* and *Ijtihād*," *Islamic Law and Society*, 4 (1996): 234–304.

Wolfson, Harry A. *The Philosophy of the Kalam* (Cambridge, Mass.: Harvard University Press, 1976).

"The Terms *Taṣawwur* and *Taṣdīq* in Arabic Philosophy and their Greek, Latin and Hebrew Equivalents," *Muslim World*, 33 (1943): 114–28.

Zayd, Muṣṭafā, ed., *al-Maṣlaḥa fī al-Tashrīʿ al-Islāmī*, 2nd edn. (Cairo: Dār al-Fikr al-ʿArabī, 1348/1964).

Zebiri, Kate. *Maḥmūd Shaltūt and Islamic Modernism* (Oxford: Clarendon Press, 1993).

Ziadeh, Farhat. "Shufʿa: Origins and Modern Doctrine," *Cleveland State Law Review*, 34 (1985–86): 35–46.

Ziadeh, Nicola A. *Sanusiyah: A Study of a Revivalist Movement in Islam* (Leiden: E. J. Brill, 1958).

Zuḥaylī, Wahba. *Uṣūl al-Fiqh al-Islāmī*, 2 vols. (Damascus: Dār al-Fikr, 1986).

Zysow, Aron. *The Economy of Certainty: An Introduction to the Typology of Islamic Legal Theory* (Ph.D. Dissertation: Harvard University, 1984), **2–3**.

INDEX

In classifying entries no account is taken of the letter *ʿayn* and the Arabic definite article *al-*.

Lightning Source UK Ltd.
Milton Keynes UK
UKHW041934170319
339342UK00001B/23/P

9 780521 599863